THE GOOD COUNTRY

Individual, Situation and Society in Saurashtra

THE GOOD COUNTRY

Individual, Situation and Society in Saurashtra

HARALD TAMBS-LYCHE

MANOHAR
2004

First published 2004

Published thanks to a grant from the Department of Social Anthropology, University of Bergen.

ISBN 81-7304-417-1

Published by
Ajay Kumar Jain for
Manohar Publishers & Distributors
4753/23 Ansari Road, Daryaganj
New Delhi 110002

Typeset by
A J Software Publishing Co. Pvt. Ltd.
New Delhi 110005

Printed at
Lordson Publishers Pvt. Ltd.
Delhi 110007

Contents

PREFACE 7

1. Saurashtra: The Past in the Present 11
2. The Capitals of Saurashtra: Images and Impressions 33
3. Provincial Towns and the Limits of Urbanity 60
4. Urban Scenes and Situations 80
5. Centres of Pilgrimage 100
6. Devotion and Segmentation: The Goddess 122
7. An Individual among Individuals in a Complex Society 146
8. Decontextualizing the Person: *Jangal*, Fields and Roads 168
9. The Individual's Burden 184
10. Public Transport: Dealing with the Other 206
11. Praj and its Social Life 232
12. Rural Settlements: Hamlet and Village 260
13. Rural Settlements: Process and Power 286
14. Hierarchical Discourse and the Image of Society 304

BIBLIOGRAPHY 331

INDEX 347

Preface

I first came to Saurashtra in 1973, and when I returned nine months later, the plan for the book seemed clear. It would concentrate on the opposition, evident in the peninsula, between merchants and rulers, between the bourgeoisie, then dominant, and the remnants of the old, feudal society. I wrote some papers on the theme, then got absorbed by research on South Asian immigrants in Norway. Meanwhile, I read an article by Howard Spodek, and his subsequent book (1974, 1976)—and it all seemed to be there. Here was a competent analysis of the very opposition I wanted to describe.

I realized however that I must go beyond Spodek's analysis, to show the broader, cultural implications of that pattern. Specifically, I wanted to deal with religious tradition, which Spodek did not cover extensively—his was, after all, a book on urban-rural integration. To do that, I had to trace the history of the divide between martial Rajputs and non-violent merchants in Saurashtra's history.

This brought me back to the eighth century and did not simplify the task of writing a book; a thesis completed in 1992 was neither readable nor publishable. It did cover much of the ground I wanted to reconnoitre, however, and led me to write a handier volume (1997) in which I dealt with the emergence of traditional society through the middle ages. I tried to construct an image of the past from an anthropologist's point of view: not history in a strict sense but a representation and analysis of the past that lurks behind the conception of the present for people in the peninsula.

As I finished that book, I finally felt free to attempt the present volume. The reader may find it sketchy, for it lacks much of the detail that makes anthropology scientific. I paint a picture of a region the size of Denmark, with a slightly larger population. Clearly, I have been doing anthropology in a region rather than of it, and so I report on my own experience: the reader will find a mixture of sketches, situational detail, second-hand data, and attempted analysis. I hope, however, that the latter will make my intentions clear.

This book, then, is the result of a long period of gestation and so I have debts towards a large number of people, too many to be mentioned here. Haribhai Patel and Jayant Meghani, however, were such close friends and helped me so much to find my way in Saurashtra, that I must thank them especially. At the other end of the process, I realize how the influence of my wife, Marine Carrin, has changed my way of thinking and writing about my experiences—a process of gradual growth for which I thank her. In my way of doing anthropology, however, this work reflects, above all else, my association with Fredrik Barth, who first suggested to me the choice of Saurashtra for study. The references to his work speak for themselves in identifying the source of a very large part of the ideas I put forward here. I take the opportunity to thank him for years of inspiration and advice, but above all for his unfailing friendship. No scholar could be more true to his ideals, to his friends, and to his lifelong project of exploring human and social diversity. This book is dedicated to him.

Mas de Labat HARALD TAMBS-LYCHE
July 1999

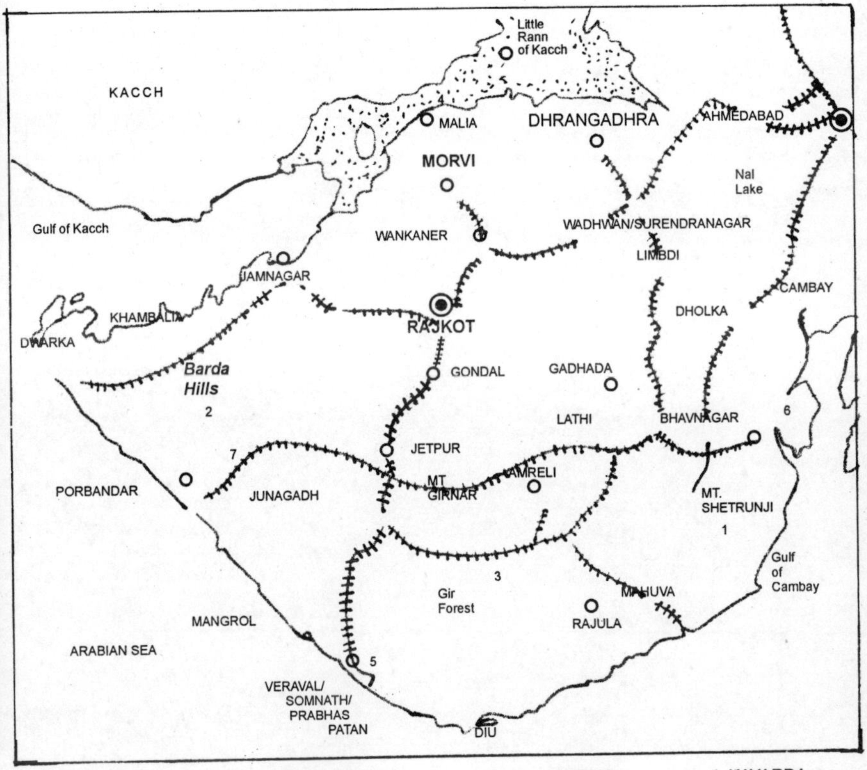

1. PRAJ
2. PACCHATARDI
3. JAMBUR
4. KAYARDA
5. SUTRAPADA
6. VELAVADAR
7. RATADI
8. CHICHOD

FIG. 1: SKETCH MAP OF SAURASHTRA. (THE NUMBERS REFER TO VILLAGES MENTIONED IN THE TEXT.)

CHAPTER 1

Saurashtra: The Past in the Present

The past, predestined, populous and over
Clings in the dampening leaves, the smell of petrol,
On the brown northern heights where I remember
Highgate and Hampstead in a fine October

ANTHONY CRONIN

My first view of Saurashtra was splendid. We came flying towards Mumbai from one of the Gulf ports, and suddenly I saw the whole peninsula, dominated by the Girnar—that holy mountain whose presence runs through the history of the region like a red thread, signalling, to sailors, the approach to the 'dangerous coastal waters of Gujarat's most prosperous ports'.[1] In front of the black mountain, I even glimpsed the yellow buildings of Junagadh, where I hoped to make my headquarters, as had rulers and viceroys in a line stretching back to the times of Ashoka.

When I entered the city through one of its gates, making my way through the steep streets to the rock on which the old fort[2] is perched, it was odd that the soda-seller outside the city walls, from whom I rented my bicycle, might not appreciate the sacredness of the site—sacred, that is, in the romantic anthropologist's view. But then he was a Pathan immigrant whose family had come a few generations ago. I came to realize that a large numbers of people, in Junagadh and Saurashtra as elsewhere in India, are immigrants. Their history is not tied to the place, yet the soda-seller and others rooted in the Muslim world may appreciate Junagadh as the best example, in Saurashtra, of Middle Eastern town planning and architecture. This progressive aspect of Muslim rule was praised by the Nagar Brahmin who was the Pathan's sleeping partner in the shop, as by many other Nagars; for centuries, they have identified themselves with the Muslim rulers. The Jains, merchants and rivals of the Nagars, prefer to note their own temples on the Girnar and the remains from Buddhist times[3] as examples of Junagadh's greatness before the days of Muslim 'tyranny'.

These are but examples of the multiple pasts of Saurashtra, as seen by various groups. Among the images, two stand out. The first is constructed from heroic tales of warriors (mostly Rajputs) fighting for dominance, village by village, over the barren lands of Kathiawar, their name for the peninsula. In another, contrasting view, the merchants see Saurashtra—as they call it—as a holy land of the distant past, vaguely associated with classical India. To them, this golden age was ruthlessly torn apart by the strife of feudal rulers, until independence brought a return to civilization—and to merchant dominance. There are other pasts, too: each community may prefer one to another, one version of myth to that proffered by their rivals or opponents, but images of warriors and merchants dominate, even in none of them constitutes the continuous narrative that a historian might extract from the mythical material.

For the warriors, one such myth deals with the battle of Bhuchar Mori, in 1591, when the Moguls gained control of the peninsula. The battle was lost, yet the Jhala and Jadeja Rajputs are still proud of their role in it. Sometimes it is seen, like the battle of Chittor for Rajasthan, as a defence of Hindu values against Muslim aggression. Sometimes it is constructed as a last stand for the independence of the peninsula from the mainland—which in the present context is an anti-merchant and anti-Congress position, since Congress is associated with the merchants and they are linked, by those identifying with the warrior past, with the mainland. In both cases, descent from a warrior who fell at Bhuchar Mori implies that there is the blood of heroes in one's veins.[4]

For the inhabitants of Sorath, the south-western part of the peninsula, a series of stories relate to the Chudasama dynasty which ruled Junagadh from AD 875 to 1470. Some concern the conquest of Junagadh by rulers of Gujarat, the last, by Mahmud Begada, again pitting Hindus against Muslims. Almost 400 years later, the Mahia Rajputs of Chichod dreamt of restoring Chudasama rule—a hopeless project crushed by the British, though not without trouble.[5] Even now, there is a tendency to identify the old raj at Junagadh with the idealized, Hindu kingdom, as well as another strain that affirms the difference between the peninsula and the mainland.

Merchant myth goes farther back, beyond the fall of Vallabhi in 788. Its Maitraka rulers, originally vassals to the Guptas, were patrons of art and religion, and the city was a commercial centre. In merchant tradition, its fall symbolizes the lapses into barbary that characterize the medieval period.[6] Vallabhi has additional significance for the Jains, for it was here that the Jain canon was edited, at two large assemblies, held around 300 and 453.[7] The latter meeting also led to the definitive split between the Svetambara and Digambara sects, so for the Svetambaras, who dominate Saurashtra

Jainism, these debates form part of their myth of origin (Tambs-Lyche 1997: 17).

The fall of Vallabhi frames the myth of the Goddess Khodiyar. She is at the centre of a whole cycle of stories, which involve the Chudasamas of Junagadh. These narratives lay down the charter for traditional society, concerning gender, what Harlan (1991) calls the ethic of protection, and the duties of a king toward his people.[8] Khodiyar becomes the mythical founder of the traditional, Rajput-dominated society of Kathiawar, and by destroying Vallabhi, she terminates the golden age of the merchants. Here the opposition between the Rajput and Merchant past is particularly clear.[9] While Khodiyar is the most important goddess of the region, there are others: in the Rajput and rural idiom, every clan or caste is supposed to have its own goddess, whose story is its foundation myth.[10]

THE INTEGRATION OF MULTIPLE PASTS

Viewed from the common present, the multiple pasts indicate dissonance and contradiction. The myths constitute arguments (Leach 1954: 264ff) about how society should be constituted, understood, and ruled. The definition of Saurashtra as a society, then, is not found in any single myth, but at the point of convergence between them.[11]

Where do the myths converge? Not, certainly, in some unitary 'caste system' within which every community finds its place. Yet when Merchants and Rajputs criticize each other, they constitute a discourse in which groups construe their myths to show superiority and inferiority, inclusion with superiors and exclusion of inferiors.[12] In doing so, they create the bits and pieces of a hierarchical order, one that never appears as an integrated whole. The discourse is hierarchizing and converges on a hierarchical image of society; but this image cannot be complete because its elements are contradictory. Surely, if societies exist they do so as culturally constructed[13] objects, and not as realities out there. Indeed, I would argue, such convergence in discourse is the essence of what a society can be, if we want to avoid reification.[14]

Such distinct constructions of societies stand opposed to the universal presence of social organization. Elements of organization (Firth 1950) may be observable and have a claim on objectivity that images of distinct societies cannot have. It is to this level we must look if we want to go beyond people's own constructions, to ask with Durkheim whether there is a common reality to which alternative constructions refer.[15] But social organization must be universal to be viable as a concept, since it makes of society (in the singular) a universal, continuous presence. Durkheim's insistence on the objective existence of society seems far more defensible if we talk of society in this singular sense.[16] But if social organization is continuous, an important part of social discourse concerns the creation and maintenance of boundaries.[17] Though merchant and martial traditions view the region differently, the discourse must follow a minimum of rules to be intelligible to the opponents. These rules are essential to my analysis here.

This book deals with the present.[18] But 'history is the process by which society shows itself as what it is' (Dumont 1957);[19] as time integrates the social with the cultural dimension. Historicity, then, is not the memory of events but

> the totality of cultural models by which a society produces its norms, in the spheres (domaines) of knowledge, production and morals. Cultural models which constitute the endeavours (enjeux) of cultural movements which fight to institute social forms conforming to the interests of the various social categories' (Touraine 1992: 423)

Thus, communities interact and argue, according to the rules, to create inequality or social stratification.[20] Our multiple pasts belong here. They form part of the dwelt-in world[21] of people in Saurashtra.

THE PHYSICAL PRESENCE OF THE PAST

Landscapès and buildings, as culturally constructed objects,[22] are part of this lived-in world. Saurashtra is studded with physical memorials of its long history. On an ordinary day one may see palaces—crumbling in decay or freshly painted—temples well or vaguely known, pass through town or village walls by ornate gates, or holes punched to let traffic pass; one may stroll along the tanks built by former rulers to furnish a city with water, or cross a river on a bridge built by British or Indian engineers. In Saurashtra, which in British times consisted of some two hundred princely states, such objects and the meanings attributed to them are particularly rich and various. They stand for the past in the present, even if people may have only vague ideas of their history. Like myth, their meaning is convergent rather than shared, as the same object may mean different things to different people. Though temples do not carry the same message to believers and unbelievers, they are temples alike to both. The remnants of village and city walls bear witness of former strife to the non-violent and the descendants of warriors. A landscape may have held meanings that are now lost, yet many are still grasped, while others are re-invented[23] to serve the present as tradition.

Thus the mental map[24] of Saurashtra is equally an image of its history; places are located in space but, also, in that indeterminate past to which myth and history contribute. In spite of the vast difference between Indian civilization and a simple culture such as the Baktaman, there is a parallel: sites in space are precise while points in time are vague (Barth 1975: 18). Since Indians, unlike the Baktaman, know very well how to calculate time,[25] this parallel makes one reflect on how abstract the concept of linear time really is. Dates do indeed exist with regard to past events, but are seldom ordered into sequences. Even when people know about linear history, this is not how most of us, most of the time, spontaneously organize our view of past events.

But the past is there, incarnated in physical objects. This is so whether we hear that an old fort was built 'by some chief' or whether his name is known. It testifies by its purpose to a past state of society. And this tumultuous past is usually compared, explicitly or implicitly, negatively or positively, to the present. If some objects legitimize the present state of things by their existence, others serve to delimit the present from the past, providing that element of contrast which the anthropologist recognizes in myth.

GEOGRAPHICAL AND SOCIAL SPACE

Just as history is cannot be reduced to linear time, the perception of a country cannot, in the minds of most people, be reduced to a map where the specifics of place are reduced to universal signs. Saurashtra consists of real towns and villages, not examples of the abstract category 'village', and they are all different.

The region, being a peninsula, is well demarcated, and the precise location of the boundary towards the mainland is of minor importance. As noted, however, its two traditional names, Kathiawar and Saurashtra, carry different overtones. The first, used by Rajputs and their clients, stresses the distinctive character of the region and its difference from the mainland: the term Saurashtra, on the other hand, is used by merchants and the urban middle classes and rather identifies the peninsula as a region of Gujarat. A third term, Sorath, has been used in Muslim tradition and stresses the importance of Junagadh: the same term is used for the south-western part of the peninsula, dominated by that city.

Apart from Sorath, most regions of the peninsula are identified, by name, with their dominant communities. Jhalawad in the north-east and Gohilwad in the south-east take their name, respectively, from the Jhala and Gohil clans of Rajputs. The north coast is known as Halar, from the Hala branch of the Jadeja Rajputs, who dominate the region.[26] The centre of the peninsula is sometimes called Kathiawad, since the Kathi community dominates much of it—though their dominance has weakened since the eighteenth century. Babriawad in the south is named after the Babria Rajputs, whose dominance, too, is weak. Modern district names are sometimes used instead of these traditional terms; thus Gohilwad corresponds very broadly to Bhavnagar District, Sorath to Junagadh District, and so on. Others again refer to the old state units. Thus Porbandar is in Junagadh District today, but it makes perfect sense to talk of villages within the boundary of old Porbandar State as being in Porbandar.

Thus in general the division of the region refers to political units, whether in terms of traditional caste dominance, old princely states, or modern administrative subdivisions. The political nature of this classification carries a certain ambiguity. Thus a Gohil Rajput from Lathi may prefer to locate his town in Gohilwad, avoiding Amreli, the name of the modern district, which is associated with Kathi territory. Lathi was in fact a Gohil state, and spent much of its history fighting its Kathi neighbours. Most inhabitants of Palitana, however, would probably accept identification with Bhavnagar district, even if Palitana, too, was an independent Gohil state often at war with Bhavnagar. But Palitana was surrounded by Bhavnagar on all sides from the eighteenth century, and geographical contiguity seems to have triumphed over historical precision.

What I want to stress, is that natural regions are submerged by political history, so that geographical identification follows the latter. True, certain regions stand like the Gir forest in the south, a legendary shelter for outlaws, and the Barda Hills in the north-west, still forested and something of a no man's land in the eighteenth century, stand out by their natural characteristics. There are several other areas of *jangal* (wilderness) such as the salt flats towards the Rann of Kacch in the north, or the salty Bhal coast north of Bhavnagar, and the legendary badlands of Okhamandal where Dwarka, the pilgrimage centre, is situated.

Whether forest or salt flats, all these regions may be designated peripheries, while each of the politically demarcated regions indicates a centre. The map is complex, for there are several centres and more peripheries. Traditionally defined, regions in Saurashtra centred on princely capitals of varying importance,[27] surrounded by the lands on which their revenue was based. Very generally we could structure the map around three towns that were the capitals of the most important states from the eighteenth century until 1947: Junagadh, the centre of fertile plains south-west of the Girnar mountains, Jamnagar in the middle of a fertile black soil area on the north coast, and Bhavnagar at the northern end of fertile plains in the south-east. Since Independence, Rajkot in the middle of the peninsula has become the undisputed centre, but this is due to modern communications, industry, and administrative importance rather than natural factors. Till then, the town and state remained small in spite of being the seat of the British resident.

In each of these sub-regions, the centre-periphery axis was not so much a question of distance as of population density and size of villages, both closely related to the quality of land. This correponds to important emic frameworks for classifying settlements. Large villages are seen as better or higher than small ones, while even the largest village is inferior to a town. In this connection, *gamda*—(of the village, village-like) carries an overtone of the rustic, the culturally inferior. But villages also differ in quality—taking their status or prestige from the kind of people they harbour, and the kind of social relations they allow. The rule seems to be that the best villages are those where landowners are distinct from, and served by, a good sample of inferior castes. Thus there is an overall, we might say hierarchical, clue to how spatial communities are placed in an overall order. Beyond the village is the hamlet, occupied by a single caste, which marks the periphery: the hamlet is usually in, or close to, the *jangal.*[28] But we must be wary of reifying this order, as more than a rough guide to social space. Discoursing on good and bad villages, town culture and corruption or hamlet honesty and jungliness, people in Saurashtra see their region as one of diversity, of many and irreducible differences between people and places—more pertinent than whatever the casual traveller sees.

THE META-LEVEL OF CULTURE

Concepts of space and time are assimilated to the 'analog' rather than 'digital' mode[29] as conceptualized by the local people. Yet in a sense the conceptualization transcends specificity. This is the level where anthropologists used to look for the essentials of a culture, the most logical and consistent efforts coming from the diverse proponents of structuralism. For India, the three-dimensional models of Marriott (1989) are of great interest, for he assumes structuring to be explicitly present in the emic models, rather than assimilating emic concepts to implicit, universal structures, as Levi-Strauss tried to do.

But prior to structuring, we need to know what bits and pieces go into the structure, (without taking for granted that they do form a structured whole)—and that the structures that govern, say, the historical narratives of warriors and merchants are the same or even similar. In other words, while Marriott is convincing on certain types of structured thinking existing within Indian culture, the scholar cannot be sure that this is how his informants think. First one must grasp the elements that enter into the construction of the dwelt-in world (Ingold 1996: 112-18) for the inhabitants of Saurashtra. To do so, I prefer to stay close to experience—my own as well as that my informants communicated to me.[30]

But communication implies concepts, and to describe and interpret experience one enters a discourse. One is looking, then, for the rules of discourse, as centering on the nature of human relations and social organization in Saurashtra. Knowing the rules may not necessary to operate within a culture, for they need not be conscious. Yet I suppose that in learning to operate within a culture, the sum of specifics would be unmanageable if there was no underlying principle according to which they are organized. Viewed as a system of storage and retrieval, cultural knowledge can hardly be completely haphazard.

As Ingold notes, the concept of dwelling encompasses building, or construction and any opposition the given and the constructed disappears (1996: 114-15). In the discourse I analyse, however, the distinction between the given and the constructed reappears, is itself constructed, as a device for situating oneself in the world and reflecting on it. Thus we shall see that people take caste for granted, but consciously try to transcend its implications. Indeed, the opposition between the given and the potential, the necessary and the possible, would seem to be the definitional core of what Ingold calls environment (1996: 117) as opposed to nature, reality *for* as opposed to reality *of*.[31]

The dwelt-in world of people in Saurashtra—and indeed elsewhere—is constructed, and this construction stems from their daily experience. That world is indeed a continuous field of relationships (Ingold 1996: 117), some to objects, some to people. To adopt this basically interactionist view is not to deny structural relations between the categories at a deeper level, but rather to suppose that such construction is a bricolage[32] rather than an ordered, quasi-scientific process. If cosmologies can remain in the making (Barth 1987), so can dwelt-in worlds. The problem with constructionism thus lies in the supposed holistic blueprint[33]—which I feel, distinguishes the engineer's work from that of the bricoleur—rather than in the potential of building materials.

THE PROBLEM OF CASTE[34]

It is tempting to view the Indian caste system as made up of numerous caste subcultures within a cultural whole (Sinha 1967). This would be fine if culture could be defined as custom, confounding thinking and action into a reified whole, thus making of caste a basic identity which people realize—unquestioning, as it were—through action. But we should be wary of taking caste for granted. Most people I met are acutely aware both of the caste element in their identity and of their wish to transcend it in thinking about themselves and society. While this does not exclude thinking in terms of caste, thought and consciousness may cross boundaries that remain central to social organization; as a trite example, many of my friends like to think of cross-caste 'love marriages' even if they themselves will marry within the caste. We need, therefore, to distinguish clearly between the categories people refer to, and the way they act.

Some of the most important categories that people in Saurashtra use, to identify others and to understand their own society, are not castes but the wider groupings that I call estates, following Weber's use of the term[35] to describe Western society. In Saurashtra, the principal estate categories are *darbars* (landowning, politically dominant groups), *vanias* (the prototypical merchant communities), *maldharis* (pastoralists) and *kheduts* (peasants) (Tambs-Lyche 1997).[36] Each category contains a number of castes, which share cultural traits and perspectives in varying degrees. Situated as members of an estate, individuals to an extent share the cultural perspectives (Hannerz 1992) traditionally and commonly associated with it, as regards society, culture, and their own place in it.

Thus there are several levels of categories between individual and society, and caste is only one of them. To an extent, caste and estate are levels of a common dimension. But each estate does not simply subsume a given number of castes. Thus the category of Darbar includes Rajputs, traditionally dominant in the greater part of the peninsula; Kathis, who dominate the central region, and some other castes wherever they are dominant. As for Vanias, sometimes most merchant castes are included, sometimes only the 'real' Vanias viewed as a caste, though the latter group includes a large number of sub-castes. Maldharis include the camel-herding Rabaris (who mostly have cows these days) and the Bharwad shepherds; but traditionally, the Charan bards and the Ahirs (who have long since settled as agriculturalists) are also included. Kheduts are, above all, the Kanbis and the Kolis, but other castes may be included when they are, effectively, peasants. So we note a certain ambiguity: Ahirs may be seen as Maldharis when referring to tradition and religious practice; as Darbars when they control land; and as Kheduts when they only till it. In former Junagadh state, they are nicely poised between the three categories, since they were the main agriculturalists and furnished the village headmen, while their pastoralist past looms large in the mythical foundation of the state (Tambs-Lyche 1997: 32-5, 37). Yet the control of land was reserved for zamindars.[37] Instead of a nice order of building blocks fitting into progressively larger boxes, we have a series of categorizations at different levels, which vary according to context and defy any simple order we may construct.

The classification of castes by estate varies with not only the sub-region of Saurashtra, but also with the semantic field (politics and landownership, tradition and religion) with which we deal. Moreover, people in Saurashtra identify themselves and others by a wide range of other categories also, including geographical origins, occupation, and other dimensions such as *jangli* (savage, primitive, hillbilly) or indeed *saheb*—a category which is difficult to pin down conceptually but easy to recognize in practice. How—or why—are we to privilege those among these various categories that refer to caste? (McGilvray 1982, Levinson 1982). This is a perspective emerging from Berreman's article on urban interaction (1972)—too often ignored—with which I have dealt earlier (1979, 1993). There, and from the situations I describe below, it will be seen that caste alone cannot account for the complex set of categories that enter into the definition of the situation. People in Saurashtra, as I think elsewhere in India, play consciously on these multiple categories, and we shall need to look closely at the rules that regulate what Mead (1934: 329) calls relativity in situational encounters. But the categories are also linked to a series of implications which cannot all be consciously present at the same time for any single actor, links which form a part of emergence (ibid.) and which may sometimes intrude to disturb the message that the actor wishes to convey.

Members of different groups view society from different perspectives and the same person may adopt various perspectives in changing contexts. Situatedness, which can hardly be separated from historicity as Touraine defines it, must be our starting point for thinking about caste. How do members of different castes, in Saurashtra, view society from their own place in it ? And what does each of them make of 'society'?[38]

I have argued that members of the Patidar immigrants in London (1980; 23-5) have to take most of the workings of British society as given: they could not change the rules of such central mechanisms as the housing or labour markets. In this sense, their community was encompassed by British society, an environment over which they had, and saw themselves as having, little influence.[39] The ecological analogy made it seem apt to use the term niche for the position they carved for themselves within the encompassing society (Tambs-Lyche 1973, 1980).

How well does such a perspective fit the situation of a single caste such as the Kanbi/Patidar category in Saurashtra ? Castes, we have seen, are differentially situated and variously defined. In traditional society, power was of the greatest importance; some communities controlled a set of relations which they, as a group, had been instrumental in creating and which, conversely, played a part in determining their view of themselves.

Thus the Darbars felt that society was theirs to control, at least so far as landholding and politics were concerned. Its members should be protected (Harlan 1991) but also chastised when the constructed order was disturbed. Environmental constraints, for the dominant castes, were clearly the realities that governed political strategies: what were the chances for dominance or independence, or the dangers of submission?

Conversely, merchant castes were conscious of being a minority, which had to deal with rules partly defined by others. Yet they were also capable of re-casting the image of society as a whole to fit their views. They could go beyond pragmatic rationality, as stated by a Patidar in London: 'Society must see to it so that people can do some good business'.[40] Such reasoning was evidently present when merchants chose to migrate from one princely state to another, as they frequently did (Spodek 1976: 25). The conditions offered by a ruler, and the prospects of trade, were certainly environmental constraints in relation to their choice: but they were sometimes able to influence the ruler's policy, since he depended on them to finance his army and other projects.

Pastoralists had to deal with much of settled society as a given, but could maintain a partial independence from it. Regions offered different regimes of pasture, with varying social constraints on grazing. In this sense, factors resulting from natural and social processes were both environmental.

Peasants were largely at the mercy of the dominant landholding castes and, sometimes, of the merchants; yet they too moved quite frequently.[41] The availability of land and contractual conditions for its use were important environmental factors here. But, as for the merchants, their services were in demand: and when invited by a ruler to settle on his land, terms were negotiated.[42] Peasants certainly saw themselves as a central element of society; they identified with a society over which others, generally, held control. Such control was relative, however, and an important factor in choosing a particular village might be the local strength of their community. Sometimes peasants were, juridically but more often factually, their own lords: but this advantage was usually to be had where soil was poor or water scarce, since the best land was controlled by others.

As for artisans, economic considerations might determine whether or not they settled in a certain village, for example, enough work to make a living.[43] Still, there was an active demand among landowners or peasants for certain services—which influenced the relative position of craftsmen. They were often included in the *ter tansali*, and so participated, with partial commensality, in the node of social relations controlled by the dominant caste. Such participation implied a degree of identification with this grouping, which opposed the merchants culturally and ideologically, and formed, if any element could be said to do so, the majority within the traditional pattern (Tambs-Lyche 1992, 1997).

There were important differences among craftsmen, however. The carpenter was usually included in the *ter tansali* [44] but the shoemaker, an untouchable, was not. Shoemakers sometimes lived inside the village walls and were far more integrated into the mainstream of village life than the arch-untouchables of Saurashtra, the Waghris (P.G. Shah 1967). The latter are excluded from village society in most ways. They live outside the walls in hutments where nobody else would like to be seen. In the 1970s they still had to wear a pigtail and clothes showing both wear and tear. Yet the Waghris, widely believed to have tribal origins, have been in Saurashtra longer than most.

Thus there are vast differences in the way members of different communities experience their relation, mediated through their caste membership, to the larger society. It is this insight which is reflected in the criticism of Dumont, for taking a Brahmin's point of view. But this distortion is hardly less defensible than taking the point of view of the Rajput, as Tod undoubtedly did, or that of the untouchable, as some writers[45] have done. Critics often leave out the obvious, that any emic or insider's view is necessarily partial. Indeed the Brahmin view may well be the only one that seriously attempts a representation of society as a whole and as seen from the inside.

Dominant castes and merchants have very different ideas of their society. In any case, most castes are minorities, and actors must adapt, in very different ways, to varying conceptions of society as controlled by others. Individual perspectives are equally real, yet none represents a global or objective view of the caste system. If we try to construct an objective view, whether by way of theories of social stratification or by adopting a simplified Marxist approach, we shall surely fail in defining the distinctiveness of the caste system.

What then is a caste, beyond the fact it is different from others? Let me return to the Patidars. Among the immigrant Patidars of London, successful entrepreneurs are the ones to imitate and identify with, if one wants to be a 'real' Patidar.[46] Much the same is true of Patidars in Gujarat;[47] some members of the caste are better Patidars than others. As Pocock underlines, this implies that the limits of the Patidar category are vague. The term was first used for an elite group within the larger Kanbi caste; to this day, opinions may differ whether a particular person is a Patidar or just a Kanbi. The prototypic Patidar has become part of tradition, and it is natural for the ambitious Patidar to identify with this ideal, which has now become a presence in Saurashtra, as more and more Kanbi peasants aspire to entrepreneurial careers.

I have used the term 'natural' consciously, for the positive qualities are seen as inherent in the individuals of the caste. I have argued elsewhere (1991b), that the identities of groups in the social order and those defending their present position in it, are differently structured. In an expansive mode, identity centres on prototypes (Rosch 1978) which serve as models for the rest of the community. Identification with these qualities is gratifying, and Patidars are notoriously caste-proud. They may accept the higher purity of Brahmins, the superiour valour of Rajputs,[48] or the inborn business flair of the Vania, but in terms of the sum of inborn qualities, the Patidar feels second to none.

Members of stigmatized castes, on the other hand, explain away those inherent qualities of the caste which are common knowledge. Thus the fishermen of Sutrapada (CVM 9) accept the impure nature of their calling, but claim once to have been Rajputs who lost their land as Mahmud of Ghazni fought his way to destroy the temple of Somnath.

Caste groups whose position is threatened are notoriously wary about their boundary towards lower castes—what Pocock calls exclusion (1957a). This concern with boundary maintenance leads to concentration on the difference from inferior others.[49] This corresponds to Thoothi's view of castes closing in on themselves as a defensive strategy when they or their society face a crisis (1935: 19). Conversely, members of such groups may well be inspired by change: thus successful fishermen elsewhere may serve as prototypes for members of the Sutrapada community, and serve to open up their defensive view of themselves.

But the prototypic nature of Patidar self-definition takes us further,[50] for such large castes can be imagined communities (Anderson 1983) only: no single person can have first-hand knowledge of the limits of the caste. As caste limits become conceptually fuzzy, Kanbi/Patidars marry their girls to Anavil Brahmins and take wives from Saurashtra Kolis.[51] Another obvious example is the Gujar/Ahir/Goala caste cluster, much too vast and widely spread for its boundaries to be clear and consciously demarcated.[52] Yet there are also castes which number only a few hundred, where each member may quite conceivably know, or know about, every other.[53]

Thus in concentrating on caste as a general concept we are led astray. For a fisherman the question is not caste in this abstract sense. His concern is, rather, whether fishing can be made into a more honourable and profitable occupation, or whether it is better to get out of it altogether. Both are conceivable in the modern Indian context, but caste solidarity may be useful for the first, while for the second it is irrelevant or even harmful. The contradiction between mobility and belonging is as pertinent here as for the Italians of Cornerville (Whyte 1943). Caste, then, may persist not by its link to a fundamental conception of society, but since it remains functional in several singular contexts. Its function depends on which caste we are talking about, where and when: fishermen's struggle for betterment and Brahmin claims to intellectual excellence are different and opposed social phenomena. To understand caste in Saurashtra, we must talk of many and different castes.

THE POSITION OF THE MERCHANTS

The opposition between rulers and merchants is fundamental in Saurashtra. We can follow it, setting martial values and sacrificial cults against non-violence, vegetarianism and spiritual devotion (*bhakti*), from the beginning of medieval times to the modern period.[54] But Pocock has argued for an alternative view, which merits discussion here.

He cites the example of an old Vania from Central Gujarat who, in his youth, had been to the temple of Ambaji[55] where he received the *tilak* 'from the blood of the sacrificial beast and brought a blood-stained handkerchief home with him as a blessing for his family'. Pocock thus infers a 'recent interdependence of the pure and impure, vegetarian and bloody cults'. 'For this Bania in his youth the violent cult was as necessary a part of his world as the non-violent' (Pocock 1973: 76-7).

Such interdependence cannot have relieved the relationship of its conflictual nature: the evidence of opposition is clear. I agree, however, that there has been a recent and important change, increasing the distance between these two poles of Hinduism. The change has been surprisingly sudden in Saurashtra,[56] following the collapse of the old political system in which the Goddess, as well as the king, was central. In mainland Gujarat, similar changes seem to have taken place much earlier.[57]

Before we discard Pocock's argument, let us note the curious relationship between Ambaji and the Jain temples of Mount Abu. According to a well-known myth, the Jain temples were built at the instigation of Ambaji herself. Jains still go to Ambaji. Though they do not participate in blood sacrifice, the link is not broken, and one wonders if the break with the past is as sharp as Pocock implies. The relation of the Goddess, even in her terrible[58] form, to Jainism, the most non-violent of religions, is indeed far from clear. And though the Svetambara Jains of northern India (in contrast to the Digambars of the south) have little room for Hindu goddesses in their pantheon, the latter do appear in several mythical contexts.

But let us consider another example of links across the gap between violent and non-violent cults. The royal house of Mewar maintained a relationship with several religious institutions (Stern 1973).[59] Among them we find the Nathdwara temple, abode of Shri Nathaji, the main incarnation of Krishna to the members of the Vallabhacharya sect.[60] They are predominantly Vanias; this is a Vania temple, and a decidedly non-violent cult.

The story of how this temple came to be associated with Mewar has been told elsewhere.[61] Faced with Aurangzeb's order to destroy important temples, the priests of Shri Nathaji took the image away into the deserts of Rajasthan, where after several adventures they were welcomed by the ruler of Mewar. He received the party as they entered his state, and the Jagirdar of Dilwara gave a village to the God. This gift was confirmed by Jagat Singh, then ruler of Mewar, in 1736-7. Later, in 1803-4, a tax of two rupees, payable by every village in Mewar, was granted to the temple. Once established in the state, rulers clearly deemed it in their interest to strengthen their ties to the Vallabhacharya temple and devotees.

The relation between the temple and the royal house of Mewar thus takes on a distinctly political character: the king is not a devotee, but a protector. Support to the Nathdwara temple must be seen as an act of goodwill towards a community which, at this time, was assuming considerable economic influence in Mewar. The king's involvement follows, then, from his relationship with a rising group of Vanias, ready to compete with the established Jains. Such goodwill must have been good for credit. Beyond this, we should be wary of assuming too much for the religious involvement of the king. Thus the goddess-worshipping king protects the god of the Vanias; in Ambaji, the Goddess herself protects the Jain shrines of Abu. We know that Jains had earlier suffered persecution from Hindus in Rajasthan (Nevaskar 1971). Is it too far-fetched to think that the protection of a Hindu ruler underlies the relation between Abu and Ambaji? The point here is not to conjecture history, but to point to the structural dilemma, of remaining non-violent in a highly violent society, unless somebody is keeping peace by force of arms. Since medieval times, rulers depended on the Goddess for their powers; thus on a structural level, she protects even those who have no specific devotion for her.

The relationship between ruler and merchant was not always conflictual, as shown by the large number of Vanias who, in one state or another, occupied the office of *dewan*.[62] The two groups depended on each other; only the activities of the merchant could raise the petty chief to the status of a real king (Tambs-Lyche 1997). We should not be surprised at finding alliance, even mutual respect, as well as animosity. But such alliance seems to have been a matter of political convenience, and occasional ritual or religious links have not affected the fundamentally opposed notions of religion that characterizes each party. It is their interests that keep rulers and merchants together. Likewise, it is religion and culture which keep the parties separate, in spite of the links.

This relationship is indicative of the character of society in the region. It is not the ritual order but power that, in the last instance, act to integrate society in Saurashtra (Tambs-Lyche 1997). But while power relations dominate social life, they refer to values that can be legitimated only through hierarchizing discourse. In the relationship between these two modes of ordering reality we must seek the key to understand interaction and the society it constructs in Saurashtra.

THE RIGHT OF THE SUFFERING

There is, however, another point on which discourse converges. I have shown (1995) how the several forms of ritual suicide found in western India—the *traga* of the Charans,[63] the fasting to death of Jain monks, and the death of the warrior in a hopeless battle—follow a common logic: they provoke disaster, through supernatural agency, for the agent seen to have caused the act. But Vidal, in an excellent study of Sihor state,[64] goes much farther (1995). Whoever suffers from a wrongdoing, will try to show that he is in the right by making his suffering public. This is as true of the feudal lord who sees his rights violated—by the king, for example—as it was of Gandhi when he showed the immorality of British law through satyagraha. Different as rebellion, suicide, or political non-violence are, they refer to a common semantic grid where the onus is on identifying the immoral agent. Basic here is a common understanding that it is wrong to provoke suffering. We cannot reduce this morality to a norm; it is a principle beyond the specific norms applying to any single situation. In the last resort, it is the moral order which acts—through agents such as gods, goddesses and men—to restore itself, but supernatural agency is clearly helped if public opinion takes a stand, making the vengeance of the Goddess, or public support for Gandhi's actions, strictly comparable.[65]

Gods and men do not live in separate worlds in the Indian context (Wadley 1975). The Durkheimian idea that God, in the last resort, is society itself, is never far. On the one hand, then, *dharma* stands for an image of harmonious, morally integrated, ideal society. But the world of the Gods may be as wrought with dissidence and conflict as the human one. Thus the appeal to divine justice is not bound by society's laws, nor by an orderly catalogue of abstract, moral principles.[66] Efforts at codification but against two obstacles: the human agents who each maintain their right but seldom agree, and the divine agency which intervenes, casuistically and concretely, as when the Goddess kills the unjust king.

POWER AND THE INTEGRATION OF SOCIETY IN SAURASHTRA

We have seen that religion was a divisive rather than integrative factor in the traditional society of Saurashtra. It was the network of power relations, mixing political and economic factors, which kept traditional Saurashtra together. I have tried (1997) to show how this worked, in the field of power, land and lineage, to integrate agrarian society with the state. Local and regional division of labour coincides with caste and political control to form a coherent pattern. In traditional society, this coherence creates a link between relationships of interdependence and distinctions of rank, similar to what has been described (Beck 1972, Zimmermann 1982) as the cluster of right-hand castes in Tamil Nadu.

As the medieval chiefdoms grew into states, this pattern could be maintained only at the cost of integrating the merchants, whose interests coincided only in part with those of the rulers, and whose networks transcended the limits of the state. As in Tamil Nadu, where they would be seen as a left-hand group, the merchants remained outside the fields of landholding and power.

The traditional power structure, with its split between ruler and merchant set in a social space which retains both wilderness and village, is not an integrated set of relationships but rather a dispersed network. Pastoralists, like merchants, would belong to a left hand constellation. They contribute to the traditional state but do not form part of its agrarian backbone. Thus, while any informant may provide a rough ranking of castes, the relative egalitarianism of the *ter tansali*—subordinate allies of the Darbars—is a salient feature of caste in Saurashtra, setting it apart from more systematically hierarchized structures elsewhere.

As elsewhere in north India, the village temple is lacking: religious integration across rank differentials is conspicuous by its absence. The closest parallel to a common village sanctuary is usually a Rama temple, but this is clearly a Rajput institution. It stands for the village only in so far as it represents the Darbars and legitimizes their dominance.[67] The village goddess of south India is unknown here. Instead, goddesses are specific to caste and/or function, while the more important, cross-caste goddesses such as Khodiyar typically have their temple in the wilderness. It is as if this source of power lies physically and conceptually outside the community, as do other sources of the sacral in kingship.[68] The legitimation of these powers was partly appropriated by the dominant community when Rama temples were built.

Today, Rama's identification with Rajputs has been partly replaced by his image as the ideal ruler of all Hindus, regardless of caste. The change does not imply just a changing role for one particular God, for the very role is new. The traditional Rajput State was defined in terms of caste dominance and its coercive character was not veiled: every Rajput riding a horse or carrying weapons, such as the *kuvadi* battle-axe,[69] was a symbol of caste dominance and its power base. The Rajput state was not an imagined community in Anderson's terms, but an alliance of communities led by the king, and though we may see these communities as imagined to a degree, none approach the level of abstraction of the Hindu community. For proponents of the new Rama cult, however, these abstractions rise precisely to the level Anderson identifies, with Rama as a national symbol.

The all-Hindu Rama replaces, therefore, not his Rajput namesake but the shady figure of Ashoka evoked by the Buddhist wheel of India's national flag (Marriott 1955). We see a decontextualization of the Rama cult, replicated on a humbler level by the tendency of Khodiyar to become a regional goddess for an imagined community of Saurashtrians. This decontextualization detaches cult from caste, leading to desacralization of caste community and sacralization of regional and national units. The process is similar to what Anderson sees as necessary concomitants of the rise of nationalism,[70] though absent from his analysis and possibly from the Christian context.

The dissociation of cult from caste does not imply that castes are disappearing or even declining in importance. But as the links between hierarchy and religion are weakened, the emerging order may well be one of competing interest groups, more or less ethnic in character, which oppose each other in a new, wider field, ultimately delimited by the imagined community of the nation-state.[71]

NOTES

1. Ibn Majid, cited by Chaudhuri 1990: 113.
2. *juna gadh*: lit "old fort". Today the fortress is called the Uparkot—'upper castle'.
3. Caves and one of Ashoka's inscriptions.
4. The Jam of Navanagar (Jamnagar) led the anti-Mughal confederacy at Bhuchar Mori: the battle involved the people of northern Saurashtra, and so the Gohils of Bhavnagar, for example, are not really concerned with this legend.
5. I describe this village later. See also Tambs-Lyche 1997: 293-4.
6. See Tambs-Lyche 1997.
7. The difference in dates relates to various interpretation of the sources, which do not concern us here.
8. Tambs-Lyche 1991a; Carrin and Tambs-Lyche 1993.
9. See Tambs-Lyche 1997.
10. I have attemped to sketch the gradual development of these myths elsewhere (1996).
11. I have dealt with the construction of the region in these terms elsewhere (1994).
12. I borrow these terms from Pocock (1957a).
13. As recent debate shows, construction may be a dangerous term [Ingold (ed.) 1996: 99-146]. Here I use it broadly to separate abstract objects, necessarily products of thought, from observable and concrete ones. Saurashtra is a peninsula: the *concept* of peninsula is culturally constructed, but as land largely surrounded by sea it is an observable object.
14. As Leach put it: society is not a thing, it is a way of ordering experience (1961: 304-5). See the discussion in Ingold (ed.) 1996, 57-98, particularly the presentation of Marilyn Strathern (ibid., 60-6).

15. Durkheim 1896. I am of course aware that no such observation is possible without concepts. Still, I would maintain that the concreteness of observation implies the possibility of recognizing an object despite divergent ways of conceptualizing it.
16. See, e.g. Strathern in Ingold (ed.) 1996: 60-6. Strathern prefers the term 'sociality'. I agree with her in seeing society as a quality rather than an entity; the continuous production of social links rather than the object for which Durkheim and Radcliffe-Brown used the organic metaphor.
17. Most obvious here are ethnic boundaries as seen by Barth et al. (1969). I suggest that ethnicity is only one of several ways making boundaries, such as class and nationalism. All have in common the dissection of an unmanageable mass of social life into smaller, bounded units which are 'easier to think'.
18. I use the term 'present' broadly, since my fieldwork spanned some twenty years (1973-92), and this implies change.
19. By his own admission, this statement also expresses the views of Evans-Pritchard (1962: 46-65).
20. I am referring to the debate which opposed, in the sixties, Pocock and Dumont to comparativists such as Bailey, Berreman and Barth, mostly appearing in 'Contributions to Indian Sociology'.
21. Ingold's term ((ed.) 1996: 112-18), not to be confused with Schütz' 'life world' (1964). Ingold stresses that we live in and with the physical and biological environment, of which we form a part: 'culture' is not external to 'nature'.
22. Cf. Appadurai (ed.) 1986.
23. The term is used here in the sense of Ranger 1993.
24. Cf. Gould and White 1974.
25. See Appadurai 1981.
26. Burgess' introduction to Amarji 1882: 2.
27. This is less so in the case of Kathiawad, for in this geographically central part of the peninsula soils were poor and irrigation difficult, so that it was, in social and political terms, a peripheral region.
28. I shall later construct an etic grid, where different village types are brought into a common framework.
29. I take my use of these terms from Bateson (1972).
30. We shall see later, however, that some of Marriott's ideas do fit the pattern of interaction I observed.
31. These definitions form part of Ingold's critique of the term construction, but I am less willing to throw out this concept.
32. Lévi-Strauss' term (1962: 26). But while he assumes the 'bricoleur' to proceed by structural rules, pre-existing yet unconscious, I feel with Barth that structuring results from the process of bricolage itself.
33. Ingold (ed.) 1996: 129.
34. I cannot but cite the remark with which I.P. Desai, the great Gujarati sociologist, greeted me when I sought his advice: 'You Westerners are all the same. You

think only about caste. Caste is not very interesting. There are many themes more important in India!'

35. Weber 1948: 81-4. This is the usual translation of *ständer*.
36. One might perhaps add artisans (*shilpi*, *naukari*) but this category is seldom spoken of in these terms.
37. Zamindari was introduced to Junagadh after the Muslim conquest in 1470 and persisted until 1947.
38. The term society refers here, not to an objective entity but an image serving as a holistic reference for each particular, positioned view. In so far as these views are engaged with each other through discourse, they necessarily converge on some such holistic image.
39. This perspective did not arise only from the Patidars' situation in Britain; it incorporated immigrant experience from East Africa, Fiji, Mauritius and South Africa. It also a reflects a rise from peasantry to an important merchant and entrepreneur community in Gujarat itself.
40. I recall, here, the distinction between pragmatic and symbolic activity as sketched by Cohen 1974.
41. Spodek 1976: 26. Amin's two monographs from mainland villages (both undated) underline this tendency of peasants to migrate in search of better land or tenancy contracts.
42. Jacob 1842: 12-13; Spodek 1976: 27-9.
43. This perspective emerges clearly from Beidelman's classic study of the 'jajmani system' (1961).
44. 'Ter tansali'—lit. thirteen plates, referring to commensality. These are the castes most directly related to the agricultural division of labour dominated by the landlords, or else (as in the case of pastoralists) allies of the dominant caste. The groupings are similar to what Mayer (1958; 1960: xxx), writing about Malwa, calls 'allied castes'. See Tambs-Lyche 1997: 112-13.
45. See, e.g. Berreman 1961 and 1973; Kolenda 1990, Khare 1984, Lynch 1969, or Kapadia 1996.
46. See Tambs-Lyche 1980, 1991b.
47. Pocock 1972, Tambs-Lyche 1997: 123-8.
48. This is more doubtful these days, since Patidars and Rajputs are political rivals and youth from the two groups sometimes clash in violent fights.
49. Tambs-Lyche 1991b; see also Barth 1969.
50. Pocock 1972, Tambs-Lyche 1997: 140-1.
51. Enthoven 1921: 245-7; Pocock 1957a,1972; Tambs-Lyche 1997: 132-3.
52. I have made some inquiries about the relations between Ahir and Gujar in Rajasthan. My view reflects that of my assistant, Inder Dan Detha, who knows these communities well. In Bengal, I met Goalas affirming they were 'really' Ahir. (1997: 151-2).
53. Pocock 1972. Some Brahmin castes, for example, are very small (Enthoven 1920).
54. Spodek 1974, 1976; Tambs-Lyche 1997.

55. This is the main sanctuary of the goddess, near Mount Abu.
56. Tambs-Lyche 1982; 1992: 391-2, 1997: 306-8.
57. Muslim rule here, since AD 1298, has weakened the influence and prestige of Rajput culture—making it significantly different from Saurashtra and Rajasthan. Merchant culture was not similarly affected.
58. The terrible form of the goddess demands blood sacrifice, which is (or should be) anathema to Jains.
59. I have discussed the goddess' role in Rajput kingship elsewhere (1992, 649-53; 1991a, 1996, 1997).
60. For the specific nature of this image, see Clementin-Ojha, 1990b.
61. Tambs-Lyche 1992; 549-50; S.R. Sharma 1971, 29-30 and notes.
62. Tambs-Lyche 1992: 86; Spodek 1976. The common idea that Gandhi's father was the only Vania to occupy such a position, seems to result from the intensification of conflict in the last hundred years or so of British rule. In Rajasthan, at any rate, it was quite common to have a Vania as minister of a state—see Qanungo 1969: 50-9.
63. The *traga* was a demonstrative form of suicide practised by the bardic caste, and the sacredness of the Charan's blood made it a terrible retribution for whoever provoked it.
64. This state is in Rajasthan, around Mount Abu, bordering on Gujarat.
65. It is interesting to compare this notion of divine justice with the 'bhuta's justice', as it emerges from our recent study in South Canara (Carrin and Tambs-Lyche 1998).
66. Though Indian history is not lacking in such attempts.
67. Rama, the God-king, incarnates the ideal Kshatriya (warrior).
68. Cf. Heestermann 1985, Galey 1989.
69. Horses and certain weapons such as the *kuvadi* were monopolized by Rajputs and other Darbars.
70. The decline of a sacred language-scripture; the desacralization of the king, and the development of the concept of linear, parallel time—see Anderson 1983: xxx.
71. A.M. Shah (Shah and Desai 1988) seems to think along these lines.

CHAPTER 2

The Capitals of Saurashtra: Images and Impressions

Heureux ceux qui sont morts pour des cités charnelles.
Car elles sont le corps de la cité de Dieu.
Heureux ceux qui sont morts pour leur âtre et leur feu,
Et les pauvres honneurs des maisons paternelles.

CHARLES PEGUY

Probably no region in India—can claim as many ex-capitals in a limited space as does Saurashtra; there were more than two hundred political entities defined, during British overlordship, as 'states'. Some, it is true, held no more than one or a few villages; their chiefs had no judiciary powers, and there was little about the ruler's seat to justify the term 'capital'. But there remain a large number of towns where the ruler lived in a palace and held court in a grand manner. Bolstered by the security of the 'Pax Britannica', these rulers were able to spend large sums, no longer needed for defence, on the development of their domains, and much was spent on the capital city itself.[1] Spodek highlights the imbalance between the capitals, embellished and improved, and other towns of the peninsula.

At the end of the eighteenth century most of these other towns served as intermediate links in the system of administration and revenue collection; they had local markets but 'fostered little trade and manufacture; they did little to welcome members of these professions' (Spodek 1976: 4). Their main elite was a part of the ruling lineage, its head responsible to the ruler. The base of its power and position was the control of land revenue. Such towns remained 'urban'.

But in the capitals and some larger towns, a second group–variously consisting of merchants and moneylenders, different professionals, artisans, and soldiers—constituted a truly urban elite (Spodek 1976: 5). Trade and manufacture, calling for a community of merchants, were necessary for a ruler's prosperity. Revenue from trade passed directly to him, bypassing the feudal intermediaries, and so he could finance an army outside their control. Trade, then, was at the very base of state power; without it no ruler could be more than a chief. The integration of the countryside with the city was a product of the state, and though some villages and minor chiefdoms remained independent of larger states, we may see traditional society as a set of regions, each centred on a ruler's capital. Nowhere are the multiple pasts of Saurashtra more present than in these capitals (Spodek 1976: 5).

The capital was a node of power networks centring on the king. Other networks, such as that of the merchants, were subsidiary. Capitals grew or declined according to the fate of their rulers, until the states dissolved into republican India. Today they bear the marks of their former lords, which contribute to the specific image of each town.

PALACES

All the ex-capitals have palaces, which stand as a memory to the rulers that built them, and so recalls their rule. In this world of vanished princely states, palaces are indeed things of the past, but many still stand.

Rajkot's palace was centrally located, on a rocky cliff overlooking the river. The slope is much easier on the other side, and most of the old city, down to the gates which still stand, is on this hill. Of the palaces I have seen in Saurashtra, Rajkot's has fared the worst in recent times. Much of it has been razed to the ground, though the rubble is still left and the site has not been built up. Left standing is one wing serving as the prison—apparently it served the same purpose in princely days—while another houses the District Forest Department. These, however, occupy only a part of it, and along the empty balconies and in some empty rooms beautiful woodcarvings can still be seen. When I went to look at them, I soon realized that nobody else did—though one old Forest Department employee came forward to show me around. As I strolled about it became clear to me that this palace had been consciously erased from memory by means of physical destruction.

Indeed, the last ruler was hopeless, busying himself with wine and women, and making his Dewan sell off the state monopolies to finance his follies. Yet a generation earlier, Lakhaji had been one of the finest rulers in Saurashtra, and the one most sympathetic to the independence movement. He created the first elected assembly in any Saurashtra state, to advise the ruler (Wood 1978). Of these pasts, the most recent explains the destruction of the others. The demolition of the palace speaks for the lack of respect in which Rajkot's new urban regime held the memory of its rulers.

Things are very different in Bhavnagar. It was a larger state and there are more palaces; those in the city centre now serve various administrative functions, their monumental character lending a sense of continuity to the new age. But the former 'Garden Palace' is still the property of the ex-ruling family. Conspicuously white-washed in its splendid, well maintained gardens, it lines a street which has become part of the suburbia of the town's middle classes, and seems to invite positive comments on the old times, common in Bhavnagar. People like to stroll in front of the well-kept gardens of 'their' garden palace, though the descendants of the ruler, live in Bombay and do not lend their elegance to the social life of the town. The fact that they still maintain their palace so well is appreciated as a kind of public service to the city. And, while any reference to the ruling family would seem out of place and at worst a reactionary political statement in Rajkot, Congressmen and other republicans don't mind giving credit to the ex-rulers in Bhavnagar—even if the freedom-fighters of the 1930s had to leave Bhavnagar and take refuge in one of the British enclaves of the peninsula—or, indeed, in Rajkot. There, the message of the palace demolition is underlined by the fact that the buildings of the British 'Civil Station' remain a prominent feature of the city centre. It is, indeed, as if the British remains are seen as consistent with Rajkot's image of modernity, while the remnants of princely rule are not.

In Limbdi, too, the ruler withdrew to his garden palace, leaving the buildings in the town centre to public institutions of the new order, with one palace donated to the Ramakrishna mission. The imposing headquarters of this organization are a permanent reminder of the ruler's religious leanings, the more conspicuous since the Mission has few followers in Limbdi. While the ex-ruling family still inhabits the garden palace, one hears few positive comments on them in the town; as if they are blamed for withdrawing from public life. It is a strange fact that the ruler took away the image of Jamboo Ma, the *ishtadevata*[2] of the ruling family, from the village temple where she was accessible to his subjects, to instal her in his now private palace. Perhaps, since she was once responsible for restoring the family to power, there is suspicion that the ruler's descendants hope she may do so again.[3]

Dhrangadhra's palace is in well kept, almost like Bhavnagar's, but it remains on the outskirts of town and people do not stroll by it, as they do in Bhavnagar. Here lives one of the last living princes to have actually ruled; a highly respected man in Saurashtra, he is the vice-chancellor of the Rajkumar College in Rajkot. This college, founded as an institution exclusive to the ruling class—in the real sense of the term[4]—is still a prestigious school. In spite of this, the palace in Dhrangadhra now seems as separate from its town as that of Limbdi: few speak of the ruling family in town, to praise or criticise. People are much more concerned with the Swaminarayana sect,[5] which seems the most active and influential node of cultural and political life in Dhrangadhra these days. To the traveller entering the town, the large yellow palace is very conspicuous but townspeople hardly seem to notice it.

Not so in Jamnagar. The ex-ruler's Land-Rover is often seen about town, but the glances that follow it are not always friendly. If we follow it back to the palace, we see how it must be difficult for him to maintain the estate. The sad state of the garden attests to the fact that the royal family no longer plays a role in the city's life. There is an aura of decay: a brace of Cadillacs rusting in the old stables, which are more or less falling down, does not help. In Jamnagar they whisper, rather than talk, about the family: there are rumours of smuggling. Strangely these rumours are old, for Jamnagar was accused of smuggling in British days: present whispers may well be mere echoes of that past. All this in spite of the legendary Ranjitsinhji, one of the greatest cricket players between the wars. While the palace is no more a civic asset, the extensive town planning of the ex-rulers remains a source of pride. In a way, then, the absent prince remains a presence in Bhavnagar, while his colleague's presence in Jamnagar has become largely irrelevant to the townspeople. Their respective palaces symbolize this state of affairs, but are also important elements in constituting it. Wankaner's palace, serving for a while as an ultra-luxury hotel run by the ex-ruler, still dominates the little town completely. The 'palace' of Lathi, however, once home to Kalapi, Saurashtra's great poet to inadmissible love, fades into other buildings of the main street as Lathi has, to all intent and purposes, become a village.

In what was once the most magnificent of Saurashtra's capitals, Junagadh's palaces have all become public buildings: I have met patriots who praised the achievements of the old state, but none who complimented its rulers. This is to be expected since the last of them, having tried to accede to Pakistan, left in a hurry, taking as many of his wives as he could along with him in a DC-3. The most glorious royal marriage in Junagadh in this century was that of his favourite dog. Such happenings make good stories but may not secure, for the ruling family, a favourable image in the memory of his former people.

Still, nobody has thought of demolishing the Junagadh palaces. Perhaps it is not the memory of the ruling family that counts, but the memory of the times when the town was a capital. Junagadh, declining in relative importance since Independence, cherishes these memories. So does Bhavnagar, since in spite of continuing importance the town has lagged well behind Rajkot. The latter city, as we have seen, has no use for the old palaces, perhaps since its present importance far outshines anything that happened there in the time of the princes.

The fate of palaces, then, is highly diverse: they mean different things to different people. Obvious symbols of the past, their present symbolic value is highly variable. This variation, however, truly reflects the character of the town in which they are found.

TEMPLES

Except in a few places like Dwarka, great temples do not dominate the cityscape in Saurashtra to the extent that they do in south India. In Madurai the deity was the eternal ruler, and the king her servant, a position which made him a sacred king,[6] but in Saurashtra there was no sacred kingship. Goddesses such as Khodiyar who sustained, created or undid kings often had their main temples outside the city, in the wilderness or *jangal*.[7] Their shrine in the city might be relatively modest, even in the case of Hinglaj, that intriguing goddess who seems to be far older than the Jadeja rulers who, we are told, brought her to Jamnagar.

Temples to Rama were more obviously royal. Thus, opposite Dhrangadhra's city palace we find a large and relatively imposing example. It is built in the same style as the palace, but its street front is lower; the palace outshines the temple and not vice versa. Moreover, the blazon of the Jhala Rajput rulers of Dhrangadhra is clearly visible on the lintel of the main door to the sanctuary.

I have commented (1997: 84-6) on the relative place of Rama and the Goddess in the legitimation of Rajput polity. The Goddess is the king-maker, but in religious terms the king is simply her devotee. The annual buffalo sacrifice to the Goddess was a state ceremony, but such sacrifices might also be held by others: the cult of the Goddess was not a state cult. The Rama cult was however sponsored by the king and dominant Rajputs at the village level. Rama as the ideal ruler came to stand for Rajput identity, and for the image of his rule propagated by a ruler. In this sense, the Rama temple of Dhrangadhra might be seen as a state temple. But townspeople today choose to ignore this aspect of the past of what is now a public sanctuary, and which has gained in importance since Rama became the emblem of Hindu fundamentalism. The link to the old rule has been broken, while the deity's political role remains important. The idol of the traditional

Rajput state now stands for Hindu opposition to the secular polity.

Some rulers preferred Krishna. In all cases, however, the monumental downtown temples that rulers built to legitimate their rule, have been detached from this original purpose and have taken their place among the other temples of the town.

Temples are treated in the plural sense in Saurashtra. A village or city does not have a village or city temple, as it has in the south. In general, Saurashtra temples always belong to specific communities or sects, those built by the old rulers often being the only ones to be 'public' in the sense of having government-appointed trustees and an administrative structure that goes beyond community organization.[8] Thus temples become landmarks of the several communities in Saurashtra; their position, prestige and age become effective metonyms of the position of the community itself. Knowing the town's temples, then, one knows something of its history, as well as its social make-up. No wonder that community members invest heavily, when possible, in improving their temple, and that the decay of a sanctuary is dreaded, as it is taken to symbolize the decline of the group.

The large white temple one sees on a hill dominating most of Bhavnagar is that of the Nagar Brahmins, once the richest and by far the most prestigious community in town. They were ministers and bureaucrats, but also bankers and businessmen. They inhabited the richest quarter in town, with beautiful woodcarvings on their substantial houses. Now these are decaying, as the fortunes of the group have declined since Independence, but care is still taken to maintain the temple. Yet, in spite of its dominant position, there is no doubt in Bhavnagar that this is a Nagar temple and in no way a city temple.

Most temples are associated with a caste or a cluster of closely allied castes. The Vallabhacharya Havelis—which strictly speaking are not temples but the palaces where the Maharajas[9] of the sect live with the idol of Krishna—are identified with the Vanias, and transcend subgroups among the Vaishnavite wing of these merchant castes, whereas Jains tend to have separate sanctuaries for each subcaste (Banks 1992).

But the Swaminarayana temples, which have an important place in most towns, transcend caste. They stand as the symbols of yet another way to create community in India: that of the sect.[10] Here, the buildings are identified with the sect as a whole. The differences among the Swaminarayana sects are more important to insiders than to outsiders. The sect is seen not just as a religious phenomenon but a broad social movement, which people identify with a number of important positions:

militant opposition to sacrificial cults, and animal sacrifice in particular; vegetarianism and teetotalism; and, above all, a puritanism inciting members to save and invest, which in the popular view of members and outsiders alike has been the main factor behind their economic and social success. The buildings of the Swaminarayanas, and in particular those of the 'new' sect;[81] stand, therefore, as symbols of modernity, progress, and a particular form of Hindu revival. We shall return to the Swaminarayanas later.

In opposition to this, Goddess temples represent the past. As they remain the most important and popular class of temples in Saurashtra, there are constant innovations to adjust Goddess-worship to the exigencies of the present. Still, the associations made, in the first place, regarding these temples are to the bonds between the Goddess and a particular Rajput clan or caste, by way of the often well-remembered myths. These myths are probably the largest single class of oral memory that makes the past of Saurashtra present to its inhabitants.

PUBLIC WORKS AND TOWN PLANNING

The town walls and gates are among the most obvious and imposing monuments of the past, as are the old forts scattered over the countryside. Their presence serves to remind the inhabitants of their tumultuous past. The state of these monuments varies, but this variation seems due to different exigencies of modern traffic, from one town to another, rather than their identification with a particular, remembered rule. Thus Rajkot's walls are in better shape than most: but the old town that they shield is now a small and rather peripheral part of the city. Similarly, Wadhwan retains its walls, as nearby Surendranagar arose in British times, around the railway station. In Dhrangadhra and Jamnagar, varying parts of the walls have been torn down, leaving the gates to stand as monuments. Both cities retain enough of their fortifications, however, to mark the townscape profoundly: it must be impossible for their inhabitants to be unaware of their historic importance. But Bhavnagar's walls were removed in princely days and are scarcely remembered. Indeed, none of the old capitals—except Rajkot—is as removed from the feudal past as Bhavnagar, whose identity seems bound to trade, commerce and that flourish of liberal culture we tend to associate with the bourgeoisie.

Well remembered, and a popular spot for outings and picknicks, is Bhavnagar's large tank, which provided the city an excellent water supply in princely times. It was built by Shri Azam Gaurishankar Oza the Dewan in 1871-2 and named after him (Yajnik 1889). Its popular name, Gaga-talao, conserves the nickname (Gaga) given to this popular figure. Today the lake is too small for the growing population, but in public appreciation it still attests to their ruler's concern for his city. The tank in Dhrangadhra is smaller, but even more beautifully adorned with temples and pavilions, and is equally popular for excursions. Yet here I heard fewer remarks praising the old rulers for their foresight—even if, since Dhrangadhra has grown more slowly, the tank is probably better adjusted to modern demand.

Bridges, like tanks, are often named after the rulers that built them, though some have changed their names—mostly on paper—to commemorate all-Indian heroes like Gandhi, Nehru or Sardar Vallabhbhai Patel. Only in Junagadh have the old rulers' names disappeared, except for their tombs. The names of British engineers and administrators remain in use to a surprising extent, as they are still important figures in local history—partly, no doubt, since indirect rule sheltered the people from many of the negative impacts of colonialism.

JUNAGADH: THE ANCIENT FORTRESS

I have told of my first view of Junagadh from the plane, with its spectacular position under Mount Girnar. It is equally impressive from the plains. Entering by one of the gates, the town rises in front, and the high parapets of the fortress merge with the mountain peaks beyond, on which may just be discerned some white temples.

Junagadh is beautiful, and, dominated as it is by its fortress and its sacred mountain, its existence needs no further explanation. The sacredness and the military aspect merge even further as, in the soft sandstone under the fort, a number of ancient caves are found, dating from Buddhist times. We must note, too, the presence of one of Ashoka's inscriptions.[12] Tod's impression of the city, which he visited in 1822, closely reflects my own:

> From whichever side Joonagurh is viewed, the mind is immediately carried back to the earliest period of history. . . . It is venerable from its age, and romantic from position, while its numerous massive square towers, and crenellated parapet, give it an appearance of strength and dignity. Assuredly it had as much claim to the one, before the invention of gunpowder, as it still has to the other. (Tod 1971; 362)

In short, the town has a character derived directly from its history and monuments. Its age and dignity have lent Junagadh pride of place among Saurashtra's cities, and there is some resentment, in Junagadh, regarding the recent and phenomenal growth of Rajkot.

The stereotyped view of Junagadh and its inhabitants, in Saurashtra, is in tune with these impressions. The town is seen as beautiful, and its inhabitants as traditional; but initiative or capacity for innovation is seldom ascribed to them. Its rulers were known for conservatism and absolutism well before the flight of the last Nawab to Pakistan, in 1947. But Junagadhis themselves, like other citizens of Saurashtra, share a nostalgia about the 'good old days' of princely rule. They reject forcefully the idea that Junagadh's administration was worse than that of other princely states, and cite examples to defend their view; thus Junagadh had the first college in Saurashtra apart from those of Rajkot and Gondal, which were meant for the education of the princes. This nostalgia is not felt in the countryside, however, where the disappearance of zamindari goes unmourned.

Junagadh is probably the most traditional of the large cities of Saurashtra. The city is still dominated by the palaces and mosques built by the Nawabs, their Islamic architecture and daub colour lending a uniform aspect to the scene. This aspect has not been spoilt by modernity, nor have the buildings been overloaded with those numerous protuberant add-ons that travellers know so well from most Indian cities. Trade and commerce is still found in the bazaar, each street named for the craft or trade found there, as obviously planned by the rulers, in the manner of Islamic cities.[13] A traveller from the western Asia would easily feel at home here. The town walls—much too large for the population of some five thousand Tod found there—still coincide with the extent of the main urban area, whose plan corresponds largely with the sketch he made in 1822. An exception is the north end of the old city, marked 'jungle' in Tod's sketch. Here, the relatively recent streets lack the planned aspect of the older quarters (Tod 1971: 361-2). We might conclude that the city stands witness to an almost unbroken cultural continuity.

Yet there have been dramatic breaks in its history. Tod found Junagadh in a state of 'ruin and decay'. In the eighteenth century, however, Junagadh had been the most powerful of the Kathiawar states, and the treaties of Colonel Watson upheld its demands on *zor-talabi*—a kind of tribute—from most other states of the peninsula. Towards the end of that century, however, long wars with Bhavnagar weakened Junagadh and must have depleted the treasury. The great Dewan Amarji was murdered in 1784, and a period of internal strife followed. Junagadh cannot then have been a safe place for merchants, and peasants, too, must have suffered from the continuous passage of armies.[14] Even if the famine of 1791 added greatly to the difficulties of the people, the decay and depopulation observed by Tod must have been, to a large extent, the result of the collapse of the political order.[15] Tod, partisan to his Rajputs, was no friend of Muslim rulers, but he clearly saw the decay and poverty as a result of misrule.[16] It is interesting to see that 'The most numerous classes are the Nagar and Girnara Brahmins. In nearly equal numbers may be the Mooslems, and the rest is made up of the agricultural and artizan classes, as Aheers, Kolis, &c. &c.; there being few, if any, Rajpoots.' (ibid.)

The Nagar and Girnar Brahmins had vested interest in the place. The Nagars were landowners as well as bureaucrats; the Girnars held specific rights as temple priests in this centre of pilgrimage, and they, too, held land. Muslims, of course, were also likely to be connected to the state and its bureaucracy, especially the army. While Tod notes the presence of artisans and agriculturists, they must have been few, if, as he states, the two Brahmin castes and the Muslims formed a clear majority. Tod does not mention Vanias at all, nor the other trading classes identified by Amarji. The obvious conclusion seems to be that traders, craftsmen and lower-class people had left the town in large numbers, leaving mainly those inhabitants who were unable to realize their assets by going elsewhere.

The *Tarikh-i-Sorath*, however, though written at about the same time by Amarji's son Ranchodji, gives a very different picture:

> In this country have been settled from time immemorial—Girnara Brahmans, Ahers, Khants, Kolis, Parmar Rajputs, Vaghelas, Vala Rajputs, Chudasama Rajputs, Sarasvati and Soratha Brahmans, as well as Surthi people. There are also Lohanas and Bhatias, whom king Naughan brought from Sindh. The governors and Naibs of the Ahmedabad and Dihli Sultans maintained Sayyids, Baluchis, Lodhis and Afghans in various offices, paying them salaries and pensions; but the cultivating classes immigrated from Gujarat (Amarji 1882: 27)

But the description of Ranchodji may refer to the city as it was in his father's time, when the city was flourishing, when Junagadh,

> . . . though it had been founded on a remote, forested hill . . . nevertheless had a great variety of artisans producing textiles, turbans, headdresses, dhotis and petticoats. They manufactured silk stuffs, like those of Ahmedabad and Surat, called *mashru*, *atlas*, and *panchpate*. Painters, dyers, workers in shells, engravers, embroiderers, and tailors had their workshops as did perfumers. Bazaars had an abundance of produce and Bohoras, Khatris and Bhatia castemen carried on trade. (Spodek 1976: 13)

Most of the trade and manufacture indicated was clearly intended for local consumption; there is no indication of significant long-distance trade. Apparently, most of this activity had gone by 1822. True, the end of the eighteenth century saw a decline in traditional forms of trade and manufacture in India. These were the decades when British goods, bolstered by colonial trade policies, replaced indigenous manufactures. The decline of Surat at this time is well known. But such decline was not universal.[17] Bhavnagar was a rising commercial centre at the time, challenging Junagadh's military and political position. 'The ancient castle' had, in fact, lost its position as political centre of the peninsula.

Junagadh's decline was thus due to political factors.[18] This generalization is substantiated by the state's response to piracy at sea, when the Nawab, unable to protect trade, simply 'closed the most infested ports' (Spodek 1976: 12). Junagadh was a political centre due to its military advantages and its strong fortress; in its shelter trade might flourish, but trade was never a primary factor in shaping the town.

When the town was depopulated in 1822, people must have gone elsewhere. The mobility of the urban population is underlined by Spodek;[19] it contributed to what he calls the 'enormous volatility' of the city-states (1976: 32-3) with which the population of a city might rise or fall quite abruptly.

Such groups would return to their cities. The population of Junagadh in 1961 was 95.900, almost twenty times higher than Tod's estimate. But if the city is far from poor in an Indian context, the explosive growth of Rajkot and even the expansion of Bhavnagar and Jamnagar have left it far behind. Even today, administration and other services, rather than trade and manufacture, remain the mainstay of the town's economy. Junagadh has thus retained its character. Fortress and temple, centre of pilgrimage and administration, it was always the least mercantile of Saurashtra's cities. Its romantic beauty reflects these functions, and the position of Nagar Brahmins in the town—they are nowhere more important—reflects the relative absence of trade and merchant communities. Yet these continuities only underline Junagadh's dependence on its place in the networks of power. While Junagadh is an outstanding example of a town dominated by its political role, other towns were equally influenced by politics.

JAMNAGAR: THE PARIS OF SAURASHTRA

Jamnagar is not particularly old, having been founded in AD 1539 or 1540 (JMG: 622). It is not strictly a port; the actual harbour is at Bedi a few miles away. Economically, this makes little difference, for Jamnagar grew and prospered as a centre of trade.[20]

I have noted elsewhere (1997) how Jamnagar's situation near the mouth of the Gulf of Kacch has been an important factor in this growth. When it was founded, the Portuguese were busy establishing complete control over shipping to and from the Gulf of Cambay, through their bases at Diu and Daman. They had been burning Gujarat ports as far north as Mangrol on the west coast of Saurashtra. Whether intended or not by its founder, Jamnagar may have given Gujarat an alternative outlet for trade at a time when many merchants wished to avoid the Portuguese, since their control of the Gulf of Oman was much less complete.

Navanagar, as it was then called, prospered with the decline of Portuguese power in these waters, as the Bhatias, the outstanding traders of the city, came to dominate the trade on Oman and Zanzibar. For the shipping Westerners associate with the word *dhow*, Jamnagar has been an important centre at least since the seventeenth century. This commercial prosperity was the basis for the growth of the port over and above its local rivals—from chiefdom to an early modern state through the sixteenth and seventeenth century. It was the first of the Rajput states of Saurashtra to reach this stature. Junagadh, its main rival, was the seat of a Muslim viceroy of the Gujarat Sultanate, later of the Moguls. Its strength came from land revenue, and trade thrived under a power umbrella. In Jamnagar, it was instead the prosperous trade which provided the funds for military expansion and control of the countryside (Tambs-Lyche 1997).

Even now, the modern port is of regional importance. But other activities were added to the sea trade. There is marble in the nearby hills, copper at Khambhalia, and pearl fisheries in the Rann of Kacch, while the town was known for its textile dyers and for silk and gold embroidery.[21] Janaki (1966) lists Jamnagar as one of the 'diversified' towns.[22] But Jamnagar is also a place of idiosyncrasies, which can be ascribed to the interests or whims of the rulers.

What strikes the visitor to Jamnagar, is the wide avenues and well-planned central areas. This aspect, utterly different from that of Junagadh, is again due to royal policies. Jamnagar, says Spodek,

> . . . attempted to build a 'Paris of Saurashtra'. The ruler tore down slums at the centre of the city and replaced them with new government offices and private shops. He cut wide roads through densely populated communities, destroying homes and businesses as he went. These new roads were open only to motor traffic; they were closed to the bullock-cart transportation customary in Saurashtra. Spacious new suburban subdivisions were planned. Some were built, but most remain until today as unexecuted blueprints in the Jamnagar Municipality Planning Office. (Spodek 1976: 45)

This extensive rebuilding of the city was undertaken by Jam Ranjitsinhji. 'One of my earliest concerns', He wrote in his 1924-5 administrative report that one of his first concerns was 'to improve the sanitation of the city and its health, which was not of the best, with chronic visitations of plague, cholera and malarial fevers, which medical efforts could not combat or control. In 1914, I took in hand a wide scheme of city improvement . . . .' (JMG: 500). The effects are pleasant, and Jamnagar has avoided the problems of congestion and public health so common in Indian cities. Apparently this was exactly what the Jam wanted: Spodek's description of it is perhaps a little uncharitable. The rebuilding may have been brutal, but then so was Haussman's in Paris. And, if the 1932-3 report is to be believed, there were resettlement schemes too: 2000 'cattlemen' were moved 'outside the Khoja gate where new and commodious buildings were erected for them' (JMG: 500).

The old walls and their gates were retained, lending character to the city. 'Its charm', says the Gazetteer, '. . . lies in the combination of old and new' (JMG: 501). The plans may have proved too grand for execution, but the result stands witness to the way in which Saurashtrian rulers lavished attention on their capitals (Spodek 1976: 45). Typically, Ranjitsinhji was not the first Jam to rebuild the city; his ancestor Ranmalji had done so, though on much smaller scale, in the 1830s, while Meraman the Dewan, had rebuilt the fortifications of the town in the late eighteenth century (JMG: 151).[23] The castle that dominates the centre, situated in the middle of an artificial lake, was built in 1839-45, ostensibly to 'provide relief work for the people affected by famine' (JMG: 624). The fort surrounding the lake could hold a thousand soldiers.

In Saurashtra, everybody knows of Ranjitsinhji's world fame as a cricketer. Says the Gazetteer, he 'naturally made Jamnagar a nursery for geniuses in cricket'. The same work goes on to mention a number of these, who have been—there is no mistaking the pride here—'Jamnagar's gift to cricket', and finally to note that 'The present Jam Shatrusalyasinhji is also a good cricketer' (JMG: 542).

But Jamnagar is, above all, remarkable for the number and character of its medical institutions. Most spectacular of these is the Solarium. This consists of a thirty-foot high tower on which is mounted a rotating wing with ten chambers. It was built to the ideas of one Dr. Saidman, whose similar structure, at Aix-les-Bains in France, was designed for solar treatment of tuberculosis, skin diseases, rheumatism, rickets, malaria and certain types of cancer. An electric motor makes the wing revolve; it makes one round in sixty minutes. This expensive and ingenious device, built in the 1930s, is now the only one of its kind, as its French counterpart was destroyed during the war (JMG: 555).

Ranjitsinhji also built the Irwin Hospital, to which has since been added the Ba Shri Sajuba Female Hospital, the Ma Shri Tejuba Maternity Home, and the Victoria Jubilee Hospital. The old state also had hospitals in Khambhalia, Dhrol and Dwarka. Though hospital facilities have been considerably extended since independence, Jamnagar State was certainly well advanced in this field for its time (JMG: 552-4).

The rulers also promoted Ayurvedic medicine. In the eighteenth century, during the rule of Tamachi, the royal vaid is said to have controlled an outbreak of plague. Eminent vaids served Vibhaji (1852-95) and 'laid the foundation for the revival of Ayurveda'. In 1940, the ruler and his queen founded an Ayurvedic Society, financially supported by the State. An Ayurvedic library and museum were established a year later. Encouraged by the rulers, Pranjivan Mehta and his collaborators translated the classic, *Charaka-Samhita* into English, Hindi and Gujarati. Six volumes each were published in 1946. A large building called the Dhanvantari Mandir was built to house these activities, with an auditorium seating 800, and an Ayurvedic Vidyalaya came into being. Today, the city is home to the Institute of Ayurvedic Studies and Research, the Central Institute of Research in Indigenous Systems of Medicine, and the Gujarat Ayurveda University. There are four Ayurvedic hospitals. In these developments, which have made Jamnagar a national centre of Ayurveda, the ruling family has played a central role (JMG: 565-7).

But cricket and medicine are only two of Jamnagar's idiosyncracies. Its policies were enigmatic at times to the British, with whom the state was not popular. When in the second half of the eighteenth century, Bhavnagar entered into an alliance with the British to curb piracy, Jamnagar chose to protect its trade by an alliance with the pirates (Spodek 1976: 12). Later, and even today, it has been known as a haven for smugglers, including traffic in illegal migrants to the Gulf—for which Jamnagar is ideally situated. Today, the town is an important Air Force Station, with other military establishments as well, and one of the centres of offshore oil exploitation. Diversified, ever renewing itself, influenced strongly by trade and industry, Jamnagar is very different from Junagadh. They have only one factor in common, the dominant role of the former rulers in shaping their character.

BHAVNAGAR: SYMBOL OF THE LIBERAL AGE

Less spectacular to the visitor than either of the two preceding towns, Bhavnagar nevertheless has a character all its own. It is relatively a modern city, founded in 1723. The foundation of this port initiated a policy of promoting trade, and this stress on economics became a *leitmotif* in Bhavnagar's development. If Junagadh was dominated by politics and religion, and Jamnagar by trade balanced by the sometimes idiosyncratic policies of its rulers, Bhavnagar stands as a symbol of the 'liberal age' in Saurashtra; open-minded, pragmatic, and free—a viewpoint shared by the British, with whom the rulers sought an alliance.

A glance at the map explains why this was good policy. Bhavnagar's immediate hinterland was small at first, and the port had competitors close by, notably Cambay—once the main port of central Gujarat—and Gogha. To gain the upper hand in this situation, Bhavnagar sought and realized an alliance with Surat, and this led to the British connection once Surat came under British control (Tambs-Lyche 1997).

Tod visited Bhavnagar in 1821, and his observations provide an interesting contrast to his comments on Junagadh. He observed 'the crowds of wealthy merchants traversing the streets, from whom, as the poet Chund says, "cities derive their beauty;" and in this point of view, Bhaonuggur was certainly beautiful' (Tod 1971: 260). He liked the ruler, who received him courteously, but was shocked in his 'Rajput prejudices' by the fact that the traditional minstrels at the palace had been replaced by Arab tabors and other incongruities

> . . . whether of things animate or inanimate, the conclave was the most motley I ever beheld. Arabian and Rajpoot costumes were here commingled, and every thing had a sort of amphibious aspect. The hall of reception was embellished by handsome glass lustres, but these were hoisted by double-blocks, evidently belonging to the dock-yard, and which might have reeved the halyards of a first-rate top-gallant sail. . . . (1971: 261)

The ruler was proud of his musical clock, especially since he had bought it for a tenth of its original price at a sale of the Peshwa's effects. Tod spent the evening admiring the Chinese toys of the ruler's smallest child, and saw the port, where the ruler proudly showed him his little navy. Half the ruler's revenues, says Tod, came from the port, in spite of a decline in traffic; it had once been two-thirds.[24] An anecdote, too, shows the ruler's interest in trade: one of his largest ships had been seized by the British, since it was carrying slaves from Mozambique. The ruler felt it highly unjust that he should be held responsible for the merchant's dispositions; he had, he said, simply rented out his ship (1971: 263-4).

It is clear that Wajesinhji, the ruler, was trying his best to be modern. Tod is amused by the incongruities that result, but the British view of Bhavnagar was, in general, highly positive. The friendship had, however, been threatened by an episode which shows that Wakhtsinhji, the then ruler, was still a Hindu king. During the famine of 1813-14, some low-caste people killed a cow for food. Wakhatsinhji punished the offenders with death. The British, after considerable deliberation, took away his rights of civil jurisdiction, as also of criminal justice in three parganas. This serious blow is said to have hastened the death of the ruler—though the rights were later restored to his successor (BDG: 73-4). Still, Bhavnagar was Britain's oldest and truest ally in Saurashtra. And the characteristics that made it a progressive state lasted till the end of its existence.

Typically, Bhavnagar is not a walled city, though it was built as such. The walls are long gone; I have not found the date of their removal. The town plan reveals a distinction between the older and the more recent parts of the city, but the transition is gradual; expansion would seem to have been almost continuous since the town was founded. The gazetteer describes the old walled city: the castle (*darbargadh*) was in the centre, surrounded by the high-caste quarters. The main street traversed the city from Ghogha Gate in the south to the Khar Gate, leading to the port in the north. It was the main shopping area, while the bazaar occupied several side streets. Streets and lanes were narrow, and divided the old town into *wads* populated by the various communities, whose status generally diminished as one got farther from the centre. On the fringe of the old town lived low-status or peripheral communities such as 'Harijans, Vaghris, Bharwads, etc.' (BDG: 567, quoting R.K. Trivedi 1961: 389-90).

But unlike Junagadh, where a similar pattern still structures the town, or Jamnagar, where the old centre has been entirely rebuilt and re-planned, in Bhavnagar the old centre has remained a nucleus around which the modern town has developed. The bazaar and many public buildings remain in the cente, though some government functions and several schools and colleges are located in the new extensions, and new markets have come up around the dock estate, catering to the wholesale trade (ibid.). As the town grew, the ruler moved to the suburbs too, building his Motibag Palace surrounded by gardens. Later this, again, was replaced by another palace outside the town, the Motibag becoming the state secretariat (now it houses the Collector's office and the District Panchayat) while the 'State lancers, infantry parade ground, jail and police lines which were formerly outside the town now stand in the midst of extended suburban and town planning area' (ibid.).

This description gives an impression of continuous growth, is substantiated by Trivedi's comments in his survey of Saurashtra industry on the eve of the Second World War (1939: 567-8). In Saurashtra, such relative harmony between growth, planning and maintenance of the original character of the town is unusual. More than anything else, it shows how the ruler's view of his capital coincided with the requirements of economic growth. For the rulers were highly interested in town planning, preparing 'a model Town Planning Scheme which gave birth to the well-planned residential area named Krishnanagar with separate zones for the location of industries' (BDG: 568). The total area covered by the Town Planning Scheme of the former rulers was 1500 acres; it was planned for a population of 48,000. A progressive aspect of the Scheme was the provision of low-interest loans on easy terms by the then Darbar Bank (BDG: 485). Typically, too, Bhavnagar had the peninsula's first organized municipality, in 1872; the Act regulating it was extended in 1875 and in 1894 to include nine other cities in the state. Together with the development of village panchayats from 1929, these developments stand witness to the progressive nature of the rulers (BDG: 475 ff).

The beginnings of a modern water supply system date to 1887. The first state school dates to 1852, the Samaldas College (now part of Saurashtra University) 1885, and educational grants were offered by the State from 1884 (BDG: 477 and 498-9) onwards. Bhavnagar now has no less than seven colleges for Ayurveda, commerce, law, technology and science. It also houses the Central Salt and Marine Chemicals Research Institute, as well as six *pathshalas* for the teaching of Sanskrit, four of which date to princely times. More unusually, the state even provided special schools for untouchables, who were exempt from fees. With this emphasis on education, it is hardly surprising that Bhavnagar has earned its name in the liberal arts. A student friend told me of a game he had played with his mates; each of them was to go out and find a poet in the shortest possible time. They all returned within a couple of hours, each bringing a poet along. . . . While I cannot subscribe to the literal truth of the saying 'Everybody in Bhavnagar is a poet', I certainly met a surprising number. One can hardly fail to do so; poets and artists, lovers of literature and folklore, abound.[25]

The town has the best bookshops in Saurashtra, including those run by the two sons of the town's most famous author, Jhaverchand Meghani. His recreation of Saurashtra folklore made him the 'national author' of the peninsula. As he was a follower of Gandhi, even the relatively liberal rule of Bhavnagar became too strict for his views, and he wrote some of his works in British territory. Even so, the town has kept its liberal reputation. This cultural aspect, which stands for Bhavnagar in the popular imagination, is not all that is Bhavnagar today. It is also an important industrial centre, second in Saurashtra only to Rajkot, as well as a regionally important port. All in all, the progressive politics of its rulers has made Bhavnagar the most well-balanced, economically, socially and culturally, of the peninsula's urban centres. This is not to deny the occurrence of strikes and industrial conflict.

RAJKOT: OLD AND NEW

Rajkot is a very different city. Here, the contrast between old and new is striking. Old Rajkot, the centre of a minor state, was a small town, walled, built on a low hill, and on a traditional layout. Its fate may be symbolized by the remains of the palace, now largely in ruins, as noted; one wing is occupied by the Forest Department, perhaps symbolizing, by its dilapidated surroundings, the state of vegetation in this part of the peninsula.

With the exception of Lakhajiraj (1890-1930), the rulers who lived here were not noted for their progressive policies (Wood 1978). In fact, it was rather a sleepy place. When the British decided to locate their Residency in Rajkot, the choice was due less to the importance of the place than its central location; moreover, here the Resident avoided too close contact with any one of the important rulers. In Rajkot he could be impartial. Once it had become the centre of British influence in the peninsula, however, Rajkot also became the node of a road and rail network that the British sponsored. Modern Rajkot took off from there.

Lakhajiraj might have deserved a place in the collective memory of the town. Yet unlike those of Junagadh, Jamnagar or Bhavnagar, the old rulers of Rajkot have no real place in living memory. This may not be entirely their fault, for among the inhabitants of modern Rajkot few can have any idea of the old times. The vast majority of the town's inhabitants are recent immigrants.

Today's Rajkot, then, is a very different place indeed. A visitor may even fail to notice the existence of the old town. Modern Rajkot is a post-Independence phenomenon. Buildings, new and often large, are set in spacious grounds; there are parks and greens, and the whole impression is rather pleasant but lacks completely the romantic dimension of the 'older' cities. The old centre remains apart, almost like a museum; it has not developed with the rest. Between the old and the modern city are the remains of a third Rajkot: the British enclave, suitably embellished for its political function, and situated on what looks like a rather dry cricket lawn. The former British Residency looks both pleasant and inoffensive, and the neo-Gothic Barton library and museum is still a central landmark in the town. It is from these much lower buildings that we may trace the decline of the old fortified city and the rise of the vast expanses of modern Rajkot.

The fourth Rajkot grew up in British times between the Residency and the old fortified town. Here is the market that grew with the increasing importance of the British administration and the central location of the town in the peninsula's railway system. This is the most lively part of Rajkot today, but the growth is in the suburbs, industrial, commercial and residential, that have appeared all round the town.

The expansion continues, with new housing estates coming up all the time. Some of the housing is in cooperative estates, offering an opportunity for continued geographical clustering by caste; but I am not in a position to state whether such clusters are really typical. Where I lived for a while, there was a concentration of people from the *ter tansali*; Rajputs of low-to-medium standing, urbanized Bharwads, Kanbis and Ahirs, and others. This was a lower-middle class suburb. One of my friends, on the other hand, recently built a house in a quarter where many doctors, engineers and lawyers live: here, high-standing Patidars live among Vanias and Brahmins. Class may be more important than caste here, but the correlation between them is equally clear. The new suburbs are not restricted to a single caste but a cluster of different castes sharing a similar class position.

Rajkot is the industrial centre of Saurashtra, with modern industries. One very important sector is the production of oil engines and pumps for irrigation, an industry which evolved not through investment by the old merchant communities, but by the entrepreneurship of the Kanbi/Patidar caste. A crisis of growth around 1980 re-structured the industry, as many of the smaller companies had to close down due to fierce competition. Thus the successful ones have long since outgrown the small-scale sector, and the Kanbi/Patidar caste—known as Patidar rather than Kanbi in Rajkot—has a predominant position in the city. The growth rate has provided opportunities for entrepreneurs of very diverse backgrounds, and it is a striking that, in spite of its quick growth, *bastis* or shantytowns remain small and temporary in Rajkot. There is no real slum of the size and importance usually associated with Indian industrial cities. While the demand for housing is intense, building activity seems to absorb much of the growth. At the same time, it seems, *bastis* are soon displaced by new developments and therefore do not attain any degree of permanence.

Traffic is dense; only in Ahmedabad have I seen more two-wheelers than in Rajkot. Girls ride mopeds to school, and the occasional girl in trousers even rides a motorcycle. The town has the greatest density of ice-cream parlours I have ever seen, replacing the teashop and traditional sweet-seller; in Rajkot, one meets one's friends in the 'parlour'. These are largely middle-class venues; but it is less easy in Rajkot than elsewhere in India to draw a line between the middle-class and other townspeople.

These are all signs of modernity, yet in spite of appearances Rajkot may be less Westernized than many traditional cities. All the material goods of the modern world are there, and the town has wide international business connections. But English is seldom spoken, there is no bookshop of note selling books in English, and few Westerners are seen here. The non-vegetarian restaurants are almost all in Indian style, as are the hotels.

Incidentally, the ice-cream parlours and sweetshops provide a lively market for milk products, and Westphal-Hellbosch found several thousand Bharwads[26] settled on the fringes of Rajkot. They seem still to be there, in spite of the statement by the director of the large and modern state dairy that the peasant castes—notably the Kanbi/Patidars—have taken an ever larger share of dairy deliveries. This indicates, as inquiries confirmed, that there is a lively market in direct sales from Maldharis to customers. Motorcycles loaded with milk jugs and ridden by pastoralists in traditional dress are a common sight.

Apparently, nowhere in Saurashtra are we further away from traditional society. Modernity, whatever is meant by that ambiguous term, has come further in Rajkot than in any other town of the area. But as the example of the milkmen illustrates, this may be a spurious conclusion. The persistence of tradition is indicated by the strength of caste organizations and even by musical taste. It is the cassette producers of Rajkot who cater to a revival of the traditional myths of the area. Thus cassettes recording the myth of Khodiyar sell well. Another new development, by 1991, was the large number of stickers, on cars and motorcycles, carrying the slogans 'Jay Mataji', 'Jay Khodiyar Ma', outnumbered those referring to Rama. The latter, however, was present in the form of a duetto from the televised *Ramayana*, between Sita and Rama. It was by far the most popular tune played in restaurants and other public places.

In 1991, I found several of my friends enthusiastic about the BJP, the fundamentalist Hindu party. They showed a concern with the past that, in the midst of Rajkot's modernity, seemed extreme. 'You should really say Kathiawar, not Saurashtra', my landlord reminded me; he was a Jhala Rajput, employed in the state dairy. 'Yes', I retorted, 'we must not forget the battle of Bhuchar Mori!' My landlord grew enthusiastic: 'Ah! You know about Bhuchar Mori!'—and we were led into a discourse on the glorious past. Clearly, in the spring of 1991, the local branch of the BJP was less concerned with the Ayodhya issue; would come later. The main thrust of my landlord's argument was a protest or reaction against the role of the Congress in what I have elsewhere called the 'merchantization' of Saurashtra (Tambs-Lyche 1982).

The BJP supporters I met, all came from the 'thirteen castes' which used to be the mainstay of the feudal system, and included Rajputs and Bharwads. They were all immigrants to Rajkot, in the sense of having their family roots elsewhere. During my 1991 visit I could not ascertain whether this was typical or true of other cities. But the people I knew, were clearly concerned with the kind of revitalization of tradition that today, in many parts of the world, confronts modernity. In Rajkot, the post-Independence trend—an ever-increasing influence of urban and merchant values as against those of the Darbars—had reached its apogee. It was actively countered, by 1991, by a revitalization of 'traditional' values associated with Rajput dominance and the time of the princes.[27]

Perhaps I am a romantic, but I had no difficulty in seeing what my friends and associates were nostalgic about. To side with them is another matter, of course. I still ask myself what happened to the nice outdoor restaurant, sited on a roundabout on the outskirts of the city, where I had several good meals in 1989-90. It was run by two Memon brothers, Muslims of course, yet not to my eyes obvious 'fundamentalists' or hard-liners. When I returned in 1991, the restaurant was gone. Were the Memon brothers victims of the Hindu-Muslim conflicts of the intervening period ? I do not know, and perhaps I never shall, for nobody answered my questions in the matter, nor seemed to remember the restaurant had ever been there—which made me suspicious.

DHRANGADHRA: 'A BACKWARD PLACE'

These sketches will give the reader an idea of the very different character of some of the main cities of the peninsula. Whereas Rajkot has decisively outgrown its princely past, Junagadh, Jamnagar and Bhavnagar are still heavily marked by it. In Dhrangadhra, on the other hand, the past seems lost but the reason cannot be growth, for it is, in the view of some inhabitants, a rather god-forsaken place. It seems the very opposite of Rajkot's dynamism. Perhaps the past is not lost but stowed away consciously!

The royal family still lives in its garden palace on the outskirts of the city. Their city palaces have been taken over by the new administration, and the Rama temple, opposite the old city palace, is now run by a public trust and open to everyone. The city centre was nicely planned by the rulers, but the turn-of-the century townscape, with its moderately impressive buildings in Indian gothic, is now overgrown, as by mushrooms, by the strange outcrops that Indian city building seems to grow.

As a whole, the royal imprint on the town is a thing of the past. Important to present-day city life is the Swaminarayana temple, to which people stream for the Sunday *satsang*, men entering from one street, women from another. The general impression of Dhrangadhra is that it has been ruralized since Independence. Its main industry, the saltworks with the salt research institute, is still active but has not expanded greatly. Expansion, such as it is, has come from the numerous small shops serving the rural population, and has not produced the elegant, modern middle class we find in Rajkot and Bhavnagar. The resulting dominance of the small bourgeoisie probably explains the architectural decline of older buildings, the absence of any newer, grand building schemes, as well as the cultural dominance of the puritanical Swaminarayanas sect.

THE VARIATION IN FORM

Cities were and are centres of power; their changing fortunes an expression of changing power relations. This is true not only of the capitals, but also smaller towns. The only available sociological studies of these towns are those of Mahuva by Desai (1964) and Pandit (1965), and of Jetpur by Véronique Dupont (1995, 1996). Mahuva is typical only on an abstract level, while Dupont's study mainly concerns industrialization and commerce. More generally, Janaki has classified the various towns by the occupation of their inhabitants (1966). Basing himself on the 1961 survey, he arrived at the categories indicated below (Fig. 2).

The agricultural towns may be seen as very large villages. As towns they are small and peripheral: but their large number points to the fluid boundary, in Saurashtra, between rural and urban settlements, which is significant. Among manufacturing towns some have grown around a single industry, such as Mithapur near Okha with its large cement works. Here, the relatively modern factory towers over the city. But they also include Bhavnagar, which has considerable industrial development, but is too diverse to give the impression of a factory town. Towns classified under trade and commerce are not important centres, but local or regional markets, serving surrounding villages. The really important markets are found in towns that harbour other activities—and which for the most part were capitals in princely days.

Diversified towns (not fitting into the other categories)	28
Agricultural towns (more than 37.68 per cent work in agriculture)	24
Manufacturing towns (more than 26.62 per cent in this activity)	10
Trade and Commerce (more than 20.3 per cent in this activity)	7
Household Industry (more than 13.48 per cent in this activity)	6
Construction (more than 3.74 per cent in this activity)	6
Mining (more than 7.12 per cent in this activity)	5
Transport and Communications (more than 36.43 per cent in this activity)	5
Other services (more than 38.71 per cent in this activity)	4

FIG. 2: JANAKI'S CLASSIFICATION OF TOWNS IN SAURASHTRA (1966)

Household industry includes a number of different activities, while mining includes fishing in the Indian census categories. Rajula, with its important quarries, is perhaps closest to being a mining town in the proper sense. The towns classified under transport and communications are all ports. Construction is perhaps a rather doubtful category, indicating growth rather than a regional specialization (Janaki 1966: 20-36). Visitors to Rajkot may feel they are on an enormous construction site, at the rate the town is growing. Even so, this city is classed as 'diversified', which is obviously true.

Janaki's 'functional classification' tells us more through its negative than positive implications. It shows the diverse character of the towns, and at least hints at an explanation. Thus of the three Class I towns—with more than 1,00,000 inhabitants at the time of the 1961 census—Bhavnagar is classed as a manufacturing town, while Rajkot and Jamnagar stand as diversified. Rajkot has more industries than Bhavnagar, but as the metropolis of the peninsula has a large percentage of administration and other services. The four Class II towns are all differently classified; Morvi under construction, Junagadh under trade and commerce as well as other services, Porbandar under manufacturing (it is a port but has a large cement factory) while Veraval, the most important port of the peninsula, is classed as diversified.

The most important conclusion from Janaki's survey, then, is the lack of a locational pattern of specialization, determined by market considerations. Typically, the largest occupational group is that engaged in 'other services'. This group includes 'doctors, lawyers, teachers, engineers and others engaged in professional and other services'. Its importance indicates the administrative and political functions of the Saurashtra towns. 'As such they have attracted the administrative class of people as well as those in personal and professional services' (Janaki 1966: 40).

Even functions like manufacturing are linked with the political structures of the past. Their location is seen as 'a haphazard growth, developed with the encouragement of individual entrepreneurs or with royal patronage. Some of them defy all principles of the economics of location' (1966: 40-1). Their distribution still reflected, in 1961, the diverse enterprises—usually politically initiated or motivated—that Trivedi described in 1939. The mercantilistic policies of the princes is the central factor here. The effects of the free market, as envisaged by Ojha (1945), had not yet affected the pattern to any great extent. Certainly there have been developments since then, notably the growth of manufacturing industries in Rajkot. Outside this centre, however, the old patterns are still in evidence: cultural and political history far outweighs the logic of the free market.

THE UNDERLYING POWER STRUCTURE

To understand Saurashtra's towns we must therefore start with the power structure underlying their genesis and growth. *On the eve of British rule,* says Spodek,

> the cities of the peninsula served as nodes of two systems of power. One was based on landholding, headed in most places by a chief of a Rajput-caste lineage who made the city his capital and armed fortress. . . . Cities with rulers of greater power and imagination attracted a second group of elites as well; a truly urban elite based not on control of land but on control of capital, expertise, and personal connections. (1976: 4-5)

Thus even in the city Spodek gives primacy to the first of these nodes, whose interaction underlies not only the structure of towns but of the whole peninsula (Spodek 1974, 1976; Tambs-Lyche 1982). Yet we should here note the other urban interest groups: the Nagars—Brahmins whose ancestors were landholders, but who had become the archetypal community of higher-level bureaucrats and administrators; the Khawas—'slaves', glossed by Spodek as 'illegitimate children of the rulers' who often held important administrative and military posts; the Mahajan, as the political arm of the Vania merchants, variously organized as guilds and committees; the mercenary armies; and the artisans (Spodek 1976: 13-23). The layout of the towns still reflect this multiplicity of groups by the division into pols, wads or mohallas. Spodek characterizes the city as

> the cockpit in which all these groups worked, sometimes for their mutual benefit, sometimes in opposition to one another. Struggles for power declined when one authority inside or outside the peninsula could assert and maintain paramount power. No single pattern characterized all the cities of the peninsula at any one time nor any one major city through extended periods (Spodek 1976: 5).

Spodek (1976: 109) sees the traditional urban-rural relationship in Saurashtra as the exploitation of peasants and the countryside by the cities, though he stresses the interdependence of peasant and ruler as constituted within the system (1976: 4). Saurashtra, then, provides an illustration of the importance of political factors in the creation and life of urban centres (Spodek 1976: 105-14; cf. Sjoberg 1960: 231). These factors create similarity at the structural level, while the human agency inherent in this common structure produces a variety of forms. Junagadh, Bhavnagar and Jamnagar, the three most important capitals of pre-Independence Saurashtra, are as dissimilar—in architecture, town planning and 'atmosphere'—as are Prague, Amsterdam and Copenhagen. Thus beyond the generalized view we must examine the differences which make, of the cultural image of each city, a part of the shared knowledge that is 'the past in the present' in the culture of Saurashtra.

NOTES

1. Thus, in 1908-9, Junagadh spent 21.896 rupees on the capital through its municipality, and 10.589 on the fifteen other municipalities in the state. The next fiscal year, Bhavnagar spent 65.117 rupees on the capital and 28.266 on nine other towns under its jurisdiction. By 1927-8 Junagadh's spending had risen to 72.349 for the city and 65.336 for the other towns—now seventeen—while Bhavnagar, in 1934-5, spent 225.983 rupees on the capital and 98.537 on the provincial towns (Spodek 1976: 46). There is a tendency towards more even distribution in Junagadh: this is partly due to the growth of Veraval and other towns, partly to the relative stagnation of Junagadh. Junagadh's impressive set of monuments dating to the eighteenth century gave it an architectural dignity that other capitals aspired for.
2. The *ishtadevata* is the chosen deity of a person, often taken up by his descendants. Gradually, the deity may thus become a *kuldevata,* clan or lineage deity, though the two may also remain separate.
3. See Tambs-Lyche 1992: 517-18; 1995, or, for the original story, Sharpe 1931.
4. It was built for the sons of ruling families only.
5. See below, also Tambs-Lyche 1997: 294-301; 1992: 560-638; Williams 1984; Pocock 1973.

6. See e.g. van den Hoek 1978, Harman 1989.
7. For a discussion of this concept see below.
8. Temples which remain private may restrict access and avoid admitting Untouchables, while public temples are bound to do so by law. This may be one reason why few temples have gone public.
9. The Maharajas are not priests, but descendants of Vallabhacharya, the sect's founder. They are responsible for the Haveli. See Tambs-Lyche 1997: 248-50; Thoothi 1935, Pocock 1973, etc.
10. This point that sects are created communities may probably be applied to most Bhakti congregations in India, but it will become clear later that the Swaminarayans are more communitarian than most.
11. i.e. the Yogijipanth.
12. See also Rushbrook Williams 1975: 276-82.
13. See e.g. Lapidus 1967; Sjoberg 1969.
14. Amarji's sons—among them Ranchodji, who wrote the *Tarikh-i-Sorath* (Amarji 1882), were highly active. Their opponents at times included the Nawab himself. Sections of the army rebelled several times because they were not paid, and states like Porbandar and Gondal interfered (Wilberforce-Bell 1915: 157-63, Tambs-Lyche 1997: 279-82).
15. As Tod approached Junagadh, 'all was barren . . . but every thing denoted that the tyranny of man was the chief obstacle to prosperity; and here, unfortunately, the people have to contend against the double operation of political and religious antipathies, their governor being a Mahomedan' (Tod 1971; 359-60).
16. Of the Nawab he says: 'His revenues are scanty, and his views of ambition circumscribed as the belt which hems him in; he lives amidst ruin' (1972; 361).
17. An excellent analysis of the trends, for northern India, is found in C.A. Baily, 1983: 112-13. There, Delhi, Agra and Lahore lost their metropolitan importance, while Lucknow and Benares expanded. These changes were mainly due to political reasons. Most other cities remained relatively stable.
18. Spodek states that Junagadh's trade was due to its political importance, and not vice versa (1976:13).
19. 'Most urban groups in the region', he says, 'were not strongly attached to place.'
20. One of its shipowners wrote the only manual of traditional Indian Ocean shipping known to me, as late as 1945 (Vaidya 1945). This trade was then flourishing in the wake of the wartime boom.
21. See e.g. Rushbrook Williams 1975: 287-8.
22. I shall return to Janaki's study below.
23. Thus Burgess noted in 1874-5 that 'being a comparatively new city there is not much of antiquarian interest about it' (Burgess 1971: 188).
24. It now amounted to some 700,000 rupees (Tod 1971: 264).
25. I was surprised to meet a poet whose project was to recreate the spirit of

Housman's 'A Shropshire Lad' in modern Gujarati. Most poets I met were however, moderns.

26. Bharwads are traditionally shepherds. See Westphal-Hellbosch 1976: 26. See also Tambs-Lyche 1997.
27. See also Tambs-Lyche 1994b.

CHAPTER 3

Provincial Towns and the Limits of Urbanity

> The stars come there at night and sprinkle their bitter grains of salt
> over mountains and hillsides
> and the old cities of Auvergne—so thay will stay hardy
> and still a while longer.
>
> ROLF JACOBSEN, translated by ROGER GREENWALD

The predominance of political factors is not confined to the ex-capitals of Saurashtra. It runs through regional urbanism, and in this chapter we shall look at some provincial towns with this perspective in mind, and then pose the question of urbanism as a variable in regional culture. Rather than seeing urban life as different from that of the village, I propose a double perspective: there is a continuity in social form but a tendency, in popular culture, to think of the urban and the rural as opposite poles. Yet beyond the urban pole there is the metropolis, making the actor aware of what it has become fashionable to call a global perspective. And we shall see that a conception of the wilderness lies beyond the village pole.

Certainly, the existence of such an awareness, at the local and regional level, of being part of a wider world is a general feature of contemporary human life, as writers like Hannerz (1986, 1992) and Appadurai (1986) have argued. I hope to show, however, that people in Saurashtra have their own way of situating themselves in this wider world. In this sense, globalization does not make culture uniform but extends its diversity to new themes.

TOWARDS SOCIOLOGY: MAHUVA

Turning to Mahuva, we are in a province: there is a sleepy aspect to the town, so that even the trucks seem to be older and smaller than elsewhere. We know a good deal about Mahuva, for it has been the subject of two excellent monographs (Desai 1964; Pandit 1965). It is located on the Gulf of Cambay some sixty miles south of Bhavnagar city, close to a creek, making it a fair port for country craft. It may be an ancient place; myth makes it the natal home of Krishna's wife Rukmini. Less mythically, inscriptions attest to the town's existence since the fourteenth century, though there is reason to think it is much older. Under the Sultans of Gujarat and in Mogul times, it was a 'port of some trade' says the Gazetteer (BDG: 598). Several temples date to the fifteenth century. Mahuva was independent from 1740 to 1784, after which it was conquered by Bhavnagar.

While the town has certainly changed since the early 1960s when Desai and Pandit wrote, it remained recognizable in 1973-4. Even in 1980, when I last visited it, little seemed to have changed. In the 1960s, the port exported groundnut, groundnut oil, oilcakes and onions, while its main imports were timber and tiles, coming from as far as Kerala by country craft. Desai assumed a hinterland of some thirty miles for the port, roughly corresponding to the southern part of Bhavnagar district. The timber trade operated on a more distant radius (Desai 1964: 5). Timber and woodwork are associated with Mahuva for people in Saurashtra, and the wooden toys of the city are well known, as its ivory carvings used to be. Beyond its wholesale trade in timber, Mahuva is mainly a local market town, characterized by commerce and administration (Desai 1964: 5). Janaki calls it a 'diversified' town (1966: 46).

Settlement is dense; 70 per cent of the population of 32,732 (BDG: 597) lived within the old centre, an area of less than a square mile. Two main roads crossing each other divide the town into four quarters, with a square (chowk) at the crossroads. Here stands the residence of the former rulers, the Darbargadh. It was intended to change it into a 'shopping-cum-cultural centre', owned by the Municipality.

> The buildings around this centre are not very high structures and present the look of staleness and stagnancy heightened by neglect. The shops on both sides of the two roads present this look. Some of the buildings . . . were built in the late 19th century . . . also a few houses built in the early 20th century without breaking with the past . . . they give the impression of being apologetic to tradition for being new and to the new for being traditional. Among the 19th century buildings the Vaishnava temple called Haveli and the Jain temple are architecturally different. The internal plan of the houses and their external look as also the plan of the town are all traditional. They are typical of the patterns of the houses and towns in Saurashtra. (Desai 1964: 13)

A minor break of continuity was a new quarter constructed outside the old town before the First World War and named after Percival, then British agent in Bhavnagar State. Another new quarter was under construction in 1961 (Desai 1964: 14). From 1948, with the Municipality controlled by the then Praja Socialist Party, electricity and piped water were introduced, and the roads metalled. The two public gardens were improved, one of them with a swimming pool; the hospital was extended and modernized, and health care generally improved. Yet, says Desai, these changes did not affect social relations,

> not even the tap water. Women, instead of gathering at the well, now gather at the common public tap . . . and gossip as they did formerly at the well. . . . But the women have appreciated the introduction of water taps and they have made a folk song praising the then municipal President for it. The electric lights . . . may have introduced a change in the personal habits of the males who now gather at night in the central place the chowk and at another end at the centre, mainly frequented by the Muslims. Women now go out more frequently to the public gardens one of which is reserved for them. But the roles expected of them and their structural position has not changed in Mahuva. (1964: 13-14)

Desai discusses whether the new suburban developments have changed settlement patterns significantly. He does not want to be conclusive, but stresses that 'caste, kinship and friendship' were main considerations when plots were allotted in the then most recent settlement. Two Muslim households were placed at one end of the area; two untouchable households were placed near their employer at his explicit request (1964: 15-16). Desai concludes that a change in social relations 'or in the ideas about them is not as radical as the changes about the choice of site of the settlement, changes about the external look of the houses and their internal plan and the plan of the whole new town. . . .' (1964: 17).

Mahuva is a peaceful place, provincial in every sense. The educational level is 'very low', states Desai. It had one big factory, a cotton spinning mill, employing about a thousand workers in 1956, when Desai's survey was made. Other industries were small, and the total industrial workforce was put by him at around 1500, excluding casual labour (1964: 6-7). Thus while 40 per cent of the household heads were employees, 46 per cent were self-employed. The latter were mostly shopkeepers at different levels, or carters. 5 per cent were employers, while 8 per cent were classified by Desai as non-earners (retired, pensioners, widows). Even the cotton mill, says Desai, should not be seen as the 'large, impersonal business and industrial houses' that we find in modern times. He concludes that Mahuva is essentially a pre-industrial town dominated by trade (1964: 8), representative of a certain type of small town in Saurashtra. Its way of life is 'more a variation of the rural area than a variation of the urban area. The words "urban" and "town" are to be understood in a very special sense in Mahuva and such other towns in India' (Desai 1964: 9). Pandit (1965), dealing with the economy of the town, confirms this impression.

Desai, then, confirms that town and village in Saurashtra form a continuum. And yet, no village shows the complexity of Mahuva. Desai estimates that there are some 55 castes among the Hindus alone, who constitute 78 per cent of the population. Muslims, the remaining 22 per cent, are also divided into a number of castes, or 'endogamous groups' as Desai prefers to call them. Like most Gujaratis, he includes the Jains among the Hindu population (1964: 9). Settlement patterns, with Hindus and Muslims dwelling separately, are still determined by caste. This is not obvious to the casual observer, says Desai, but looking more closely one finds

> social intercourse regulated according to the principles of the caste system. Those persons of the lower castes who are living in the higher caste areas are conscious that they are living among a different caste. They would say proudly that we do not like to leave the place because we are accustomed to the neighbourhood of the higher castes. The higher castes also speak patronisingly about them saying that though the belong to such and such a low caste they are like us. . . . (Desai 1964: 10)

Pandit stresses that no Vania does any kind of low-status work in Mahuva. He may work as a clerk elsewhere, but 'the higher the status enjoyed by his family in Mahuva, the greater the compulsion to leave it, to avoid "service" or at least becoming a "blue-collar", in Mahuva' (1965: 18). Clearly, all emigrants did not return.

Caste, then, is not just a principle of residential segregation in Mahuva, it remains a principle of social integration too. Caste institutions are maintained, and most castes have their Panchayats. 'Among the Banias', says Desai, 'the Panchayat is called Mahajan'. This term is sometimes used for what we would call a guild in Gujarat.[1] Desai comments:

> For the whole town there is a big Mahajan. We would call it the Town Committee. It is not at all powerful today though it exists and owns huge property. Property is also owned by the white collar caste Panchayats and the Panchayats of the Muslims. The caste Panchayats are stronger than the Mahajan. . . . Someone . . . remarked that the functions of the Mahajan are being taken over by the Municipality. This is true with regard to some functions. We shall more profitably observe the Municipality as the forum of the new force in the town than as a civic organisation with its municipal functions. (Desai 1964: 11-12)

'MERCHANT SOCIALISM' IN MAHUVA

The 'new force' referred to is the Praja Socialist Party which, when Desai wrote, was in complete control of the Municipality. As Desai, a communist, puts it:

> Though the P.S.P. separated itself from the Indian National Congress, as the Socialist Party it could also be interpreted as thrown out by the Congress or the nationalist movement when it was no longer required after the anti-imperialist phase of the nationalist movement was over. (Desai 1964: 18)[2]

We may wonder why the Socialist Party should gain power in such a sleepy and traditionalist place as Mahuva. The local party was built by a landowner

> whose grandfather was the contractor for the collection of revenue for the feudal chiefs. He thus had prestige, respect and also the economic security inherited from the traditional feudal society. This heritage helped him in securing the respect of the well-to-do in general and the businessmen in Mahuva in particular, residing in Mahuva and outside it in such places as Bombay and Calcutta. They could receive him and could give funds to a respectable man like him. Of course, they also had faith in his personal qualities of integrity and ability. But why should they give funds for Mahuva which had very little to do with their everyday life in Bombay and Calcutta? Their regard and patriotism for the place of birth was the pre-requisite for their contribution. . . . (Desai 1964: 18)

The group behind 'socialist' power in Mahuva was therefore, sociologically speaking, similar to other merchant and white-collar groups that drove the princes and their supporters from power in post-Independence Saurashtra (Tambs-Lyche 1982; 1997: 304-8). The PSP's strength must be understood in the context of Mahuva; it represents a 'young group' which became the advocates of independence in Mahuva from 1942 onwards. 'Socialism', says Desai, 'provided them with an ideology as distinct from the Congress ideology of the traditional group of the town', which belonged to the moderate wing of Congress. Both groups represented vested interest, and 'the P.S.P. has more businessmen and well-to-do people as its members and sympathisers than the Indian National Congress has in Mahuva'. The achievements of the group are not contingent on any ideological principles save the desire to serve the community (1964: 18-19), for 'neither the new ideology nor the new interests have any firm footing in Mahuva. . . . The P.S.P. group which is the symbol of the new is accepted because it adjusts to the old and does not give the impression or the feeling that they are different from the rest in their way of living or views of life' (Desai 1964: 20).

But clearly, the PSP represents some interests more than others. While their power base is traditional it is not universal; the leading PSP group

> is the higher caste group which economically ranges from the middle to the higher income groups and occupationally it largely belongs to the category called business. Though all castes are represented in the group, the white collar ones are the brains

of the group. . . . The belief about the P.S.P. group that they are serving the people . . . has the same social roots as the belief that the Mahajan of the town served the interests of all. (Desai 1964: 20)

Interestingly, Pandit notes that the 'distribution of occupations of their choice' among her informants, 'would suggest a high preference for independence and/or skill among these low background families . . .' (1965: 19), an evaluation which the lower groups share with the merchants. This kind of value orientation was common in urban Saurashtra in the 1970s and early 1980s, but rather less so since then. In Mahuva, however, this might have been a local tendency strengthened by the conquest of the town by Bhavnagar in 1784, when the local ruler was displaced. And he, too, had a short ancestry: Mahuva had been an independent state only since 1740. Thus the town lacks the dynastic tradition of the capitals I have described, and even of many smaller towns, which still had a ruler to their name. Since Darbar power was vested in Bhavnagar, local and class interest may have coincided to some extent. In the context of princely rule, the provinciality of Mahuva consists precisely in the absence of a prince. The young group, then, may have been faced with less of the feudal past in Mahuva than would have been the case elsewhere. Their opponents were other merchants, organized through the Mahajan, who, like their counterparts in other cities, supported the Congress. The Mahajan may not have served 'the interests of all'; it was, above all, the political arm of the business community. In a longer, historical context, it must be seen as one of the main parties to a continuous power struggle between merchants and rulers (Spodek 1974, 1976; Tambs-Lyche 1982, 1997). It is in these terms that Desai explains how the PSP group, as successors to the Mahajan, came to represent the whole community.

The mercantile group which was the leading participant in the struggle against the feudal political authority in Saurashtra and the merchant capital still play the dominant role in the economy of Saurashtra and Mahuva. In Saurashtra and in Mahuva, in the organisation of social, economic and political power and ideology this is the force to reckon with. . . . (Desai 1964: 20-1)

Desai's study of Mahuva is thus an excellent case of that 'merchantization' process which characterized Saurashtra in post-Independence days (Tambs-Lyche 1982). With the collapse of princely power, the Mahajan, with the social forces behind it, was the only organization effectively able to take over political responsibility.

Mahuva was always a port and a trading centre. One might expect its leaders to be champions of free trade rather than 'socialism', however parochially conceived (Desai 1964: 19). But as a trading centre, Pandit explains, Mahuva has declined.

> Post-1918 competition in trade, growth of railways and development of other ports in Saurashtra led to the break-up of the old houses, and the new generation, or rather the new blood took time to come up. Right now the creative energy shown in Mahuva in Municipal life may be only one aspect of the new upsurge. They are building the social over-heads, shaping the new elite and forging the changed elite-norms and roles by one of those silent social processes that precede any major social transformation. (Pandit 1965: 84)

Thus, what started off as a merchant bourgeoisie, constituting their power through the Mahajan, has been transformed not only through independence and its new institutions, but also through the impoverishment of the town and its trade. In a sense we have here the radical elite of Marxist historians, the impoverished bourgeoisie. The old merchant families, when they have not migrated, have become a cultural elite, drawing on an economic base which is now as much white-collar as it is commercial.

JETPUR: A TEXTILE TOWN

Cotton became the leading cash crop in Saurashtra in the nineteenth century. It was exported, unprocessed, in loose bales, but then a ginning and pressing factory was established at Wadhwan in 1866, followed by a spinning and weaving mill at Bhavnagar in 1873. Cotton textiles became the most important industry in Saurashtra until the 1950s. The cotton trade was favoured by the British, and fostered economic competition between Saurashtra's princely states (Dupont 1996: 111-12).

Jetpur was among the few Kathi states of any size which resisted the expansion of Junagadh and its Rajput neighbours in the eighteenth century. Colonel Walker praised its rulers as 'reformed Kathis'. Like their caste-fellows in Chital, they had acquired a reputation for protecting merchants and artisans. Jetpur was situated on the old road from the mainland to Junagadh, and when the British started improving the roads from 1865 onwards, the Rajkot-Junagadh road on which Jetpur was situated was among the first to be bridged and metalled. The bridge over the river Bhadar at Jetpur was a major construction, opened in 1877. The railway reached Jetpur in 1881 (Dupont 1996: 112-13). The Kathiawar Gazetteer (1884: 242) describes the town as a centre of trade: it had 13,085 inhabitants according to the 1881 census.

Jetpur's growth was due to the absence of duty on imported goods, while cloth was exempt from octroi. This attracted traders, who imported cloth even from Japan and Europe for re-export to British India (Dupont, 1996: 113; Trivedi 1970: 38). The rulers also invited artisans: 'around 1813 the first families belonging to the Khatri community—traditionally cloth-dyers and printers—were called from Kalavad in Jamnagar district to develop dyeing and printing crafts and trade in Jetpur'. A hundred years later, some hundred artisans were engaged in these activities (Dupont 1996: 115-16). Memons, a Muslim community, were to become an important section of Jetpur's traders. But in 1885, there were Hindu-Muslim riots at Moharram, leading many Memons to migrate to Burma, where their community was already well established in trade. During World War I, many of them returned with capital to Jetpur, where they built a substantial part of the bazaar, being now among the richest traders in the town (Dupont 1996: 113-14).

With independence and the end of princely rule, tax and octroi policies were standardized and Jetpur lost its comparative advantage. Moreover, many of the Memons, supporters of the Muslim League, left for Pakistan, and the resulting economic depression led Vanias and artisans to move to Bombay. The Municipality estimates the loss of population in these years at some fifteen thousand, so the population hardly increased from 1941 to 1951,[3] in spite of natural growth. Dyeing declined, and cloth-printing became the main industry of the town (Dupont 1997: 114-15). But the Memons left spacious property which was sold cheaply, and Khatri entrepreneurs as well as refugees from Sindh (some of whom were Khatris, too) used this opportunity to establish themselves (Dupont 1997: 119).

Hand-printing of textiles is said to have expanded considerably during the Second World War, and then, in 1947, screen-printing, a properly industrial technique, was introduced—by a direct descendant of one of the first Khatris to have come to Jetpur a hundred and thirty years earlier, but at the time active in Ahmedabad's cloth trade. His was the first enterprise to adopt screen-printing in Saurashtra. In 1954 he went to Japan to study new technologies, and with these his group expanded to became important in the Indian context. Other entrepreneurs followed suit, so that there were 110 screen-printing units in Jetpur in 1970, and no less than 1,200 around 1985. Though these were all small-scale units, they in turn led to considerable development of ancillary activities, so that the town expanded quickly, reaching 1,14,000 inhabitants by 1988 (Dupont 1997: 116-18).

Jetpur became something of a showcase for the Saurashtra and Gujarat governments, who favoured small-scale industrial development in several ways. The Municipality helped too, by reducing octroi in 1963 and extending the legal delay of paying it. Even more important was the integration of production with marketing through job-work, which meant that the cloth merchants provided the printing entrepreneurs both with cloth and credit. The 'merchant heritage', says Dupont, was an essential factor in promoting the kind of entrepreneurship we find in Jetpur (Dupont 1997: 119-20).

The printing business is dominated by family firms. The Khatris still dominate the industry in Jetpur, owning 43.7 per cent of the sari-printing factories, but they are closely followed by the Kanbis (33.5 per cent), who own two-thirds of the ancillary establishments. Vanias, Lohanas and Brahmins are also active in the industry. Traditional knowledge of the trade explains the position of the Khatris.The rise of the Kanbis, here, is typical and reflects their growing importance (Dupont 1997: 122).

Since the 1980s, there has been a diversification of production, with more stress on export to other Indian states as well as abroad, to east Africa, the Western Asia, Europe and north America. But the widening market strengthened the position of dealers, leading the entrepreneurs to group as the Jetpur Dyeing and Printing Industries Association. They were faced by the association of the dye and chemical merchants, which had some 110 members in 1988-9, and an association of cloth brokers. Though sandwiched at times between demand for credit by dealers and cash by suppliers, the printing industry continues to flourish, as an example, first, of the capacity for adaptation of the traditional trade and craft communities, and secondly, of the dynamism of the up-and-coming Kanbis.

Jetpur is therefore the very opposite of Mahuva. Far from being a sleepy provincial town, it is vitally alive in its industry and its links to Indian and international markets. But Jetpur was once a capital, and the main factors behind its expansion were of a political nature. As we have seen, the character of Saurashtrian towns derives from specific histories of politics and power.

GOGHA: THE FORGOTTEN PORT

If Mahuva's trade has declined in relative terms, that of Gogha has—for all practical purposes—disappeared. This process was well advanced even by 1822, when Tod visited it. The declining port, he says,

> . . . is now merely a nursery for seamen. . . . Still, Gogo has a venerable air, and its dusky walls, which must have defended it against the pirates always abounding in these seas, give it an imposing and picturesque aspect. The southern face, with its numerous round towers of unequal height, cannot be less than one thousand two hundred yards in length; yet this is much less than the western side, where the

fortifications have been destroyed, apparently undermined by the sea. . . . (Tod 1971: 250)

Today, the rest of the walls are crumbling, too. Yet Gogha was once the centre of the Gohils, who may have been pirates at the time. In the sixteenth century it was important enough to be sacked and burned by the Portuguese. Now it is little more than a village. Still a mahal headquarter, it had 5,472 inhabitants at the time of the 1961 census. Yet no visitor can avoid the impression of a glorious past. The mansions along the waterfront are in an advanced state of decay, but their carved-wood balconies are still impressive; and in 1974 the harbour was still full of ships, though most were wrecks rotting in the mud of the sheltered harbour. Outside the old centre, which is the port, pastoralists graze their goats on the ruins of much of the town's residential quarters.

Gogha is situated on a promontory reaching into the Gulf of Cambay some ten miles south-east of Bhavnagar. Its history reflects the competition of that port and its antecedents. During the sixteenth century it was an entrepot for Cambay, but suffered when the latter lost its trade to Surat. Trade declined in the eighteenth century and 'A place of consequence' under Vallabhi, Gogha declined under the Gujarat kings (AD 746-1298), when Cambay flourished. By the fourteenth-century Gogha was a base for 'Musalman soldiers of fortune' untill the Gohil chief Mokhdaji took it and Piram island in 1325 and 'levied toll on all ships passing up the Gulf'. This was not tolerated by Muhammad Tughluq, who took Gogha and Piram in 1347 and killed Mokhdaji, but left Gogha to Mokhdaji's son (BDG: 581; Tod 1971: 265: Tambs-Lyche 1997: 78-9). By 1390 the Gohils paid tribute to Muzaffar Khan, first of the Ahmedabad dynasty, and in the fifteenth century it probably had Muslim governors. By 1503 it was 'entirely a Muslim town having a great traffic as the port in a fat and wealthy land'. By 1513 it was 'a very large town' trading with Malabar and Aden; but then the Portuguese burnt it in 1531 and 1546. By 1591, it seems to have recovered as an entrepot for Cambay. In 1612 the British considered it for a factory but rejected it; the agent Whittington found it a 'poor town'. The Portuguese again burnt it in 1614, yet it retained some importance in the seventeenth century. But Surat now became the area's main port (BDG: 581-3). Gogha, passing from the hands of one Musalman noble to another (1730-51), taken by the Peshwa (1751-5), recovered by the Nawab of Cambay (1755) and again (1764) taken by the Peshwa, was under his indifferent and not very faithful managers, who were not quite able to compete succesfully with its pushing rival Bhavnagar. In 1803 when it came under British management the trade of Gogha was almost gone (BDG: 583).

The British promoted Gogha as a trade rival to Bhavnagar with mixed results; by 1850 it was 'a thriving town with over 8,000 inhabitants and a growing trade'. By 1860-4 it was 'a rich town, and one of the chief cotton ports of Saurashtra'. Cotton boomed in these years due to the effects of the American Civil War. But then came the slump in the cotton trade.[4] The history of Gogha shows how its fortunes have been determined by its political environment. In trade, too, power was the ultimate factor.

In the present century, Gogha has had only limited importance. But for as long as the sailing vessel traffic remained important, it still had a role. When trade passed through other ports, it remained a nursery of seamen, and still is, on a limited scale. Ships were registered there and shipowners resided in waterfront mansions well into the century. As a centre for the dhow traffic Gogha probably prospered during the Second World War, when traditional shipping boomed due to the shortage of modern ships. Its subsequent fate followed the decline of the sailing vessel as a viable means of transport. Muslim shipowners seem to have stayed in business longer than Hindus. Tod described the majority of the seamen as Hindu; this does not seem to have been so at the end.

In Gogha's coffee shops, old *nakhodas* (skippers) were still chatting about the old days as I visited the town in 1973-4. They were mostly Muslim. With its long and stormy past, a decrepit but peaceful present, and no obvious future, Gogha represents the changing fortunes of trade and shipping on the coast. For as long as the past remains visible there, people of the area will be reminded of the role that the sailing vessel once played in the economy of the region.

RAJULA: A SMALL 'INDUSTRIAL' TOWN

In the far south-west of Bhavnagar district lies Rajula. In contrast to Gogha, Rajula is full of life. This is due to its quarries: Rajula is an important source of building stone. Looking more closely at the people in the market, in the teastalls and cafés, one is conscious of the popular character of the town, dominated by a variant of working-class culture. Ice-cream is available, but there are no parlours. While men in simple but traditional dress abound, there are few middle-class men in Western dress. There are few women in the streets. Money is clearly present, but the bazaar is conspicuously lacking in goods for the middle classes. Business is dominated by the Kapol community (ADG: 624), but there are few of the verandah houses typical of merchants. Strolling in the town, I was conscious of friendliness but felt rather out of place—it was clear that tourists do not come to Rajula.

Is Rajula a town or a village? Its size makes it a small town, while the lack of merchant and middle-class culture makes it feel like a village. It is cultural complexity, not size, that defines urbanism in Saurashtra.

FROM URBAN TO RURAL: MANGROL AND LATHI

Gogha is one example of a town that declined to a village over the centuries. Much shorter is the process of decline which followed the demise of princely rule, and a series of small capitals have become villages. Their ruralization is due to loss of political independence and to centralization of commerce. Better transport facilities have changed the radius of operation of commercial enterprise; what once demanded presence on the spot, can today be done at a distance of a few miles. The second process is not independent on the first, for the prince and his court formed the clientele for the merchant, and while tolls and duties at state boundaries were an impedinent to commercial interests, local commerce was bolstered by protectionism.

Mangrol, between Veraval and Porbandar on the west coast of the peninsula, and Lathi, on the boundary between the Gohil and Kathi areas in east-central Saurashtra, may serve as examples of these processes. Both were once capitals of smaller states; both are today reduced to village status. Mangrol had Muslim rulers, while Lathi was ruled by a junior branch of the Gohil Rajputs. Not only are the rulers' 'palaces' empty today, this is also true of many of the merchant mansions, with their exquisite carved-wood verandahs. Merchants have left these places for better prospects elsewhere.

What we see, then, is the reverse of the process that once made Chital the capital of a small state. A merchant, tells the story, came to the Kathi chiefs of the village, offering them half the property he had lost in Amreli (his town, plundered by Junagadh) if the Chital chiefs could recover it for him. They did so, but wanted to kill the merchant and keep the whole lot when a Kathi woman advised them to give up their share to the merchant. The happy merchant brought in others of his kind, and Chital prospered to become a real little state (ADG: 59-60; Tambs-Lyche 1997: 68-9). This is how political and commercial interest united to form a state, but in Mangrol and Lathi, this symbiosis is gone. In these small capitals, the disappearance of the power nucleus entails the disappearance, too, of the business community.

VILLAGERS IN TOWN, TOWNSMEN IN THE VILLAGE: TWO EXCURSIONS

While interactions of town and village are ordered along a continuous axis, the two loci of social life generate images that are polarized. There is an image of the town, relevant to villagers, and an image of village life, held by townsmen. I shall exemplify these complementary images by describing two excursions. One, made with Muslim friends in Praj, took us to town to make merry; the other, organized by a sociologist friend for his students, was intended to initiate them into the charms of village life. Each of these excursions exemplifies what townsmen or villagers look for in the other, and show this otherness as an integrated part of their own definition of self and home. Certainly, the townsman's image of the villager's innocence and the villager's dream of city lights is as European, or indeed American, as it is Indian. The point here is not whether Indian ideas are different from Western ones, but to explore those conceptual patterns which seem to be important in the setting of Saurashtra.

In Gujarat alcohol is banned. Palm toddy is an old tradition, my folklorist friends told me—but not where it could be found. Fishermen, I am assured, have an alcohol problem but I never located their source of drink. Prostitution is evident in the appropriate quarters of Surat, but I never saw similar quarters elsewhere, though I am told they exist. Gujaratis may be no better than other people, but most 'badness' is well hidden.[5] While Saurashtra is a sober place, young people like fun. So my friends and I, in Praj,[6] decided to have a go at the real life. Didn't we share, the Muslims and I, the non-belief in Hindu taboos on alcohol, tobacco, meat and fish?

I think it was Ismail—the Khoja son of the biggest *pan*-shop in the village—who got the idea. Yet it might also have been the Teli,[7] one of the select group who gathered at the Pir's grave.[8] He was a small round man with a moustache as big as his smile, and an easy sense of humour. Also with us was my cook Bahru[9] who was not a Muslim, as he stressed when talking about birth control, but almost untouchable—a Jogi by caste—and so he had few qualms about purity. He, too, was a jolly kind of guy.

We would live it up, go to town together. Yet, we were not going for girls, nor alcohol, which was felt to be both difficult to find, and dangerous.[10] Tobacco was no problem; we all smoked, not least the bidis Bahru was rolling daily, in Ismail's shop. Meat, too, was considered dangerous, for the restaurants serving it, in Bhavnagar, were not of the best, and many people we knew had got sick from meat gone bad. So what was left was fish. Nobody ought to know about it, however, since even some of our friends might not like the idea that we were fish-eaters.

Thus we did not leave the village together. I had some business in town anyway, and so had the Teli, so the two of us came separately to the bus station to meet Ismail and Bahru, who travelled together. Once in town we stayed together, joking and enjoying ourselves, sometimes looking at film posters. We approached the side street where the Rajput Lodge was situated; like many non-vegetarian diners in this part of India, it was discreetly located on the first floor, entered by a dark and narrow staircase. For safety's sake, we entered two and two, so our errand would not be obvious to anybody watching. Obviously, the occupants of such restaurants are not visible from outside. Moreover, there are private rooms, small cubicles sheltered from the main room. Those who eat at such places prefer not to be seen by other customers.[11] We appreciated this in case someone from Praj should have the same idea; we surely did not want them to tell on us.

We enjoyed the meal. I do not know whether beer or alcohol would have been available[12]—we certainly never asked. The fish was quite tasty, as it was heavily spiced in the Rajput fashion; this was just as well, for all four of us were sick the next day. We would have liked to go to a movie afterwards but time was getting on, and to arrive by a late-night bus would have been too conspicuous. We had a walk, a smoke, chewed a *pan* and, returning on the same bus, took care to sit separately. The negative consequences of this excursion concerned only our stomachs. From all other points of view, it had been a success, and villagers did not seem to be talking of it. Apart from the fish, and the pleasure of good company, the main thing was to have been to town together. In that sense, the experience was no different from that of Yorkshiremen in Soho.

If the first excursion was informal and even a little secret, the second was an official event. My friend, a sociology teacher, had included a field excursion in his course. The idea, he told me, was that urban students should get a taste of village life. This was to bring them back to the roots of Indian society, and the base of a progressive understanding of Indian society—a 'discovery of India', in fact. Second, the outing was to show them the reality behind some basic sociological variables, present in the contrast between city and countryside. It was hoped that students would develop some feeling for the charms of rural life, so as to counteract their youthful cult of the cinema, the city, and the culture of the West.

My friend and another teacher, the students, and myself went by bus. The village, north-west of Bhavnagar, had been chosen for several reasons. It was a fairly typical agricultural village, medium-sized (some 1,000 to 1,500 inhabitants, thus much smaller than Praj), and there was a farmer there, known to my friend, whose farm was acknowledged as a model of enterprise and development. This farmer, a college-educated man who had returned to his lands, was doing all the right things; new crop varieties, studious use of fertilizers, well-planned irrigation. He received us and showed us his fields, making a little speech on the improvements he had effected; it was followed by some well-chosen words from my friend, on the potentials for agricultural progress if farmers would only adopt new and better techniques.

We then toured the village, seeing some of the artisans at work. The teachers made apposite remarks: the students put a few questions. Students were then allowed to roam by themselves, trying to find interesting objects of study: they would all write an essay, afterwards, on their visit. They were then to gather at the largest temple in the village, and the only one which had a *pujari.*[13] He was known as something of a personality, a follower of Bhakti who had adopted his own style of worship and had his own philosophy. He had spent some years as a renouncer, roaming the countryside and living on alms. He had then come to this village, where he found the temple without a priest; he liked the place, and began to do *puja* there. It was a temple dedicated to Shiva, but he was more inclined to Bhakti, so his worship included a great deal of singing. He had a good voice, and had been able to buy, or had been given, a harmonium. We spent the afternoon idly listening to his songs and chatting with him.

Stressing how happy he was living 'like this' in a village where his style of religiosity was appreciated, he underlined the importance of a simple life unencumbered by material worries, and the joy that his devotion should inspire others. One should not get stuck in ritual or theology, he felt. Expressing one's existential happiness in joyful praise of the lord was the important thing. The songs, mostly his own, were of Vaishnava rather than Shaiva inspiration, but the conception of love found in them was not devoid of eroticism; indeed, he had been to Bengal and seemed to have received some inspiration from the Krishnaism of that province, where the tantric and erotic presence is far greater than in Gujarat. He was not a Brahmin; and as an ex-renouncer he did not tell me his caste; but I think he must have been Sanyasi or Yogi, one of the low castes whose members serve, traditionally, in a priestly function.

He was no puritan, and his joy was helped, too, by consumption of hashish (*ganja*), as was evident from his vividly rolling eyes. In fact, he was well and truly stoned. This fascinated the students, but as my friend the teacher said, if we had known that he was like this, we should perhaps not have come. *Ganja*, he stressed, is not a good thing, and he sincerely hoped his students would not be inspired to take it themselves. A small speech on the subject, made later as we returned to town, took care of this problem.

The visit was concluded by an excellent dinner, served by the villagers, though I understood that the college had been subsidizing it. As the food was being prepared, my friend lectured more formally on the sociology of urban-rural contrast, reminding his students of Parsons' pattern variables and the opposition between Durkheim's organic and mechanical solidarity. We were all in a good mood as we boarded the bus to go back.

The cannabis-smoking priest had, however, slightly tarnished the image of the countryside that the teachers wanted to present to their students. Found in numerous school-books, the village here becomes a metonym for the 'real' India, unspoilt, innocent, harmonious, and ready for the Gandhian approach to social and economic uplift. The ideology behind the trip was clear: to counter the thrill that urban lights effect on youth, to show how interesting and even exciting the agricultural transformation could be. In the 1970s, many students thought of the future in terms of migration to the West, to Bombay, to the City in general terms. This was the dream that the trip to Bhavnagar, made by my village friends and myself, had reproduced on a humbler level.

As in the West, the urban-rural opposition revolves, ideologically, around two dimensions: one, practical and economic, assimilates the city to progress and expansion while the village signifies the past and decay. Another, moral and cultural, opposes the moral dangers and excitement of the city to the virtuous and simple rural life, where the only danger is boredom. The Gandhian ideology, stressing that village virtue and socio-economic development may go together, may indeed have acted as a brake to the 'flight from the countryside' in areas like Gujarat, though its effect may have been stronger among the middle classes than among peasants. It has provided motivation for educated youth to work as teachers or social workers in villages, and for students to return to their ancestral lands as progressive farmers, like our host during the village outing.

In both cases, those who return to the village come to occupy high or at least highly respected positions in it. An ordinary teacher, who would disappear among the masses of the lower middle class in the city, becomes a 'somebody' in the village. For those who remain 'ordinary villagers', however, the city remains attractive.

Villages and towns may both be called *gam*, which means village, but also the native place.[14] In this sense, hamlet, village, town and city are all situated along the same axis, but the variable of size is conflated with the degree of prestige, so that a good village (*saro gam*) and a big village (*moto gam*) become synonymous. Thus some 'big' villages are smaller, in actual population, than some 'small' ones, as when fishermen's or quarry labourers' settlements are compared with agricultural, multi-caste villages which, quite clearly, are 'better'. This hierarchical ordering implies that one's *gam* enters into the total rank or prestige one can muster. But this rank is in its turn influenced by the position one holds within that *gam*. Thus the loss of status when the city boy becomes a village teacher is offset by his relative importance in the village. And the descendant of a famous Dewan of Bhavnagar, who lives on the outskirts of Praj, is a source of prestige for the village even if he cannot be said to be very popular there.

THE *BEENTO* IN SAURASHTRA

People migrate, but they also return. Villagers go to town and come back; townsmen (especially teachers or social and health workers) sometimes return from the village to their urban origins. I came across no obvious linguistic counterpart, in Saurashtra, to the couple *bush* and *beento* that Hannerz (1992: 228-30) notes in Nigeria. When denouncing 'ignorance and rustic, unsophisticated, uncouth conduct', urban Saurashtrians may use *khedut* (peasant) or the adjective *gamda-*: there are other terms. But there is no obvious counterpart to *beento*, though the image of the returned immigrant is standard fare in popular literature and films. In fact, this image, in Saurashtra, differs from the one Hannerz gives us from Nigeria:

> During the sojourn abroad, the *beento* had acquired an advanced education, and so he (for there were rather fewer she *beentos*) could claim a privileged position in an expanding, at least in part conspicuously meritocratic, national social structure. But hardly less important for the definition of the *beento* as a social type was the general sophistication which he had acquired abroad, a savoir-faire with regard to the way of life of the metropolis, and an intimate appreciation of its finer points. (1992: 228-9).

Such figures exist in Saurashtra, too, though relatively few in number.

But there is something that doesn't fit Hannerz' description. For Saurashtra, the metropolis is, above all, Bombay. The pictures and the pop music are dominated by that city, as is the standard of elegance in restaurants for the middle classes or the fashions of women. Compared to Bombay, only minor cultural roles can be discerned for Delhi or Calcutta. There are other sources of culture certainly, like Hong Kong and Western movies in the Video Halls (which did not exist in the 1970s), but one must go to Ahmedabad to find a cinema screening Western films. Imported magazines are extremely rare, and while you can get any of the Indian, English-language papers and periodicals in Rajkot, one must rise early to get a copy of the *Times of India* in a smaller place like Dhrangadhra. By the way, while the video halls were spreading fast as the 1980s grew into the 1990s, they hadn't got to Dhrangadhra, either, when I was there in 1992. Satelite television was not really a presence, either, though you could get the BBC World Service on your screen at big-city hotels. But no hotel I stayed at, in Saurashtra, had such amenities: clearly very few people in the peninsula have access to them.

'The beento stands, as it were, at the intersection where Wallerstein meets Bourdieu', says Hannerz (1992: 229). But in Saurashtra, the two have not yet met. On the cultural front, Wallerstein's global system is still some way off, while the elite that controls the cultural capital in Bourdieu's sense, is still overwhelmingly Indian. This does not mean that Rajkot businessmen stay at home; they may be closely involved in wide-ranging commercial networks, but while they are glad to export their products, they import only a few cultural items.

It is not easy for the visitor to Gujarat to decide whether he is in a provincial ('culturally backward') part of the world, on a humble visitor to a proud and self-sufficient civilization which has no need for Western culture, or whether there is yet another answer. We are, indeed, close to a centre of civilization, the Gujarat that may have been the world's richest country when European merchants arrived in the sixteenth and seventeenth century. The cultural pride of Gujarat took a beating from the encounter, which did not break it but brought out, stronger than in Calcutta, a traditionalist attitude as a defensive refuge against foreign influence. Later on, Gujaratis discovered, as merchants and migrants, that they could deal quite adequately with the West with a minimum of cultural accomodation;[15] and this has become the model, to this day, of integration with the World System. The elite capable of dealing with the West has become the model for any number of young gentlemen in town. This, no doubt, is another reason for the importance of the 'merchant model' (Tambs-Lyche 1980) in

Gujarati culture: the merchant shows the way to being modern and Gujarati at one and the same time.[16]

In short, there are many and good reasons for travel elsewhere, but it is the 'Mumbaiwallah' who is the real *beento* in Saurashtra. It is the Mumbai 'sing-song' which is adopted by the English-speaking, scooter-riding belles of Rajkot, even those who replace their sarees with jeans. It would seem indeed, from the number of Arab visitors to Mumbai, that this city remains the metropolis not only for those Indians who go to the Gulf for work, but for their hosts and employers as well. The city's central position in the culture of the region is, of course, underpinned by the popularity of Bombay films.

TOWNS OF SAURASHTRA: AN OVERVIEW

Towns have different characters, related to their origin. Some are built around their fortress, others are based on a marketplace; ports have a character of their own, as have centres of manufacture, of which the modern industrial city is a special case. Then there is the pilgrimage or temple city. What is special about Saurashtra, however, is the influence the political system of the princely period has had on towns. Many are marked by their past as princely capitals, and so the functional classification is muddled, as we have seen (Janaki 1966). The capital may have started as a fortress, but it attracted merchants to form a marketplace, artisans for manufacture, and no capital was without temples, which might then well acquire importance in their own right. Thus towns in Saurashtra are multifunctional, and recent history has modified their character only to a certain extent. This implies the coresidence of a large number of castes. Today almost every community in Saurashtra is found in the cities.

This is important, for as A.M. Shah has pointed out (Shah and Desai 1988), our image of caste as an orderly, ranked system is marked by the bias of village studies in Indian sociology and anthropology. The town shows a more competitive order, where rank remains important but the order is fluid. The hierarchies of the villages, therefore, are continuously confronted with the blurred ranking order produced by urban competition. Any attempt at defining a regional caste system from a village point of view is therefore misleading. On the level of social relations, networks cover villages of very different form as well as sectors of the city. As for conscious models of society, villagers and urbanites know of each other and their image of caste is influenced by both situations. Thus, whether we analyse caste as a set of social relations defined by interaction, or as an emic model to represent the types of social being found in society, we need to refer to a regional level to get a reasonably precise idea of how the 'caste system' is constituted.

NOTES

1. Caste or subcaste, guild, town and temple committees, and sect membership are elements of social organization which we may distinguish analytically, but which combine and covary in a number of ways among Gujarati merchants. See Tambs-Lyche 1997, 224-55.
2. I.P. Desai was a radical, and his remarks on the PSP should be read in that light, as should his judgements about caste: he was vehemently opposed to casteism and the tendency of Western scholars to concentrate on caste to the exclusion of other themes.
3. In 1941 Jetpur had 28,406 inhabitants; in 1951 there were 28,444 (Dupont 1997: 115).
4. 'due to the fall in the value of cotton and the spread of railways, the trade of the ports of the Cambay Gulf have been greatly reduced. Whatever trade remained, was generally attracted towards Bhavnagar by the lowering of tariffs and making of good roads. The average annual value of trade at the port of Gogha for the five years ending 1871-72 was £ 159.310 . . . against the average of £. 81.196 . . . for the five years ending 1877-78' (BDG: 583-4).
5. According to the newspapers, three tribal girls were held captive in a Rajkot flat for weeks until they were liberated by the police. They were bought or captured quite cheaply in some other state.
6. I shall describe this village later.
7. The caste of oil-pressers. Locally, they are more often known as Ghanchis.
8. I describe this group later.
9. In fact it was his wife who cooked for me, but he brought me the food and collected the money.
10. Less so because of the police than rumours of methanol (which makes you blind) circulating in the black market.
11. In places like Bombay one assumes that separate compartments are useful for secret love-affairs.
12. As 'special tea', perhaps, an arrangement known from some other places in India.
13. I use this term rather than priest, since while responsible for the temple, he was not a Brahmin.
14. Thus when asked 'what is your *gam*', one may well answer Ahmedabad or even Bombay.
15. I had a forceful impression of this when doing my fieldwork on the London Patidars (1980).
16. We might say that Gujarati identity becomes part of a world-wide ethnoscape (Appadurai 1991) rather than being tied to place.

CHAPTER 4

Urban Scenes and Situations

> The world of a child's one town, renascent, in rage unfurled
> Between Cwmdonkin railing and black-faced Inkerman Street.
>
> VERNON WATKINS

In Saurashtra, the distinction between town and village is fluid. Lathi was once a town when capital of a minor state; now it is rather a large village, but the architectural remains of its glory do not indicate that it was very different then. Praj, a large village, is in some ways as urban as Lathi. Towns differ in size and atmosphere: the sleepy provincial mood of Mahuva, the hustle-and-bustle of Rajkot; the architectural unity of Junagadh or Jamnagar, the mystery of Prabhas, the temple town near Somnath, or the matter-of-fact communication centre of Surendranagar. From the character of towns I turn now to scenes and situations from the urban end of the rural-urban continuum.

Towns offer a wider range of social scenes, and of situations to be defined, than villages. Moreover, town life includes a larger range of situations where the other is unknown, and a better opportunity to observe the process of defining the situation. This process is crucial to an understanding of the lived-in world. Two qualities distinguish situations and the management of identity in urban settings. First, certain traditional situations and identities find their full expression only in towns. Secondly, there are new cross-caste identities, exemplified through middle-class clubs, that are as yet peculiar to cities. Thus while variation is continuous, a distinction can still be made between urban and rural social life. To some extent, we must assume, urban identities and situations provide the 'models' for those of rural areas. For as a large village is a good one, and ranks above smaller villages, so the towns rank above them, and the big or famous towns above the small or unremarkable ones.

PUBLIC AND PRIVATE IN SAURASHTRA'S CITIES

The categories public and private are often applied to space in the Western city, the general assumption being that streets are public; privacy starts at the front door or garden gate. If such a conception is a little simplistic in the Western context, it is far more so with regard to the cities of Saurashtra. One specific pattern of the traditional city is excellently described by Doshi (1974). In old Ahmedabad, the social geography can only be understood by reference to the local concept of *pol*. Every traditional dwelling in the old city is located within a *pol*, where houses are grouped a round courtyards or in a dead-end street. The *pol* is usually closed by a gate. This enclosed area belonged to members of one caste (in some cases a cluster of closely-related castes), though it might include settlements for their workers and servants. These *pols* thus constituted a space neither fully public nor entirely private in our terms.

Ahmedabad has long streets with a scarcity of cross-cutting passages. Between the streets are the *pol*, placed back to back. Most examples of traditional Gujarati wood-carving are to be found inside the *pol*, street fronts often being modernized without much taste.

The Ahmedabad pattern is not however, universal. Junagadh has no counterpart to the *pol*, and the spatial marks of caste are less obvious. Instead, the plan ressembles medieval cities of the West, in that streets are allocated to the named trades still associated with them; other streets, indeed, carry caste names. Yet these are streets, not *pol*; in this sense, Junagadh is typical neither of Gujarat or Saurashtra, but of the *vilayat* of its founders—the Middle East. Bhavnagar follows a different pattern, which may derive from its historical links to Surat.[1] As in Surat, the *paras*—called *mohallas* in Surat—are quite discernible and indicate a number of dwellings belonging to a single caste. But unlike Ahmedabad, the Surat *mohallas* and Bhavnagar *paras* are not closed by a gate. Instead, the houses of the *paras* and *mohallas* are often back-to-back, so that the lanes themselves constitute the social boundary. There are exceptions; in the Nagar *para* of Bhavnagar, for example, we find enclosed courtyards of the *pol* type. Generally those sharing a courtyard belong to the same minimal lineage, with quarters for servants sometimes included. Among other towns following the same arrangement, we note Mahuva. The centres of Jamnagar and Dhrangadhra have planned streets, but beyond them the pattern ressembles Bhavnagar, rather than Ahmedabad.[2] Whatever the particularities of each city, however, clustering of dwellings by caste is the common, traditional pattern.

This tendency extends to quarters of the city, commonly identified with particular castes. Thus the clustered dwellings of the *pol*, *mohalla* or *para* indicate one point on a variable stretching from private to public, a point near the private end. The larger quarter is closer to the public end, but still seen as belonging to certain groups of people. This is true even of squares and other forms of open space located within the quarter, as is most noticeable in the evening, when local people gather there to enjoy a sherbet, betel, or a cigarette at the appropriate shops. The atmosphere here, dominated by the locals,[3] is quite distinct from that found in spaces used by the public at large.

A PARTICULAR COURTYARD

One hot day I had been struggling with some very sandy roads close to the Rann to arrive at the small town of Malia, once capital of a small state. From the main street bazaar I turned into a side street leading to one of the few substantial buildings of the town, which was marked by the sign of the State Bank of Saurashtra. Entering the gateway to the large court I realized that the building had an even more important past: it must have been either the aministrative headquarters of the old state, or, indeed, the palace itself. Appreciating its relative grandeur in a kind of Indo-Britannic style, I was suddenly hailed by a well-dressed, spectacled person.

'Excuse me, Gentleman, but I must ask where you think you are going?' Taking him for a bank employee, I said I was just admiring these grand buildings of the bank, when he added: 'In fact, you see, the bank is only the front building; where you are is private grounds. And, I may add, I live here'. This charming introduction, of course, made it clear to me that I was, in fact, speaking to the owner of the palace, the heir to the *gaddi*[4] of Malia. I excused myself, explaining rather awkwardly that I had taken him for some director of the Bank. 'Oh, but you are perfectly right', he answered, 'I let part of the palace to the Bank in return for a job. But I am working in Rajkot, not here'. And a little later he added, not without visible regret: 'These days I even have to look like a Vania'.

What is more central to us here is that the former ruler had put no demarcation between the private grounds of his palace and the area let to the Bank. I suppose everybody knows, in Malia, at what point they are entering their former ruler's private domain. Social position, and not material fences, demarcate private space here.

THE IMPORTANCE OF BEING AHIR

The prevalent form of business district in most Saurashtra towns is still the traditional bazaar. Even Rajkot has a large bazaar. It is not old, yet its structure is traditional, though the allocation of space to different trades seems less systematic than in other towns. Large semi-modern shops break the continuity of market stalls. This is less true elsewhere. But even in the traditional bazaars, there are variants to the general form.

In the traditional bazaar each trade has its place. Shops trading in cloth are usually found in the same street or lane; similarly the ironmongers, shoemakers and shoeshops, and so on. In Junagadh, a typical Islamic city, separate named streets indicate each trade. In Bhavnagar, more typically for the region, the central market forms one complex, where only narrow lanes are found, and the grouping of trades, though still quite marked, is less rigid. In both cases, trade generally coincides with caste, though there is some overlap. The caste of Bhowsar (cloth-printers) in Bhavnagar, for example, no longer practise their original craft but share the textile trade with other Vania castes. Still, their shops tend to be close together within the area of the bazaar dedicated to the cloth trade.

In general, the bazaar is dominated by the merchant castes—Vanias, Lohanas, and, in Jamnagar, Bhatias. But there are exceptions. In Jamnagar I spent some time with the proprietors of a trading company, Ahir & Co., dealing in the most traditional of Vania trades—grains and agricultural inputs.[5] They stressed how being Ahir gave them a special niche in the market, catering to Ahir agriculturalists.

Here, a pattern emerges which is alternative to the traditional occupational specialization: caste networks, based not on occupation but rather on what Grönhaug (1978) calls fields, are utilized economically. Earlier, Kanbis (becoming Patidars in the process) have established themselves in trade, and it is probable that their initial trading activity was based on marketing the agricultural produce of caste members.[6] If this trend continues, we may see an important shift away from the traditional pattern of ethnic stratification in Saurashtra and Gujarat, marked by the link between caste and occupation.[7] The change had certainly begun when the nascent Bombay bourgeoisie—groups like Parsis, Voras and Gujarati Vanias, among others—scrambled for positions in the nineteenth-century colonial metropolis. To an extent, it is a pattern we might see as traditional in urban India (Shah and Desai 1988).

The shift, here, would be towards a pattern of field-based ethnic groups reminiscent of the situation we find in the USA. Spreading through a wider range of occupations while keeping their distinctness as social and cultural groups, castes would come to resemble American ethnic groups. But though the trend is visible, it has not yet gone that far. Caste is still heavily linked to occupation. The changes, however—and this is where the American parallel is useful to us—may not invalidate the importance of caste as an ethnic and organizational factor.

THE RADIO SHOP

All over Indian towns, one hears music. Much of it comes from cassette shops. Manubhai's business, in one of the larger towns, seems brisker than it is because friends and acquaintances—many of them young come simply to listen to the music. Though every listener does not buy, most buy something sometimes, and Manubhai feels it important that his shop should not seem empty; this might dissuade customers. When somebody plays a cassette, somone else might hear it and come in to buy. There is, in fact, a steady trade in cassettes. Radios and cassette players are sold too, but not everyday. The crowd makes the shop a centre of information, however, and I used it as such, since the best newspapers—and certainly the English language ones—disappear early in the morning. And then, most of the interesting news is not in the papers.

Manubhai tends the shop, but with the crowd of youthful music lovers, there is always someone to take over for a while. Manubhai's nephew is also working part-time in the shop. It is difficult to tell 'shopkeepers' from 'customers'; rather there are 'insiders', some of them close friends who buy a cassette now and then; while others simply know Manubhai well and will tell outsiders that he will soon be back. Among the customers are smart young officers from the military camp nearby, entering with their elegant wives asking for the latest Mumbai cassettes, sometimes before a provincial shopkeeper can get hold of them. At the other extreme are the Rabari or Bharwad pastoralists come to town from distant hamlets.

Manubhai is a Lohana by caste. But the group who gather at his shop, come from a number of castes, mostly sharing a middle-class background, and customers come from all castes and walks of life. Among the insiders, the tone is rather egalitarian though Manubhai is the boss. So he remains with rural or low-caste customers; when the military officers come, however, he becomes their eagerly polite servant.

Shops such as Manubhai's are important nodes of social life. The time spent there is not simply a business transaction or a chance to hear music. Information is exchanged; people from different caste and class backgrounds get together: friendships are formed that transcend such barriers.

RAMBHAI'S GUEST HOUSE

I will not say where Rambhai has his guest house, since it is the only respectable establishment of its kind in its town. The town is large, but traditional, and what people in Saurashtra call 'backward'. Rambhai is an

Audich Brahmin, whose father was the *karbari* of an important state and he maintains that this state was the best administered political entity in Saurashtra. He claims, too, that most of the important archives of the state are in his possession.

The guest house is nice and clean and quite comfortable by traditional Saurashtra standards, and Rambhai is keen to maintain its reputation. Customers should be respectable and well behaved. He likes to sit with them in the evenings, in the hall by his office, where a number of clients and acquaintances also come. The latter are his lodgers or working for them; thus the secretary of the trucking company that hires an office from him in the back of the building. The secretary is a Koli, from a low farming caste, so this is a cross-caste venue. But the host always presides; he is the owner and a Brahmin to wit, and likes to show off his general culture. He is, in fact, quite knowledgeable and well versed in traditional culture, and has read several Puranas of which the *Vayu Purana* seems to be his particular favourite.

The conversation is structured according to rank.[8] Rambhai speaks, and the others are generally content to listen. This, at least, is true of the clients from the town. But not all guests share Rambhai's conservative views, which make him a staunch supporter of the BJP. Businessmen or bureaucrats, some of them are rather 'secular' in their outlook, express their differences of opinion with deference. Not so the uncouth anthropologist, who once felt he should apologize to Rambhai for the assertions he had made one night . . . yet on the whole we got on well, though I had difficulties with Rambhai's view, that only a Brahmin would be able to understand Hindu thought; as he put it: 'It is in our blood'.

Similar discussion groups form in other guest-houses of this type. I may cite the hotel I used in Mahuva, as well as a small guest-house in Rajkot where I spent some time. The Mahuva hotel-keeper liked to show off his skill in palmistry, and generally seemed to elicit discussion on religious and philosophical subjects. The Rajkot man never spoke on these matters: he was not a Brahmin like the others, but a Patidar. Yet some of his guests were highly religious; when the discussion took a philosophical bent, the host grunted in a down-to-earth but good-humoured manner. In this way he remained the host who let his guests indulge. In both cases, these were establishments tended by the owner himself, so that he became the natural centre of the group, and his authority structured the group discussion. Like Rambhai's guest house, these places had a number of regular customers, who knew the owner, and sometimes each other, well.

Who were these guests? What struck me in Saurashtra, was the relative absence of Western-style, luxury hotels. This is striking when one observes the travelling public, which include the very well-off as well as the unquestionably poor. Both extremes, I concluded, tend to lodge privately, with business associates or with family. In the guest houses you meet the frequent travellers among the in-betweens: salesmen, auditors, certain types of business or engineering consultants, public or private employees on temporary detachment to another town. Many of them travel to more or less regular schedules, so that guests may know each other not only in a particular guest-house, but meet frequently, at different places, on their rounds. Needless to say, these were the people to ask for advice, when I arrived at a new place, looking for accomodation.

These people form a significant part of the public, for they travel all over Gujarat and have access to discussion and information that is, in many ways, a privilege. They are a significant part of the fabric of networks that integrate the region and makes it, in spite of the problems of displacement, a realistic object of study.

NEW FORMS OF ASSOCIATION: THE CLUB

In shops and guest-houses, members of different castes associate. Friendships and acquaintances developed in such places, cut across caste lines. We may doubt that they modify basic identities, however, for members of different castes have always been in contact, in traditional as well as modern settings. But the club is a new social form, deliberately set up, where the inequalities of caste are consciously put aside.

In Bhavnagar, one of my best friends belonged to such a club, constituted for the plain pleasure of membership. I went on an excursion there with ten men from the age of thirty upwards, including millworkers, a college teacher, a lawyer, and an assortment of others. While all were in the medium income group, our 'class base' might well be seen as rather mixed. The group was also quite mixed in terms of caste—though seven out of the ten were Muslims.[9] Others, like my friend, were Kanbi/Patidar. There was no untouchable, and no Brahmin either.

We went to Gogha, where we borrowed one of the many empty houses by the waterside. We had brought our food, which we prepared for the weekend; some sleeping-gear; playing-cards, and bottles of liquor. It was a friendly affair; nobody got drunk, and the sums that changed hands over the card table were quite symbolic.

What was still quite clear, was the basically norm-breaking nature of the occasion. We broke norms, however, not to hurt anybody or even act in a demonstrative manner. Instead, norm-breaking was an individual statement of ideology from each of us; we felt liberated and vaguely progressive, while the necessary secrecy underlined the friendship of people across caste, religion or occupation. The latter aspect seemed most important to me, apart from the fact that we were having a good time. From the verandah of the derelict house we could see the moonlight on the harbour with its many wrecked sailing ships—and this romantic view certainly influenced our mood.

The 'Friends' Club', was a cross-caste affair, which had then existed for some two years, but had already changed its name. It was started by a Brahmin from the income-tax department, and some two-thirds of its members still seemed to work in that office. Many of them, but not all, were Brahmins. This club had a more formal tone than the first. We went on a picnic to the coast near Gopnath, and when we met, all participants in the tour introduced themselves rather formally to the group. The gathering was less lively, and we mostly discussed in groups of two or three; only on the return trip did the talk start to move freely. We visited a Goddess temple by the seaside; several of us taking a 'bath' (by hitching up our trousers). The temple was Shaktist—'in the old days they even sacrificed humans here'—so the card games did not conflict with the spirit of the place. A visit to an old hunting lodge, belonging to the Raja of Bhavnagar, rounded off the trip.

In Junagadh I became friends with three young men who used to gather at a particular milk-shake joint across the street from the then only modern hotel in town. They introduced themselves as members of the Rotary Club in Junagadh. Two of them were bank employees; the third an accountant in the Public Works Department. The latter was an elegant bachelor of the Audich Brahmin caste, working in the district branch of the Civil Engineering Department of the Government of Gujarat. His father had been the Rajpurohit of an important state. 'For a bachelor like me', he said, 'it is difficult to find housing; a bachelor is regarded as 'hot'.[10] A lover of Western films, he was always eating at 'Murlidhar', the restaurant where travellers and bachelors meet in Junagadh. Tastes modern and traditional mix in the individual; this man may well represent the younger, urbanized middle class in the peninsula. To some extent, this is true of 'Murlidhar' himself, the owner of the establishment, who had taken part, as a soldier, in the European campaigns towards the end of World War II, being among the first British troops to enter Oslo.

One of the bank employees was from Rajpipla in eastern Gujarat, and though he worked in Junagadh, his wife and children were in Gandhinagar. He hardly had time to visit them; what spare time he had was spent visiting his old father in Rajpipla. Their separation from the family, forced by the need to find work, was certainly an important factor in keeping the group together. Bachelors or family men, the group of friends complemented each other in their need for good company.

The Rotary Club was multi-caste. The secretary, a Jain Vania, ran a typewriting shop; his wife was a PhD in Sanskrit. At the time, the secretary's main interest in me was the information I might give regarding possibilities for migration. It turned out that we had common friends; a Jain Vania family based in El-Obeid, Sudan, whose sons I had met in London. The treasurer, on the other hand—a college teacher—was more interested in discussing religion. He was appalled at the self-interest evident behind apparent conversions. In both cases, tradition and modernity might be seen as underlying poles in the conversation themes; most of all, however, I just want to share with the reader something of the variety of themes, related in some way or other to coping with 'modernity', that kept the club members talking to each other and to myself.

I do not know what other activities the Rotary Club was organizing; I never went to meetings. But their pleasure in the simple gatherings at the bar, in the conversations taking place, was unmistakeable, and, in spite of the prestige of the Rotary, not very different from what I experienced in the less formal clubs mentioned earlier.

The club seems to provide a cross-caste venue for like-minded individuals who, not only in the case of the excursion to Gogha, see their organization as an expression of individual tastes and likings not catered for by traditional fora. As such, it is a modern institution. We shall see that religion, too, offers the opportunity to express personal preferences. The club, however, has the advantage that it does not involve ideological or religious issues except the taste for a certain style of leisure. To understand what the club is really about, then, we may refer to the discussions at Rambhai's guest-house, to which the club represents a healthy and, I think, liberating contrast, for caste and rank should be undercommunicated in the club. No doubt, the club fosters its own hierarchy, but this does not necessarily coincide with traditional or professional status outside the club setting.

Perhaps for this very reason, the club tends to unite individuals who are, relatively speaking, near equals. There is clearly a limit to the degree of social difference that can be undercommunicated or ignored, even in the separate sphere of club activities. Typically, the club is cross-caste in its membership, and recruits its members on the basis of common individual tastes as well as a certain commonality in terms of social position. Thus the core groups in clubs often work in the same firm occupation. Club members may have different backgrounds, but they have to come to terms with similar problems in their individual lives. So the modern club offers its members an escape from the stringency of family and caste.

The themes discussed in the club resemble those discussed by farmers in their fields, with additions related to the common experience of urban life. We have noted how the bachelors of Junagadh's Rotary Club enjoy their (modern) milk-shakes together while eating their dinners (traditionally) in Murlidhar's Lodge. They discuss the problems of being a bachelor in a family-oriented society or of being away from their families with whom, traditionally, they ought to reside. Again, the themes discussed at Ghogha were those of coping with life in a situation characterized simultaneously by the modern and the traditional. And, like the discourse of the cashier of Junagadh's Rotary Club, these talks often turned to religion. This excursion went much further in breaking norms: eating together irrespective of caste, as well as indulging in the forbidden pleasures of drinking and card-playing. These are highly respectable, middle-class men, whom one would not suspect of such shocking behaviour in other contexts.

CASTE IDENTITY

Surely, these examples show that daily life, in the city as well as in the countryside, is never lived within the limits of a single caste. Networks and friendships cross-caste barriers and, in many cases, 'class' is as much a factor as 'caste' in deciding with whom one has a friendly and informal relationship. Yet caste remains the obvious group of reference: though the question '*Apna jati shun chhe*?'–'What kind are you ?' has many possible answers, caste being the obvious one. Unlike some other regions of India I have visited, like the coastal district of South Kanara, Karnataka where quite a few people are reluctant to state their caste, no such reluctance is felt in Saurashtra.

In numerically small castes, the caste also constitutes a network of acquaintances: thus when I spoke to a bookseller in Bhavnagar—an engineer who had started this business only recently—he not only identified himself, quite readily, as a Shrimali Brahmin, but also quickly located a caste-fellow in Praj, one of the village's few remaining grain merchants. This would hardly be possible in the case of Kanbis or Kolis, far too numerous in any region for all the members to know about each other. And yet, when talking, say, of a particular shop, a Kanbi interlocutor will often remark that the shopkeeper in question is a Kanbi, though he has no particular ties to that person. In the first case, then, there is a real connection by network; in the second case, an identification by category.[11]

Regardless of this difference, it is striking how members know the 'story' of their caste and are able to give a potted version of it on all occasions. Thus, one evening, I chatted for a couple of minutes with a young man I met at Gogha Circle—one of those places, in Bhavnagar, where people gather in the evenings to smoke a cigarette, chew a *pan*, or have an ice-cream while meeting friends. The young man, a Bachelor of Commerce, was a Mewari Brahmin. His caste, he said, had followed Mirabai when she left her husband and court in Rajasthan and came to settle in Saurashtra. Thus they came 'three to four hundred years ago', becoming a subcaste separate from their fellows in Rajasthan. The young man's father was farming some twenty *bighas* (a good size of medium farm) in Amreli District. The son would be happy to farm, but had wanted to secure a good education first. The point here, is simply that such a crop of information in a few minutes is usual and conventional. It was simply the young man's way of making his identity clear to me, his way of introducing himself. The identity which one presents, readily, to others includes caste membership and some information about the caste if it is small and not generally known by all. Then there is a brief family and personal history to complete the picture.

REFERENCES TO THE 'GREAT TRADITION'

Such conversations may, however, turn into an argument concerning status, in which standard, all-Indian references may be given an unusual twist to make a point. With the Shrimali Brahmin bookseller, mentioned earlier, we got to chat on religious matters. He was a Shaivite, but not, he said, a follower of Rama—who of course is, in principle, an incarnation of Vishnu, but whose followers may include castes which were once devotees of Shiva (Ghurye 1962: 198-9; Tambs-Lyche 1992: 145-7). To explain his position, he reminded me that Ravana, who had abducted Sita, was a Brahmin. But then he noted:

> Ravana was a very learned and a very wise man. It is true that he is described as a demon, since he abducted Sita, but that he had to do, for he had understood that his special duty in the world was to fight Rama, so that Rama would become known and honoured. To do that, he had to abduct Sita, to entice Rama to follow him and

attack him; but even if he abducted Sita, he did not touch her—he just teased her.

Then, he described the bridge that Rama built to get to Shri Lanka, a description which carried an implicit as to the greatness of Indian engineering in the old days—the bookseller was, it will be remembered, an engineer, and had been working on steel wire for structural use in a Bhavnagar factory. I may note in passing that in spite of these Brahmanical references to religion, much of his stock was Soviet technical literature, translated into English.

Noting the willingness to regard Ravana as an ancestor, I asked the bookseller if the demon might have been, like himself, a Shrimali Brahmin. No, said he, for his caste comes from Shrimal, not far from Ajmer in Rajasthan, whereas Ravana came from Shri Lanka. In fact, I have since learnt, a particular re-working of Ravana's role in the *Ramayana* is not too unusual, but crops up quite frequently in Brahmin circles.[12]

In a similar way, one comes across surprising variants of the four-varna system. One Lohana, the son of a cloth-merchant from a village near Gondal, gave the following version: the four varnas are Hindu, Kshatriya, Vaishya and Shudra. Lest it be thought that this was simply a renaming of the first (Brahmin) varna, he then added: 'Members of the first varna are Brahmins, Vanias, Lohanas and Patels (Kanbi/Patidar). Kshatriyas are such people as Bharwads and Rajputs. Vaishyas are, for example, the Malis (gardeners), Bhangi (sweepers) and so on . . . the Shudras include the Waghris'.

This classification of course, includes the Lohanas, his own caste, in the first varna. It would probably be too radical to exclude the Brahmins: but note that the three other groups in the 'Hindu' varna are all, today, rivals in trade. While Lohanas are accustomed to give pride of place to the Vanias among their commercial rivals, the inclusion of the Kanbi/Patidar (Patel) seems to acknowledge that large numbers from this caste, too, have become businessmen. If we assume this as the basis for their inclusion, we may note that such Patidars, like Brahmins, Vanias and Lohanas, are strict vegetarians—quite often, Patidar entrepreneurs are Swaminarayanas. The four castes included in the first Varna, were ranked Brahmin, Vania, Lohana, Patel. This relative ranking would probably be quite widely accepted—except by quite a few Patidars, who would place themselves above the Lohana.[13] Otherwise, it corresponds to Thoothi's remark that the 'Brahmin-and-Vania' constitutes the first category of the varna system in Gujarat (1935: 119)—a feature of caste ranking in Gujarat which has been commented upon, in one way or another, by several writers. As a matter of fact, this rather unconventional definition of the first varna is far less strange to Gujaratis than to most other Indians—or Indianists.

But the peculiarities of the ranking did not stop there. By including the Bharwads with Rajputs in the category of Kshatriya, the Lohana was playing on an opposition between meat-eating and therefore 'barbarian' castes and the 'civilized' vegetarians of the first varna. In terms of inherent qualities (*guna*) the former are *rajasic*, while the latter are *sattvic*. This, too, then, is a rather logical classification, resting firmly on traditional thinking even if bent to produce an unconventional result.[14]

The Vaishya category, as defined by this informant, do not call for much comment: since the merchants have been moved to the first varna, only artisans remain for the third. But then something unusual happens when Bhangis (sweepers) are included, for this effectively amounts to denying the barrier of untouchability! Here, indeed, is a theme for further research, for it is not the only example I have found, of the blurring of this barrier in Gujarat (Tambs-Lyche 1997: 129). Why this should be so, is far from obvious, for in practice untouchability is very much a fact of life in Gujarat even today, with such important issues as temple access for untouchables still largely unresolved. The question needs far more study than I have been able to do so far. With untouchable craftsmen included among the Vaishyas, the residual category of Shudra becomes quite clear: by mentioning the Waghris, often regarded as ex-hunters of tribal origin, we reach people unanimously placed at the bottom of Saurashtra's stratification system, outside the pale, as well as living outside the village walls.

I note this example as one of the most interesting among several unconventional formulations of caste ranking in Saurashtra. There was considerable individual variation here, though the variations were generally, and usually in an obvious manner, related to the speakers' own caste position. Looking at the system in this way, 'from below', as it were, there is indeed no obvious consensus in the matter. At the local or regional level, relative rank is an object of active discourse and not a question of reference to an unanimously recognized, all-Indian standard. Like the myths Leach (1954: 278) speaks of, caste and varna ranking orders do not make for a chorus of harmony but for a language of argument.

But there are rules to the game, which may be discerned clearly from the above example. There are four varnas, and they are ranked. There is no way of avoiding the inclusion of Brahmins in the first, nor, in Saurashtra, of pushing the Rajputs out of their place in the second. The main issues of debate finding the best place, in the overall ranking, for one's own caste. This affects the place given to other castes. Thus all good reasons for including the Lohanas in the first varna, such as vegetarianism, a clean occupation (trade) and a generally *sattvic* nature, necessarily include the Vanias, too. A Lohana cannot get away from the fact that, in these terms, his caste is inferior to the Vanias. For a Vania, the same principles might lead him to claim near-equality to Brahmins: he, in his turn, might exclude the Lohanas.

The second point of debate, then, is clear: what role should vegetarianism and a *sattvic* nature be accorded in constructing the ranking, as opposed to the 'traditional' pattern where Brahmins occupy the first and merchants the third varna ? The latter point of view is held by Rajputs and concerns the relative rank of warriors and merchants, the two groups opposing their interpretations of each other. The inversion of the all-Indian order, by placing merchants higher than warriors, is indeed very common among Gujaratis.

The third point of debate is whether to accord prime importance to untouchability, and where to draw the line between untouchables and other castes. The distinction is certainly less clear than one would think, and it seems to me that it is particularly blurred among the merchant castes. Perhaps these strongly vegetarian groups see themselves as so far removed from lower, non-vegetarian castes that the distinction loses some of its significance. It may also be that their version of Vaishnavism makes less of ritual distinction than ritualist, Shaivite orientations.

The traditional concepts define rules of discourse where fitting the argument to the frame forms part of its legitimation. People in Saurashtra do not agree on how society is or should be constituted: but they address the question in a common idiom that is part of all-Indian tradition.

A CROSSROAD OF ITINERARIES

We already met Mr. Khan, who runs a bicycle-and-soda shop in Junagadh. This combination of trades is common in Saurashtra and easy to explain: as people bring their bicycle with a broken chain or a flat tyre, what is more natural than having a soda while waiting? Mr. Khan also sells fizzy drinks. His home-made soda brought good profit, he explained; 24 of the 25 paisa he demanded for it. As his name indicates, Mr. Khan is a Pathan. He came to Junagadh in 1956; his family came from the environs of Peshawar. The sleeping partner of the firm is a Nagar Brahmin from Junagadh.

Strolling among Junagadh shops you discover the extent of migration. The owner of the Sindh Panjab Rajputana Lodge, a non-vegetarian restaurant, is from Rajasthan. The tailor I met at Patel's tea shop originally hails from (Soviet) Turkestan; his father migrated to Mangrol on Saurashtra's west coast before he was born. He himself moved from there to Junagadh; there were not many Turkis in Mangrol. In Junagadh there are quite a few.

At the post office, I met a young Anglo-Indian born in Karachi, come for some railway work. He was thrilled that I was from Norway: 'I have an aunt in that town', he exclaimed. Was he thinking about Norwich? Another young man wanted to stress his ties to me, shouting 'Hello! I am also a Christian!' Typically, he did not mention his caste—most Christians in Saurashtra are untouchables or come from very low castes.

Close by the shop of the photographer I shall cite shortly, I met one of the many young men eager to migrate to the West. He had his eyes on Canada, then still open to migrants. His friend, a Brahmin born in Kampala, had chosen Uganda citizenship just before Idi Amin's expulsion of Asians, and now found himself back in India. These were some of the people I met in a few days in Junagadh. What struck me was the number of itineraries leading into or out of Saurashtra; in this most traditional of Saurashtra's cities, individual fates create a vast network of ties. Ancestry and migration binds people to remote corners of the world.

This is true even in villages: I was swimming near Veraval, when I was joined by a man from the fisherman's hamlet nearby. He was a good-looking fellow of twenty-nine years, in 1973. 'I see you are no Chapati-wallah', was his greeting. He introduced himself as Ismail Yusuf Italian. Yes, he was Italian; his father had gone to fight some war—probably the Ethiopian conflict or its world war aftermath—but had left on a dhow for Gujarat. Becoming a Muslim, he had settled here as a fisherman. Gujarat and Saurashtra may have lost the central position they held in the trade networks of the seventeenth century, but are still at the crossroads of numerous individual migration routes. As noted, I had acquaintances in common with the secretary of Junagadh's rotary club, the links in the chain passing by London and El-Obeid (Western Sudan). And indeed, it suffices to sit for a while in any typical Muslim café in Gujarat, to meet people hailing from, and having been to, a large sector of the Islamic world.

Faced with such evidence, the conception of caste as a closed system is difficult to defend. Too many communities have their origins elsewhere, while others have long been engaged in out-migration. Globalization, in this sense, is nothing new in Saurashtra, and our conception of Indian society must take this into account. Rather than an abstract principle underlying the whole, we should try to grasp the Indian way of accommodating difference to the exigencies of sharing territory and polity.

THOUGHTS ABOUT THE WORLD

'In India', said a Junagadh photographer, when I came to him to develop a couple of films, 'there is so much philosophy—so many different Dharmas. And in India, there is Vidya, but Vidya means mysticism—thinking. So it all goes in circles, this kind of thinking. Because people think, and think again, but that is not science.' A middle-aged man who had dabbled in drawing and painting in oil, he was born in Junagadh, but got established as a photographer in Bombay before opening a studio in his home town. He is a Lohana, a community usually believed to have come from Sindh.

The photographer went on to talk of perception and the nature of reality. Drawing on personal experience, he said: 'Take colours; you may say that the sky is blue, but in reality it has several colours. Light is very important. You have to see where the light comes from. You have to make your selection. This is true also of society'. The statement might have come from a Paris impressionist of the 1880s. His reflections are inspired by his professional; he is a good photographer, who has won several prizes for his work. His remarks made me think about the epistemology of anthropology; the light in which we see society is important. He, like some of us, wanted to view things in a perspective coming from outside the society itself. We may see this as Western influence, and his critical remarks on dowry and other traditional institutions mark the photographer as a secular and progressive-minded individual. But the context is as Indian as he is himself, wearing a *kurta* and a *dhoti* with the 'Gandhi cap' hanging on the wall.

We may usefully contrast him with an engineer, having introduced some of his own ideas to public sanitation, who now had his own technical consultation business. He was from south Gujarat, but we met in Rajkot, where we stayed at the same guest house. He was a rational and efficient man, devoted to his work. Yet our conversation soon took a different turn. 'Have you thought about the final questions—life and death?'. It was clear that he spent much of his spare time reading and thinking about such matters. In fact, he would like to retire, he said, to devote all his time to these 'really important matters'. He is not unusual; I remembered the restaurant owner I knew in Coventry, who had not only realized this ambition but become a kind of saintly and spiritual leader of the local Hindu community. He reminded me, too, of several politicians of the princely states, who on their retirement had a hut built in their garden, where they studied religious philosophy when they were not receiving old friends and, incidentally, through these discussions exercising a remote but significant influence on the affairs of state.

THE ASHRAMA OF A NEW SECT

The engineer shared these interests with Jagatbhai, a Charan—member of the bardic caste—teaching sociology in a regional college. One day, he told me of a new sect which had just come to town. He was interested in seeing them, and so I joined him.

The new establishment was part of the Brahmakumari Mission. This organization was started in 1937 by one Baba or Dadaji, who was born in Hyderabad (Sindh) in 1876 or 1877. In 1936 he had a revelation, realized that he was God, and founded the sect. He is seen as a reincarnation of Shiva, who is identified with Light. In the iconography of the sect, the Godhead is shown in the form of a luminous egg with the pointed end upwards. Their philosophy is built around the cycle of the four ages (*Yugas*), telescoped down to a period of 5,000 years. Each age lasts 1,250 years or 84 generations. Thus each soul has 84 lives in one *Yuga*. We are in the *Kaliyuga*, and the end of the world is near; then the cycle will start all over again. The atomic bomb is one of the agents which will destroy the world—and that year, in 1974, India in fact exploded its first 'nuclear device'.

The headquarters of the Brahmakumari mission is Nasik, from where they publish their material in Hindi, Gujarati and English, including the periodical *World Review*. In the new centre we found an instructive pictorial exhibition, explaining the tenets of the sect. In style, this presentation recalled the rich glass paintings of modern Jain temples. The Brahmakumaris claim to integrate all religions, but criticize the Hindu 'pantheism'. God is not everywhere, though he knows everything. Predestination is rejected; their insistence on a free will is rather similar to Christian ideas. The world is like a play, they say; the first half is happy, the second tragic. During the first half, the individual soul becomes a Deva; in this our second half souls remain men. Sins are acting on the soul of man, and they are responsible for his sad state during the *Kaliyuga*.

The sect does not have temples, but ashramas, which they call *vidyalayas*, places of learning. In Bhavnagar, as I believe elsewhere, most inmates were women, though men may also join. They wear white clothes, like Svetambara Jain renouncers. Other devotees are lay followers. The landlord of one of my other friends had become a follower of the sect. A medical doctor, he used to drink a lot, had an uncontrollable temper, and beat his wife and children. Now, his conduct was much better. Thus, concluded my secularist friend, religion may do some good.

Jagatbhai was quite impressed by this new sect. 'Ultimately', he said, the function of religion is to maintain some moral order in society. So most religions start out with some ideas about this moral order, and most of them keep some of these ideas. The Jains have non-violence, the Muslims their idea of Brotherhood. Hindus have a thing about tolerance, and Christians are great on charity. But even so, with time these religions have tended to degenerate. The moral ideas are no longer carried out in practice. So the Jains, for example, will go to their temples and do their *puja*; and then they go back to their unsavoury business practices.

Jagatbhai, himself a scholar, was impressed with what he called the scientific method of the sect. Clearly, science here did not stand for empirical research. Rather, he found a certain logical consistency in the Brahmakumari ideas, as he had, as a student, in the ideas of Jainism. Jagatbhai did not join the new sect, but I was interested by his careful assessment of what they had to offer. He evaluated their teachings against standards of philosophical and psychological satisfaction, from a strictly individual point of view. He was looking for a religion that could integrate, for him, the intellectual and the moral dimension, and thus conciliate his intellectual quest with his existence as a moral being in society.

What he assessed was the philosophy; he did not seem to consider the sect in terms of the social dimensions of membership. Recruitment to the Brahmakumari sect is individual, and the doctor mentioned does not spend much time with other Brahmakumaris outside the ashram. This is very different from the communitarian character of the Swaminarayana sect, so powerful in Gujarat, which Jagatbhai detests.

THE CITY: ESCAPE FROM CASTE RULES?

It is often said that the complexity of the city offers an escape from the hierarchy of the village. What I have shown of city life here may bear this out. But we shall see later that interaction in the village does not conform, either, to the strict hierarchy supposed to exist in India. Nor will it do to think of the village in terms of tradition, opposed to the modernity of the city. The city is too old, in India, for that. Its importance with regard to caste must be seen from a different angle. Only here, a representative range of known castes can be simultaneously present.

Caste is not a rural phenomenon, for no village contains more than a section of the castes needed to form a 'system'. Small villages in Saurashtra have only a few castes, and in large villages, interaction rules resemble those of the city. Villages are not microcosms of caste society but rather the limbs of a city-centred region, which historically, in Saurashtra, often corresponds to one of the old princely states.[15] Only in the region, then, is a large complement of castes simultaneously present in a single geographical location. And while they are absent from the villages, they are still present in the mind of the villager.

This complement of castes corresponds to what we might call a regional caste system. Only at this level may we speak of system, if we or our informants think in terms of functional analysis or its common-sense equivalent. Yet as a system it cannot be a closed one, since immigrants are legion and many castes, in their turn, have taken part in the Gujarati diaspora. Moreover, the range of castes present in the region will include groups in comptetition as well as in symbiosis, groups of similar as well as complementarily different status—in other words, a set too complex to form a 'system' in the organic sense. The Brahmin, the philosopher or the anthropologist may well have a vision of the unity of the whole: but the view of most people, I hold, is less orderly and more realistic. It corresponds, not so much to the serene order of the imagined village community as to the hustle and bustle of the city. The villager's view of the city, then, corresponds to the view that the citizen has of it, and on this broad horizon there is complexity rather than order, competition as well as interdependence, conflict as much as order. It is a world where strangers are indeed strange and sometimes threatening, and where recourse must be had to those one knows: relatives, caste fellows and various network links. As the photographer put it, the sky may seem blue, but in reality it has many colours.

NOTES

1. For these links, see e.g. Tambs-Lyche 1997: 276.
2. Parmar (1991) feels that privacy was less of a value in Saurashtra than on the mainland, leading to a more open architecture.
3. In this sense, one may think of the traditional English pub as a parallel.
4. Literally, a cushion; equivalent to 'seat' or 'throne'.
5. The term Vania originally meant grain trader.
6. Pocock 1957b, Tambs-Lyche 1980: 35; see also Tambs-Lyche 1992: 209-10 and 361.
7. In Jetpur, the new entrepreneurs—such as Kanbis—often entered textiles as employees or salesmen, thus gaining access to the network, or field, of the trade (Dupont 1997: 121-8).
8. I return to this phenomenon later, analyzing such exchanges as 'ranking transactions'.
9. It may be relevant to note here, that nobody alluded to Hindu-Muslim relations in this context.

10. He used the English term here.
11. A third possibility is of course actual network connections within a large caste. We have seen how a similar discussion in Junagadh led to Jain Vania caste-fellows in the Sudan and London.
12. There is also a Jain *Ramayana*, where the demons (*rakshasas*) are not only the heroes, but also Jains.
13. In Britain, the Patidars clearly placed themselves above Lohanas (Tambs-Lyche 1980: 139), but the latter did not necessarily agree.
14. Such stress on the paradigms of thought rather than the resulting structures characterizes the ethnosociology of Marriott (1989).
15. Spodek (1976) aptly calls them city-states.

CHAPTER 5

Centres of Pilgrimage

Magical prospects, monuments divine-
Now all were visited.
Here we had tarried five nights and days;
Yet homeward now with loitering footsteps trod.

YÜAN CHÊN, translated by ARTHUR WALEY

PILGRIMAGE AS TRADITION

Saurashtra has often been described as a holy land, both by outsiders and inhabitants. The famous centres of pilgrimage, Dwarka, Somnath, Girnar and Palitana, occupy a special place in the memory of Saurashtra's inhabitants. Each of them is the subject of a large number of myths, of which some turn on historical events, such as the destruction of Somnath by Mahmud of Ghazni. Others must be regarded as myth, such as those concerning Krishna. What is striking to the Western observer—as long as he does not question his own myths too closely—is the way these events, real or imagined, merge into pasts that are distributed as points of reference in a rather indeterminate past, rather than ordered in a linear sequence. These points are fixed in space rather than time: everybody, in Saurashtra, knows where Dwarka is and has been since time immemorial, and in relation to this certainty the actual timing seems a minor detail.

Here, I deal with the place of these centres in Saurashtra society, and my point will be to show how variously they are integrated with that social fabric. In terms of social and political history, they have little in common. As for other towns, I shall deal with the historical patterns that distinguish each centre as a particular place in the imagery of the region. Religion is of course important here, but we shall see that other aspects of tradition, too, are constitutive of the image of each place of pilgrimage.

I shall not deal with the theme of pilgrimage as such: as Gold (1988) has shown, the motives of pilgrims and the nature of their journeys differ. I never participated, as she did, in pilgrimage. To Dwarka I went alone, and was little more than a tourist. Going to Gadhada, the sacred town of the older branch of the Swaminarayana sect, I spoke to pilgrims, ate and lodged with them, and may perhaps claim to have been a participant. My visits to the Khodiyar temple were individual, but so arc thc visits of most devotees.

The dividing line between tourism and pilgrimage is not easy to draw. Perhaps Gadhada seems closer to the real thing simply because no tourists go there: the temples are relatively modern and lacking in aesthetic distinction, the town has no outstanding characteristics, while the Swaminarayanas, who go there in some number, are very serious about their religion. To Dwarka or Somnath, people go both as tourists and pilgrims, so the atmosphere is a mixture of both. Even at Khodiyar, the families arriving by car from Rajkot or Ahmedabad seem to combine a pleasant outing with their devotion; indeed the temple is constructing a picnic spot and a playground for children to cater to such visitors.

A study of pilgrimage, then, should properly be of the pilgrim and not of the place. This is what Gold did. Starting from a Rajasthan village, she set out to demonstrate that the pursuit of *moksha,* as the ultimate goal of pilgrimage, is not 'subversive' to ordinary life, but exists in 'continuity with normative Hindu existence' (1988: 3). Indeed, she found that while her informants talked little of *moksha*, they did think and talk a lot about death (1988: 59-63). Both themes cropped up in my own talks with informants; though the theme of pilgrimage was seldom introduced.

There is an association, traditionally, between pilgrimage and suffering. This link is not always evident in modern pilgrimage, however. To climb the Girnar barefoot certainly implies a degree of suffering, somewhat akin to what Daniel describes (1984: 245-87). It will be clear, later, that getting to Dwarka was both dangerous and uncomfortable in the old days. But most pilgrimage places in Saurashtra, nowadays, are easily accessible by bus or train; at Palitana, palanquins have long been available to ease a long and hard climb. Thus a pilgrimage is, for most people I met, a pleasant excursion rather than an ordeal. I hardly met, in Saurashtra, the type of pilgrim familiar from some parts of India—easily identified as such by dress and behaviour.[1] Only in Junagadh, at occasions such as *Shivaratri*, were such traditional pilgrims seen in number. Nor did I know people who talked enthusiastically of pilgrimage, in spite of spending quite some time discussing religion. Perhaps I talked to the wrong people (but then there must be quite a few of them), yet I cannot help feeling that people in Saurashtra are more used to seeing outsiders come to their region on pilgrimage, than they are interested in joining them.

A MODERN PILGRIMAGE: GADHADA

Unlike the other places mentioned here, Gadhada's status as a pilgrimage is historically recent. It was here that Swaminarayana—the founder of the sect that bears his name—lived for many years, under the protection of the Kathi chief, Dada Khachar, who had become his disciple. Swaminarayanas talk of 'Gadhapur' as their 'Holy City', and a considerable number of sect members make a pilgrimage to the place. It has a large and important temple of the older branch (the Acharyapanth) of the sect, and guest-houses and dharmashalas for pilgrims. Going there by bus, I found that at least half the passengers were pilgrims from all walks of life—though the devotees who are really well-off come by rented coach or car. The temple, though large and impressive, was built in the nineteenth century and there is little else to see in Gadhada, so there are no tourists. Here, then, I had occasion to experience something of the 'spirit of pilgrimage'. Members of both the Swaminarayana sects come, and one senses, it is true, a certain enthusiasm to see this place which was so central to the history of the sect. But Swaminarayanas are very sensible people, so there was little of the exotic about my visit. People came in the evening, went for *Satsang*—the communal gathering that is normally held on Sundays, but more often in Gadhada, for the benefit of pilgrims—the next morning and left in the afternoon. One dresses for the *Satsang* in one's best clothes, the yellow rosary common to most Vaishnava sects and receives the yellow *tilak* on leaving the temple—but otherwise there is little to mark the pilgrim.

At the guest-house were I stayed—it had a Swaminarayana owner but it was not a Dharmashala—the conversation tended to religious themes, but there was also talk of business and ordinary small-talk. Clearly, there was a feeling of being an insider, belonging to the community, but precisely for this reason, communication was easy and informal. The very fact of visiting Gadhada made me a kind of pilgrim too, so I felt included in the group, and talked a little of my experiences of the Swaminarayanas in London; but I cannot say that the visit to Gadhada remains in my mind a religious experience. In fact, for that the pilgrims will go to Vadtal, the centre of the old sect, or to Bochasan, also in central Gujarat, where the new sect (the Yogijipanth) has its centre. In these places, as well as at the Akshar Bhavan of the new sect in Mumbai, there are large communities of monks with whom the pilgrims may stay.

I visited the Mumbai centre and stayed three days, talking to the monks and pilgrims. We ate the food of the monks (dipped in lukewarm water to kill all taste) and followed a certain monastic discipline: the atmosphere was therefore quite different—and more serious—than at Gadhada. Here, devotees came to find peace, taking their minds off daily worries; but also to learn more about their religion. I was alone among the visitors, however, to avail of the library: most preferred to listen to the monks or seek their advice. These centres function rather like the ashramas of many other sects.

My visit to Gadhada certainly brought me into contact with very ordinary people, leading ordinary lives, whose aim in making the pilgrimage was no break with their present life, but rather to sanctify it, to add an element of religious quality to an otherwise ordinary existence. In the Swaminarayan community, such pilgrimage is recognized, and a cynic might conclude that it simply brings prestige to the pilgrim; but people also spoke of 'feeling good' or 'feeling at peace' on celebrating the *Satsang* in this holy place. Swaminarayanas do not believe that pilgrimage, as such, brings release from *karma*; this comes from experiencing the presence of God in this world, and such *darshan* may come to the devotee anywhere, at any time. But going to places such as Gadhada, where the Swami lived for a long time, or Loj, where he joined and then led the ashram that became the core of the new sect (Dave 1967), certainly helps fix the mind on his exploits. Since few people go to Loj, the fact that I had been there gave me some credibility when I discussed religion with members of the sect.

Loj, on the west coast of Saurashtra not far from Mangrol, has seen better days. As in many large villages, the merchant houses are closed and shuttered, and there are few recent buildings. The Swaminarayana temple is not large, but it houses the oldest image of the saint. Iconographically it is an interesting image, since it is very close, in style and execution, to the images of Shri Nathaji, the incarnation of Krishna venerated by members of the Vallabhacharya sect. Modern images of the Swami are more naturalistic, and the new branch of the sect has cut the ties with Krishnaism. The early history of the sect, as a branch of Vashnavism centering on Krishna, is therefore evident at Loj. On my visit, I met a middle-aged couple with daughter and son-in-law. Devout Swaminarayanas, they had been to Gadhada and other places holy to the sect. There was no mistaking their emotion on seeing the birthplace of their religion. But, the guardian of the temple confirmed, not many people come.

DWARKA: KRISHNA'S HOLY CITY

On the north-western tip of the peninsula, Dwarka is known for its association with Krishna. Here he fled from Mathura, and here he established his kingdom. Krishna has been worshipped in India since before 300 BC (Banerjea 1956: 395), and Hopkins has noted that in the *Mahabharata* Krishna is always treated as an incarnation of Vishnu and a God, while Rama only attains this status in the later versions of the *Ramayana* (Hopkins 1915: 213). The main texts and myths surrounding Krishna are too well known to repeat here. Through them, Dwarka has become one of the main centres of pilgrimage in Saurashtra.

The most recent and thorough research into the arrival of the Krishna cult in Gujarat is that of Francoise Mallison. While the cult of Vishnu was certainly well established in Gujarat in Vallabhi times (Mallison 1983: 250-1) the position of Krishna is ambiguous. The term Ranchod, used both for Vishnu, in his Trivikrama form, and for Krishna, may provide the clue to an intermediary stage. This is an alternative name for the image of Krishna at Dwarka, as also the name under which the original image was brought to Dakor in mainland Gujarat. The development of the cult of Krishna, from earlier Vaishnavite cults, has been gradual, and the image of Krishna as propitiated today in Gujarat may not have been fully developed before the fifteenth century (Mallison 1983).

Dwarka's position as a pilgrimage centre, however, is certainly older than this, and belongs at least to the intermediate period of transition from an older Vaishnavism to modern Krishnaism. Dwarka's origins are steeped in myth, but recent underwater discoveries have shown that it was inhabited before the beginning of the Christian era. In the sixth or seventh century it was rebuilt (JMG: 616). Its exact age need not detain us here. But it is certain that the adoption of Krishnaism by rich merchant communities from the fifteenth century onwards has embellished Dwarka and added to its repute.

The main centre of Krishna worship in Dwarka is the Dwarkadhish (or Dwarkanath) temple, also known as the Jagat Mandir (world temple). Legend has it that it was built by Vairanabh, Krishna's grandson, and it is believed that it was finished in a single night. Historically, it is believed by some to have been built in the sixth or seventh century, and its construction is sometimes ascribed to 'Gupta Raja, a ruler on the Ganges' (JMG: 616). It is also, however, stated to date from the thirteenth century, which seems to be the professional archaeologist's view (JMG: 617).[2]

For the pilgrims, as for the inhabitants of Saurashtra, the status of Dwarka as Krishna's holy city is not in doubt. Dwarka is regarded as one of the *char dham*, one of the four principal holy locations in India, as also one of the *sapta puris*, or the seven ancient cities of the subcontinent. Today, the town remains viable mainly because of the pilgrimage; in spite of its fame it had only 14,314 inhabitants in 1961 (JMG: 615).

Krishna, or Ranchod is the main deity, but there is a shrine to Shakti Mata on the fourth floor of the main temple, one floor below the main shrine. The whole structure, of seven floors, is imposing, and dominates the town. Surprisingly, the image of Ranchod here is not the original one, which is at Dakor in central Gujarat.

> It is said that, taking pity on his old devotee, Bodano, who came for *darshan* from such great distance on every full-moon day, the God in the form of idol walked with him to Dakor in V.S. 1212 (1155 A.D.). The Gugli Pujaris of Dwarka chased Bodano to recover the idol and killed him in Dakor. The widow of Bodano offered to give the equivqlent of the idol's weight in gold whereupon the Guglis agreed to withdraw. By a miracle the idol became as light as a golden nose-ring which was all that the widow had. The Guglis were disappointed, but the Lord mercifully directed that they would find an exact replica of the idol in a particular well at Dwarka on a particular day. The impatient Guglis looked for the idol earlier than they were told to, and as a result, found an idol which, though similar to the original one, was smaller. It is said that this is the idol which is now enshrined at Dwarka. (JMG: 617)

This myth[3] has been studied Pocock (1973) and Mallison (1990). Pocock found it striking that the Guglis at Dwarka themselves tell this story. They are still the main priests at Dwarka, as well as at Dakor.

Also dating from the thirteenth century is the ancient temple of Rukmini, wife of Krishna. The Govardhannath temple is dedicated to an incarnation of Krishna particularly popular in Marwar. Damodar, another incarnation, also has a temple here, while the temple to Mahalakshmi may be included in this Vaishnavite group. Similarly, the shrines of Narsinh Mehta and Mirabai appeal to Vaishnavite Bhaktas.

The four main festivals at Dwarka are all dedicated to Krishna; on Janmashtami (*Shravan Vad* 8, in August) his birth in Mathura is commemorated. This is Dwarka's most important celebration, with pilgrims coming from all India; it has long been directly reported by All-India Radio. In the Annakuta festival the new year is celebrated by offering food to Krishna from the new crops. Holi is celebrated in Dwarka by the singing of *bhajans* and the sprinkling of water and *gulal* before the *murti*. And on Dolotsav, following closely on Holi, the *murti* is swung on the *dola* or swing. Bhim Ekadashi, celebrating Bhima (of the *Mahabharata*) may also appeal particularly to Vaishnavites.

But Dwarka is also an important pilgrimage for the devotees of Shiva. The Sharda Pith is one of the four *maths* said to have been established by Shankaracharya at the four corners of India. The present 'Shankaracharya' is the 77th in the line of its spiritual heads. There is also a temple of Shiva, here known as Ranmukteshwar Mahadev. Mahashivratri is another important festival in Dwarka.

While pilgrimage is Dwarka's main basis, it should be noted that there is also a cement factory outside the town. The hospital, established by a Bombay merchant, is more in tune with the town's character. Yet the visitor is struck by the dominant position of the temple complex, the importance of the pilgrim trade, and the number of dharmashalas. In contrast to some other places of pilgrimage, however, no sacrifice to modernity had been made by 1974, when all arrangements for pilgrims were still strictly traditional. I occupied the only single room in town: its dimensions were such that I had to open the door to put my shoes under the bunk, which filled the whole space. Pilgrims, normally, share common accommodation in the style of traditional dharmashala, though they pay hotel prices. Nor has Dwarka become a centre of tourism, in spite of its fame.

OKHAMANDAL—THE BAD COUNTRY

The north-western tip of the peninsula, in which Dwarka is situated, is known as Okhamandal, which tradition translates as the bad or difficult country. It is largely infertile but covered with a dense growth of brushwood. 'One of the most savage looking Countries I ever beheld', says Macmurdo, a British officer who visisted these parts in 1809. 'We passed no Village and the Country so completely waste that no traces of road were perceptible, nor did we see a single soul in the fields. It was literally marching through a milk bush Jungle, in some places extremely close' (Ghosh 1977: 29).

The pilgrims who came by land travelled with difficulty, and were in constant fear of robbers, who even searched the ascetic's loincloth for a few coins. By sea, the pilgrim traffic was harassed by pirates. The coast is indented by small creeks and inlets, where pirates could hide easily (Ghosh 1977: 46; Meghani 1928). Piracy is old here; Marco Polo considered the Gujarat pirates the worst in the world (Majumdar 1956: 268) and Sultan Mahmud Begada fought the Dwarka pirates in the 1473 (Chaube 1975: 66-72). He also destroyed the temples that year (Mallison 1990: 203n.). From what Macmurdo tells us we may perhaps surmise that Mahmud, too, was aware of the link between priesthood and piracy.

Tradition has it that at the time of Rai Lakka of Kacch,[4] Okhamandal was divided between the Hirole and the Chaora Rajputs. Then a band of Rathods managed to usurp the power, and intermarried with the local Vagher community of fishermen, seamen and pirates. The mixed Rajput-Wagher community became known as the Vadel. Meghani tells the same general story.[5] When Macmurdo wrote, Vadel and Vagher chiefs were the masters of Dwarka and Okhamandal. Their power centred on the island of Bet north of Dwarka, which they defended against the British during the Vagher rebellion of 1858.[6]

Robbers and pirates were integrated in the local political system. Macmurdo notes how the chiefs here do not receive land revenue—the land being poor in any case—but a share of the pirate's and robber's loot. The inaccessibilty of the country made this adaptation viable, but piracy must be explained by the strange position of Ranchod and his temple, whose

> Priests and attendants are the great instigators to Piracy. They derive a certain share of all plundered property in return for the protection of (them by) Runchorjee (i.e. Ranchodji, the form of Krishna) while (they are) at sea. It is a common practice for Pirates to promise a larger share (than the God can claim by Rule) if he will insure the success of their trip. Many vessels are actually fitted out in his name and really belong to the Pagodas which receive all the plunder which they bring. (Ghosh 1977: 46)

Macmurdo was taking part in the expedition led by Col. Walker, whose purpose was to arrange for peace and order in the peninsula. He may be biased, and exaggerate the role of loot in the economy and maintenance of the temple. But the role of the chiefs can hardly be doubted, and it seems evident that over the centuries, a kind of symbiosis had developed, between piracy and protection, between robber chief and temple management.

We may note that the Gugli Brahmins, who controlled the temple complex of Dwarka, were also active as traders. 600 of the 4000 houses of Khambhalia, a port under Jamnagar, were inhabited by them, says Macmurdo, who continues: '—they have amassed sums of money arising from the pilgrims to that Pagoda—with which they have retired to Kumballia, as affording the double advantage of security and trade' (Ghosh 1977: 27). Perhaps the security of their trade was bolstered by the alliance that their community had formed with the Dwarka pirates.

When Pocock studied the Gugli Brahmins a century and a half later, hereditary priesthood (*pandagiri*) at Dwarka had become much less profitable. Some 160 Guglis were still employed in catering to pilgrims, but most of them would happily give up this work should some more lucrative opportunity arise; they also, for the most part, combined this work with other business (1981: 325-8). The majority of the some 600 gainfully employed caste members, at Dwarka, were in secular employment (1981: 332-4). And, if many Guglis were in business, they no longer controlled important sectors, as was apparently the case when Macmurdo wrote.

But the Gugli Brahmins were not the only traders related to the temples of Dwarka. Many of them served the Vallabhacharya Maharajas (Enthoven 1920: 231). The main devotees of Vallabhacharya in this area were, however, the Bhatias, a merchant community based in Jamnagar and in Kacch. I have described elsewhere how the commerce of Jamnagar and that of the Bhatias rose together, exploiting particularly the triangular link Jamnagar–Muscat–Zanzibar (1997: 69-71). The prosperity of the Bhatias certainly accounted for Dwarka's growth as a pilgrimage centre. But today, Pocock notes (1981), the mansions that rich Bhatias had built at Dwarka are empty and decayed. Partly, the Bhatias have lost much of their commercial position with the decline of the Oman–Zanzibar route and of the old Indian Ocean trade in general, and partly, the importance of the Dwarka link was undermined when the Vallabhacharya sect suffered greatly from the effects of the 'Maharaja Libel Case' in 1860-2 (Pocock 1973: 118-20).

Were Bhatias, too, protected from piracy by some kind of alliance? Jamnagar certainly chose an alliance with the pirates rather than fighting them in the nineteenth century (Spodek 1976: 12). Bhatias were then the state's most prominent traders.

This historical background is not, in itself, our concern here. But the way in which pilgrimage, commerce and piracy has been linked in Dwarka reflects not only the kind of society that Saurashtra has been, but also the subjectivity of our present-day notions of piracy and commerce. On the north-western tip of Saurashtra, the two have been linked rather than opposed for a very long time, and the holiness of Dwarka has not suffered from the dubious foundations of its economy. It is indeed as if religion, here, stands apart from the pragmatics of moral life, as if the blessing of a pilgrimage to Dwarka had to be bought at the cost of exposing oneself to dangers that were not only implicit in, but quite explicitly created by the political regime. This is what the pilgrim's song is about, when, after describing the danger of piracy and theft, it returns to the refrain: 'In Dwarka, Ranchod is ruling' (Meghani 1928: 100-1).

SOMNATH PATAN

Somnath is quite different. The temple of Somnath is, of course, well known. Its destruction by Mahmud of Ghazni has become part of myth. Strictly speaking, there are at least three temples of Somnath; the old, the new, and an eighteenth-century replacement. It is the new temple which is now the object of pilgrimage. The old one was a ruin for a long time. Tod, visiting it in 1821, wrote of 'the "temple of the sun", deserted, desecrated, a receptacle for kine, the pinnacle . . . demolished, and the fragments strewing the ground . . .' (Tod 1971: 328-9).

Tod found only one symbol of the Sun, the 'ancient object of worship at the temple',[7] left; it was 'a globular patch of red paint, placed by the cowherds'. This should not surprise us, since Soma refers to the moon. Though the temple had been restored, its spire had never been re-erected since its destruction by Mahmud of Ghazni (AD 1026). In fact it had been restored several times; first by Kumarpala of Gujarat in 1169. It was destroyed again by Alaf Khan Khalji in 1297, restored in 1325,[8] destroyed by Muzaffar Khan in 1394, and restored soon after, only to be destroyed in 1406. Under Akbar, the *Lingam* was re-installed in the temple, till its final destruction was ordered by Aurangzeb in 1646 (JDG: 125-47).

S.H. Desai (1975) claims that the temple was destroyed nine times by the Muslims; Davis notes that 'the Muslim desecration count' had climbed to twenty-one by 1990, according to a letter to the *New York Times*. He also states that 'from the 1870s or so on, almost every author who wrote of Somanatha confidently asserted that the site had been repeatedly contested by the Muslim and Hindu communities over six or more centuries' (1998: 187). Tod found little more than a ruin: 'Mahmoud himself could scarcely have contemplated its present degradation. Even with the Hindu, all reverence for it is gone. . . . ' (Tod 1971: 343).

That the temple was deserted in the nineteenth century is confirmed by Forbes: at one time a battery of heavy guns was mounted on it, to serve as a bastion against pirates (1878: 56). Like present-day pilgrims, Forbes assumes that it was dedicated to Shiva as 'Lord of the Moon', as the name attests.[9] He describes the Lingam as the Sultan of Ghazni saw it, 'a stone cylinder which rose nine feet in height above the floor of the temple, and penetrated six feet in depth below it . . .' (Forbes 1878: 58).[10] Modern pilgrims are probably right, then; they do propitiate the original divinity of Somnath. But it is clear that there has been no continuity of worship at Somnath, as at Dwarka.

It is difficult to get a clear picture of Somnath's political history, since the accounts we have are cast in the image of Hindu-Muslim conflict. Mahmud of Ghazni probably came for the loot as much as for religious motives, but it is less clear whether this is true of later Muslim attacks. What is certain is that the town and temple was attacked frequently. The elaborate city walls underline its need for defence, and the old temple, too, was protected by walls.[11]

The Gazetteer assumes Ra Naughan of Junagadh was the ruler of Somnath when Mahmud attacked. In or about 1214, however, Vinjani, of the Dwarka Rathods,[12] established himself at Prabhas Patan, the town and fort close to the temple. His desendants the Vajas were at times quite powerful in the thirteenth and fourteenth century, while at other times they were vassals of Junagadh. Vijayraj, the last of the line, fell defending Somnath against Muzaffar Khan of Gujarat in 1406 (JDG: 125-34).

We may of course wonder whether the Rathods instituted the same symbiotic relation between piracy and pilgrimage as we observe, later, at Dwarka—a hypothesis which would help explain the constant attacks, but there is no evidence for it. In general, Patan and Somnath seem to have been partly independent, partly remotely controlled from Junagadh, in the times of the Hindu Chudasama dynasty (875–1470). Under the succeeding Muslim rulers, the temple was either ignored or actively destroyed, except for its partial restoration by Akbar. The Babis of independent Junagadh (1747–1947) do not seem to have taken any interest in it.[13] Yet they allowed Ahalya Bai Holkar, the queen of Indore, to build a new temple—late in the eighteenth century—inside the town walls of Prabhas Patan, to house the original Lingam—'cautiously placed in a secret underground vault' (Davis 1998: 197).

The ancient city of Somnath Patan—also known as Prabhas Patan or Deva Patan—is still much as Tod found it in 1821. It was defended by strong walls

> . . . worthy of the object for which they were raised. They are composed of large square blocks of freestone . . . the square towers, constructed with a bold external slope, or *talus*, only to be met with in the remains of ancient days, lend an air of beauty and strength. . . . The vallation is . . . not less than a mile and three quarters. . . . The height of the walls varies from twenty-five to thirty-five feet, and they are about sixteen thick at the base. A ditch, twenty-five feet broad, and about the same in depth . . . surrounds the whole. (Tod 1971: 335-6)

No such extensive defences are found at Dwarka, though there are walls around the main temple complex. Tod found the city too large for its walls; in 1974, however, the walls surrounded most of the inhabited quarters. These defences, according to Tod, were rebuilt after Mahmud of Ghazni's destructions by Kumarpala of Anhilwada Patan.[14] The main entrance, to the north, is of much later date (Tod 1971: 337).

Tod estimated the population of the town at under five thousand;[15] it did not seem to have grown much by 1974. It is beautiful, yet rather melancholy, for nothing seems to happen here; I hardly saw one modern building. They are in Veraval, where fishing and its attendant industries, modernizing feverishly, produce the dynamism that Patan sadly lacks. Tourists do come for the temple, but few bother to see the old town.

The town is still inhabited by the Girnar Brahmins, who have retained their monopoly on this place of pilgrimage for a very long time. There was, apparently, a pilgrim tax, but how it was distributed we do not know. The land is better here than at Dwarka and probably the Brahmins received some of their income from *agrahara* lands. They also serve at Girnar. They are a larger caste than the Guglis at Dwarka, and in 1901 they numbered 3,674, living at these two centres of pilgrimage but also in other parts of Saurashtra and Kacch. According to tradition, they were settled at Girnar by Krishna himself.[16] 'They are Vaishnav temple priests, beggars, traders, moneylenders, cooks and husbandmen', says Enthoven (1920: 231). Their connection to Krishna and Vishnu does not prevent them from serving at Shaivite temples.

As noted, however, there has been little continuity of worship at Somnath. Since its destruction by Aurangzeb the old temple was a ruin, and Ahalya Bai's temple in town never really replaced it. The memory of Somnath remained, however, and the importance of its myth rose during the colonial period. Tod's visit may have added to its fame, and it is clear that he was more impressed by the myth than by the realities he saw. Then, in 1841-2, came the 'gates episode', when Lord Ellenborough declared, to 'all the Princes and Chiefs, and People of India' that the gates of Somnath had been brought back from Ghazni by the British. They were not the right gates—they were obviously of Islamic origin—and moreover, many British saw the move as condoning Hindu 'idolatry', so the move was not a success (Davis 1998: 200-9). But it did bolster the Somnath myth. So did Elliott and Dowson's *History of India as Told by Its Own Historians*: the first of its seven volumes came out in 1849. Now Mahmud's desecration of the temple became but the best known of a whole series of similar episodes. In effect, says Davis, 'Somanatha was no longer simply the site of a single famous invasion, but rather a place of ongoing struggle between two religious communities' (1998: 209).

The modern temple was raised after independence on the initiative of Sardar Vallabhbhai Patel, whose statue now stands in front. The move had, however, a complicated history. Davis gives pride of place to K.M. Munshi, the famous writer, who first visited Somnath in 1922. The shame he felt at seeing the desecrated site, made him take on 'the reconstruction of Somanatha as something of a personal mission'. Munshi was a Congressman, a Brahmin and a nationalist: he was also a prolific author. His best known novel is *Jaya Somanatha*, published in 1937. Here, Somnath becomes at once 'a symbol closely identified with the integrity of Gujarat' and a symbol of 'national resistance to the invader' but, says Davis, the audience might equally identify the Ghaznavids with 'the present-day Muslim population of Gujarat, seen as their religious descendants'. 'Another reconstruction of the temple could symbolize successful resistance to British invaders and restoration of a preexisting order of society' (Davis 1998: 210-12).

Davis goes on to describe how Munshi won Sardar Patel over to the rebuilding project, as the Indian Army took control of former Junagadh State.[17] On Divali day, 1947, Patel announced, from Ahalyabai's temple in Patan, the plan to rebuild 'the original' temple. There was opposition from the archaeologists—since the ruins of the old temple were to be torn down—and, especially after Patel's death in 1950, from more secular-minded or radical Congressmen, including Nehru. Yet the temple was reconsecrated in November, 1951 (Davis 1998: 213-19).

Somnath's three hundred years of inactivity—from Aurangzeb to Sardar Patel—has lost for it whatever specific place it may once have held among Hindu pilgrimages. The rebuilt temple, decontextualized, seems to symbolize exactly what Munshi may have wished, Hindu and national revival, in a very general, but also partisan, sense. Not all Gujaratis or Hindus are drawn to the new Somnath. It has an appeal which is not purely religious, and attracts groups that have come to be identified with the BJP. In 1990, the party used it as the starting point for its Rath Yatra, which took the leaders to Srinagar. Yet Somnath is also a tourist place and here again it is hard to distinguish tourism from pilgrimage.

PALITANA—THE CITY OF JAIN TEMPLES

The Shetrunji or Satrunjaya mountain rises some two thousand feet from the plains of Bhavnagar district. The sides are steep and the ascent difficult—it is the perfect example of a sacred mountain, and has been a main centre of pilgrimage to the Jains for a very long time indeed. The *Tapa Jaina Pattavali* relates that the first Jain temples were built here in AD 355, while the *Satrunjaya Mahatmya*, which takes the existence of the place for granted and argues its antiquity, was certainly first composed under the kings of Vallabhi (Burgess 1977: 40). Vallabhi fell in or around

AD 788, so Satrunjaya, as a place of pilgrimage, predates the medieval period.

In contrast to Dwarka, the Satrunjaya temples, often referred to as the temples of Palitana, the town nearby, seem to have been under constant political protection and active merchant patronage. Thus under Siddharaja Jayasimha of Gujarat, the governor of Sorath was responsible for the Satrunjaya temples, as well as Somnath. He rebuilt the Jain temple of Neminatha on Girnar. This royal protection is even better attested under Siddharaja's sucessor Kumarapala (1142-73), when Jain influence was strong at the Gujarat court (Burgess 1977: 26-9), and seems to have continued till the end of Hindu rule in Gujarat in 1298. There followed a period when several temples of the region were destroyed and deseacrated, but the later Sultans of Gujarat were liberal towards Hindus and Jains, and the fourteenth century was a period of reconstruction at Shetrunji.

Akbar conquered Gujarat in 1573, and a long inscription of 1589 at Satrunjaya confirms an earlier *farman* which granted the mountain in eternity to the 'persevering and bold Hira Vijaya, the prince of Suris'. This grant to a prominent Jain also stated an interdiction on killing cows, bulls or buffaloes on the mountain, 'all property of those dying should be remitted, and none should be made slaves'—a guarantee to the Jain community. This grant was confirmed by another in Shah Jahan's time, which conferred the mountain on a certain Satidas Jhaveri and his descendants as an *inam* or gift. Confirmed within a week of Aurangzeb's accession in 1658, the grant also forbade 'the exaction of any tax from the Sravaka (Jain) pilgrims' (Burgess 1977: 31-8).

In the eighteenth century conditions for travel and pilgrimage in Saurashtra had become difficult due to law and order problems. In 1750 the chief of Palitana extended his protection to the mountain in return for a moderate sum to be paid by the responsibles of the Jain community, but in 1788 imposed a heavy tax on pilgrimage, and the relationship between Palitana and the Jains was becoming conflictual.[18] Following a petition to Elphinstone, then governor of Bombay, an arrangement was made in 1821, by which the Jain community leased the mountain for a fixed annual sum, payable to the chief of Palitana. There were complications later, as the ruler wanted to raise the rent, and he succeeded in doing so by 1866 (Burgess 1977: 38-9). Still, the problems and conflicts regarding Satrunjaya were minor disturbances in the context of continuous and peaceful control by the Jain merchant community from at least the twelfth century onwards. While paying tribute to surrounding rulers, the Jains were able to secure their temple city through good times and bad. This situation reflects the merchant influence that runs like a thread through Gujarat's history. Forbes, in the *Ras Mala,* described the hill as follows:

> Street after street, and square after square, extend these shrines of the Jaina faith, with their stately enclosures, half palace, half fortress, raised in marble magnificence upon the lonely and majestic mountain, and like the mansions of another world, far removed in the upper air from the ordinary tread of mortals . . . . Satrunjaya indeed might fitly represent one of the fancied hills of eastern romance, the inhabitants of which have been instantaneously changed into marble, but which fairy hands are ever employed upon, burning perfumes, and keeping all clean and brilliant, while fairy voices haunt the air in these voluptuous praises of the Devs. (Forbes 1878: 5-6)

This captures the feeling of this city: temples, the coolness, cleanliness and stillness of the place. And the view is splendid. Towards Bhavnagar and Ghogha, you see the Gulf of Cambay; to the north the hills of Sihor, and in the west you see the summits of mount Girnar.

Most of the temples are not very old, having been built in the nineteenth century. The seventeenth, too, was an intensive building period, while the age of the oldest extant temples is difficult to assess due to the renovation and rebuilding that has taken place. The fourteenth century is clearly represented, but Burgess, at least, was sceptical of traditions assigning some buildings to the twelfth. What is striking is less the archaeological interest of the buildings than the continuous vitality of the place, which has led old and derelict buildings to be replaced and rebuilt. The city of temples, then, testifies above all to the continuous prosperity and devotion of the Jain merchant community.

Pilgrims from such a class are not easily distinguished from tourists: most are middle-class, modern people whose personal motives may well combine both streaks of sentiment. There is no accommodation on the hill, so visitors often sleep in Palitana town, if they do not come by car from places like Bhavnagar. Here, too, tourism mingles with pilgrimage.

GIRNAR, THE HOLY MOUNTAIN

Girnar is again a very different story. Here, the antiquity of the place is not in doubt. Ashoka's rock edict is well known, and stands on the pilgrim route between Junagadh town and the mountain. Hiuan Tsang mentions the mountain as a place of pilgrimage, and states that there were about fifty Buddhist convents there.[19]

The Buddhists have long gone, but the holiness of the mountain has not changed. There is, for the Jains, an important temple to Neminath, the twenty-second Tirthankara, who is said to have settled on the mountain as a renouncer and attained salvation here. Around this temple are about fifteen others, grouped together on a ledge some two hundred meters below the summit. An inscription on Neminath's temple states that it was repaired in 1278, while other inscriptions relate to donations made in 1275, 1278 and 1281. It is certainly a very old temple. At its entrance is a shrine to Ambika, the Sasanadevi or tutelary goddess of Neminath (Burgess 1971: 166-7). Again, a fierce goddess protects the temple of the non-violent.

The relationship between Ambika and the Tirthankara is interesting, for some 130 meters above this Jain group we find the main temple of Amba Mata, also called Jagdamba ('mother of the world') who occupies a special place among the Goddesses of the region. It was from her that Khodiyar, presently the most popular of Saurashtra's goddesses, got her powers (Tambs-Lyche 1997: 25; 1991), and she is certainly one of the oldest goddesses of the western India. An inscription states that 'The destroyer of doubts and fears, the accomplisher of all human desires and wishes, who causes to be completed the designs of the devout—such a goddess is Sri Mata Ambika, the sole power whereby the prayers of man are fulfilled . . .' (Burgess 1971: 174).

This temple, too, is very old; with Neminath's temple it is certainly the best known sanctuary on the mountain. On the highest peak, some 50 meters above Amba Mata, is the temple of Gorakhnath, the founder of the Nath sect of ascetics. There would seem, from the Naths' own stories, 'always' to have been Naths at Junagadh and Girnar (Tambs-Lyche 1997: 21-2). But there are several other sanctuaries on the mountain. Indeed, the mountain has always attracted renouncers, particularly Shaivite ones; typically, Burgess found 'a substantial dwelling, occupied by one Sivadas, a yogi who has acquired great influence over the ignorant by his sanctimonious austerities and his charities—bestowed, of course, out of the offerings of his worshippers' (1971: 174). There are, and must have been for a long time, others who find that the holy mountain provides them with just the setting needed for a saintly life and career.

On Shivaratri, Junagadh is full of pilgrims and renouncers, but Shaivite monks come and go at all times of the year. Just to underline the variety of sects who are attracted to Girnar, let us note that the shrine of Kalka Mata and its environs has been known as a haunt of the Aghoris, most feared of all ascetics. I cannot resist Tod's description of his supposed encounter with one of them:

> To this awful *penetralium* the pilgrim never ventures, and the legend relates, that whoever has been so fool-hardy, has paid dearly for his temerity. A stranger

was said always to join the sacrilegious visitor *en route*, who . . . proved to be the dread Mother herself. Her rites are performed by the hideous Aghori, whose patroness she is, as *Aghoriswara Mata*, and it was a strong desire to unkennel some of these cannibals which tempted me to prolong my rugged pilgrimage. . . . (Tod 1971: 383-4)

Tod regales us with stories about 'man-eating' Aghoris. He was sitting on the peak, when his

solitude was disturbed by a being whose approach I had not perceived, and who silently took his seat before the shrine of Goruknath. A rag of cloth was his sole covering; his loins were girded with a rope of hair, and his whole frame and matted locks were smeared with ashes. . . . As soon as he was seated . . . he closed his eyes, and remained for some time in motionless abstraction. In a few minutes, there were certain indications of the spirit, expressed by contortions of the muscles of the face, writhings of the frame, and agitations of the neck and heart, as if the infernal divinity he worshipped had inspired him. . . . Having made his final obeisance . . . he departed, and clambered down the peak towards the interdicted shrine of Kalka . . . as he went off direct to the Aghori peak, said to be frequented only by his sect, it is probable that he belonged to the fraternity. (Tod 1971: 385-6)

Tod's account conveys something of the atmosphere of Girnar, the very opposite of the beauty, cleanliness and order of Satrunjaya. We are far from Dwarka, too, in spite of the dangers of that pilgrimage in former days, as well as from the relative solemnity of Somnath. Girnar and the ascetics that gather there are as various as Hinduism itself, but the accent here is on Shaktist and Tantric tendencies, rather than Bhakti. The Aghoris may be gone from the mountain, but the idea of their presence is still in tune with the spirit of the place.

My wife and I were coming down a Junagadh street on our motorcycle, when we were met in the middle of the road by what looked like the figure of death itself: Clad in black or dark ashes rather than white, in a black loincloth and with his long black hair surrounding a black face-mask, he shouted something at us: the figure was so striking that we—and both of us have met quite a few Indian renouncers—were completely taken in: we never saw anything like it. It took us a while to get over it; asking questions and trying to identify the ascetic's sect, we were able to know only that he 'must be some renouncer, possibly tantric'. This we could guess: but the Junagadhis we spoke to were evidently so used to any possible kind of ascetic that nothing could surprise them.

Unlike Satrunjaya, relatively few tourists climb the Girnar: those who take the trouble are either pilgrims or visitors of an adventurous and sporty kind. There is not, therefore, the dominantly middle-class atmosphere of the other mountain pilgrimage. But among the pilgrims religious views are as various as the temples on the mountain.

Most pilgrims still follow the advice of Tod's companions: they visit the Jain temples, then go as far as Amba Mata. Some continue to Goraknath, but few go beyond that. The further peaks are still associated with Tantrism and extreme forms of asceticism, and while it may be too much to say that people are scared to go there, they certainly think of it as a dark, mystic place.

Girnar always belonged to whoever controlled Junagadh. It seems clear, however, that during Muslim rule at Junagadh (1470-1947) the State did not interest itself in the sanctuaries on the mountain, though they did build the present steps. Nor have the Jain temples received the massive investments that we find at Satrunjaya. There is no parallel either to the funds the Bhatias spent on Dwarka during their heyday. Perhaps the very multiplicity of deities and cults present on Girnar excludes massive patronage. For those interested in the history of architecture, this is an advantage, since old temples have been left standing on Girnar, rather than being replaced by more modern and imposing structures.

Of the four great pilgrimage places of Saurashtra, then, Girnar is the one that has been least touched by political and religious change. It is probably the oldest and also the most authentic, if by that we mean that religion has been left to develop unhindered by worldly concerns. To most people in Saurashtra, Girnar is a fixed point in history. It has always been there and it is highly respected. Yet among the various places of pilgrimage it may also be the one which most people have heard about, rather than visited.

DISCUSSION

Somnath and Dwarka, like Girnar and Palitana, occupy an important place in the myth and cultural repertoire of the peninsula, but we must note that of these four important centres of pilgrimage, Dwarka cannot be safely documented before the fifteenth century[20] while Somnath seems to have been largely derelict from the seventeenth century to very recent times. In myth, however, both Dwarka and Somnath remain eternal.

Yet the social, economic and political roles of the centres of pilgrimage is hard to pin down. First of all, we have seen that their mode of integration with the political system, is as varied as their individual character. Dwarka and Somnath both had their periods of independence; both ultimately came under other rulers. Somnath became a part of Junagadh State, which always controlled Girnar; Dwarka, surrounded by the semi-independent

Vaghers, came under Baroda in 1817 (JMG: 615). The prestige that accrues from control of holy places is obvious. But in terms of regional integration, it is striking how most pilgrimage centres, visited by pilgrims from all over India, seem to have played a subsidiary role for the communities inhabiting their immediate surroundings. Their religious importance did not make them economic or political centres of their region.

Nor are they, at least not obviously, integrated in a regional network of temples, such as seems to be the case in Bengal. The pilgrimage centres seem to have been enclaves, protected partly by their sanctity at least from Hindu intruders. They served as a refuge for outlaws, without themselves playing a political role. Though the Chudasamas controlled Girnar for centuries, there is no parallel to Puri, the centre of the Orissa kingdom, and no king of the region tried to build a royal cult around them, as the Orissa dynasty did at Puri (Eschmann, Kulke and Tripathi 1978).

Medieval rulers of Saurashtra subsisted on land revenue, with the control of trade as a later development (Tambs-Lyche 1997: 68ff). But Dwarka and Somnath did not depend on land revenue: they taxed the pilgrims. There was no need for these centres to control land beyond whatever was needed for the subsistence of the priests. Since they did not depend on land, there was no need of the military organization to control it; and as for defending the temple itself, it would seem that Hindu rulers never destroyed major pilgrimage centres. The shock of Mahmud of Ghazni's sacrilege was no doubt a factor in his attack on Somnath becoming a major subject of myth.

Pilgrimage taxes or tolls must have been important to the rulers who received them. From the time of Sidharaja Jayasinha of Gujarat, we hear of taxes levied on pilgrims to Somnath. For Dwarka, the information we have is highly interesting, but the double-taxing of pilgrims by plunder may have been exceptional. We have seen how Palitana succeeded in drawing a steady income from the Satrunjaya temples. Trade with and catering to the pilgrims must have been important too; at Dwarka and Somnath this was largely a monopoly of local Brahmins, yet there may have been some revenue from this trade. Still, we know little of political attempts to control pilgrimage; no wars are ascribed to this reason in traditional history, though they may have been the reason behind more mythical explanations. The struggle for Dwarka by the Rathods is one a possible example, but no substantial kingdom is involved. As for the rivalry between the Vajas and the Chudasamas, we do not know the role played by the Somnath temple and pilgrimage. However we read the history of Somnath, its various

Muslim conquerors do not seem to have wanted to profit from a pilgrimage tax.

Many people in Saurashtra, of course, go on pilgrimage. But they do not necessarily prefer one of the regional centres. Where to go is more a question of sectarian leanings and personal preference than vicinity. The importance of these places for Saurashtrians, therefore, is not necessarily tied to their own religious travels. Rather, places like Dwarka or Girnar are symbols of regional identity. Saurashtra is a 'holy land' because Dwarka, Girnar, Somnath and Palitana are there. Their sacredness colours the image that locals as well as visitors have of the region. Even those who have not visited Dwarka, nor follow Krishna, are proud to live in the country that the God-king chose for his kingdom.

There is nothing surprising about this: Italians may be proud of Dante without reading him, as some people in Bergen, my native city, are proud of Grieg but can't stand classical music. The pilgrim places are located, above all, in symbolic space, and inform that space with a quality of sacredness which in itself is a point of reference whenever people speak of Saurashtra as their country. Places like Somnath, Dwarka, Satrunjaya and Girnar—held to be 'eternal', to have been there since history began—invest the historical consciousness of Saurashtra's inhabitants with a sense of great time depth, relativizing whatever happened later in history.

NOTES

1. For example, the pilgrims to Aiyappan's temple in Kerala, whose presence is striking in South Canara (Karnataka) where I have been working recently.
2. If the main temples of Dwarka were built during the thirteenth century, they certainly cannot have been destroyed by Mahmud of Ghazni, but why were they not pillaged in the fourteenth century? When Somnath was destroyed in 1394 the Krishna cult had not yet gained momentum in Gujarat.
3. In spite of the myth, the *Dvaraka sarvasamgraha* states that the main image is from 1559. There is no epigraphic or documentary evidence of Dwarka as a pilgrimage centre before the sixteenth century, nor was it attacked by the early Muslim conquerors (Mallison 1990: 203 and n.), which may explain why it was not fortified like Somnath. But what about the *murti* that moved to Dakor in 1155? And where was the Dwarka of the *Mahabharata* (Bhardwaj 1973: 30; 46-7), of the Puranas (1973; 62; 66; 69) or of the *Tirthavivecana Kandam*, dating from AD 1110 (1973: 72)?
4. Macmurdo places his rule at AD 1010-54, others in the thirteenth century (Ghosh 1977, 34; Tambs-Lyche 1997: 194-5).

5. Ghosh 1977: 34-40; Meghani 1928: 100-2.
6. Tambs-Lyche 1997: 291-3; Dharaiya 1970.
7. Tod's confusion here is easier to understand if we remember that sun-worship had, in fact, been important in Gujarat. The most important sun temple still standing is at Modhera in north Gujarat, and was built under the Chalukyas (eleventh-thirteenth century). But there are also ruined sun-temples at Ghumli, not far from Porbandar in north-western Saurashtra, and at Than, in the northern part of the peninsula. The Ghumli temple was probably destroyed in the fifteenth-sixteenth century, while that at Than was active much later.
8. This was done by one Mahipaldev of Wanthi (probably Vanthali).
9. Some Muslim sources ascertain that the temple Mahmud destroyed held an image, not a Lingam, as the modern temple does (Rushbrook Williams 1975: 284).
10. Forbes' account is based on Briggs' *Ferishta*, the *Ain-i-Akbari*, and Bird's *Mirat-i-Ahmadi*. These sources, then, seem in no doubt as to what kind of idol was destroyed.
11. Tod felt they must date from the days of the Gujarat kingdom, and that the walls surrounding the temple must have 'risen from the ruins' of the walls destroyed by Mahmud of Ghazni (1971: 336).
12. My scepticism as to the presence of Rathods at this early date, noted for Dwarka and based on their history in Rajasthan, does apply here, but has little relevance for our point.
13. Amarji mentions only its past fame. In spite of being a Shaivite Hindu himself, he certainly makes no plea for its restoration. But then he was, above all, a politician.
14. He gives the date as 1208; note that we have earlier given the same king's rebuilding of the temple as 1169, which is more likely to be correct.
15. In 1821, there were two hundred Brahmin houses, four hundred of Muslims, four hundred of Vanias, and the last hundred or so houses of smaller caste groups (Tod 1971: 352-3). The proportion of Brahmins must have increased, and that of Muslims and Vanias decreased, since then; but no data are available.
16. The *Prabhaskhand* states that they came originally from the Himalayas.
17. The Nawab wanted to join Pakistan. He fled, and his Dewan Bhutto—whose son and granddaughter were to become prime ministers of Pakistan—invited the Indian Army to restore law and order.
18. In 1808, the British found the Palitana chief in heavy debt—to Jain moneylenders, in fact—and 'incapable of managing his own affairs'. Unable to pay his mercenaries, he had granted the revenue of the holy mountain to them, and they actually camped on the mountain, behaving in a manner that was shocking to the Jains.
19. 'At a short distance from [Junagadh] rises Mount Yeu-shen-ta (Ujjanta) upon the top of which a monastery is established. The chambers and galleries have been mostly hollowed out in the face of a scarped peak. The mountain

is covered with thick forests, and streams from the springs surround it on all sides. There holy men and sages walk and fix their abode, and thither resort crowds of Rishis endowed with divine faculties' (after Burgess 1971: 84).

20. This is Pocock's view, and tallies with Mallison's studies on Krishnaism in Gujarat. We must of course reserve some caution here with regard to the archaological investigation of the submarine city. Yet as the matter stands, the link between these ruins and the present centre of pilgrimage poses problems.

CHAPTER 6

Devotion and Segmentation: The Goddess

> Good men, the last wave by, crying how bright
> Their frail deeds might have danced in a green bay,
> Rage, rage against the dying of the light.
>
> DYLAN THOMAS

Saurashtra has known many religions, Buddhism, Jainism, Islam and a whole series of Hindu sects and cults. Yet, from the beginning of the middle ages it is the cult of the goddess that takes prime of place, and were we to count the devotions paid everyday, her position remains pre-eminent. Since I am not concerned with a survey of Saurashtra religion but with establishing the points of reference for everyday religion, we shall concentrate on two poles of regional Hinduism—the Swaminarayanas, the most radical and important form of sectarian Hinduism, and goddess-worship.

In Saurashtra, few people avoid paying respect to the Goddess. They include the stricter Muslims, as well as the more puritan Swaminarayanas. Most others—whether devotees of a particular goddess or not—are ready to visit her temples, bow in a respectful *namaskar* and accept the *prasad* offered at her sanctuary. In this sense, the goddess unites Hindus of all sects and cults in practice: there must be few who do not, at least once a week, come to 'her place' and show at least the outward forms of respect to her.

Temples of goddesses are found everywhere. They include places of pilgrimage known all over the region, temples of restricted following familiar only to a few villages, and small shrines where the goddess has no name, and is represented by a stone or a tree. Once the trishul is painted on, the place is seen as dedicated to the goddess. It seems almost irrelevant, in Saurashtra, that the trishul is Shiva's symbol. Shiva is recognized by the Lingam: in its absence, only the goddess is there. The simplicity and namelessness of her most simple places makes one feel that Mata—used for all goddesses—is also the most simple and elementary term denoting sacredness.[1] In such cases, one should perhaps not to imply too much of a 'mother goddess' image behind the cults. Yet there are other places and situations where the latter type of *gestalt* does, indeed, come to mind.

The cult of the goddess is certainly old. In its present form, it is medieval. The origin myth of Khodiyar may be seen to mark the transition from the ancient to the medieval period in Saurashtra (Tambs-Lyche 1997). While people have turned to goddesses for help in various difficulties, the typical devotee for whom she has performed miracles is the king or chief, and she is above all the particular deity of a caste or a Rajput clan. I present here a synthesis without going into the various myths that accompany the cults.

THE CHARACTER OF THE GODDESS

There are several types of Mata or goddess to be found in Saurashtra. In a few temples we find the all-Indian goddesses (Durga, Lakshmi), under their own name. In most cases, such temples are modern and frequented by the urban middle class. They are of secondary importance.

Then there are some very old, regional goddesses, generally close to Durga. Most important among them are Ambaji at the Rajasthan border, near Mount Abu, Jagdamba at the Girnar mountain near Junagadh, and Chamunda on yet another mountain, near Sayla. Hinglaj, the famous goddess whose main sanctuary is in Baluchistan, has a temple in Jamnagar.

Hinglaj and Jagdamba provide us with transitions to the most important class of goddesses in Saurashtra, which I have elsewhere called Western Indian Goddesses (1999) since they are contiguous with the type found in Rajasthan. In all-Indian terms, this type may generally be seen as variants of Durga. In Saurashtra, the earliest example of the type is Khodiyar, whose myth of origin relates to the fall of Vallabhi (in AD 788). Similarly, the goddess Avad initiates the type in Rajasthan. Mythically Khodiyar's sister, Avad's origins date to the ninth century (Tambs-Lyche 1995). This class of goddess relates to the growth of traditional Rajput society in Rajasthan and Gujarat, and many among them are the *kuldevis* (lineage goddesses) of a Rajput clan: their myth of origin is often that of the clan. They are protectors of kings and chiefs, and the ultimate guardians of the moral order that kings are seen to protect (Carrin and Tambs-Lyche 1993). Traditionally, all demanded animal offerings—in particular the buffalo sacrifice that was at the foundation of royal legitimacy. I shall present Khodiyar briefly, as typical of, and most important among, this class of goddesses in Saurashtra.

If these goddesses guard Rajput kings and clans, they are closely related to another type, tied to a caste rather than a clan. Ashapuri, guardian of a large part of the Kanbi caste (Pocock 1957b) and Bahucharaji, goddess especially of the Kolis, are of this type. The latter, whose main temple is at the eastern borders of Saurashtra, is known for the eunuchs in her service. She sometimes enters the political arena on similar terms to the goddesses of the Rajputs, but most chiefdoms protected by this class of goddess have been small and relatively unimportant.

The two classes have much in common. Terrible to their enemies, they are capable of sustaining their devotees by performing miracles. Though unmarried,[2] they are benign as well as fierce—and thus do not fit the distinction made by Babb (1975) between fierce, unmarried goddesses and married, benign ones. In their double role (sweet young girls in some contexts, terrible female warriors in others) they resemble Durga. As we might expect, there is a tendency for their characteristics to get closer to Kali as we move from the Rajput clan goddesses to the Kanbi and Koli caste deities.[3] These two classes of goddess have another quality in common: they are all, with very few exceptions,[4] seen as deified, human women of the Charan caste, regardless of the caste of their followers. Thus the sanctity of the Charan caste rests on two foundations: the women are potential goddesses,[5] while the men are bards and genealogists of the Rajputs. Only a Charan can certify royal descent, and royal prowess must be acclaimed in Charan poetry. The more important Goddesses are indeed Charanis, as their iconography and rich mythology shows. As an example, let me sketch Khodiyar's story.[6]

THE GODDESS KHODIYAR

Momad Gadhavi, Khodiyar's father, is bard to one of the last kings of Vallabhi. So close is he to the king, that other courtiers get jealous, especially the merchants at court. They bribe the king's *purohit*, who promises to get rid of the bard. Pointing out that Momad is childless, he enjoins upon the queen the danger to her fertility if she sees the face of a sterile person. The queen complains to the king, and Momad is banished from the court. Returning to his village, he realizes that childlessness makes his wife unhappy. He withdraws to a temple of Shiva, in the wilderness (*jangal*). There he prays and practices austerities for eight days. Finally, he threatens to perform *traga*, the ritual suicide particular to Charans,[7] when Shiva appears, granting him seven daughters and a son.

The youngest of these daughters is Khodiyar, 'the limping one'. One day she plays with her sisters on a hill, when suddenly they all feel a great hunger for buffalo flesh and blood. They run downhill and kill the fine buffalo of their neighbours, devouring it on the spot. Soon the countryside is strewn with the carcasses of buffaloes, and the herdsmen complain to the king, but in vain. Then one day the king's own favourite buffalo is mysteriously dragged from the stables—as by invisible figures. The soldiers follow, and finally surprise the seven sisters in the midst of their meal.[8] The king orders that the women be burnt alive, but no sooner has he pronounced his sentence, than they disappear, vanishing into thin air. Then a voice is heard from the sky: 'You insulted our father for his barrenness, and so your family line will be terminated'.[9] As the king asks forgiveness, however, the curse is withdrawn, on the condition that descendants of the royal family marry into the local population.[10]

Through this myth, the Goddess' right to the sacrificial buffalo is established, as well as her authority over the king. The rights of the goddess' people, the bards, are also vindicated, and finally there is an explication of the fall of the kings of Vallabhi. They did not respect the goddess and the bards. It seems clear that the position of the Charans at court is a later development, as is the cult of the goddess such as we know it, so Khodiyar's myth is, in fact, the origin myth of medieval society with its particular, Rajput-dominated, social system (Tambs-Lyche 1997: 26).

The sisters must now leave home and establish themselves elsewhere. But the sisters tease Khodiyar, the lame one, saying she walks too slowly: reaching her destination, she will find others established in her place. Weeping, Khodiyar begs Jagdamba, the older goddess residing on the Gir mountain, to take her 'to her abode': she puts her dagger to the neck in the gesture that, for a Charan, signifies the decision to commit suicide. But Jagdamba blesses her and assures her that she will become a far more important goddess than they. Thus she achieves ascendancy over her sisters.

Later, Khodiyar, as an established goddess, is sought out by the childless queen of Junagadh, who susbsequently gives birth to the prince, Naughan. When Junagadh is conquered by the king of Gujarat, the king is killed in battle and the queen mounts the pyre to become a *sati*. A maidservant saves the baby prince and takes him to a chief of the Ahir pastoralists, living in the forest of Gir. To fool the Gujarati governor of Junagadh the chief takes his own son there, and beheads him in front of the palace, so that the governor believes it is Naughan who has been killed. Khodiyar then comes to his aid, and through a series of miracles

Naughan is installed as king of Junagadh. This makes her the *kuldevi* of that dynasty—the Chudasamas—for whom the Ahirs remained soldiers and close allies (Tambs-Lyche 1991).

Khodiyar emerges in a series of stories, as a divine *person*, with her own life history as well as a long line of subsequent appearances and miracles. Though certain themes appear in the hagiography of several goddesses, the events are seen as specific to the story (*katha*) and deity involved. Most of these goddesses are said to have been Charanis living at a particular time and place. Whenever the visitor wants to know more about the deity, it is these stories that are brought forward.

They always include sequences which establish a link between the divinity and a particular devotee or group of devotees (usually both, as when the myth establishes a link between a goddess and a king). In such cases, the king is seen as a historical person and the event as a historical event, but at the same time the king stands, for his entire clan. Rajputs always link with a particular goddess through their clan. Sometimes, it is a whole caste (*kaum*, *jati*) which relates to a goddess in this way. The goddess becomes, as it were, a mark of group membership and a symbol of group solidarity. Thus, some time probably in the late fifteenth or early sixteenth century, the Gohil chief Shadulsinhji is said to have had a miraculous vision of Khodiyar, and so she became the goddess of the Gohils (Tambs-Lyche 1992: 492-8).[11]

The degree of devotion to the particular goddess may vary considerably between individuals. Some will affirm their personal devotion in no uncertain terms, only adding that they have this link in common with the rest of the group. Others will make a distinction: 'We are the followers of X, but I am myself devoted to Y'. This distinction marks another level, where the link between goddess and devotee hinges not on myth but on some event in the individual's life.

The goddess cults went through a period of relative crisis in the 1970s and into the early 1980s. The temples were still active, but seemed to suffer from 'Sanskritization'. Other cults were seen as purer, more in tune with the times, and more intellectually satisfying. The cult of the goddess was in danger of becoming 'folk' religion, at which the cultural elite looked askance, preferring the purer and more textual male gods, along with their spouses, to the unmarried goddesses of regional tradition. But there are signs of change recently, as if the goddess, going along with the changes in society, caters more closely to individuals and their problems. During the 1980s the trend seems to have turned, and the goddess is returning to the forefront of Saurashtra Hinduism.

ON THE WAY TO THE KHODIYAR TEMPLE

Khodiyar's main temple is situated some ten kilometres north-east of Bhavnagar, not far from her natal village of Roisala. Before reaching it, we pass an interesting temple to Nani Khodiyar—'Little Khodiyar', which may be interpreted in two ways. It is small, as opposed to the big temple; and it is devoted to the goddess as a child. Central to the small compound is a banyan tree, with a small tank on its south-western side. The south-western wall of the tank is bisected by a yoni. There is no Lingam in this yoni. In front of the tank—on the south-west—there is a trishul, placed slightly to the right, between the yoni and the tree. The main image of Nani Khodiyar is in front of the tank, looking north-east: this would normally classify her as a fierce goddess.[12] Between the image and the tank is another trishul, again slightly to the right.

The image itself is a row of seven very stylized heads with Khodiyar's in the middle. Hers is the largest, though she the smallest sister: the size of the heads diminish symmetrically on each side. They are painted red, with black eyes, but no other features, except Khodiyar herself who has black hair worn long, and a conical silver headdress.[13] Slightly behind this image, to the left, is a linga of Shiva; this seems to indicate that he is subsidiary, here, to the goddess. In front of it there is a trishul on the right and a small image of Hanuman on the left. On the right side of the main image is another statue of the goddess, slightly more figurative and dressed in silver.

The three priests of this small sanctuary have their quarters in the north-east corner of the compound. Bearded and wearing their long hair loose, with ochre loincloths like some Shaivite monks, it seemed clear that they were not Brahmins though they did not tell me their caste. They would not enlarge on the religious significance of the place either. Probably, this smaller sanctuary has been established by a group of wandering ascetics. Yet they would seem to have succeeded, for quite a few devotees stop here on the way to the main temple.

So they do at the temple to Navadurga where the road to Khodiyar's temple leaves the main road. Khodiyar is sometimes seen in Saurashtra as one of the nine Durgas, and is the same kind of goddess. Here, the priests are Brahmins. It is quite typical, here as indeed elsewhere in India, that an important temple should grow these auxiliary establishments in its neighbourhood. These may or may not be connected to the main temple by story, but if devotees stop there, some of the popularity and income spill over to the smaller establishments. This may be reason enough for their existence.

THE TEMPLE

Khodiyar's temple is situated all by itself in a small valley near a source—as her stories tells us it should be. The first building that meets the eye, as we approach the compound from north-east, is a large dharmashala for pilgrims, with restaurants and tea-stalls in front. Three more tea-stalls and a few shops for books and pictures of the goddess, stand to the left of the dharmashala, just before the entrance to the temple, which is at a slightly lower level, occupying the south-western corner of what is now the parking lot. The cars are parked under banyans, however. East of the temple is a platform raised a foot above the ground, where I was told goats and cocks were sacrificed in the old days. I describe below the temple as I saw it in 1974 and 1979.

Because of the banyans one does not have a good view of the temple itself. It is a very simple structure, possibly quite old, with multiple, square and undecorated stone pillars supporting a more or less flat roof, with only a small dome to adorn it. The temple is painted light green. In front of the entrance are a large number of trishuls, painted red, and a square pit of stones with a sharp stone in the middle. Coconuts are broken on this stone, and a few cows stay around to lick the juice.

The devotee first goes to the coconut vendor at the north-western side of the temple. I was not sure whether he was part of the temple staff: his price, one and a half rupees for a coconut in 1979, was well above the market rate. You then go to the breaking stone to have the nut broken properly. It is absolutely necessary that it should break into two equal halves, and that this should be done at one stroke. Thus most devotees let one of the priests break the nut. I felt that these requirements hailed directly from animal sacrifice, where the goat's head should be severed at the first stroke, or else. . . . The devotee takes his two half-nuts to the pujari, who gives him back a piece from a large heap received from devotees. This is the *prasad*. If the devotee brings other offerings—like money—he receives more coconut in return. Finally, the devotee proceeds to Khodiyar's image and makes obeisance to her.

The pujaris at the Khodiyar temple were Brahmins who inherited this work from one generation to the next since as long as anyone could remember. Like the ascetics at Nani Khodiyar, they were bearded and wore their hair long, but were fully robed in white. They were Shaivite Brahmins but I was never able to get their subcaste—most people I spoke to did not know. Nor did I get a good picture of the organization and economic base of the temple. What is clear, however, is that in the 1970s the priests managed the temple themselves, without public trustees or other outside influentials. They evidently lived from the incomes of the temple—the offerings of devotees and possibly some arrangement with the stalls outside. In the days of Bhavnagar State, or so I was told, they received a subsidy from the prince. Their quarters were in the north-east corner of the temple, but their families apparently lived elsewhere. At that time, too, the priests at this temple were not held to be vegetarians, and one of them was peacefully smoking in the back of the temple during one of my visits.

Here, as at Nani Khodiyar, the goddess faces east. This was a full figure, but still rather sketchily sculpted from stone, and painted red. There was a relaxed atmosphere about the temple. Most visitors being from Bhavnagar and surrounding areas, there were no modern improvements apart from (rather infrequent) buses, and one certainly did not feel that the temple or its priests earned much money. Typically, I remember a rickshaw driver who had left his key in the dashboard. One of the numerous temple monkeys stole the key, and devotees were enjoying the spectacle as one of the priests tried to—and eventually succeeded in—bargaining an exchange of a banana for the key.

Tourists did not go there—very few came to Bhavnagar anyway. On my way back to town, in 1974, I had to descend from my bicycle several times as people asked me, 'How was the temple?' Since I did not have a research permit, my friends strongly advised me not to go back—I would have been too conspicuous.

THE KHODIYAR TEMPLE IN 1990

When I came back to the temple in 1990, many things had changed. There were more people, and more of them came by private car, from Rajkot or from Ahmedabad. Many of them did not know much about the goddess: 'my family came from Saurashtra', said one young man, 'and I understand she is a very important goddess, so I came to see her'. There was quite a lot of whitewash, the whole place was neater, though the buildings were the same. But the priests were not. Now there was a committee of appointed trustees in charge, and they had simply sacked the old priestly families, who apparently did not answer to modern standards. As one of the dynamic young priests of the new order put it, 'they were completely uneducated and practically illiterate'. One initiative now taken was to renovate a couple of older temples close by, including the one which, I was assured, was the oldest of all Khodiyar temples. This may be true, for it is on a small rock overlooking the pond formed by the source, which fits the description in some of the old stories. There was also a new, more naturalistic image, and better dressed. But then, they were also going to have a picnic ground on the other side of the car park, and a children's playground on the old sacrificial platform. The temple itself would be renovated . . . people had felt, said the young priest, that the situation at the temple had degenerated to a level unworthy of an important goddess such as Khodiyar. Cash offerings (suitably augmented) had replaced coconuts, so there was no longer even a semblance of sacrifice—and the monkeys, too had been chased away. They made 'too much noise'. Whatever these changes may be worth in religious terms, Khodiyar's popularity has certainly increased, as the number of visitors show. I have mentioned how her name now figures prominently on stickers and inscriptions on all kinds of vehicles. But the modern Khodiyar is to some extent a decontextualized version of the old one, less attached to particular groups and more a mark of regional identity.

THE GODDESS AND HER DEVOTEES

What does the cult of the goddess mean to devotees, what does it do for them, and what do they themselves do? I shall start from the point of view of the devotee who chances to come by a goddess temple and, more often than not, decides to enter and offer his respects. What is involved in this simple action, and what does it tell us of popular Hinduism?[14]

Susan Wadley is, I think, close to the truth when she groups Hindu gods and goddesses, demi-gods and demons all together under the heading of 'powerful beings' (1975: 54). As a good friend, an Ismaili Muslim, put it when we both made our devotion to a goddess temple near Praj—being a Muslim is no reason not to respect[15] the goddess. Indeed, the openness to pay respect to any deity one may come across, indicates a view of the world as inhabited by a whole series of beings more powerful than man, whom one had better respect, since their powers are not precisely known or demarcated. In this context, the goddesses are simply one of the generic categories of such beings, in Saurashtra by far the most numerous, and, in this sense, important class. At this level, then, one should not make too much of either the individual identity of any particular goddess, nor of any qualities they may have in common. Indeed, this is an important point made by Pocock (1973). This level of interpretation corresponds with the perspective of a general public, where individuals have no particular relation to that deity. It is important to stress this aspect, since it always coexists with relationships, between the divinity and the individual, that exist on other levels.

In spite of the danger of specifying too closely the generic qualities of Matas, there are some common denominators, and the first, not surprisingly, concern their gender. In general the Matas are feminine. But in order to avoid the conclusion that they are mother-figures, it is important to explore the meaning of femininity. Very briefly, this refers above all the the distinction between *purusha* and *prakriti*, where the latter stands broadly for matter as opposed to spirit, so that the goddess rules creation, which to some schools of Hindu philosophy is an illusion. Feminine deities therefore control most matters of this life, which explains at once their importance for most people and their subaltern position in more Brahmanical views of the pantheon.[16]

MIRACLES, DHARMA AND THE INDIVIDUAL

Kholidas Parmar, the late folklorist of Saurashtra, was not by caste a follower of the Goddess Khodiyar. Her devotees are, above all, the Chudasama Rajputs of central Saurashtra and the Gohil Rajputs of Bhavnagar district. Kholidas was a Koli from the Rajkot area. But he had a serious attack of smallpox when still a very young child, and his parents brought him to Khodiyar to save him from what seemed certain death. They sacrificed a goat to Khodiyar, and Kholidas survived, becoming a devotee of Khodiyar for the rest of his life.

Such stories, which are numerous, makes it relatively easy to distinguish this level of personal allegiance to a goddess from that of a group, provided that we adopt a narrow time perspective. For it is clear that the miracles or events that figure in contemporary life stories are seen as ontologically similar to those that happened a long time ago, and which are best remembered when they helped found a kingdom or establish the cult of the goddess. Indeed, all foundation myths of kingdoms in the area seem to be of this type, which develops into a standard form between the twelfth and the fifteenth century (Tambs-Lyche 1995a). The goddess always establishes herself by a miracle, which at once proves her real nature and changes the world around her in some important way. Thus Khodiyar, the first goddess of this type, establishes herself not by founding a kingdom but by destroying Vallabhi in the eighth century. The pattern is persistent, from Khodiyar's saving the Chudasama dynasty of Junagadh in the eleventh century, till the minor Goddess Jambu Mata's help in placing, in the mid-eighteenth century, on the throne of Limbdi the Jhala rulers that remained in power there until 1947.

The proof of the goddess' powers is her ability to influence, as by miracle, the events of this world. The use of the term miracle, here, needs clarification. If we accept, as her worshippers and most Hindus do, that she has the power—indeed, that she *is* the power—necessary to make the world change or even go on, then there is nothing 'miraculous' in her doings. When the goddess destroys the unjust and protect those who adhere to dharma, she is fulfilling her role in the world. Miracles are, so to speak, only the 'natural' form of her intervention with us ordinary mortals. What is special, then, about miracles is not their occurrence in general, but the specifics of each case. Khodiyar implicated herself in saving the infant prince Naughan of Junagadh[17] for two obvious reasons: Naughan was supported by some of her truest devotees and his case was just. Add to this, his protector sacrificed his own son, and we see why Khodiyar was, so to speak, compelled to help (Tambs-Lyche 1991). As for the Gohil chief Shadulsinhji, his outstanding devotion to the goddess is why, after some cajoling by the king, the goddess actually appears (Tambs-Lyche 1992: 493-4). And what is proved by Kholidas Parmar's story is not Khodiyar's powers to save a dying child—doubted by no devotee—but the devotion of his parents and, perhaps, the fact that the young child was worthy of her love.

This latter point is crucial. In stories of the goddess, the devotee should not doubt her powers: indeed, the cruellest sort is reserved for those who do not respect her. The accent is on active respect as much as inner feeling: to honour the goddess is to be active in her cult, usually by sacrificing to her. Traditionally, the sacrifice was a buffalo, goat or cock according to the position of the worshipper and the seriousness of the case. Typically, when the goddess herself speaks through a medium, she takes time to specify the nature and amount of whatever is to be sacrificed.

The fundamental structure of any story concerning the goddess' miracles turns on a transaction: the devotee sacrifices to get something in return. True, this calls to mind the Vedic sacrifice. Indeed, Brahmins did officiate in the great buffalo sacrifices that, once a year at Navratri (Dasahra) re-established and legitimated the kingdom. But the goddess myths speak little of Brahmins, and most sacrifices are administered by the sacrificer himself. Moreover, these sacrifices are made in anything but a ritual idiom: it seems that for the goddess, it is the content, not the form, that matters. We do, indeed, see a tendency to accept a morality close to that of the *bhakti* cults, where the spirit of devotion is more important than the material resources of the sacrificer: but in such cases the goddess herself often arranges matters, as when she says to the poor chief—having no buffalo to sacrifice—that he will find an animal grazing in a certain spot, which will subsequently be the sacrifice (Forbes 1878: 426-9). Here, the usual transaction—a buffalo for the powers of a chief—is effectuated, even if the goddess has to arrange matters by providing the animal herself.

With all its variants, then, the transactional nature of the devotee's relation to the goddess is clear. Her powers are unquestioned, but human access to her assistance is limited. And, in most of our stories, this access depends on an additional condition: no sacrifice works if the sacrificer is acting contrary to dharma.

This is an important point. In stories where the sacrificer is not supported by his goddess, there is a recurrent theme, also present in a large number of cases where the sacrifice invokes aid against the unjust. Break of dharma, in such cases, is usually illustrated by attacks on female chastity. The unjust king runs after the wives of others, and is destroyed. The chaste maiden is violated, and the goddess turns her wrath loose. It is as if the protection of women stands for the whole moral order (Carrin and Tambs-Lyche 1993).

I have proceeded, here, as if there was complete contiguity between the goddess myths, dating back for centuries, and the imagery which relates to today's devotees. In Saurashtra, however, the goddess stories seem, more than perhaps anything else, to form a link between the present and the past—here indeed, the past is still present. If there are no more kings, men still desire other men's wives. Today's miracles may be less spectacular than in the past, but is not the survival of a sick child as good a miracle as any other? The goddess' powers, certainly, are as real to people as the power of god to the best of Christians. Daily life has changed, but not the need for divine protection, and so cars, trucks and scooters sport stickers hailing the goddess of the owner's choice.

NAVARATRI

The forms of goddess worship have changed and so has Navaratri,[18] the nine nights dedicated to the goddess in September/October of our calendar. Among middle-class people Navaratri is now mainly associated with communal *garbo* dancing and singing in honour of the goddess. Thus schools and colleges train in advance for their Navaratri spectacle, which of course means that the specific links between a particular goddess and a single community dissolve into a celebration of what may be characterized as common Gujarati culture. To some participants, the dancing has become folklore: to college boys and girls, it is an interesting occasion for observing the other sex since boys and girls dance together, though in separate, concentric circles. Participation at this level in no way excludes a deeper relationship to the goddess, but the public celebrations probably contribute to putting more group-specific and formal ritual in the shade. For the Rajputs, and especially the rulers, Navaratri leads to Dasahra, the tenth day, when the buffalo sacrifice that was the most important state ritual, took place. Unlike in Rajasthan, where princely families still celebrate Dasahra in a semi-public manner,[19] the descendants of the Saurashtra rulers do not host important Dasahra celebrations nowadays. Sacrifice of animals is forbidden in Gujarat,[20] so while I strongly suspect that cocks and probably goats are still sacrificed, nobody would tell me about it. In any case, the ritual is not public.

POSSESSION

Possession was traditionally associated with such sacrifice. Sometimes the *bhuvo*—the sacrificer who generally (but probably not always) was from a low caste,[21] was himself possessed: sometimes another person acted as the medium.[22] But it seems true for Saurashtra, as for Gujarat (Pocock 1973) that possession by the goddess is no longer as popular as it once was. No doubt possession used to be a central feature of the Navaratri, but now it is mostly the lower castes who incite the goddess to manifest herself in this way. I describe, in the chapter on Praj, Bhagatbhai's efforts to become a medium of the goddess. A Kanbi shopkeeper who is neither rich nor poor, his new cult seems to express a personal religious quest rather than a move towards higher status. His religiosity may be respected, and people do come to see his attempts at getting possessed, but it makes him in no way a leader. This may well be because possession is associated with low status rather than high, so Bhagatbhai is already closer to the top than the bottom of the class of people who interest themselves in it.

This, at any rate, seemed to be the situation in the 1970s. And as far as I have seen, the recent revival of goddess cults has been precisely at the cost of possession and sacrifice—the revival benefits a vegetarian and bhaktist version even of goddesses that manifested vehemently, through possession, their lust for meat in the past. To give an idea of possession as it may have existed in Saurashtra, I shall describe a case I observed in Marwar (Rajasthan) in 1980. There, several ritual practices are still current, which seem to correspond to those my informants described from their own past.

My guide, Inder Dan Detha,[23] and I were touring the region on bicycle, when he took me to an old temple dedicated to Ambaji. The sanctuary is on a small peak rising out of the dry plains, and surrounded by a small grove. Below the main temple, on the plains, a yogi, practicing tapas or austerities, had established his ashram. He came nine years earlier, liked the place, and started to take care of the small temple he found abandoned. Visitors naturally pause at his place to pay their respects and give a small gift.

Entering the grove, at the foot of the stairs leading to Ambaji's temple, we see two large stones. On one of them a tiger is engraved, the design on the other is hard to identify. On each stone there is a point surrounded by two concentric circles, explained to me elsewhere as the 'eyes' of the goddess, though Inder Dan, sceptical of this interpretation, sees them simply as marks that the stones belong to her. They certainly mark the entrance to her domain, and are followed ten yards beyond by a third stone, bearing the design of a tree. This marks the grove as sacred: no trees here may be cut. Advancing further, the impression of sacred space grows stronger, as innumerable stones are painted with the red marks of the goddess. Then I notice something about the trees. There is a strange smell, and going closer I realize that the branches are covered with dry goat skins, evidence clear enough of the ongoing tradition of animal sacrifice. According to Inder Dan, people still come from some forty to fifty kilometres around to offer goats here. At one time, buffaloes too were sacrificed.

As we climb, we first reach some remains of fortifications, built by a Rajput ruler to defend the temple.[24] Then comes an old cave temple, which may well have used in Buddhist times as Inder Dan thinks, though the sculpted pillars may be a little later—fifth to ninth century, perhaps. But the cave has given the goddess one of her names—Andheri Mata, 'the blind goddess', living in the darkness. Above this cave are three temples, of various age, and the murtis of the goddess, too, reflect several different periods of the cult.[25] The goats would be decapitated on the small sacrificial platform beside one of the temples. The head of the animal would then be brought into the temple and offered to the goddess with elaborate prayers—lasting, probably, about half an hour. Then, the head is cooked: though the pujari may be offered a piece, it is the sacrifiant who consumes the head.[26]

We were looking at the temples when a man arrived. It was in the early hours of the afternoon: the pujari had come. He started lighting a fire in the porch of the temple, and then a man and a woman, evidently a couple, arrived. Without further ado, the woman knelt before the fire, facing the goddess, and began beating her palms rhythmically on the floor, shouting.[27] Then, perhaps entering into trance but speaking in a normal voice, she spoke on behalf of the goddess: 'She says it will be ten maunds (about fifty kilograms)'. The man answered her: 'That means you are again going to have this breakdown? That means I shall have to give another four maunds!'. 'Oh', said his wife, 'the six maunds were for the people who came (to be feasted during a former seance of possession). These four maunds are for the goddess'.

After this introductory fixing of the quantities of grain to be given to the temple, the woman changes her voice. Now it is the goddess speaking, the voice is high-pitched and angry. 'Why did you feed these people in my place, why not do so in your own house?' Clearly, this remark relates to the grain consumed by the guests, the goddess claiming, implicitly, that she herself got nothing. 'Oh but the goddess is everywhere', answers the husband somewhat meekly, 'so there is no problem'.

His wife again changes her tone, shouting '*Mata, mata, mata . . .*' and she begins to tremble. The pujari speaks: 'If you are not good, I will make a fireboard of you'—referring to a form of exorcism, applying burning cowdung to the skin of the possessed person. Clearly, the woman is now possessed by a spirit, who answers: 'I do not mind that'. The priest then asks, 'Who is this spirit in you ?'

'Why do you want to know ?', the spirit answers, defiantly, but as the pujari makes a move towards the burning cowdung, the answer comes: 'I am the wife of the man who sleeps in the porch'. This refers to a woman who died some twenty-five years ago, possibly a suicide, and her husband, as we understand, is now destitute. 'How did you come to know her', asks the pujari, referring to the living woman, and the spirit answers: 'Oh, she is a very good friend of mine now'. There is little need, here, to explain the implicit threat: if the husband will not answer to the woman's demands, she may well 'join the spirit' (commit suicide?) and so, again implicitly, her man will find himself as destitute and wifeless as 'the man who sleeps in the porch'.

It is the husband's turn to defend himself, explaining to the pujari: 'Now she does not work, she feels she is inhabited by an evil spirit, she is becoming absorbed by this spirit. . . .' At this point, the priest takes some lumps of burning cowdung from the fire, placing them in a small brass vessel which he covers by a piece of coconut shell.[28] All three, priest, husband and woman, now pray to the goddess to heal the woman.[29]

Actually, the woman's skin is never burnt, for as the priest approaches, she suddenly falls forward, her forehead touching the ground, as she rocks her head violently from side to side. The spirit in her shouts, then: 'I promise to leave, I'll go away, I'll go away—if I come back I'll eat your shit!'. The spirit leaves: the woman sits back, returning to a normal state. She goes up to the image of the goddess and salutes the deity quite peacefully. The husband says, to the pujari: 'I will bring her back four times and give you four maunds for the goddess'.

We learn that the man has been away a long time, working in Ahmedabad. While he was away, his wife, alone in the village, has been 'absorbed' by an evil spirit. Now the man is back, promising to look after her, and to bring her back to the temple. They first tried to feast friends and relatives at the temple, but this did not work: as we have seen, the goddess claims that nothing was left for her. Finally, we understand that the husband has promised to offer his wife a silver bracelet.

Though this is a ritual of exorcism, and the pujari performs it at the husband's cost and request, what is striking is the woman's control of the proceedings. She speaks with several voices, and apparently changes easily and abruptly between her several identities as the spirit, the goddess, and herself. These sudden and easy changes seem to imply that she herself may be conscious of her several roles and able to manipulate them. Moreover, these changes—immediately accepted and recognized by her husband as well as the priest—implies a considerable range of implicit knowledge, a traditional grid which makes every new statement or move fit into place.

Bhagatbhai's attempts at a possession cult in Praj, which is described later, was more innovative, and so more explicit: the shivering that marked possession lasted longer and was more pronounced: the sounding of horns started the whole sequence, which was, altogether, conceived as a spectacle. The example from Marwar shows another mode of possession by the goddess: a private, expiatory rite. Other examples from the region, such as possession by the *hijadas* (eunuchs) who serve the goddess Bahucharaji (Westphal-Hellbosch 1976: 59-61), show the wide range of possession phenomena in Saurashtra. In most cases, the goddess is involved: either it is she who manifests herself through the medium, or she controls possession rites which take place under her auspices in sacred space dedicated to her. Though less popular than before, and more clearly limited to medium and lower castes (roughly speaking, from Kanbis downwards)—possession still offers a major form of access to divinity in the region.

THE GODDESS AS ORACLE

The goddess also inspires many an oracle. This too, was a practice generally said to have been more common earlier, and to have included the higher castes to a greater extent. Higher castes tend, more often, to consult astrologers, though the two practices are not contradictory. Thus, having more contact with middle-class people, I did not observe any important oracular session. But I did meet, in a large village close to Dhrangadhra, a woman who serves regularly as an oracle inspired by the goddess. Shaktibai is the wife of the headman of the village, which is dominated by its majority of Kolis. She also serves as the medium of the goddess Bahucharaji at Navaratri and, occasionally, at other ritual occasions. But most of her oracular sessions, which I understood take place almost daily, are of the simpler kind. Thus when I was there she had just finished a divination by grains[30]—taking a lump of grain in her hand, she counts the grains: an even number produces an inauspicious or negative answer, an odd number a positive one. She knows a number of other divinatory techniques: but this is the simplest and cheapest one, and the one most often resorted to. Even in this practice, however, it is the goddess who answers the question posed: Shaktibai is positive that any power she has, comes from the goddess.

Medium and oracle, Shaktibai also serves as counsellor to village people in many matters. Even Rajputs and Kanbis ask her advice, she says, but smiles when I ask if Vanias come. It may happen; but generally such people have little faith in the goddess.

Shaktibai's village is quite large but traditional, and the region around Dhrangadhra is generally considered 'backward'. Moreover, it is a Koli village, so the influence of the higher castes remains limited. Her considerable renown and prestige in the village should be seen against this background. Such oracular practices are found all over Saurashtra, though their simplicity and private nature means that one has, so to speak, to stumble into them to observe them. Most such oracular mediums, then, would be known to, and serve, a local and limited clientele. But taken together, they do constitute a commonly used resource whenever people are faced with dilemmas and problems.

This kind of divination is dominated by the goddess. Lord of the material world, she is the one able to tell the future or intervene in practical matters. Though astrologers, too, deal with such questions, their advice is generally more expensive. As for the stars, they determine fate mechanically: they do not intervene as the goddess does.

THE NATURE OF DEVOTION TO THE GODDESS

The goddess is of immense importance to most people in Saurashtra. Her interventions range from the rise and fall of kingdoms to the matter-of-fact questions of daily life submitted to Shaktibai's grain oracles. There is continuity here, from the simple to the most complex problems, and from the humblest devotee to the mythical king. This continuity brings me back to the distinction between individual and group devotion. Naughan's experience made Khodiyar the goddess of all the Chudasamas, and Shadulsinhji's vision brought her the future devotion of Gohils. Group devotion is seen to stem from an event concerning an individual, at least initially; and so while it is convenient, in a synchronic perspective, to distinguish the individual's attachment to a goddess from her acceptance as protectress of a group, these two levels are not radically different. They are seen, rather, in terms of process; even today, one individual's experience may cause his family members to share his devotion. Individual stories may refer not to a miracle happening to that person, but to his or her father, or another close ancestor. If we do not see, today, the formation of new Rajput clans, this is not because miracles are absent but because the clan's story tends to start with the founding of a political domain, something which in the present context is evidently impossible.

Devotion, then, is not only transactional in terms of the sacrifice itself: it may be seen as a continuing process, where the devotee is acknowledging what the goddess did for his ancestors in the past. The transactional idiom transcends the distinction between individual and group levels. We may extend this idiom to outsiders, who happen to pass by a goddess temple: whether known or not, the goddess must have helped somebody in the past, worked some miracle, upheld dharma in some way, to earn her place in the pantheon. Worshipping her, one honours one of those powers that keep the moral order in shape. To do so costs little and might turn out to be more important than one thinks.

There is thus a whole scale of belief involved. There is a certainty, on an existential level, of having been helped or even saved by the goddess, which comes forth in individual life stories. Then there is knowledge of a historical kind, that she has helped ancestors in the past. Finally, there is belief, in the sense that any goddess is thought capable of the miracles she must have operated, in the past, to become a goddess. This belief, strictly speaking, is just a deduction from first principles, but it is also a way of dealing with uncertainty;[31] when in doubt, follow the accepted course of action.

THE UBIQUITOUS GODDESS

The goddess is ubiquitous since her manifestations run the whole range from certainty to not taking a chance with the unknown: from individual experience to general good sense; from object of intense individual devotion to the formal nod towards a customary cult. In this sense, she can be all things to all people, and so she can mean somcthing even to groups of followers whose main religious allegiance lies elsewhere.

To the king or chief, the goddess—always a particular, named divinity—was the one to whom he owed the kingdom, whether a few generations or hundreds of years back. This event made him dedicate the annual buffalo sacrifice to her. Consequently, this sacrifice was the ceremony of state par excellence, and its performance the symbol of statehood. When, sometimes, ministers or other important men imitated the king's sacrificial act, this amounted to claiming chiefly status and must have been seen as a highly political move. In so far as people felt or practised allegiance to the ruler, the sacrifice was theirs, too, for the ruler was seen to act for his subjects as well as himself. In a bad year, the ruler might increase the stakes of sacrifice hoping for the goddess' aid.

Thus the goddess was responsiblc for the worldly power needed to maintain dharma, but equally for good crops and human fertility. Here, again, the logic is dual: good crops or healthy children are at once rewards for dharmic conduct and the deity's recompense for ample sacrifice. One does not work without the other, since the goddess both controls fertility and protects dharma. The link is made particularly clear when female chastity—incompatible with promiscuity but associated with wifely status and motherhood—is made to stand for dharma. This perhaps explains why the deity is feminine, and why every woman is a potential goddess insofar as she incarnates *shakti.* These aspects of goddess cults are as important when we talk of the goddess of a clan or caste, as of her role as maker of kingdoms. Only the chief is missing in the former case.

THE GODDESS TODAY

This latter point is important, for while the princely states have disappeared, the rest of the goddess' functions are unaltered in principle. In terms of what the goddess is able to do for her followers, little has changed as we enter the modern age. But the virtual disappearance of her most prestigious devotee, the king, has changed the patterns of allegiance. No longer tied to a political centre as its foremost religious symbol, the ex-state goddess has become less exclusive in her following and more easily accessible to all. Khodiyar, especially, as Saurashtra's most important regional goddess, now receives and accepts (we assume) offerings from devotees who, formerly, hardly bothered with her. Conversely, several minor goddesses, like Jambu Ma of Limbdi, have sunk into oblivion and disappeared from public view.[32] In other words, even among goddesses the new economic and political order has wrought changes. Deprived of royal support, a goddess now depends on the extent of popular support she or her temple priests can mobilize.

This may seem, at first, to be largely a quantitative change: well-known goddesses extend their following while minor divinities lose theirs. But the change also breaks up links between deity and devotees on the group level, so that goddess-worship comes to revolve increasingly around its two poles: individual experience, and general recognition. In good sociological jargon, then, goddess-worship becomes more individualistic.

This implies that the social characteristics of goddess cults move closer to those of Bhakti sects, which, at least in principle, are open to anyone who feels the love of the deity concerned. This, of course, privileges individual experience over group solidarity, unless that solidarity, as in the sect, is itself founded on communal experience. No wonder, then, that I heard an old man sing bhajans[33] to fierce old Shakti Mata of Dhrangadhra. He was surrounded by visitors—mainly women—who admired his performance and seemed to find it apt. Yet this intrusion of Bhakti emotional religion is surely foreign to the sacrificial and transactional ethos of traditional goddess-worship.

THE DEVOTION OF BHURO BHARWAD

The story of Bhuro Bharwad seems tome typical of this mixture of old and new, of Shaktist and Bhaktist themes, which is becoming current in the goddess cults of Saurashtra. Bhuro is a devotee of Khodiyar, but vacillating in his devotion. His best cow is always returning from the pastures empty of milk, as if somebody had been milking her in secret. One day Bhuro decides to follow the cow, which plunges into a pond and disappears. Bhuro follows her to the bottom of the pond, where he sees the cow being milked by a wondrously beautiful young girl. Not realizing to whom he is talking, Bhuro scolds her for stealing the milk of his cow. Khodiyar—for it is She—answers him laughing: 'I have done you a lot of damage by taking your milk. Take this as recompense'. Thus saying she gives him something bound up in a cloth, but Bhuro cannot see what it is. He takes his cow away and finds himself back beside the pond.

Bhuro believes the girl has given him just a sack of pebbles. Only when he comes home and shows them to his wife, does the woman realize it is gold; immediately, however, the gold turns again to pebbles. Bhuro understands that his lack of faith has cost him the goddess' blessing. He implores her again, and finally appearing before him, she confirms the loss, but as he is now becoming a true devotee, she promises to make him the richest and happiest among Bharwads (Mehta 1978: 38-40).

The story underlines the link of the goddess to the cow, as well as to fertility and plenty. Gold is exchanged for milk, stressing the value of the latter. More importantly, ritual and sacrifice are not the central element, but devotion, and Bhuro is referred to as a Bhakta. This is not just a matter of words, for throughout the story the devotee's belief is central. It may indeed be seen as an example of the merging Bhaktist and Shaktist strains in Saurashtra Hinduism. The story is probably modern. Mehta notes: 'This story appeared in "Paramartha" and has been written according to that version, with some added modifications (improvements)' (Mehta 1978: 40n).

TOWARDS INDIVIDUALISM

Goddess-worship used to be closely related to caste and clan solidarities, so that individual devotion would be circumscribed by the person's belonging to a group. There are exceptions to this, for we have many stories of individuals approaching goddesses that do not, at that point of time, belong to the group. But since the point is made explicitly, one has the impression that they are, if not contrary to norm at least unusual in the statistic sense of normality. Today this is changing, as if what was exceptional is becoming normal. It is not the ties between the goddess and her community that are changing however, but rather the kind of content individuals look for in their relation to the deity. Thus the Bhakti or devotional element has become stronger, while the powers or *shakti* of the goddess, no longer attached to the chief's role, are becoming generalized towards a wider range of roles, with power in the political or military sense losing its central position.

For the individual, then, religious choice is becoming wider, and less tied to particular roles or tasks. The paradox is that the choice of modern, individualist worship implies allegiance to a group, as for the Swaminarayana, while the older cults, freed from many of their old functions, are now open to an individual form of worship which can be made independent of social ties.

NOTES

1. Pocock (1973: 41-2) seems to share this view, noting that no image of motherhood is attached to the word.
2. There are a couple of exceptions to this rule; see Tambs-Lyche 1999.
3. This may be true of others, such as Momai Mata, the dumb goddess of the Rabaris, but we know very little about them.
4. One such exception is Shakti Mata, the clan goddess of the Jhala Rajputs. For a discussion of her case, see Tambs-Lyche 1996a.
5. They are also said to be potential *satis*. See Tambs-Lyche 1992: 490-523 and 1997: 188-90.
6. I present these stories more fully in Tambs-Lyche 1992: 437-89, and 1997: 22-6 and 32-5.
7. Charans practised the *traga* in a various contexts. They stood surety with their life for political agreements or loans; the *traga* was proof that injustice had been done, and the guilty had a Charan's blood on his hands. See Tambs-Lyche 1995b. See also Vidal 1995.
8. There are variants to this story. Some are discussed in Tambs-Lyche 1992 and 1997, as cited earlier.
9. According to one myth they actually do so, and the intermarriage produces the Vala clan of Kathis.
10. Most of my informants gave Khodiyar as the goddess of the Gohils. Yet Virbhadra Singhji, himself a son of the last Gohil king of Bhavnagar, gives Chamunda as the clan deity (1994: 216). He obviously knows best, but even so, the link between Khodiyar and the Gohils is important.
11. Fierce (malevolent, inauspicious) goddesses normally look eastwards, while benign ones look west.
12. The shape of this headdress might indicate a *jota,* 'matted hair', but this seems unlikely since the black hair also flows down each side of her face.
13. For a recent and full discussion of this concept, see Fuller 1992.
14. The verb *manvun,* which he used here, expresses both devotion, in a strict sense, and a general feeling of respect. To distinguish between the two shades of meaning, Gujaratis rather qualify the subject: 'I personally or particularly respect . . . '. This of course implies a degree of tolerance.
15. These two phrases are very gross simplifications. I return to some of these themes in the concluding chapter. See also Tambs-Lyche (ed.) 1999.
16. Naughan is said to have acceeded to the throne in AD 1030.
17. I was unable to study Navaratri in Gujarat: my visits never coincided with it. I did observe two Navaratris during my fieldwork in Britain. There, the folkloristic dimension clearly dominated the scene.

18. It must be juridically private, or it would be a ritual challenge to the sovereignty of the Republic.
19. Nobody would specify the law in question. When I asked lawyers, they answered that animal sacrifice was forbidden, but added that it had never existed in Gujarat—which is manifestly untrue.
20. Virbhadra Singhji (1994) feels most of them were Kolis.
21. Pocock (1995: 45-55) has better material on this than I have, and these generalizations are partly based on his examples.
22. Inder Dan's hospitality and guidance was invaluable to me in Marwar—as it has been to numerous other anthropologists.
23. As sacred space is usually seen as inviolable, I refer to Jain's work on the goddess cult among the Mina (1973). Here we find traditions of capturing and taking away the image of the goddess in order to transfer her protection from her old protege to one's own group.
24. The temple used for animal sacrifice is straight above the cave, facing north. The sacrificial platform is just south of it. An inscription says it was built by Shaktidan in SV 1889 (AD 1832-3). Here the goddess is shown killing the buffalo demon, but, contrary to contemporary images, she is not riding a tiger. Another temple, looking south, has several old images of varying iconography (one shows the goddess holding a snake), and seems to be disused. A third, facing south, may well be the oldest building but has a modern murti where the goddess, riding a tiger, is flanked by Brahma, Vishnu and Shiva.
25. This description relies on Inder Dan's information. The procedure corresponds broadly with Vedic rules for sacrifice (Malamoud 1976; 1989: 211ff) and is similar to that found elsewhere, as at Kalighat in Calcutta. Ghosha (1871: 60-6) gives the *Yajna-mantras* used there (Beane 1977: 221-5; S. Bouez 1986: 887). There is reason, then, to assume that goat sacrifice in Saurashtra is and was quite similar.
26. We had difficulty making out the words, which sounded like 'Aghori' but might have been 'Andheri', the epithet of the 'blind' goddess, shouted indistinctly.
27. The coconut is a common replacement for the sacrificial animal: the same dagger and the same movement is used to split the nut and to behead the animal. Both must be done with a single stroke. Here, the piece of coconut shell may represent the woman's skin to be burnt: it may also represent the sacrifice, or even the skin of the spirit, who is then both burnt and offered to the goddess.
28. As far as I could understand, the woman returned to her normal voice for this prayer.
29. Virbhadra Singhji mentions this 'grain looking' as a common type of oracle in Saurashtra (1994: 220). According to him, they are particularly used to know the outcome in case of illness.

30. We see here a parallel to the way Esser's subject—to whom we shall return—is acting.
31. Jambu's case is instructive here, since she has been 'saved' from her neglected country sanctuary and is said presently to 'sit' in the garden palace of Limbdi's ex-ruling family.
32. Devotional songs in the bhakti tradition.

CHAPTER 7

An Individual among Individuals in a Complex Society

And the trees were black, the mountains gone and the rain
still falling around me
Later when I the singular lay awake

ANTHONY CRONIN

THE SECT

Goddess-worship is individual as well as collective. Yet like caste, kinship and family, it tends to refer, directly or indirectly, to traditional society. It hardly serves as a base from which to observe the conception of the individual. Other categories like occupation are ambiguous, for some are traditionally caste-bound, while others are modern, which means that we think of them as a matter of individual choice. Sect membership,[1] however, is often seen as an individualist element in a society where caste, as generally perceived, limits individualism.

Yet, if we approach Hinduism with classical Western sociology in mind, the sect appears at first paradoxical. Seen as an individualist form of worship, it creates, as we shall see in the case of the Swaminarayanas, a community where the cult is collective and even celebrates the community. This community does not become a caste or a caste-like social formation, however, as Dumont would have it (1966a: 237-42), and shows for the much older, southern sect of the Virashaivas. Though tending apart from unbelievers, the Swaminarayanas remain to this day a cross-caste community, whose members marry non-sectarians of their own caste. The collective nature of the cult creates community, but this coexists with caste solidarity. Pocock (1973) has shown the role they play as heralds of a new kind of Hinduism, opposed to the old popular cult of the goddess. Their cross-caste community, he says, replaces the 'symbiotic' intra-caste order with a clear-cut opposition between purity and impurity. Caste and sect do, indeed, intersect as Srinivas suggested in an early article on

Gujarat (1958), and such cross-cutting ties contribute to the complexity of present-day Saurashtra society.

In Saurashtra, as generally in Gujarat, sects are an important feature of regional Hinduism. They are mainly inspired by *bhakti*, a cluster of religious ideas centred on individual devotion. This is the case for the Vallabhacharyas,[2] who after 1600 became important among the merchant castes, and contributed to the rise in status of the Bhatias of Jamnagar district.[3] Several other Vaishnava sects have been active in Gujarat.[4] But the first sect to recruit in large numbers from different castes, and break the correlation between sect and caste membership, were the Swaminarayanas. How, then, does the sect function to modify the links between actor and caste, between tradition and behaviour, that I have outlined earlier?

THE SWAMINARAYANAS

You cannot move far in Saurashtra without coming across the Swaminarayanas. Today, along the main roads, large posters invite drivers to stop for meditation and thought at one of their numerous temples. These are found in all towns of importance, and in some large villages. Politically and culturally, the sect has become a major force in Gujarat (Hardiman 1988). This is especially true of the 'Yogijipanth' or Akshar Purushottam branch, which split off from the main sect in the 1940s. The story of the sect has been told elsewhere.[5]

Among all Vaishnavite sects, the Swaminarayanas are the most puritanical as well as the most numerous. The parallel with puritans extends to their economic role; they may be seen as representative of the 'new' bourgeoisie of Gujarat, as opposed to the older Vania groups, who together with Parsis and certain Muslim sects dominated the early industrialization of the state.

A SATSANG IN BHAVNAGAR

Among Swaminarayanas, the word satsang stands for two interrelated concepts. It is the community of believers, literally the society of truth or the true society, and as such it denotes the sect as a whole. But it also refers to the Sunday gatherings that are the focus of the ritual week. Unlike many other rituals, the satsang is usually well attended; especially in the Yogijipanth, which is in general far more vigorous than the older sect.

I shall describe such a meeting, as I knew it in Bhavnagar. The satsang starts at four p.m. on Sundays, but only a few of the local members had arrived by that time. Gradually, however, they came. Taking off their shoes, newcomers greeted those already present with a 'Jay Swaminarayana'—the universal mutual greeting of sect members. They approached the image of Swaminarayana by the central aisle formed by those already in attendance, and prostrated themselves, lying flat on the floor with their arms stretched towards the image. One does not approach this god among men with the simple namaskar used for ordinary gods and goddesses. Then, turning to the man in charge of distributing the prasad—a householder of the congregation—they knelt in front of him, touched his feet, and again uttered, 'Jay Swaminarayana'.

Prasad was given, accompanied by a return of the same greeting. The newcomers then turned toward the main body of the congregation. If still few, the newcomer bows to touch the feet of all individually; when quite a number are present, he will do so to a few prominent members of the congregation, sitting in the front row. Then he takes his seat. This greeting of the congregation—rather than just the image—is an integral part of the proceedings. This is the satsang, the true community, and it is itself holy. Dave, the Swami's biographer, stresses that 'Satsang is the only means for ultimate redemption or for absolute brahmanization' (Dave 1967: 152). Swaminarayana himself has affirmed that 'The eternal truth sat is atma (the individual soul) and Sat is Paramatma (the universal soul, i.e. God). The contact of atma with Paramatma is Satsang' (*Vachanamrita*, Gadhada, III, 39, cited by Dave (ibid.)). The polysemy of the word 'satsang' serves to identify the communion of the soul with god as well as the community united in communion. Greeting the congregation as if it were divine is quite pertinent, as the solidarity of the congregation becomes a metaphor for the closeness to god achieved by its members. The greeting, then, offers a perfect example of 'Durkheimian solidarity' in a religious context. We shall see that this is not the only way in which the sect members emphasize their belonging to a community.

On this occasion the satsang started with a long tape recording. This was a 'sermon', where readings from the texts were interspersed with comments and elaborations. As far as I could ascertain, most citations were from the *Shikshapatri*, a 'catechism' or handbook of central teachings which, unlike the learned and complex *Vachanamrita*, is read by all literate believers. The *Vachanamrita*, compiled by the Swami's successors, contains his original sermons in an edited form.

These tape recordings, common in the temples, are often read by the current incarnation of the Swami himself. For, in the Yogijipanth, leadership of the sect is by election; human in so far as the last incarnation appoints his successor, but, in religious terms, made by god himself, since each incarnation, like Swaminarayana himself, is deemed to be god. The word of god, then, is quite literally carried, by monks using modern communications, in taped form every Sunday to each important temple. I do not know how regularly the same practice is followed in temples in Britain, East Africa or America, but I am certain that sermons are carried by air to such far-off places on the more important ritual occasions of the year.

After listening, thus, to the word of god, the congregation chants the *Swaminarayana Mantra*. The mantra consists in a repetition of the name Swaminarayana. In the version used by the Yogijipanth, the words Swami and Narayana are sometimes juxtaposed, giving an added stress to the assertion that, as the Swami is Narayana (god), so Narayana is the Swami. God is identical to the Swami, just as the Swami is and was god. 'According to Shree Swaminarayan', says Dave, commenting upon the *Vachanamrita*, 'God does not descend. He simply manifests' (1967: 138). Without repeating my discussion elsewhere (1992: 607-18), we see here the gradation of beliefs between the old sect and the new. For the former, the Swami is only an incarnation of Krishna, who himself incarnated the high god, Vishnu; for the Yogijipanth, the God-Swami is well beyond the intermediate stage represented by the High Gods of Hinduism.

This temple in Bhavnagar belongs to the new sect, which in a way has parted from its Vaishnavite foundations, yet the next two songs we chant show the continuity with that tradition. '*Shree Hari jay jay jay Hari*' uses the term for god common to all Vaishnavas and is sung to an old Vaishnava tune. This was followed by '*Hare Krishna*', again part of the wider Vaishnava tradition. The latter sequence was rather short, however, as if none should doubt that Krishna is, indeed, a minor figure in relation to the all-important Swami. The singing is communal, but is structured by the exchange between a leader and the body of the congregation. The former constantly varies the theme, and his variations are repeated by the others. It struck me how the communal singing produces a collective religious feeling. The community of song seems to touch everybody's soul. As in the case of the greetings, the collective spirit of Swaminarayana worship is very much in evidence.

In conclusion to the singing, the names of all the incarnations recognized by the sect are recited in chronological order. At the mention of each incarnation, the name is greeted by a 'namaskar' by each and every member of the congregation. Including the 'spiritual hierarchs' of the new sect, this recitation is, of course, particular to it.

The next item was a recitation from the scriptures, accompanied by a commentary by the resident sadhu of the temple. The change, in tone and level of voice, between the recitation and the commentary was quite marked. Clearly nobody should be left in doubt as to what is the word of god himself, and what the humble interpretations of his servant. The former, though in Gujarati, borrowed its style from Sanskrit religious recital, while the commentary was made in common speech.

Now is the turn for the lay brothers to perform in the proceedings. On this occasion six members spoke, including myself. First, three lay brothers each made a short speech, comparable to 'bearing witness' in some Christian sects: people will tell others how, in particular circumstances, they were helped towards the good religious life by Swaminarayana himself, or by their membership in the sect. Sometimes the speech takes the form, familiar to students of Western low-church movements, of 'I used to be a sinner until . . .'. Then I was urged to speak, so I told the congregation about my experience of the Swaminarayana temple in London and the positive effect it had upon the community and spiritual life of Gujaratis there. This brought a long comment, the gist of which was in appreciation of my interest in the sect. One of the lay brothers then sang a new hymn composed for the visit of Yogiji Maharaj—then the living incarnation of Swami Narayan—on the occasion of his visit to Jamnagar some time earlier, followed by another lay brother, singing his own composition. The song was followed by a short speech. Finally, there was another spell of communal singing, before the satsang was concluded by *arti* before the image of Swaminarayana, of Yogiji Maharaj, and of Pramukh Swami, who at the time shared leadership of the sect with Yogiji.

On this occasion, the congregation numbered some hundred to a hundred and fifty men. It will be noted that I have not mentioned the women. They were behind a screen, in the rear of the temple. It is extremely important that sect members should not see the other sex in the temple, and so I cannot tell how many women were present. It seems, however, that women usually outnumber men, as is indeed common for temples of most kinds in Gujarat.

Apart from my presence, smoothly integrated, as we have seen, in the proceedings, this was quite a typical satsang both in programme, duration and size of congregation for the place. There is another Swaminarayana temple, belonging to the old sect, in Bhavnagar, and they seem to be as numerous there as the Yogijipanth. I assume that something like one thousand individuals attend satsang on a typical Sunday in that town.

Elsewhere too, traffic to and from the satsang attests to the sect's popular appeal.

THE COMMUNAL ASPECT OF SATSANG

It is clear that the communal aspect of satsang is very strong. While the sect does not oppose caste, no distinction apart from gender is made during rituals. While older, respected members of the satsang sit at the front, this is common usage rather than a rule, and such members may come from a wide range of castes. In speech, sect members are always referred to as brothers and sisters. Outside the temple, members greet each other with 'Jay Swaminarayana'. This communal solidarity is not a matter of ideology only. It is actively instilled in members by the ritual proceedings. Greeting, or paying obeisance, to the congregation as such, is only one example. Singing in unison, swaying together to the rhythm of the Swaminarayana mantra, members are made to experience this community as a very real emotional fact. It would hardly be possible, even for an observer, not to experience some of the same feeling.

While the Swaminarayanas are the only Gujarati sect of Bhakti tradition of which I have personal experience (apart from a few Kabirpanthis) I felt much of the same spirit among Bengali Vaishnavas. Brief meetings with Gujarati Vaishnavas in England gave a similar impression. There is a special atmosphere felt wherever Bhaktas meet to sing bhajans together. In the Indian context, this is a trait setting sect apart from cult; while the latter may be practised individually, the sect is defined precisely by a sense of community. Still, this is a very general observation, which allows for further distinctions.

The emotional dimension of worship as felt among Yogijipanthi Swaminarayanas go beyond any similar phenomena I have observed, and perhaps the most remarkable aspect of it is that this emotional quality is not compromised by the size of the gathering. Attendance at London and Bombay temples only serve to strengthen this impression. The temples of the older sect, the Acharyapanth, never produced the same emotional effect in me; in every sense, the Yogijipanth bears the stamp of religious revival, so the most obvious parallel I can think of is the revivalist groups of low-church Christianity.

While the satsang is the main weekly occasion in any Swaminarayana temple, there are prayer meetings everyday. The Bhavnagar temple has a small library and an upstairs room for study; such facilities are common in the larger temples of the sect.

As Dumont noted, the sect here serves as an 'egalitarian island' within the larger, hierarchical structure (1966a: 237-42). Within the sect, rank is not relevant. Outside, caste affiliations remain important. But the sect is also an agent of what Srinivas called Sanskritization (1952, 1961, 1967). To be a Swaminarayana implies vegetarianism, teetotalitarianism, and being a non-smoker.

THE SECT AS AN AGENT OF SANSKRITIZATION

To outsiders, sect membership stand for customs associated with the prestigious merchant castes. This particular path of 'Sanskritization' is typical of Gujarat.[6] Sect membership may serve aspirations to higher caste rank, or higher 'standing' (Pocock 1972) within the caste. The sect was an important element in the rise of mainland Kanbis to Patidar status, imitating the merchant castes.[7] In Rajkot too, the term Patidar is now universally employed,[8] though in general the process has not gone so far among Kanbis of other peninsular towns. Some other castes similarly benefit from their sect membership. Still, the membership does not, as Fuchs (1965) implies, base itself on the lower castes; sect members are concentrated at the middle level of the caste system. Seen from the higher-ranking groups, sectarian practices help 'inclusion', while they aid sect members in 'exclusion' from stigmatized practices (Pocock 1957a). According to the position of the caste, sect members may or may not form a separate section; this tendency is stronger among low castes. Among higher castes, Swaminarayanas tend to intermarry and interdine freely with caste members of other religious persuasions.

SWAMINARAYANA CHARANS

One of the famous conversions in the sect's early history was of Ladu Barot, the great Charan bard, then called sadhu Brahmananda, and subsequently recognized as one of the greatest poets of the sect. His conversion was particularly important[9] since Charans held a key position in the Shaktist cult and ideology which underpinned the old princely order. Traditionally, they are Shaiva and Shakta, the foremost devotees of the goddess. Yet some are Swaminarayanas, among them the brother-in-law of Jagatbhai, with whom I visited the Brahmakumari mission in Bhavnagar. The whole family of his in-laws belong to the sect. They were converted during the years the Swami stayed at Gadhada,[10] so the conversion took place some 150 years before.[11] The members of the sect are vegetarians, which sets them apart from the rest of the caste; but they still intermarry quite freely with them.

Jagatbhai stresses the difference between Swaminarayana and traditional Charans, and has quite strong views on Swaminaryanas, in spite of—or perhaps because of—his close family ties to them. His views reflect his profession, as a sociologist.

You know, there is this theory of Weber about Capitalism and Christianity. Actually, there is some basis for a comparison with Swaminarayanas. They are doing the same thing. They are shrewd businessmen and they are always keeping away from spending. You know what the *Shikshapatri* says: '*Avta vedhu kerch na karo*'—Don't spend more than you earn. This is one of the main moral tenets of Swaminarayana Dharma. My grandmother, who is a Swaminaryana, often gives me this advice. I respect it, because it is her religion, but I do not always follow.

Swaminarayans are known as misers. You know, when I was staying at hostel in my college days, some Swaminarayan boys were there. They would be nice boys, they were not offending anybody, very peaceful. But at the same time they would not spend a single sou on us. They would at most give us a cup of tea, they would always offer a glass of cold water, but they would never say 'Look here, I got these nice preparations from home', and so invite us to join. That is typical. Swaminarayans will not spend money on you unless they are sure of something in return. That is why, in my opinion, we do not like to have matrimonial bonds with Swaminarayans. It is true that there is no barrier to intermarriage, but we do not prefer. The reason is that we know that even if they are often very rich people, they will not give us even five thousand rupees. Others will, and that is why we prefer to be connected with them.

One is reminded of the story of Ladu Barot and the two chiefly ladies of Gadhada.[12] Ladu was found of ornaments, and liked to dress well; the ladies taught him that such bahaviour was not just vain; it might tempt others—women, for example, as they found Ladu handsome—to sin. With their association to the court and the need to appear in public, members of the bardic caste were less than frugal in their traditional spending pattern. Indeed, Jagatbhai was often looking for ways to gain some extra money—by small enterprises such as diamond-cutting—but he was no businessman and his ideas never seemed to pay. His finances were not always of the best and his judgement about relatives unwilling to lend money may have been based on experience. He was, however, very generous; visitors never left his house on an empty stomach. We may conclude, then, that the opposition between 'traditional' and Swaminarayana Charans is not just a matter of religion. It is a question of life styles; puritanism contrasted with a courtly manner inherited from feudal times. This opposition is certainly clearer among Charans than among members of less aristocratic castes; but similar remarks on the frugality of Swaminarayanas were often heard among them, too.

A PROMINENT MEMBER OF THE SECT

If Swaminarayanas are frugal, they are not necessarily narrow-minded. Take doctor K., who belongs to the elite among the sect members of his town, taking an active part in temple affairs. He belongs to the Acharyapanth, the older branch of the sect. He is a man of considerable reading, and, like many Indian intellectuals, well acquainted with the Bible. During his student days in London, he was given a beautiful bible by a British friend, which he keeps as a cherished possession. Tolerant and broad-minded, he is good company; to the anthropologist, he showed a great deal of understanding.

Dr. K. comes from the Vania group of merchant castes, and his views of the Nagar Brahmins, the former elite of the city, are not complementary. 'The Nagars', he says, 'are of no account today. Their time is past.' But they have kept their houses in their old quarter of the town, and many, he says, simply live off the rent. Their big houses are often used as offices. Such a house can bring a rent of a thousand rupees a month,[13] enough to live comfortably. 'So many Nagars are doing absolutely nothing. They visit each other, they chat about the old days, and have a good time.'

There is a note of contempt here. I understand that it is the 'laziness' of the Nagars, in particular, that Dr. K. finds insupportable. He has himself built up a highly respected medical practice and owns his own hospital, clean, modern and efficient. The Nagars have the resources to do well, but make no use of them. He himself—like many sect members—has followed an ethic of hard work as inculcated by their teachings. Again we see that streak of puritanism—similar to what Weber (1930) analysed for Protestant sects—in the Swaminarayana spirit and community. An undeniable success in these terms, Dr. K. may feel his 'spirit of capitalism' scandalized by the unashamed 'leisure class' lifestyle of Nagars (Veblen 1934). But we also recognize in his remarks a theme in the history of the region, the antagonism between Vanias and Nagars. This opposition refers to the wider one between merchants and rulers, since Nagars upheld the old feudal regime. Bureaucrats as well as Brahmins, Nagars epitomize not just the political but the religious order of the old days; sometimes they were jajmans of blood sacrifices denounced by Swaminarayana and his followers (Tambs-Lyche1992: 596-9; 1997: 299-300). But the Nagars themselves were more refined, being the main proponents of Shankara's version of Advaita in the region. On a hill overlooking the city, the Shankaradeva temple, patronized by Nagars and with Nagar priests, was the most prominent in town. Now visitors are scarce.

Beside building up his hospital, which is now known all over Saurashtra, Dr. K. has found time to produce a commentary on the *Shikshapatri*. He is chairman of the local temple committee of the Acharyapanthis. Yet he is tolerant of other Swaminarayana sects. 'There are no substantive differences between the four Swaminarayana sects. The difference is due to some minor variations. In the case of the Yogiji/Shastri Maharaj group (i.e. the Yogijipanth), these two were great holy men, but they were also not completely without personal ambition. So they left Vadtal[14] to set up on their own.' Still, he assures me, differences remain minor. 'While in London, I visited the Yogiji Maharaj temple. I paid my respects and did my worship. It is not impossible to go to both temples. Quite a few people do so, and no harm is attached.'

Dr. K. himself was brought up a Swaminarayana. He points out that he has never in his life touched meat, wine, or tobacco. 'You will find', he says, 'that the Swaminarayanas in the villages lead a purer life (than their neighbours). They are economically better off also. They do not spend foolishly on small luxuries like tobacco or sweets.' Again, then, we note that streak of 'capitalist ethic'.

Comparing such views with those of my traditional Charan friend Jagatbhai, shared by many Brahmins and Rajputs, I was reminded of Pareto's 'lions' and 'foxes' (1966: 256ff), those rising in society and those who have seen better days. More specifically, traditional high-caste people tend to emphasize a fixed hierarchy, while Swaminarayans and such rising castes as the Patidar underline a state of flux. Thus when T, a Nagar Brahmin, indicates that Shiva ranks above Vishnu and, implicitly, Shaivites above Vaishnavites, his reasons are given as permanent and philosophically grounded. Such ranking has nothing to do with present-day success or failure; it is indeed an order beyond the vagaries of power relations. Dr. K. and other Swaminarayanas, on the other hand, are the 'foxes' of the situation; Swaminarayanas do better than others and challenge the hierarchical order. Their emphasis is on competition rather than permanent rank relations. This competitive order contains an egalitarian and individualist element, but is mingled with the symbolism of the old hierarchical order; abstaining from meat, wine and tobacco have, for centuries, been symbols of high rank in the very order they see as changing. For sect members, the superiority of vegetarianism over meat-eating remains as important as ever. But by adopting such measures, anybody may 'better themselves'. Rank becomes a matter of achievement rather than ascription. This implies a move towards the 'individualism' often identified with modernity and Western society.

I shall return to another mode of liberation from the social order, where the sect's leader, like other gurus in India, legitimizes the break of certain social ties, normally following a life crisis. In such cases, the existence of religious community serves to underline and maintain this legitimation—but liberation from family constraints is replaced by submission to the guru and the sect's rules, just as sect members escaping from caste hierarchy adopt the rules of an alternative, more competitive order. Individualism, here, does not stand for liberation from rules, but the opening up of alternative life courses implying a choice between different sets of rules for living one's life. This is no different from similar processes elsewhere. If we accept, as Weber or Durkheim did, that Protestantism brought individualism to the West, we also realize the social controls involved—if not always as strict as Hawthorne shows, in *The Scarlet Letter*.

The presence of sects such as the Swaminarayanas—open, in principle, to all—extend the field of inividual choice for potential members but control behaviour strictly once the choice has been made. In creating alternative life courses, they act principally to increase further the complexity of social life in the region.

THE LIFE-WORLD

Coming to grips with this complexity demands a regional approach, since any local unit offers but limited access to it. Yet no regional study can deal properly with social organization, unless it is done by a large team of anthropologists.[15] To map social relations locally is ample work for a single scholar, yet social organization links the individual to the system: in renouncing these links, we are left with the persons we meet, and glimpses of the system as they see it. I try to present such glimpses here, of caste and society as seen from various points of view; of cities and monuments as people in Saurashtra see them; and some aspects of Hinduism as seen by devotees. All these, then, should be read as efforts at situating the individual within the region.

In contemporary India, most people do not live within a village universe, nor a single-caste one. They, like us, live in a world too complex for any individual to grasp. They are certainly situated, but their social horizon does not form a boundary. Rather than cling to a rock, they navigate in a sea of social life. This is what I did: like them, and learning from them, I tried to make sense of the complex world we shared for a while.

This world corresponds to what Schutz called the life-world of individuals (1964, 8n), which represents the subjective point of view of actors and is 'the only but sufficient guarantee that the world of social reality will not be replaced by a fictional non-existing world constructed by the scientific observer' (1964: 8). But the only subjectivity to which I have access is my own. We enter, here, the fundamentally impossible task of anthropology, of trying to construct the subjective life-world of others. Schutz partly comes to our rescue.

> My experience of the world justifies and corrects itself by the experience of the others with whom I am interrelated by common knowledge, common work, and common suffering. The world, interpreted as the possible field of action for us all: that is the first and most primitive principle of organization of my knowledge of the exterior world in general. . . . (Schutz 1964: 9)

But only part of our project is rescued, for in fieldwork we only come to share part of our informants' life-world. I do not know how it feels to be a Saurashtrian. I simply think that I have a better idea of it than most outsiders. As Barth puts it: there is nothing to prevent us from 'progressively equipping ourselves, through participation in the social intercourse connected with planning and interpreting acts, with the knowledge and insights needed to make increasingly intelligent guesses at what is going on as further events unfold. . . .' (1993: 160). In short, we gradually acquire some of the knowledge implicit behind our informants' actions, and learn, from our association with them, to act on these implicits ourselves:

> . . . not by a hermeneutic reading in solitude of certain cultural products, but by knowing an increasing store of the premises for people's actions and interpretations, and entering into the dialogues and interactions of others whereby their experiences are shaped and shared . . . this learning is embedded in the social process of participation; and it is immensely simplified to the extent that the anthropologist is able to perform it in the context of practice. . . . For it is in practice that the appropriate keys of interpretation are linked with the appropriate contexts and events to which they are applied—a linkage it is highly questionable one could reconstruct post hoc, from logic and first principles. . . . (Barth 1993: 160-1)

My fieldwork involved too much travel, too much shifting around, to know any great number of people intimately. Those I knew best, as friends and colleagues, became too close for me to visualize their motivations in general terms, or to disclose their intimacies. But the discussions I had with them enter into my interpretation of the behaviour of others. Still, a large part of my material is anecdotal; stray meetings, situations observed, discussions which were interesting, but not repeated. Yet the basic assumption remains, as Barth puts it, that we may best break into 'the enchanted world of others' at the point where events become acts, in Weber's sense:

> . . . and by directing our analysis in both directions from the point at which an event occurs: to its preconditions, and to its consequences.
>
> To the actor, the event of own behaviour is an act by virtue of the intent that shapes it, i.e., what the actor sees herself/himself as doing, and why this is desirable and feasible: this is its 'meaning' and, to a large extent, determines its form. To other parties, on the other hand, event becomes act through interpretation, through the way its purposes and entailments are understood at the time of its manifestation.
>
> In the short or in the longer retropect, or in anticipation of encounters, people reflect on these intentions and interpretations and shape them in the forms of 'plans' and 'experience' respectively. Various templates, imagery, dialogues, and musings are no doubt involved. . . . (Barth 1993: 158)

With Bateson (1936), I assume these various forms of imagery, necessary for the interpretation of events as acts, to be essentially of the same epistomological nature, whether they are those of the anthropologist, or of his/her informants. The way in which I try to save something of my informants' life-world, then, is by basing my models on elements which I think must be basic to their perception of their world. Thus I assume that the vivid experience I have of Saurashtra as a land, where the past is ever-present in monuments and memories, corresponds to a similar though varying consciousness of the past in the minds of most Saurashtrians. We then move from time into social space, as I describe the various scenes in which people of Saurashtra act out their social life. This involves them, as it did myself, in definitions of situations, which I describe and analyse.

I have shown bits and pieces of an image of Saurashtra, mythical or historical events as well as places and settings for interaction. I argue that these cannot form a single image common to all, since different communities do not share the same perspective: moreover, we must assume that each individual has only a partial vision of the region. I do not believe in a complete model of the social world, present in the minds of members, for my knowledge of my own society does not form such a structured whole. Rather, we orient ourselves in a social space, with continuities and boundaries, formed by identities and ideologies, where history as an ongoing process knits together strands of which present positions are but the temporary end points (Barth 1983).

Barth's recent work on Bali represents a major attempt to bypass simplistic images of society. Stressing the need to accept the complexity of society as real, rather than hiding the rubble behind a nicely constructed analysis, he feels that

> . . . our experience of social life should lead us to accept as plausible this view of disorder, multiplicity, and undeterminedness. Why then does it seem so difficult for anthropology to embrace it and develop it as a basis for theory? One reason may be that it goes against the grain of received intellectual standards of excellence. . . . We must rebel against this scenario. . . . Culture, society and human lives . . . do not come in this puzzle format. . . . (1993: 5-6)

Thus, presenting a picture that is neither global nor analytic, neither holistic nor subjectively viewed from a single viewpoint,[16] I hope to avoid the claims to objectivity that post-modernists criticize. My description reflects no vision but my own, but is, I feel, a kind of knowledge close to that held Saurashtrians. I take the reader into the region the way I came to know it, as one individual among others in a highly complex society, trying to sketch the region according to ideas some of its inhabitants have of it. Yet I translate into anthropological tradition by calling on the comparative perspective, as a realization, above all, that all perspectives are relative.

Hannerz (1992) uses the term perspective to gloss the manifold views of a culture as experienced by differently situated actors. Caste as categorization must be kept apart from the subjectivity inherent in the term perspective, for while some perspectives may be identified with castes, and caste is important for the actors' situatedness in Saurashtra, we must not confound it with the thinking subject. Similarly, the role caste plays as a framework for social relations, must be distinguished from the web of relations as spun by the actors themselves.

Such deconstruction corresponds to post-modernist criticism. But I want to proceed beyond the stand which tends to equate anthropology with literature. Many problems we confront can be expressed through fiction, but the anthropological monograph, as a literary genre, differs from the novel. The latter, by consciously constructed ambiguity, invites the reader to use fantasy, while the anthropologist tries, successfully or not, to avoid being ambiguous. The novelist's carpentry in constructing his novel is usually hidden to the ordinary reader: the anthropologist's way of building his argument should be clearly visible. A good monograph may well make a tedious novel.

MODELIZATION: THE NEED FOR CLARITY

It is this difference which leads us to modelization, to cope with the need for clarity. It is surely true, as the critique of positivism in the early 1970s made clear, that models do not pertain to the object, they are products of our own thinking.[17] Our models are not theories, and cannot be tested by the hypothetical-deductive method.[18] Their main usefulness lies in their being good to think. But—and this to me is what makes anthropology a science—the constraints of modelling serve to store, on the conscious level, the logical processes by which an interpretation has been made. Thus they may be retrieved, criticized and improved upon by the reader.

By modelling, I part from experience acknowledged as subjective, to express myself within a formal, though still subjectively constructed, framework. To construct models, I believe, is to play at reproducing, by a set of formal rules, our subjective image of what happens in reality. We then manipulate the various inputs of the models, to see if the consequences of our manipulation correspond to the outcome of the events we have observed (Barth 1966). To the extent that these outcomes conform to real processes, we may then formulate theories to postulate that the factors corresponding to our model inputs are, indeed, the reasons for the form social life produces.

With these points in mind I turn to the problem of constructing a model to link my observation of persons with those of large-scale social phenomena. We need a model of the agent facing his world. We must analyse action in a set of terms which allow us to depict the confrontation of the individual with those presuppositions for his own thinking, which he must use in order to orient himself towards action. This means going beyond the level of agency to which Barth refers when focusing on individual choice (1966), for we are concerned to break down the category of the actor himself. I have found no better way to tackle this problem than the one suggested by G.H. Mead (1934).

THE 'I' AND THE 'ME'— EMERGENCE AND RELATIVITY

Mead distinguishes between 'emergence' and 'relativity', which he relates, respectively, to the 'me' and the 'I'. The agent, as such, is always an I; whenever he reflects upon himself, however, he (or she) must, necessarily, do so in terms of the 'me'.

In Mead's terms, the 'I' is cross-cultural; while the 'me' must be expressed in the terms of the culture to which the person belongs. I do not think we need to argue the presence of the 'I' in the Indian, or any other, context. Whatever the motivations of the 'Indian' as an agent, he is clearly manifest in his choices, his actions, his behaviour—whether more or less standardized, norm-oriented, or holistic in his views than his Western counterpart. Such variation must be part of his conception of himself, his 'me'. If this conception was produced by the 'I' independent of others, there could be no variation in such images as between cultures, and any semblance to a 'Homo Hierarchicus' (Dumont 1966a) could be no more than a metaphor.

We must concentrate, then, on those attitudes of others which, assumed by the single human being, come to constitute the 'me'. Dumont's view (1965), that the 'modern conception of the individual' is external to India, and has entered the Indian mind only in certain Westernized settings, begs another question: what kind of personhood is formed by the processes that constitute the 'me' in the Indian case?

THE 'ME' IN SAURASHTRA

The angle from which I will attack this problem, in the context of Saurashtra, is the categories used to describe various kind of people met in diverse situations. The underlying assumption is simple: any conception the individual has of herself or himself will necessarily be expressed in terms of the categories he or she shares with relevant others.

Let us consider the category caste. The Patidar must be considered a caste category today; yet a hundred years ago, this was not so. Today's Patidar families were Kanbis then. Thus Pocock 'cannot give a substantive reply based upon territorial limitation, political institutions, or a body of shared custom . . . we cannot draw an arbitrary line . . . the distinction between Patidar and Kanbi is hierarchically relative' (1972: 153). The Patidar caste has neither clear boundary nor organizational unity (1972: 66). Hierarchy within the caste is as marked as intercaste hierarchy. Intermarriage with other castes takes place both at the top and bottom of the caste. This caste category, then, does not coincide with a bounded group. This is true of several other castes in Gujarat.[19] The lack of fit between group and category is an important element of the system, not an incidental occurrence, and recalls Leach's remark:

> . . . when social structures are expressed in cultural form, the representation is imprecise compared with that given by the exact categories which the sociologist, *qua* scientist, would like to employ. I hold that these inconsistencies in the logic of ritual expression are always necessary for the proper functioning of any social system. (1954: 4)

The very imprecision of the category Patidar is consistent with Leach's ideas; it makes the term functional as part of a language of argument. Politics within the Patidar caste, indeed, tends to concern itself with alternative regulations of custom seen as appropriate to the essence of 'Patidardom' (Pocock 1972). While such thinking contradicts a map of society marked by clear boundaries between groups, it is, as we have seen, consistent with conceptualizating Patidar as a prototype rather than a bounded category (Rosch 1978; Tambs-Lyche 1991b). Pocock stresses the different nature of castes: some really are groups, some are not (1972: 54). And then, as I have shown, many of the stereotypes held about kinds of people in Saurashtra relate to the level of estate rather than that of caste.

This shifts our focus, making the system of categorization largely independent of any 'objectively' existing group. Rex (1970: 139 and *passim*) in a perceptive work, argues the need for such 'typifications', 'ideal types', or 'stereotypes' as necessary correlates of any complex society, needed to make sense of the environment and produce 'models of interaction' enabling us to 'orient conduct' towards each other. We should expect, then, the proliferation of such categories in such a complex society as India.

A number of diverse categories are used to define persons in interactional situations, in Saurashtra as elsewhere in northern India (Berreman 1972). These categories are not mutually exclusive; they are simply somewhat apt and therefore prototypical in nature. They relate to estate, caste, regional identity, occupation, education, religion, and other real or imagined social entities. The main feature they seem to have in common is their function in characterizing a salient, prototypical, feature of the person in question. Clearly, we have to use a wide range of alternative categories if we want to characterize the formation of a concept of 'me' in Saurashtra. How, then, does the individual choose, among a large number of interactionally adaptable categories, those most apt in each situation? And, how does he structure his choice to construct an image of the 'me', sufficiently consistent as an identity for him to live with ?

Fluid as social life is, 'social structure' has become a loaded term indicating a position hard to maintain. There remains what Nadel called 'structuring' (1957: 156) without which orientation, or indeed description, becomes unmanageable.[20] While recurrent processes may structure the lives and identities of individuals (Barth 1972a), and provide elements for social organization (Firth 1950), only the larger time-scale seems appropriate for processes that structure our view of 'society'. Thus we return to the role of tradition in the image that informants, as well as myself, build of Saurashtra.

TRADITION AS EMERGENCE

'Emergence' is used by Mead to describe the preconceived knowledge of nascent social situations, the knowledge the I uses to define them (Mead 1934: 329ff.; McHugh 1968: 23ff.). In situating this knowledge culturally, we must look for whatever such knowledge is shared by people in Saurashtra. This brings us to tradition as a central element of emergence.

Important parameters of living in Saurashtra must be seen as a partly shared heritage, marking places and social positions on a kind of map to which most people refer and which stems, ultimately, from their view of the history in which their ancestors took part. Thus we return to what most actors, in Saurashtra, would agree to see as traditional society. This construction may not correspond to the actual pattern of social relations at any definite point in the past. Nor, as we have seen, does everybody have the same image of tradition. Like the ideas people have of society in the present tense, the conception of traditional society is but a reference point beyound actual experience.

As such this knowledge is, precisely, 'the past in the present' (Bloch 1978); communicated and shared, it cannot be direct and individual experience. Rather, it is the store of cultural presuppositions or 'structural assumptions' (Bateson 1958: 24) that the individual has incorporated as his tools for thinking about social life. For Bateson, these premises are the building-blocks of 'cultural structure', which he sees as closely related to tradition, provided the latter term is

> . . . stripped of all reference to the past or to diachronic processes. When so stripped, 'tradition' can only mean the given facts of a culture, facts which are 'given' as premises. Thus it comes about that the word 'tradition' is sometimes used in synchronic analysis as a synonym for 'cultural structure' as here defined. (Bateson 1958: 24)

Tradition, then, in Mead's terms, becomes part of 'emergence'. The cultural premises that enter into the tradition of Saurashtra are fundamental to the emergence of individuals, but the latter differs since no individual is the bearer of all the elements that make up tradition, a term I would reserve for the collective level. Unlike Bateson, however, I avoid the term structure when referring to this level. Epistemologically, it is only too easy to confound, as I feel Dumont (1966a) does, the structure ascribed to a phenomenon with the structuring perspectives we introduce by our interpretation.

The term structure, then, is used here for premises inherent in the models, emic or etic, that I construct as heuristic devices to interpret social or cultural data. It denotes, following Lévi-Strauss (1958: 305), a degree of structuration inherent in the thought process, as opposed to properties inherent in empirical reality. But as he also notes, what the anthropologist thinks, his informants are also capable of thinking, so this distinction must not be confounded with the emic-etic dimension. When researchers such as Marriott (1976, 1989) construct emic models, designed to interpret indigenous cultural premises, it is they who model what they see as premises of Indian thought.

These models clearly refer to a different level from those, clearly etic and depicting human interaction in general, which I borrow from Mead (1934) and Barth (1966). But the two levels translate into each other, for the cultural premises we are talking about appear as an implicit of emergence with Mead or as principles beyond the values and categories of Barth's models. In Goodenough's terms (1957, 1961), emergence is the stuff of which 'models for', as well as 'models of', are constructed; standards for 'deciding what is . . . for deciding what can be . . . for deciding how one feels about it . . . for deciding what to do about it . . . for decoding how to go about doing it' (1961: 522).

TRADITION AS LEGITIMATION

Through emergence, social situations are seen as conceived, constructed and acted out using tradition: concepts and conceptions which, though constructed through history, may be conscious to the actor on the level where Malinowski (1954: 101) would locate 'myth as charter'. Myth is not history, but legitimizes an imagined tradition (Hobsbawm and Ranger 1981). This point is crucial, for, as Verdier puts it, the argument that something was done or said in a certain way in the past, may legitimate what is to be done in the present, not so much in terms of rules as of examples: in her French village, each custom has its own eventful history (1979: 80-2). The term tradition ceases to make sense if we leave out the dimension of time altogether (Boyer 1990). Thus Ranger, whose ideas on the invention of tradition were seminal, now prefers to speak of re-invention (1989). Still, the legitimacy of the traditional way of doing things saves us a lot of trouble.

While a few individuals may spend time and effort rethinking the foundations of their social world, most of us depend on ascribing a degree of permanence to social arrangements, to concentrate on the mutable as opposed to what is held to be constant, when we are confronted with social situations to be defined. As Rex notes (1970), we have neither the time nor the energy to analyse our bases for action every time we act. These premises include elements that are acquired by what we, somewhat nebulously, are used to call 'socialization'.

I wish to avoid Bourdieu's concept 'habitus' (1977), and stress instead the potential of the individual to question the very elements others see as fundamental. Bourdieu's concept assimilates too closely the distinct dimensions of orientation and action, knowledge and behaviour. Mead's concept of emergence avoids the ambiguity of Bourdieu's approach, making a sharper distinction between presuppositions for, and the resultant choice of, a mode of action. The individual may take the elements of his emergence as self-evident—but this does not prevent him, at the next instance, from confronting them, in order to analyse his own presuppositions. Manipulating the various inputs that constitute emergence, we produce a subjective image of our own activity, constructing as it were, our view of why we choose to act as we do.

Most of the time however, most of us have no inclination to do so. By referring to tradition we save our energies for the task to be accomplished, here and now. Tradition provides us with a ground for our motives, as if we could build our action on something fixed or given, instead of engaging in a continuous process of invention. Our tendency to turn to tradition indicates a preference for the given over the mutable. In other contexts, we feel restrained by tradition, as indeed by what I have called environmental constraints, in our effort to create or invent.

But the distinction between the given and the mutable is not absolute. Geographical and social space are conceivable to actors only in terms of the categories used to describe them, so any such description merge factors seen by actors as given and those which, for them, are negotiable. I have distinguished (1980) environmental (given) from social (negotiable) constraints on individual choice, but since the distinction must be seen from actor's point of view, he or she may relocate it. Brox notes that 'If, some years ago, one came to a Newfoundland fishing village and asked why there were only small boats beached, one would get the local explanation that the north-west winds made bigger boats impossible. Now it is much more likely that the answer will be that it is the fault of the government, as it has not built a molo' (1972: 68-9).

What was due to nature has become politics: the frontier may move when people interpret their surroundings differently. In the same way, traditional concepts like caste become mutable once they are challenged—even if the challenge is unsuccessful. Once defined as debatable, caste opens up for conservative or radical views: even when opposition is muted, organization for specific caste interests changes its character. Today, caste in Saurashtra is less a parameter of traditional thought than a dimension of the socio-political world too useful to discard.

Tradition, like culture, may be embedded in individuals, but it also influences them from a supra-individual level (Keesing 1976: 184), which, I have argued, presupposes real time-scale. Paradoxically, what is supra-individual is also infra-individual: any single shared cultural perception forms only part of the individual's life-world. Concepts such as 'status', 'role' or 'position' (Linton 1936; Radcliffe-Brown 1952) were designed to describe the point at which the individual articulates with 'culture', 'structure', 'society', and similar constructions, and cannot be divorced from the reifying view implied by the latter (Jackson 1972: see also Strathern, 1996).

The insight that such concepts are reifying constructs does not invalidate them; the world of experience is necessarily constructed. In substituting tradition for structure, I am not saying that tradition lacks structure, but that the disjunction of time from structure is spurious. Even if the idealized traditional society is static, it is not timeless, for it belongs unambiguously to the past and this is what provides it with legitimizing authority, to be read as charter (Malinowski 1954)—or even as a kind of anti-charter, as what we would like to get away from. Such pre-existing constructs provide alternatives for action in everyday life that are known and seem predictable as to their results, saving us insecurity and the extra cost of rethinking the situation rationally.

In the Indian context, the qualities associated with various categories of people, such as caste, are sometimes seen as 'natural'. Such implicits are clearly part of emergence, but their relevance, in any given situation, may vary. The actor must identify, not only actors but types of situation. Here, the setting plays its part. Thus I base my description of social life in Saurashtra on an inventory of scenes, dealing partly with the perception of situatedness, and partly with patterns of action deemed appropriate to each. The aim is to define the givens that actors feel they must take into account, pertaining to types of situations to which different rules apply. Starting with the physical setting, I try to outline the way its particularity is categorized and the situational rules perceived. These rules also influence the typology of personnel that comes to be relevant in each case.

NOTES

1. For Weber, certainly, sects as known from protestantism were vehicles of individualism (1930).
2. For this sect see Esnoul 1964, Thoothi 1935, Brent 1972, Clémentine-Ojha 1990a.
3. I have dealt with this theme elsewhere (1997: 69-71). See also Pocock (1973: 108-20).
4. Thus the Sri Vaisnavas campaigned actively in Saurashtra in the second half of the nineteenth century, and built temples in Khorasa and Mahuva. Rangarajan (1996) lists fourteen castes of converts, plus Barots, Kathis and Lohanas, mentioned elsewhere; all of medium to high status. She notes that the Ramanandas have more followers than the Sri Vaisnavas, and that some of the latter went to the Swaminarayanas 'on the psychological ground that it was after all an offshot of the parent body' (1996: 170).
5. See Williams 1984, Tambs-Lyche 1992: 560-638; 1997: 307-14; Pocock 1973: 122-57.
6. We might speak of 'merchantization', but I have used the term earlier (1982) for the way the whole of Saurashtra, in the post-Independence period, came to be dominated by merchant castes and their values.
7. Shah and Shroff 1958; Shah and Desai 1988; Pocock 1973; Tambs-Lyche 1980a, etc..
8. H.G. Patel, personal information.
9. Tambs-Lyche 1992; 587-8; 1997, 296-7.
10. In central Saurashtra.
11. I.e. before 1973, when we met.
12. Tambs-Lyche 1992: 560-1; Dave 1967.
13. In 1973-4.
14. The centre of the old sect, in Charottar on the mainland.
15. We might refer to Warner's teamwork on Yankee City, which led to a series of monographs.
16. Such a subjective viewpoint is of course implied by the term 'analysis'.
17. Lévi-Strauss, in effect, dealt with this problem as early as in 1952, stressing that the structures he writes about exist in the mind of the writer, and not in the object itself (1958, 305).
18. A distinction which Barth has made clearly (1966): epistemologically, his 'models of social organization' are, like Lévi-Strauss' structures, products of the researcher's mind.
19. Notably the loose Koli category (Shah in Shah and Desai 1988, see also Tambs-Lyche 1997: 128-32), but also, it seems the large category of pastoralists variously called Ahir, Gujar or Goala (1997: 151).
20. I prefer Nadel's term to 'structuration' (Giddens 1986) or Strathern's 'sociation' (e.g. 1996:64), though there are parallels between the terms. 'Structuring' has the advantage over Strathern's term, of covering the ordering of thought as well as social life, while Giddens, too, refers mainly to the latter.

CHAPTER 8

Decontextualizing the Person: *Jangal*, Fields and Roads

The valleys crack and burn, the exhausted plains
Sink their black teeth into the thorny veins
Straggling the hills' red thighs, the bleating goats
—Dry bents and bitter thistles in their throats—
Thread the loose rocks by immemorial tracks.
Dark peasants drag the sun upon their backs.

ALUN LEWIS

PERCEPTION OF LANDSCAPE

Towns and temples, palaces and public works, all products of culture, stand witness to the past. But what about the landscape, most 'natural' of our surroundings? The answer is that the category of landscape is itself a product of history: landscapes are cultural, not natural, phenomena.

In the Rajput school of painting—the most relevant in the context of Saurashtra, perspective and the sense of distance is generally lacking. Nature is a backdrop, not a subject in itself. True, the sky and weather figure as a seasonal thematic; but there is a difference, for this aspect of painting is tied to conventions which link the seasons, like the *ragas*, to states of mind. Much the same can be said for Indian poetry. By Western, and certainly by Norwegian, standards, nature poetry is conspicuously absent. It is dangerous to generalize from art to cultural attitudes; but it seems safe to note the absence, in Saurashtra, of that celebration of landscape *per se*, that love of nature as an aesthetic category, that we find in modern Europe.

JANGAL

Much of what a European would see as nature would, in Saurashtra, be included in the term *jangal*. Here, as elsewhere in India, *jangal* does not refer to lush and thick forest (Zimmermann 1982: 8-9). The stress is on wilderness of any kind, as opposed to community and civilization. *Grama* and *aranya* were the Sanskrit terms for this opposition (Malamoud 1976, Heesterman 1985: 18), and the contrast is still fundamental to any description of settings for social life in India.

In Saurashtra, the *jangal* is usually dry, grey to brown, with few trees and a lack of shade and shelter. Meghani (1929) describes a world, before modern roads, where people travelled across open country, for business, visits, or any other purpose. Present-day travellers follow the roads, and often use public transport, entering another set of scenes which I describe later. In the 1970s one might still see Rajputs or Kathis travelling cross-country by horse; but even then, riding was mostly a sport and travel by horse was unusual. As even those who walk prefer the roads, the travellers of the *jangal* have diminished radically, and the wilderness has become wilder.

Large tracts of open country are left to the pastoralists, who use them thoroughly, roaming freely between villages. The herdsman and his flock are seldom far off. The proportion of shepherds to the total population is quite high in some parts of Saurashtra; and the number of goats—who will eat anything, given a chance—is constantly increasing. Yet I never heard of disputes about grazing rights in open country, in spite of evident overgrazing. Sometimes, herdsmen build temporary dwellings in the wilderness, and there are hamlets inhabited entirely by them, quite different from agricultural villages.

In a sense the wilderness belongs to the pastoralists. For others, '*jangal*' implies danger: one never goes there alone. To do so, implies some unlawful or dubious business. Similarly, thieves and 'bad people' are said to inhabit the open land. For most people, then, the *jangal* is not part of the social world but an antedote to it. We might expect references to *bhuts* (spirits) or other supernatural beings, but I heard few such remarks, nor does one talk much about wild animals, and in fact little game is left. It is people, outsiders to 'society', who represent danger, and pastoralists are seen as strange, outlandish and fraught with mystical power. Thus villagers talk of the Bharwads pastoralists as *bhuts*, and Enthoven comments:

> The Bharvads do not quarrel with the name. We are Bhuts, they say. If a villager is asked why are Bharvads Bhuts, he answers: they are so stupid. Their wildness, their sudden and weird appearance among their sheep, a small heap of blankets rising into a huge figure, give point to the nickname. Their fitfulness is also uncanny, suddenly bursting from stolid dullness to frantic rushings and the oddest shouts, yells and calls. . . . (1920: 119-20)

Westphal-Hellbosch adds: 'As a wanderer in the desert a Bharwad is conversant with the "Bhuts", the terrible spirits of the wilderness, or is himself a Bhut. This conception the Bharwad takes quite lightly or even accepts' (1976 : 13).

The mystification of the pastoralists is even clearer in the case of the Rabaris, traditionally camel herders, who used to roam more widely and have less to do with villagers. Finally, the pastoral origins of the Charan—whose men became bards and genealogists, while the goddesses of the region are recruited from their women—certainly form part of the aura that surrounds this very special community. Bharwads and Rabaris, whose women never became goddesses, tend to have their own female deities, and these are sometimes inaccessible to members of other castes. My efforts at seeing the image of Momai Mata, the 'dumb' goddess of the Rabaris (Westphal-Hellbosch 1974: 160-9), never succeeded; she is said to be black. This goddess has special powers; according to Trivedi, the Mer agriculturalists of Porbandar district appeal to the Rabaris to intervene with her to produce rain. The Mers also light their *holi* when they see the smoke of Rabari fires, since the herdsmen are seen as closer to the relevant powers (Trivedi 1961: 19-20).[1] Krishna, the cultural hero of the pastoral communities, was black, like the dark goddesses. His position as an outsider, as a 'tribal' facing civilization, is important to the discourse concerning him; this is why he is rejected at first from the assembly of kings, in a well-known episode of the *Mahabharata* (Rajagopalachari 1973: 100-1).

The pastoralists are outsiders since they are associated with the *jangal*. A pun is made on the terms Bharwad and Rabari, as both caste names are given folk etymologies derived from the word *bahar* or 'outside'. The effect is to construe the pastoralists as savages, not to civilize the landscape. This stress on the boundary of nucleated settlements emphasizes the lack of a truly 'rural' atmosphere in Saurashtrian villages—if 'rural' is taken, as it often is in Europe, to indicate a degree of intimacy with 'nature'. There are no peasant homesteads in the fields: in Saurashtra, all agriculturalists live inside the hamlet or village. The forces feared when venturing into the *jangal* are not 'natural' as standing above and beyond society; they are rather anti-social, in that they represent the dark side of the social experience.

The Indian *jangal* was not always natural. Well before the Christian era, Kautilya advised rulers to dig hidden trenches and plant thorny shrubs as a defence around their camps (1998: 82), and this advice was probably followed. Rulers in Saurashtra often left wilderness as a screen against neighbouring chiefs (Le Grand Jacob 1872: 121). Even impregnable Junagadh was protected by *jangal*, as Tod found in 1822 (1971: 361).

The king was the upholder of Dharma, so without a king, how could there be a Dharmic state? The *jangal* is home to powers that Dharmic kings do not control, and temples of the uncontrolled, 'fierce' goddesses are situated in the *jangal*. Often, too, a fierce goddess is posted at the village or city gate, as is Bhadrakali in Ahmedabad.[2] In such a world, are needed goddesses to guard against intrusions at town and city walls, where the fields end and wilderness begins, at the seashore, and, indeed, on hills overlooking the landscape. Beck (1970) notes similar sites for such temples in Konkunad. In Saurashtra, some of the older goddesses have their temples on mountain peaks; Jagdamba at Girnar, Chamunda at Sayla. I have described such a hilltop temple above. The original temple to Khodiyar stood on a smaller rock, but overlooking the river Shetrunji.

If modern Norwegians see nature as good, and abhor its purity being invaded by dams, power lines or other signs of civilization, this attitude is but a lasting effect of nineteenth-century romanticism. Earlier Norwegians, like modern Saurashtrians, saw the wilderness as inhabited by anti-social or anti-cultural forces. In this view, the graduality of post-romantic landscape painting makes no sense; there is a sharp dividing-line between civilization and wilderness. Indeed, Norwegian stave churches were guarded by 'dragons' facing the wilderness to chase away roaming spirits.

In Saurashtra, where civilization ends there is at once the *jangal*, opposed to the social, civilized and human world, and home to powers that rule where man's domain ends. It is beyond the limits of safety for a villager or a townsman; one crosses such land in the safe company of others. It is the realm of the pastoralist, but this is what makes the Bharwad shepherd a *bhut*.

Referring to Norway again, one is conscious there of a strong element of nature pantheism: God is present in nature, and this view relates to the concept of the individual, whose very essence is to be found in nature, too. Norwegians seek the wilderness to find themselves, and escape the disturbing influence of others. To them nature is sacred, while society is profane. Things are very different in Saurashtra. The wilderness is the abode of sacred beings characterized as malevolent or anti-social. Man belongs to civilization, but the civilized and the wild each have their representatives in the divine world. Neither society nor wilderness are profane.

The Norwegian example—which may find its closest parallel in parts of American tradition—is an extreme case; in most of continental Europe the idea of nature as sacred is less salient. Yet the abstraction of man into nature is a radical element in the Western conception of the individual. With that idea, society becomes profane: and this is exactly what the Indian social order is not. For Hobbes, society follows natural laws; morals are a product of society and not a prerequisite for social life. The concept of Dharma as represented by Indian tradition is, certainly, far removed from the Hobbesian social universe.

One night at the banks of the old reservoir of Bhavnagar, with a friend I watched the rains arrive, lightning crossing the dark sky, several at once. I do not doubt the awe he felt, faced with this superb natural spectacle, was the same as mine. His appreciation may have been coloured by centuries of cultural sentiment concerning the rains, which I was only beginning to appreciate. Yet, I hold, it was the natural spectacle and not our culturally coded appreciations of it that brought us together. Similarly, I remember watching the stars with another friend as we camped overnight in a school yard, somewhere in north Gujarat. Here, I noted the difference, in the constellation of stars, from my home skies. Yet, and in spite of the astrological knowledge common to Indians and lacking in my own background, our appreciation of the clear, star-studded sky seemed of an identical nature.

Our reactions to decontextualized nature, then, are the same. The reader may find such remarks trite. Do we not know that humans are similar regardless of culture? Yet such reminders are, I think, needed. We must not forget that the Western concept of the individual is as constructed and (in an epistemological sense) arbitrary as Indian conceptions of a more organic and integrated world. No object, not even thunderstorms or stars, transcend such representations; only subjects can do so. Yet it is only in the confrontation with an object that the subject is conscious of itself.[3] While such objects are perceived through a filter of cultural representation, and the subject's view of itself[4] is a similar construct, the confrontation as such is transcultural: the experience of culturally coded objects as well as those which are at the margins of such coding, is universal. Of stars or thunderstorms, the awe I recognize in my friend, is the same kind of awe I feel myself, even if coded differently.

What is particular about our Western concept of the individual is that it is decontextualized, abstracted from its social parameters. So too the concept of nature. And, considering the social and cultural parameters of Indian landscape painting, ought we not to see a link with the equally contextualized concept of the person in India?

At any rate, stars, skies and *jangal* share the quality of being timeless. Unlike the cultural objects I have described earlier—temples, palaces, towns—they are not productive of specific, social identities. They are not the past in the present. If tradition, visible and tangible through experience of such objects, divides Saurashtrians from each other and Indians from Westerners, a thunderstorm or starry sky unites. One relates to the contextualized person, the other to the decontextualized individual.

In Saurashtra, society and wilderness are part of a single world, penetrated by sacred forces: yet within this universe, *jangal* and village represent opposite poles. The whole of this world is of a moral, and therefore religious nature; it is inhabited by gods, men, and demons, and the difference between these classes of beings is one of degree, rather than of radical oppositions.[5] Man is somewhere between gods and demons, and partakes of the character of both. The whole is produced and maintained by Gods and humans together: the *jangal* may be as man-made as the village, and human agency is not materially distinct from divine agency, though Gods rule men.

What does all this tell us about the conception of the individual in India? Certainly, the individual is not the generalized natural state of man, product of Western reflections. The Indian concept is differently mediated, in relation to a cosmology including different kinds of beings, demons, men and gods. But as subjects, we must all relate to these different conceptions, which are part of ourselves and also something beyond the subject. The process of constructing the distance between the subject and such conceptions must be essentially similar, and it is this process that we, as anthropologists, stand a better chance than most to recognize. Watching stars or thunderstorms with Indian friends, I get closer to this process, than in discussing social and cultural matters. In the latter case, we both construct an opposition, not between the I and an outside object, but between the culturally constructed me and other constructions.

THE INDIVIDUAL

If individualism is seen as typical of Western society, there is a tendency to assume the opposite for India. Though Dumont admits the presence of the individual agent, he has consistently stressed the absence of the concept of the individual from caste society (1965; 1966a: 22). In India the anthropologist is faced with a strange dilemma, for at the level of common sense, I and I suppose others do experience Indians as individuals, much in the same way that we meet and interact with individuals at home.

Most anthropological debate on individualism refers to emic constructions of the individual in each culture. Yet, while people may well act on patterns present in their mind, we must not confound models for action with concepts identified, described and discussed in other contexts. The great ideas of intellectual history, such as individualism, are addressed to an explicit theoretical discourse—they are not necessarily templates for action. We run the risk, then, of talking literary history rather than describing social life.

The assumption that Western individualism may serve as a basis for evaluating the emergence of the individual elsewhere, seems to me a false start. Rather, we must build a comparative framework for individualisms, taking into account alternative constructs of the individual. Is there a recognizable way, in South Asia, of thinking about the individual which is different from the Western one? If so, what are its modes and stages of development?

I assume behaviour to be individualist when the actor tries to define an identity different from persons of his or her own class and caste: differences between these categories are not individualist. This precision is important. I speak of individualism whenever we can discern an image of the 'me' as a culturally defined unit, singular as being distinct from all others, and a logical break where the dynamics of the me change into other dynamics. The processes that form the individual must be distinct from those that constitute the person or the role. The 'me' must be distinct from the interface between the 'I' and society. In other words, individualism exists wherever an ethnopsychology may be defined in opposition to an ethnosociology. I try expressly not to delimit, in advance, the appropriate dynamics that may constitute such an image of the me.

IS THERE AN INDIAN BRAND OF INDIVIDUALISM?

I met several persons in Saurashtra who struck me as singular individuals. Why did they make that impression? I shall try to show that on the level of common sense, the supposition of a qualitative difference between Indian and European individuals does not hold. Though perhaps obvious, this needs to be said. I shall then try to deduce the kind of factors which produce singularity in each case. The analysis will be couched in terms of symbolic interactionism, building on the concepts of Mead, Goffman and Barth.

All societies must deal with the fact that individual human beings act and think individually. What is seen to characterize the Western idea of the individual, as distinct from views current elsewhere, is the abstraction of an unmarked individual essence, independent of social context. But concretely speaking, people are born into particular positions in any society, and what we call identity takes this position into account. The concrete individual is always situated or contextualized. This is true whether the position remains a constant or changes in the person's life or changes, and whether this change follows an ascribed itinerary or results from choice.

For Dumont, a person can become an individual, in traditional India, only by opting out of society, becoming a renouncer (1966a: 235-7). But in what sense can we say that the renouncer is outside society? He is occupying a well-defined role, even if it is defined by its lack of social ties. Indeed, the boundaries of society implied by Dumont are as much part of a particular, constructed image of it as are the relations within it.

The Western concept of the individual does not mean that there are no ties,[6] but these are constructed; they are not natural. Decontextualization from social life, here, becomes more real than the social, since it refers to human nature. Conversely, in caste society, social ties are seen as natural.[7] The individual represented by the renouncer is not, then, constructed at the same epistomological level as the Western concept of the individual. It is a social role defined by negation of social ties. In filling it the renouncer is an empirically observable person, not so the Western individual, who only exists in abstraction: like caste, his naturalness is constructed. We may see the effects of such constructions reflected in social life, but, like force in mechanics, we assume its existence from its effects: we see individualists, not individuals. The concrete Western person, then, is situated in society but entertains an ideology abstracting his self from the world.

We may compare the Western and Indian histories of such ideologies, though what we are then doing is literary history, not anthropology. This is what Dumont does—substituting the functional equivalent of the individual in caste society (1966b), which for him is largely represented by caste. It is on this level, too, that Marriott locates his dividual (1976), stressing that the person, in India, is less an integrated and bounded unit than a point through which a number of processes pass, underlining the continuity with, rather than the limits towards, the wider social world.

A great deal of thought has been given to this search for a construct corresponding to our idea of the individual on the level of Indian thought. But there is indeed such a counterpart, centring on the *atman*, the individual but decontextualized soul. It is this tradition of thought which made Basham (1954) feel that India was the first civilization to speculate seriously about the individual. To deal with at least two thousand years of such speculation, as diverse as it is complex, is clearly beyond my means here. Let me just recall the *Bhagavad Gita* doctrine of action with detachment, inciting the individual to distance himself from the demands of society. What is advocated is not withdrawal from the world—Krishna explicitly enjoins Arjuna to do his duty. Instead, the individual is enjoined to stand back and dissociate the ultimate reality of his self from the contextualized person that social life requires him to be. I do not see how one can deny that this is a theory of the individual, though it differs from the Western one.

BETWEEN CULTURE AND WILDERNESS: THE FIELDS

Let us return to the landscape, to the fertile soils tilled by man. In parts of the peninsula, say around Jamnagar, Junagadh and Bhavnagar, the fields of one village merge with those of its neighbours, forming large, fertile plains. In the centre of the peninsula, fields form scattered patches of arable between low, stony ridges. Yet as scenes for social interaction, fields are everywhere similar. They belong to man, but remain outside community: they are neither wilderness nor village but where these opposites meet.

Though fields are individual property, there is no fencing between or around them. Nor does one try to keep traffic from skirting fields or even crossing them when this does not hurt the crop. The subdivision of each farmer's lands into small plots necessitates much coming and going, while no signs mark the entry into private space. Yet fields are not unprotected. In Praj several farmers guard their crops at night, a male member of the household sleeping in the fields. One family used an old muzzle-loading pistol for the purpose. Those held to be thieves are the poor of the village or surrounding settlements, but also the pastoralists. There have been, and in some places still are, organized gangs to keep their animals off the fields. Yet it is equally common to invite shepherds to graze their flocks on the land to obtain manure, a service for which the herdsmen may even be paid. The varied relations to pastoralists are closely related to the timing of crops and pastoral migrations.

Thus one does not roam the fields at night with honest intentions. Such visits are for illicit purposes; to steal from the crops or engage in illicit love affairs. In the latter case, while none may see what goes on in the field, there is always the risk of being observed on the way there. This is a recurring theme in poetry and song: a girl is seen walking towards the fields, ostensibly carrying food or some other item, while the implicit sense is that a secret lover is waiting for her.

The fields are reached by causeways, paths that have not been ploughed and which rise a few inches above the soil. Their narrowness makes it impossible for two people to pass each other, unless one of them steps down in the field. Such meetings follow the norms of precedence: the person of lower rank steps aside to let the other pass. Brawls may result if these rules are violated, or when both claim precedence. The causeways may be used by anybody, so the fields are not private settings. But in the open landscape, intruders are seen at a distance, so it is still possible to be alone in the fields—which is difficult in the village.

Farmers are proud of their fields, as a central source of identity. In the old days, Rajput men tended to avoid manual labour, coming mainly to inspect the work. Since the land reforms of the 1950s, many Rajputs work the fields themselves. Farmers continually watch and judge each other's performance. Though landholding is linked to caste, a man's achievements as a farmer are his own, and while some castes are judged better farmers, the real test is always the individual's performance. This means the owner or tenant: labourers are not identified with the fields they work. Thus neighbours may respect each other as farmers, regardless of caste or caste politics. This judgement of individuals is a major constituent of the friendly groups that meet in the fields.

Visitors are a welcome diversion from work, and since one may accept hospitality in the field which, from rank or other considerations, would be refused in the village, the fields offer an opportunity to meet those you normally would keep at a certain distance. If the visitor is not an important person, however, one may just greet him while continuing work, perhaps stopping for a moment to talk. Farmers put up small huts of branches and bamboo mats to make their nights in the fields comfortable, and today these are supplemented by brick-built sheds housing the diesel pumps. By day both are used to shelter from the sun. For privacy one turns to such shacks and pump-houses, and visitors are received there: they usually contain facilities for making and serving tea. The midday meal is often taken in the field, and the hut and its precincts serves this purpose, too.

Invitation to a proper house implies, as a matter of duty, that the guest should be served food. At the very least, tea is offered. This raises the question of caste restrictions. While there are ways to avoid the kinds of food most critical in terms of pollution—generally cooked food—(Marriott 1968), rank differences must always be taken into account. In his house the host always ranks above the guest, which means that many invitations have to be refused. Offering a cup of tea is, in this respect, more neutral, and since it is difficult to offer anything else in the fields, nobody is offended. But the place also makes a difference. Nobody else may be present, but even if the visit is known, it is treated as less important, perhaps since nobody has to know what is going on in the fields. If status differences are ignored in the field, it does not constitute an open violation of the norm, as would be in the village setting.

The hut in the fields is very much a home from home and one does not enter anybody else's hut or pump-shed unless he is there. Hospitality is legion, but women are absent—female labourers do not take part directly in receiving their landlord's guest.[8] Men enjoy their rest, chat and drink tea, so the hut offers an informal and unobserved venue conveniently away from the family house or village street. Here, caste restrictions may be relaxed or observed lightly, so it is an obvious venue for any meeting, say, of a political nature, that one does not want others to observe.

Women of high caste visit the fields only to take food to their men, and prefer, when possible, to send a servant or a child. This is one of the ways in which purdah is observed. Lower-caste women are present as an important part of the workforce, and as wives working alongside their men. Female labourers are sometimes involved sexually with their employers—at least the allegation is extremely common.[9] These affairs are not seen as romantic, but rather as sexual services bought or obtained by coercion; the relations take place during work hours. But the fields are also the venue for lovers, who are assumed to meet by night, as an imagined escape from marriage and family life, seen as humdrum and unromantic.

The associaton of fields with illicit love and easy-going sociability indicates how they are perceived as a social scene. They remain outside the social controls of the village community. Situated between culture and wilderness, they are a place of work and of earning one's livelihood, but also a venue of relative freedom and relaxation. Thus the fields are where the villager can go simply for a walk. Adults seldom do, however, since people may assign some ulterior motive to such trips. Rather, a visit is legitimated by some practical purpose—to look after the water supply, to see how the crops are getting on. Young boys, however, roam the fields for pleasure, taking care—unless they want to be brave—to stay within the limits of the village's cultivated area. The fields are hence an important setting for social life. They constitute an in-between situation, neither public nor entirely private, and offer an escape from family, home, and crowded village streets. The company of males in the field takes on the informal nature of a group of friends. In this respect it parallels the club.

In the fields the individual is free to a degree, from his social position. The informal nature of conversation underlines the point, and marital problems may be discussed.

ON THE ROAD

Since the *jangal* is seen as dangerous, people use the roads to go from one place to another. Roads in Saurashtra carry a most diverse traffic, for people travel a lot. Buses, which ply between most large villages and all towns, are used by all kinds of people and are usually full. All belong to a public undertaking.[10] Tending to be the fastest-running, largest and heaviest units on the road, they dominate other traffic: almost every other kind of vehicle gives way to them as a matter of course. Trucks licensed to carry goods for others also share in passenger transport on an unofficial basis. They are cheaper than the buses and serve, to some extent, a different clientele. Lorries serving a single company—private carriers—are scarce, but there are always the 'tempos'. A Tempo, in India, is a small truck or sometimes a minibus.[11] Unlike public carriers, who are often run on a long-time charter basis, tempos are usually hired for the task or the day. One goes to the tempo-stand to hire one, as for a taxi. Taxis, though used for inter-urban transport by well-to-do people, are seldom seen outside towns. The limited use of shared taxis[12] indicates the success of the State bus company.

Private cars were scarce in 1974.[13] They are more common now, but remain the privilege of a minority. Many cars belong to government agencies or large companies. The identity of their occupants is often masked by curtains. Government jeeps are the only vehicles which challenge buses to give way.

Motor cycles and scooters were popular in towns by 1974, but seldom seen on country roads. Almost nobody, in the villages, had a bike then. This has changed completely now, but certain groups use two-wheelers more than others.[14] The pastoralist rider has become quite a figure on Saurashtra's roads, for he uses his bike a lot, and likes to be seen on it. Customized Jawas with a lot of extras, practical or ornamental, often belong to Bharwads, who tend to monopolize the milk trade wherever the government dairies do not. They make good money these days, as their bikes show.

Even bicycles were a mark of some status in 1973-4. This is hardly true any more, but they are ever-present, and used for all kinds of transport. In the 1970s bicycles carried milk for the market; this is seldom seen now.

Oxcarts, though still present in number, are less important for road transport now. When they carry people between villages, the occasion is often a marriage or some festival, and the animal and cart are decorated accordingly. A class of transport peculiar to Gujarat is the camel-drawn cart, faster than the oxcart but used mainly in and around towns. They used to be a caste monopoly of the Ravals. It seems they are losing ground now, for less camel carts are seen than before. Tractors were very scarce in 1974. Now they are common, and even used for festive occasions, where tractor and trailer may replace the oxcart. Still, tractors are not as common in Saurashtra as they are in the Punjab; farms are smaller and lands more scattered, and I would think access to the land is a major problem here.[15]

Finally, there are always a number of people who walk. Among them are Sadhus, who, though seen on buses and trains, still seem to stick to this mode of transport. Beggars, on the other hand, prefer trains,[16] and are seldom seen on the road. Then, alongside rather than on the road, there are the groups of pastoralists, according to season. There are small groups of poor people, travelling between villages.

Roads are frequented day and night. Trucks often go by night in the hot season. Long-distance buses run overnight routes. In the small hours of the morning, farmers and milkmen go to market.

There is a fairly well-defined rank order on the road. Buses dominate, challenged only by government jeeps. Everybody else gives way to these two. Trucks are next, followed by private cars, taxis and tempos. Motor bikes, cycles and pedestrians follow in descending order. There is not much social intercourse between the different categories of traffic, except the use of horn by the stronger. Within each category, there is a certain cameraderie; bus drivers greet each other, truck drivers sometimes help each other, as do motor cyclists. Yet the traffic seems too diverse, too divided by rank, to form a travellers' community. Indeed, the road may be a dangerous place, and is thought of as such.

Strangers must be careful in Saurashtra, informants said, because the people of the region are known for their violent temper. I came to respect this statement. I have seen a few accidents, and it seems common for car or lorry drivers to continue on their way if possible, even if somebody is hurt. This is partly because bystanders can get very excited when an accident has taken place, and one does not expect a chance to argue the case rationally.[17] Such incidents may not be typical, but are common enough for people to regard the road as a scene of danger, violence and fear. On the road people are strangers, and one must be careful to stay out of trouble.

Thus the road is a scene where the strong prevail, where one feels alone and vulnerable. One defers to superiors, hoots at inferiors, and looks for equals in need of alliance. The fellow who has trouble here may be the one who'll give you a hand further on.[18] Such acquaintances are valuable sice others cannot be trusted. As I received help from other motor cyclists, I noted how drivers liked to keep company with equals. 'Racing' another bike by passing and being passed established a relation where, one hoped, the other might stop and offer help if one got into trouble.[19]

In this situation, there are two possible ways of gaining security. One is the temporary alliance with equals that my motorcycling experience taught me to seek. Another is to be seen as somebody with a certain power and influence. The rank order is largely indicated by who gives way to whom; rank, here, is not a matter of traditional values but of everyday importance. The officer in the government jeep is a powerful individual, the kind of person who might make a bus driver lose his job. The strength of buses is backed by the Gujarat State Road Transport Company, a powerful organization, whose drivers have a strong union. This differs from trucks, owned mostly by small proprietors, whose drivers are seldom unionized. Truck drivers fear inspections and harassment by police, octroi (internal customs), and other officials, while buses are usually waved by.

Going down, the size and speed of vehicles remain the main factors in defining rank. Government jeeps are an exception, since people fear the official inside. Faced with insecurity, conflict, and the absence of efficient and peaceful means of conflict resolution, safety lies in avoiding conflict, by recognizing and respecting power on the road. The fact that roads were lawless and insecure in Saurashtra well before modern times underlines the point. The ranking on the road is a direct function of power.

When looking at public transport, we shall see how this order is maintained even where the lawlessness of the road is replaced by a kind of competition within rules.

NOTES

1. Pocock (1972) notes a similar relation between pastoralists and villagers for central Gujarat.
2. Or, indeed, the 'guardian goddesses' of Madurai (van den Hoek 1975).
3. As Mead would have it, the 'me' is a social construct, which results from interaction with others.
4. In becoming the 'me'.

5. This is what Wadley (1975) maintains when she talks of them all as 'powerful beings'.
6. As Brøgger insists: 'It is society that gives structure to the human repertory of emotions and that moulds and refines them into various shapes and qualities' (1993: 3).
7. The most common Hindu term used for caste—*jati*—also designates the natural species.
8. They may help in making tea, for example, but it is the host who will serve it.
9. Ghaddavi (n.d.) writing of central Saurashtra, stresses the coercive aspect. Singhji (1994) feels that low-caste women are not always averse to such liaisons, which may develop into regular relationships.
10. The Gujarat State Road Transport Company.
11. Originally three-wheelers of German design made in India, the term now stands for all kinds of light commercial vehicles.
12. A common practice in other parts of India. In Saurashtra, this is done mainly on special occasions by very rank-conscious people.
13. In 1973-4 any private car had high status; only Ambassadors and Fiats were seen in any numbers. Today the diversity is greater, Contessas and the newer Premier form the elite, with Marutis being small but chic; still, state agencies and companies often use Ambassadors.
14. Thus pastoralists use Jawas or Rajdoots to take their milk to market. These old-fashioned but sturdy bikes are popular with farmers too, while townsmen prefer the Indo-Japanese bikes, lighter and more economical. Above all, townsmen have scooters, and the two-wheeler has become the accepted means of transport for all those who can afford it. Even sweepers, in Rajkot, now make their tours on old mopeds, brooms and brushes sticking out from the back. One avoids rubbing against them.
15. It is difficult to move the tractor across other people's land, and labour is cheaper, too, than in Punjab.
16. Here they have a captive 'audience', and trains like beggars serve towns and larger villages.
17. I remember a taxi ride, passing the scene of an accident. Another taxi had run down a pedestrian. The car and its driver were surrounded by angry crowds. A little further on, another crowd, evidently mistaking our taxi for the other, shouted invectives and tried to make us stop. Shouting his explanation through the open window our driver pressed on and got away. In Bhavnagar I watched a collision between a Fiat and a truck, meeting in a narrow passage. Misjudging the situation, the truck pulled away too soon, denting the Fiat's rear wing. The Fiat driver—who did not seem to be its owner, and clearly nervous of his charge—emerged furious, swinging an iron bar two feet long. He rushed to the cab of the truck, opening the door. This was a bad move, for three men riding on the truck's platform retaliated by jumping onto the Fiat's roof—giving it a markedly convex shape. The threatening truck driver had meanwhile scared

the Fiat driver, who jumped into his battle-scarred car and drove a few metres away. The two parties shouted at each other for some time; after some heated discussion with the crowd, both drove off. No police intervened or were, indeed, called in.

As passenger in a bus, I once saw a peasant, slightly injured after an accident with his oxcart, begging us to stop and help. Some passengers laughed, and the bus went on.

18. While riding my motorcycle in the early 1990s, I was struck by the riders who stopped to help. But they were riders of similar bikes—Jawa or Rajdoot—as if a similarity in our condition was implied by our mounts. The riders of Indo-Japanese bikes, or the more prestigious Enfields, simply went by.
19. I should note, however, what happened as my wife and I returned from the Gir forest for the night. The light on my bike failed, but an Ambassador car joined us and lighted up the road for us, all of twenty kilometers back to Junagadh. I see this as a special case of being nice to us as foreigners, however.

CHAPTER 9

The Individual's Burden

> The other terror that scares us from self-trust is our consistency;
> a reverence for our past act or word, because the eyes of others have no other data
> for computing our orbit than our past acts,
> and we are loath to disappoint them.
>
> RALPH WALDO EMERSON

THE SELF IN THE EYES OF OTHERS

When a Westerner is enjoined to realize himself—or herself—it is I think understood that he must do so through action. It is action that makes the individual singular. The view of the *Bhagavad Gita* is quite different: action is socially determined and what one realizes thereby can only be well or badly done: though the person may make his imprint on action, the actions can never become the person.

But this is exactly what we, as Westerners, believe. Or is it? The consistency that Emerson refers to, in the epigraph above, can be implied only in signs shown through behaviour. 'But why should you keep your head over your shoulder?', asks Emerson next, implying that, in our image of the self, it is this very consistency that we must question. 'Suppose you should contradict yourself; what then?' (Emerson 1907: 49). Emerson, it is true, was influenced by contemporary orientalism.

Mead's theory of the self implies extrapolating social process to include the individual: it may be seen as a reaction against an overwhelming reification of the individual in our culture. The *Bhagavad Gita* seems to take sociological determinism, more akin to Durkheim, for granted, but excludes the self from it by insisting on the capacity to view social action from the outside, at a distance. Mead contextualizes a decontextualized construction of the individual: the author of the *Bhagavad Gita* does exactly the opposite. The difference here is the link between self and action, implied by the two strains of thought. The *Bhagavad Gita* distends the link, while Western individualism shortens it. So does Mead. But we are clearly talking of different approaches to a common, human problem, so that the question of reserving the term 'indiviual' for the West or using it as common denominator for the problematic, becomes a secondary matter.

FAMILY AND CASTE AS CATEGORIES OF REFERENCE

This brings us to the categories by which people are identified in the scenes I describe. Nobody, of course, belongs to a category—one may belong only to a group. Group membership as such is invisible, and we identify it only by ascription to a category, which people themselves produce, or that we ascribe to them.

Catcgories, then, are the stuff of which individuals build their image of themselves as against others. The individual's agency stands between the self and any set of categories that society may impose. Mead must have read Emerson: every educated American did at the time, and Emerson expressed some of the fundamental reflections concerning the self that led to symbolic interactionism as we know it. These are central streams of thought when we, as Westerners, reflect on the individual. To me, the key to the Western concept of the individual is precisely the consistency Emerson talks about, which 'terror' haunts the Western individual to a greater extent than his Indian counterpart. For, going from one situation to another, Indians sometimes seem to me, and I believe to other Westerners, to contradict themselves. Emerson's 'Why', directed at the Western individual, may already have been answered by his Indian counterpart.

To exemplify this point, I shall start from 'the son's burden'. The son, in the Indian context, is very much the future representative of the family, so he should act consistently with the family image, a demand the individual son is acutely conscious of. The importance of the family in the individual's life is obvious. Family life, of course, varies a great deal as between castes and classes, and while I knew a good number of middle-class families of various castes, I did no intensive study of family or household organization. Yet some general observations can be made.

The insecurity of public life in Saurashtra has as its counterpoint the security of family and kinship. It is here that the individual forms his basic identity and finds his most reliable allies in the struggle that life can be. Danger is not, here, a matter of fantasy. As an example, take the marriage of Manubhai's cousin. Manubhai, you may remember, is the Lohana who keeps a radio and cassette shop in one of Saurashtra's cities. I was present one evening of the cousin's wedding, as they were preparing for the groom to set off for the bride's village. We were supposed to return the next day. But then, Manubhai told me, I had better stay away. A rival of the groom had spread the rumour that he would join the party with his friends, and that he would be bringing a gun. 'There may be trouble', said Manubhai. 'You see, the other family also wanted the same girl'. Thus, conflict still involves families, and allies are defined in terms of kin. Safety lies in the unity of kinsmen.

But this opposition between inside and outside, between security and perceived danger, implies that the loyalties inherent in family and kinship take on an absolute character. The demands made upon the individual by his family are clearly more acute than in many other societies. While the family may be more resistant to outside pressures in India than in the West, the individual is also under greater pressure from his family. There is indeed a dialectic here, between the burden the young man must bear, as he takes on the task of representing the family, and the dream, commonly found, of escaping into renouncement, or, at least, into the semi-retirement of *brahmacharya* (Tambs-Lyche 1995).

These links may be partly responsible for what Dumont (1966a) views as absence of the individual in Indian society (Tambs-Lyche 1980, 1993). The family offers the individual a solid anchor for his identity. To function thus, it cannot be just a means of classification. It must have some important content. Inden, in his study of Bengali kinship (1976), contributes to our understanding of that elusive 'estate'[1] which constitutes the 'content' of patrilineal continuity, persisting where possessions and inheritance do not. Such substance[2] may be seen as the content to which family refers. It is the son who, in particular, is responsible for maintaining this substance, and so we shall see how young men of several castes, and mainly from the middle classes, cope with their lot.

Pressure comes not only from the internal organization of the family, but from the necessity, in a competitive and insecure situation, of sticking together to maintain or improve the family's standing. Indeed a main theme of conversation between men (and, I think, women) in informal and relatively egalitarian situations, is how to cope with family roles. Often, the pronoun we is used, referring to the extended family or caste, (the two merge almost imperceptibly into each other). For Westerners, this identification with the collective 'we' may seem a matter of the past, placing the family in a quasi-historical perspective. To grasp the specificity of the family in India, however, we must place it in the context of similar referential categories.

With the family, we enter a set of categories whose properties are different from, say, occupation, which may be stated in any particular situation or not. The family is a category which cannot be changed: but, when others are unknown, the family is not known either. More than any other category, the family links the individual to his caste. To deny one is to deny the other.

Family and caste link the individual into networks. In Saurashtra, two caste networks are fundamental to society: the kinship-based political network of Rajputs and the institution of the 'family firm' among Vanias (Tambs-Lyche 1997). According to Misra, the medieval Indian merchant lived within several 'distinct but interlinked worlds: the primary entity in this complex was the family—the extended joint family with its innumerable obligations—a syndrome which furnished him with one of his major life-goals'. He goes on to specify caste, faith, and the 'world of the market, the polis'. Intermediate between caste and market was the *mahajan* and the residential *pol*. Such a hierarchy of referential categories may be constructed for most complex societies, but the way in which they are linked with organizational groupings is peculiar to India.

I have noted the extension of an Ahir peasant/pastoralist network into the commercial sector. Such examples could be multiplied, for it is through its kinship-based networks that the caste emerges as an organizational unit capable of defending its own interests.[3] Thus the organization of craftsmen castes clearly show features of unionization. The relative importance of interest to identification does, however, differ considerably as between castes.

To generalize, caste offers an opportunity to extend kinship solidarity to a wider group, uniting for common interest as against other, similar groups. Caste thus forms part of the inside rather than outside, the pole of solidarity rather than competition, of *gemeinschaft* rather than *gesellschaft* in the complex set of oppositions we may use to characterize Saurashtra society. As such, caste partakes of the stress that the family imposes upon the individual, regulating the behaviour of members to a considerable extent. In most cross-caste arenas, the need to conform relates with the rank of the caste, and thence to that of the individual. One's caste must not be compromised, and a Vania wanting to eat meat or drink alcohol must be very careful as to who watches him do so. This stress on conformity may, however, produce its own denial, as individuals look for opportunities to transgress caste rules where this is not dangerous.[4] In discussing the individual, therefore, we need to pinpoint the escapes from family and caste stringency.

THE IMPORTANCE OF BEGETTING SONS

In the *shastras*, by which term most Hindus refer to their scriptural tradition, the salvation of the father's soul depends on the post-mortem rituals performed by his sons. He that has no sons goes to hell, or rather, his spirit will roam endlessly if the rituals are not performed. It is thus of the greatest importance to have sons. It is hard to say to what extent modern, middle-class fathers share this belief, but the joy at the birth of a son, and the relative indifference shown to daughters, is surely not just a matter of economic calculations. These, however, cannot be discarded, for regardless of older caste traditions,[5] the middle classes in India today expect to pay heavy dowries on the marriage of a daughter. The son, of course, will benefit from the dowry brought by his wife. Among the Vanias of Gujarat, the dowry is a major contribution to establishing the son's business. In fact, the transfer of the dowry establishes a triple alliance of family firms, between the father's, the son's, and the father-in-law's business. A marriage between merchant families, therefore, implies not just a transfer of capital but an extension of the commercial enterprise of both parties. Still, it is the bride's father who must invest in the future they will share. But, in the patrilineal idiom of north Indian kinship, it is the name of the bridegroom's family which is carried forward through time. And the pattern of the merchant castes is, in Gujarat, the most influential cultural model for the urban middle classes. Thus sons are the links who perpetuate that substance for which the patrilineal family is the reference, and this is even more true among Rajputs.

THE CASE OF INDRASINGH

Take the case of Indrasingh, described by Steed in her classic article on personality formation in Gujarat. He is a Vaghela Rajput, from the senior branch of his lineage in the village of Kasandra,[6] on the boundary between mainland Gujarat and Saurashtra. He was twenty-six years old in 1950, when Steed interviewed him. His father died when he was fifteen months old, so his mother brought him back to her parents' village. There, he was 'loved and indulged in', as a sister's son should be in the hypergamous pattern of Rajput kinship. Thus, his upbringing was different from the standard pattern, where the father is the one for whom 'the son has learned to show the greatest formal respect and obedience, and with whom the son has the strictest ties of religious duty; he is the man who, until he dies, controls the son's economic, social, and political rights, claims and privileges; he is the person whom the son is destined to replace in the patrilineal family line' (Steed 1955: 135-6). But Indrasingh's mother acted as his 'paternal village' conscience, and 'knowingly attempted to prepare Indrasingh for his future roles in Kasandra as a ruling overlord . . .' (1955: 136-7). Thus if Indrasingh has no recollection of his father, the patriline continues to dominate much of his life.

At ten he is betrothed, on the initiative of Kasandra's ruling chief, who is childless. He has chosen a girl from the lineage of his own mother.[7] Indrasingh's mother—as the boy himself—would rather have had a wife chosen by her kinsmen, but the chief must be obliged. Indrasingh is married at sixteen; within a year he develops symptoms of hysterical epilepsy. His mother accuses her daughter-in-law of sorcery, while the doctor recommends a second marriage. Following the advice, Indrasingh, at eighteen, marries a girl form his mother's village. She has two unsuccessful deliveries, and then dies. Indrasingh's mother again accuses the first wife, who is still childless, of sorcery. Indrasingh marries again, through the intermediary of his maternal relatives, but the third wife is too old to bear children.

If the reason for childlessness was not sorcery, argued Indrasingh's mother, 'it was harassment by the spirits of restless ancestors. . . . There was also the curse of an ancestral Vaghela woman which promised the ultimate extinction of all Vaghelas . . .' (1955: 140). Failing to beget a son and heir, Indrasingh and his mother propitiate the ancestors with expensive ceremonies performed by Brahmins. Indrasingh himself begins to fast and to worship intensively the Vaghela *kuldevi* Vagheshvari. Indrasingh's symptoms get worse, 'he used to vomit a lot, day and night'. The symptoms disappear as he takes to the old Rajput habit of drinking *kasumba*—opium mixed with water. While fulfilling his duties in running the estate of his lineage branch, he often isolates himsef 'in the upper story with his worshipping' (1955: 141-2).

Beyond Steed's analysis, couched in terms of culture and personality, we see the elements of a structural functionalist approach, which is in fact proffered by Indrasingh and his mother.[8] If the reason for childlessness, implying the end of the patriline, is not the sorcery of the in-married wife, the reason must be sought within the line itself. And here, too, though it is not clear from Steed's account, I suspect that the curse stems from another, in-married woman. The curse works like a *sati's*[9] recriminations, which she utters throwing herself on the pyre. The *sati* usually condemns the line responsible for the death of her husband, but she might turn her powers against her in-laws, if she has been maltreated by them. It is unlikely for a Vaghela woman to condemn her brother's lineage, unless—and there are examples of this—her husband has been killed by them. Such curses, and benedictions, accumulated by a Rajput lineage over the years, form an important part of what Inden calls its substance. So do lands conquered or lost, the deeds of heroism and cowardice that form its history. For Rajputs, such elements are as important as the accumulated links of marriage which, for Inden's Bengali Brahmins (1976), become the dominant element in the line's substance by the nineteenth century.

All this forms part of the burden transferred from father to son. It is of course an asset as well; but for the sonless Indrasingh, who, moreover, lives in a post-Independence situation where Rajputs are deprived of much of their land and power, it is a heavy load to bear. He, however, does his best to find a solution to the dilemma. Indrasingh is cultured rather than martial and differs, in many ways, from what Kasandra people expect from their Rajputs. Yet, on the level of village politics and the respect people have for him, he is successful. Though his style is influenced by the absence of a father, he has managed to become a good son. But he fails in the one, overwhelmingly important, respect of being sonless.

THE FEMININE IN INDIAN CULTURE AND PSYCHOLOGY

Indrasingh's story examplifies a trait which, perhaps more than any other, is responsible for the psychological particularities of Indian—or at least north Indian—culture. This is the role of his mother. It is true that in this particular case, the absence of the father, as well as early residence in the mother's village, may have strengthened this tendency. But the importance of the mother-image in structuring identity is general. Thus in *The Inner World*, perhaps his most closely argued and certainly most 'anthropological' work, the analyst Sudhir Kakar (1982a) devotes one chapter to the mother and another to the extended family; there is no chapter on the father.

The Indian father often has access to his child only after some time; as children are born in their maternal grandfather's house, the father may see the child only on the mother's return to him. The mother remains the main care-taker through early infancy, care usually seen as extremely loving and attentive to the child's every wish. Boys remain with the women of the house until the age of five to seven years. Toilet-training is gentle and gradual, as are other elements of socialization in the early years; the mother retains her benevolent image, for the child until he or she is confronted with responsibilities which quickly surpass those of Western children.

The nostalgia of childhood is turned towards the earliest years, relativized in the West by the memory of the period without major responsibilities that follow, the age of play—the childhood invented in the eighteenth century and culturally elaborated during the nineteenth. Only now is this notion gaining importance in India, and even then it is muted by a larger sense of responsibility to the family.

These early memories, which may be seen as a common cultural factor in the identity formation of most north Indians, is dominated by the mother image. For girls, the intimate relation to the mother remains; for boys, however, it is tinged with a latent sexuality considerably strengthened by the mother's sexual frustrations (Kakar 1982a). These partly result from arranged marriage and the low age at which girls marry—as well as the fact that marriage, much more than in the West, is marked by a break with the natal family and a high degree of submission to that of the husband.[10] Indian mothers transfer a good deal of their latent sexuality towards their sons; and this desire which the boy is unable to understand or satisfy, creates in him both a feeling of guilt and a fear of the mother-figure which is likely to colour his perception of sexuality and of women (Kakar 1982a). The vagina dentata is a recurrent theme in Indian myth, and sexuality becomes threatening to the male. It is seen as dark, mystical, absorbing, and consistent with the idea that loss of semen is loss of strength. Thus sex threatens individuality and autonomy, as well as the spirituality that, like rationality in the older West, is seen as a particularly male trait.

Perhaps—this is certainly Kakar's view—these factors explain the importance of the Goddess in Hinduism, where female deities are more numerous, widespread, and popular than male ones. This preponderance is as strong in the patrilineal, male-dominated north, as in the matrilineal areas of south India. Certainly, no theory of goddess worship as a survival from matriarchy[11] is needed to explain her present importance in Saurashtra.

THE ABSTRACTION OF FATHERHOOD

I cannot expand upon the mother image nor the cult of femininity,[12] but they are fundamental to the father-son relationship. In terms of the dominant dyads proposed by Hsu (1971), we have here the dominance of the mother-son relationship.[13] Stressing this dominance, Carstairs notes that the father is 'an aloof, seemingly unwelcoming figure. The reason for this is that a man, so long as he remains under his own father's roof, must keep up the fiction of denying that he leads an active sexual life of his own. Not to do so is to be disrespectful . . .' (1967; 67-8). A man should not show undue feeling for his wife and family in his father's presence. 'This taboo', says Carstairs, 'perpetuates in each generation the tension which exists between father and son; and it is very strong.' There are mutual obligations, but little intimacy.

Kakar says little about fatherhood, though he deals fully with the importance of the extended family. In a sense, the father figure is circumscribed by this larger category. But the father is more than a prominent member; he stands for the larger unit, and this may be the clue to the gap that separates father and son on the personal level, as well as to the force that the father figure still exerts on the symbolic level. In the joint family, the father image may be distributed among several individuals, as the father's brothers share his structural position, in several ways, towards his son. But more succinctly, symbolic fatherhood rests with the patriline, with its 'estate' (Radcliffe-Brown 1952) or 'substance' (Inden 1976) rather than with the individual father. Thus the father image depends less on the actual presence of the father than we are used to. Indrasingh is haunted by the burden of his lineage even if his father is dead. We shall see, in other examples, how this symbolic inheritance remains independent of the individual father.

BEING A SON: THE MODERN CONTEXT

When I did field-work among Patidars settled in London, I spent my first couple of months living in the boy's room of my landlord's house. This proved useful, for the boys, aged some nine and seven at the time, were excellent informants. What struck me most, however, was their acceptance of the ethos of their parents' community, which seemed little influenced by any countervailing influence from school or classmates.

The elder, called, by his parents, *Aku* or 'number one', would seem to be the model son. The younger—*Baku* or 'number two'—was, when I knew him, too fond of sweets and fun, to escape being seen as 'naughty' by his parents. His naughtiness was no worse, however, than most children. Being the younger, he was less bound to the responsibilities of the family than his elder brother. I later visited the family. Aku had become an accountant, established his own business, and was about to marry. The pride of the father in his elder son's achievements were obvious. Here, certainly, was an example of the good son. Yet his father had been the domineering kind—even if, in the last instance, his wife ran the household.

This impression of the good son remained with me, not only in London, but when I came to Saurashtra. Quite naturally for a young scholar, I spent much time with young men. To outline one's plans for education and a profession seemed to be, for them, the obvious way of introducing themselves. At the same time, a Western companion seemed to offer a means of airing questions beyond the limits of family or even local friends.

'Never tell my father', a young friend said, as he enjoyed smoking a cigarette in my company. He came from the Bhowsar or cloth-printer caste, which recently, and probably in part through their adherence to the Swaminarayana sect, has been accepted as a Vania or merchant community. Some Westernized Vanias smoke; Swaminarayanas, emphatically, do not. But my friends' liberties were limited to cigarettes and the occasional (and unavoidable) questions about Western girls and love-marriage. Otherwise, his discourse remained that of a faithful and responsible son. Still, the image of restrictive fathers, and sons longing for liberty, is strong in my memory of encounters with young men or boys. But they talked as much or more about their mothers, and, certainly, the family 'we' was an ever-present category. I was invited, time and again, to visit or spend a night with the 'family'; I was never once invited to 'my father's house'.

And yet, the loss of a father puts a heavy burden on a son, for now it is he who symbolizes the family as a social whole. I remember a young functionary, Mohan Lal, in Ahmedabad. Extremely thin, and obviously nervous, he showed me the house he shared with his mother, his sister and a young brother, still a boy. His home was a beautiful example of the traditional Ahmedabad town-house, situated on a courtyard (*pol*) with a common entrance, and embellished with excellent carved-wood decorations. But the decay of the house was apparent; in fact, the better-off families now tend to leave Ahmedabad's city centre, moving to the new suburbs. Trying to keep the household afloat on his meagre salary was no easy task for Mohan. But the talk soon turned to religion, as he pointed to the photo of Sai Baba on the wall. I keep praying and hoping, he said, trusting my future to Sai Baba. It was soon clear that he invested himself so much in praying—and fasting—for Sai Baba that he had little energy left; and a prosaic Westerner would probably think that all this effort might have brought greater returns—in practical and economical terms—elsewhere.

Mohan Lal's case is a close parallel to some of the cases cited by Kakar. The Guru, he stresses, owes a great deal of his importance, in Indian culture, to his role as a father-figure, replacing the image of a father lost or felt to be insufficient (Kakar 1982b).

The short story that made Mulk Raj Anand's name as a writer was his 'Lament on the Death of a Master of Arts' (1967). The student, dying from despair as much as anything, identifies himself with the smouldering hopes of his father, as the youth fails his exam. The father, distant, makes these vanishing hopes the only apparent link of attachment to his son, as he laments the investment made on his education. The reader is made to understand the lack of a real link of love and friendship between father and son.

Very similar is the case of Sundar (Kakar 1982a: 41-7). Because of poverty, his family move from the Himalayan foothills to Delhi, where his father struggles hard to maintain them. He is determined that Sundar, the eldest son, should have a college education, 'the only raft that could save the family from the ever-present possibility of sinking back into the abysmal poverty from which they had barely emerged'. Sundar is intelligent, but cannot apply himself to his studies. Still, he reaches the bachelor examinations but fails three times, while his father borrows money to keep him trying. Sundar gets jobs, but quarrels with his employers and must leave. The father berates him, there is constant tension in the family, but then Sundar becomes sick. Kakar (1982a: 43) describes his symptoms: '. . . an attack was generally heralded by a tic in the underlip, followed by a heavy, numbing sensation in the lower jaw. The feeling of numbness gradually spread down through his arms to the whole body and Sundar would keel over into semiconsciousness'. Sundar feels his plans thwarted by illness; he wants to finish his education, to realize his, or his father's, ambitions. But, says Kakar, It will be evident . . . that Sundar's symptoms enabled him to be relieved of onerous responsibilities and to receive protection, help and attention. . . . An outer deference', masks 'an inner rage that takes dramatic form in the dream of the shadow attacking him . . . the guilt and anxiety at these feelings of hostility, compounded by an intense, oedipal attachment to the mother, we would say, constitute the core factor in his illness' (1982: 47).

The illness of Mulk Raj Anand's young student is, of course, not analysed in this way. Yet we understand that illness and death provide an escape from the pressure of a father's expectations. Mohan Lal is, apparently, a different case; for his father is dead, and can no longer put pressure on him. But the sense of responsibility beyond one's powers is very similar to the other two cases.

Let me turn to a successful son. Dipak—whom I knew well in 1973-4—comes from a medium-sized town in Gujarat where his father is a businessman of some standing, a prominent member of the Svetambara Jain community, and a leading member of the Jain temple committee. Yet in his personal devotion he had developed his own cult of Shiva, whom he had placed on his prayer shelf and worshipped along with images of the Tirthankaras. This was a generally known, and Mr. Parekh's views were seen as somewhat original. He is basically a Gandhian in his political and social attitudes, representing a liberal brand of conservatism or even what we might call fundamentalism but mixed with an enthusiasm for social work. The friends of the family, too, tend to be Gandhians and some are the sons of well-known figures in the independence movement. Dipak studies engineering in Ahmedabad and is a successful student, very active in the student's debating society and other organizational activities. Dipak is also a gentle but intelligent companion, highly appreciated by his friends.

With his family background it was only natural that Dipak should be fascinated by the social message of Vinoba Bhave's successor, Jayaprakash Narayan. Inspired by him, Dipak became one of the leaders of the student movement that, staging demonstrations and strikes, sparked off the unrest that shook Gujarat in 1974 and led to the establishment of President's rule in the state—events which contributed to the establishment, by Indira Gandhi, of 'the emergency' later that year. To the people I knew in Praj, the village where I was staying, the whole affair seemed a matter for the urban middle class. Dipak, at this time, stressed that the movement was directed against the corruption of Gujarat's leading politicians.

Dipak's father did not, to my knowledge, participate. But he seemed to accept and, at least implicitly, to be proud of his son's involvement. No doubt, he recognized, and approved of, the parallel to his own youthful enthusiasms. I do not know the later history of Dipak in detail, but I hear he is successfully established and respected by friends and colleagues.

Dipak, then, is a good son; his, too, is a good father. Indeed, the father wields his authority in the household in a very liberal manner. It was difficult to visit them without feeling that a considerable degree of mutual respect and affection bound the household members together. Like other Indian fathers, Dipak's was perhaps distant, but he was also affectionate. I cannot, of course, attempt a psychological analysis here. But the atmosphere of the family was obvious. Dipak seemed to have at his hand exactly the kind of father-figure that the others lack.

Apparently, Mohan Lal is looking for the father he has lost. But on further consideration, we understand that the figure he is looking for is not the father present in the cases of Sundar or of Mulk Raj Anand's dying student. Mohan Lal has found, in the figure of Sai Baba, the very element that is so often lacking in the real, Indian father; and this distant, benevolent, but at the same time understanding figure incarnates many of the features that Dipak's father, on a more prosaic level, possesses.

Clearly, we should be on the guard against oversimplification when talking about cultural patterns in the family and their influence on the personality of its members. Indian fathers and sons are as diverse as their Western counterparts; and yet, we may generalize that it is a heavy burden that the father image poses on the son's shoulders, though the burden does not necesserily prevent the expression of individualism.

THE INDIVIDUAL 1: BEHAVIOUR DEVIATING FROM CASTE NORMS

We have already met Dipak's father, who keeps a Lingam of Shiva on his prayer-shelf, practising a kind of syncretic mixture of Jainism and Shaivism in his personal cult. Certainly, people see Mr. Parekh as an original, but it does not prevent him from being highly respected. Apparently he, as well as his acquaintances, distinguish between participation in community affairs (where he makes no attempt to impose his own, particular, religious views) and personal devotion, where he is left to his own choices.

The same distinction was made when Jagatbhai went looking for a religion to satisfy his intellectual leanings, and we visited the new temple of the Brahmakumari mission together. He spoke, then, of his religious quest, telling me how he had been attracted to the teachings of Jain monks. This personal quest did not, apparently, conflict with his adherence to the Goddess cult, proper to his caste. Nor does Jagatbhai doubt the earnestness of his Swaminarayana in-laws, though he does not like their views or life-style. The vegetarian, non-violent and economically puritan Swaminarayana ethos, we noted, is at odds with much of Charan tradition, influenced by the aristocratic values of the Rajputs they served as bards. Yet Swaminarayana Charans do not, in any sense, separate from the community. Jagatbhai's wife, a Swaminarayana, chooses to practice formal purdah, a practice not at all common to her sect but traditional among well-to-do Charan women, which contrasts bluntly with the Westernized lifestyle of her husband's colleagues. Both partners in this marriage, then, clearly make their own choices with regard to personal lifestyle, choices which differ from that of other caste members without provoking conflict.

One of my best friends, Ashok, a Jain intellectual, in turn transcended most caste norms when he came to eat with Jagatbhai and myself at the former's house. True, Jagat's wife had prepared a vegetarian meal, so my friend did not transgress his dietary norms. But we ate with our hands from a common bowl, as Rajputs, Charans and other rural people often do, stressing the cross-caste commensality: Jains, ordinarily, never take food from Charans. As an liberal Gandhian and an intellectual, Ashok opposes such caste restrictions, but in his daily life he strictly follows Jain norms. I do not think he ever told his wife that we had been eating from a common bowl, since she is stricter than he is, though she, too, approved—at least in principle—of commensality with other castes.

In these examples, we see individuals going beyond the norms of their particular caste or community. What these persons do is not conceived of as deviant: there is rather a margin allowed to those who otherwise conform to the expectations of the community. This is an important point. I am not at all sure that Mr. Parekh's particular cult would not have been criticized, even ridiculized, if he had been a quarrelsome or unpopular person. True, a particular action may be deviant, but this is not stressed if the balance of right and wrong remains such that the person remains a respected member of the community.

It is not surprising, in a comparative perspective, that Indians, like people in most cultures, should be allowed some margin in their conformity to norms. But I wish to stress the point, since conformity looms large in the view Western scholars tend to project of personhood in India. It seems clear that defining the singularity of a person, in the Indian context, is precisely to point to areas where his behaviour deviates from the norm: here as elsewhere, the very notion of 'deviance' constitutes an affirmation of the norm.

THE INDIVIDUAL 2: GOING BEYOND NORMS BY PERSONAL INTERPRETATION

We have seen that fathers in India, at least in this solid, middle-class milieu, are supposed to be authoritarian and distant. What was striking when I visited the Parekh family, was the way his wife, his daughter and Dipak all spoke freely of their opinions—the father contenting himself with assertive nods and brief remarks, as if he was quite content to let the family members speak for themselves. Yet, once in a while, the others would refer a question to him: clearly, in the last instance, he was the authority. His role was that of the benign patriarch who had no need to assert himself. This harmonious image—confirmed on several visits—contrasted with the father's obvious dominance in most of the other cases I knew (Tambs-Lyche 1995b).

Not surprisingly, Dipak was a delightful person, confident in himself without being self-assertive, and in every way a good son. One might expect his political activity to be seen as youthful rebellion, so that

Mr. Parekh would be exasperated by this deviance which might easily prolong his son's studies. But in fact, the father seemed pleased by his son's political activity. Had he not himself been an active Gandhian in his youth, fighting for ideals like those that J.P. now represented? This continuity might well be seen as a matter of substance, qualities running in the family. But while a sense of social justice and a willingness to act on it may have been seen as a family trait, the choice of active participation in politics was clearly made by Dipak himself—as was the case for the father in his youth. Mutual respect, and a degree of closeness between father and son unusual for India, was clearly seen, by themselves as by others, as an intra-individual matter, not predicated by tradition or inherent quality. Rather, in judging the father as well as the son, a distinction was made between such factors, and their individual ability to act on them.

Ismail is the second son of the largest shop selling betel, bidi and soda in Praj, a large village I shall describe later. He is an Ismaili Khoja,[14] thus belonging to a minority, but one which had a good standing in Gujarat at the time.[15] The family were generally liked and respected locally. Still, Ismail was particularly popular. He seemed to be welcome everywhere, among high and low, Hindu or Muslim. One of their employees, from the low Jogi caste, was his true and loyal friend, but Ismail deserved this loyalty, for he helped his servant in several ways, and did not hesitate to be seen with him.

Ismail sought me out when I came to the village: he never asked me any favours but seemed to find my company interesting. We discussed all kinds of matters, personal as well as things I liked to know for my fieldwork, while he took me to see the sights and the people of the village. Thus we went together to a goddess temple nearby: I was surprised to see Ismail, the Muslim, pay his devotions and receive her prasad. 'But why', said he, 'should I not respect the goddess even if I am a Muslim? Of course I am not a devotee, but I do honour her.' He took me to the grave of the local *pir*, where we joined the others in talking about the world, the moral dilemmas of living in it, and about girls. Unlike the others Ismail did not smoke. He joined the group of devotees watching the Kanbi shopkeeper, Bhagatbhai, who tried to get possessed by the goddess every Friday while a group of singers accompanied the ritual. Again, Ismail was welcome: he never made fun of Bhagat (some spectators sometimes did) nor did he mark distance as a Muslim might have done. Polite and discreet, he seemed fully at home without taking part in the actual devotion, as much as when we went to the well to bathe, where he dived better than most.

One might have thought, perhaps, that Ismail's contacts with Hindus and friendly behaviour towards low-caste people would have been frowned upon by his parents. This never seemed to be the case. Rather, I think, they appreciated his capacity to get on with everybody in the village, for it was probably he who would take over the shop. The eldest brother, in fact, was just being established in business by his father, in a small town at some distance. But then, was Ismail's amiability simply a wise strategy for a minority member running a local business?

While I cannot rule out this possibility, I never felt that Ismail's style was just a strategy. He spent a lot of time with me, time which brought him no obvious advantage. Once I asked him about this, saying I felt indebted to him for all the help and attention he was giving me. 'No matter' said Ismail—one of his very few English phrases—then he continued, in Gujarati: 'I may help you, and maybe you are not able to return that service. But then, you may help somebody else, and some other time, somebody else again will help me. It all comes back in the end'.

The rhetoric, here, may be common to many people in Gujarat: but Ismail would not have been Ismail if his words had not brought across that sincerity which made people like him; whatever the origins of his words or behaviour, it was the way in which Ismail did and said these things that made him universally liked and respected as an individual.

Dipak and Ismail act out the roles that are expected of them. There is no obvious break with norms or traditions, just an individual way of acting. Indeed, there is a conscious distinction made between a sphere in which one has to answer to others for one's actions, and another sphere, where one is apparently free to make one's own way. But Dipak and Ismail do not build their singularity on this distinction. Rather, as enjoined by the *Bhagavad Gita*, they become singular by doing their duty particularly well.

Westerners, too, do their duty while seeing themselves as individuals. The question of an Indian individualism, then, may be put more precisely: is there a difference between the Indian and the Western way of distinguishing between the individual and his role? Is the boundary between social duty and individual quest drawn differently?

RELIGION AND THE INDIVIDUAL: THE CASE OF ARJUN

Let me cite a very different case. Arjun is a high school teacher, in his thirties or early forties, working and living in Ismail's village. But he came from the city. He had problems with his colleagues at work. 'They will fire you like anything', he says—and so he had to come to Praj. Here, he said, people are very good to him. He only misses his old father, who is staying in town.

Arjun's parents were staunch Swaminarayanas. At one time he was very sick; his doctor thought he might die, as he did not take well to the medicine. Nothing more, the doctor felt, could be done. 'But', said Arjun, 'the doctor was proved wrong. We went to Gadhada where Yogiji Maharaj blessed me like anything and told me not to worry.' This saved his life.

Arjun's marriage never worked out; it was not a good match. Arjun told Yogiji Maharaj, the head of the sect, of his troubles. 'He blessed me and told me to live (like a Brahmacharya). Since then I had no trouble'. Now he lives alone. He has seen his guru several times since. He is dead now, but Arjun still feels his presence. Yogiji Maharaj, indeed, left a strong impression on everybody who met him, as I did earlier in London.

Arjun is sorry that there is no Swaminarayana tremple in the village. For the emotional support that the satsang gives him, he has to go to Bhavnagar, forty kilometres away. Then, one of his pupils, present at our conversation, reminds him that there is a temple of the sect not far away, in one of the neighbouring villages. Arjun at first says he does not know about this temple, then acknowledges its existence: but he has never been there.

Swaminarayana worship is, as we have seen, highly oriented towards the religious community, and the satsang occupies a central place. We might expect that Arjun, in whose life the sect played such a central role, would be eager to go to the temple. Sectarian difference—the nearest temple belong to the other main branch of the sect—does not worry him: he knows several of their prominent members in town, and praises them warmly. For Arjun, however, the common worship was clearly not a central element in his relationship to the sect. Instead, the role of Yogiji Maharaj in his life, the saint who had cured his illness and freed him from the obligations of married life, had made it possible for him to re-cast a rather unsuccessful life story in the mould of the true devotee. Arjun says he is happy now. Looking at him, one wonders whether this is true; he is thin and emaciated. But certainly, the positive sanctioning of his wish to separate from his wife has relieved him of a heavy burden. Now he will have no sons, and the circle of family succession is broken.

Thus Yogiji Maharaj has not only freed him from social obligations, he has also provided the material for the construction of a new, individual identity. Here, the guru seems to replace and outrank the father—a theme central to Kakar (1982). But as the chosen guru replaces the imposed father, so the religious (and individual) expectations outrank and replace the social and family-based ones. Yet, and perhaps typically, the sorest aspect of Arjun's life in the village remains his separation from his father.

CULTURALLY RECOGNIZED WAYS OF 'OPTING OUT'

Though this case is completely different from the first, they go together in showing how religion, becoming a basic element in the construction of individual identity, may serve to relieve the stresses of social existence. But they also provide an example of Brahmacharya, a recognized way of opting out of family roles. This is what Arjun did. Indrasingh did not, but considered the possibilty, says Steed,

> which he extolled in conversations with me and dreamed about. . . . Indrasingh esteemed this role for several reasons. . . . First, it permitted withdrawal from domestic affairs; second, it offered access to powers which Indrasingh found himself incapable of acquiring through following Rajput norms. . . . (Steed 1955: 134-5)

Sexual continence, as commonly believed in India, produces strength. But there is one relationship to a female which may gain, rather than lose, importance through that practice: this is the cult of the goddess, to which Indrasingh was already inclined. Vagheshvari, his lineage goddess, symbolizes the patriline towards which, a sonless man, Indrasingh failed to fulfil his obligations. It is, indeed, to the goddess that Rajputs have turned, from the beginning of Rajput culture, for sons (Tambs-Lyche 1991a).

But religious bachelorhood is important in another sense. It is seen as a halfway house to the more radical alternative, open to all Indian men: renunciation. In becoming a *sadhu* a man leaves the world and its attachments behind. More specifically, he opts out of the patriline; he is no longer a son nor will he become a father. Leaving the cycle of procreation he frees himself, in more philosophical terms, from the cycle of birth and rebirth. Free to attain *moksha*, he is converting failure into victory.

Arjun choose this halfway house but also found a guru, recalling the case of Mohan Lal. Kakar (1982b) interprets the guru as a father-figure, replacing a father lost or insufficient. Finding a guru may be the opposite of becoming a Brahmacharya, for it submits the individual to external authority. Yet the two are combined in Arjun's case: the status of Brahmacharya frees the individual from his role, while the adoption of a guru introduces him to another. There is a contradiction, then, inherent in the traditional means of opting out. The traditional renouncer adopts a guru while giving up his family, and we may well ask if the new role is really more individualist than the old one. Becoming a renouncer is a radical solution to the son's burden. The guru replaces family, lineage, and caste; not only son-hood but fatherhood, too, is rejected. But worldly lineage is replaced by a spiritual one, and though the cycle of reproduction, assimilated to the cycle of death and rebirth (*samsara*), is transcended, the subject may not become, as Dumont (1966a) would have it, an individual.

The paradox is well illustrated by the story of two farmers who became disciples of Swaminarayana some time in the 1820s. Krishnaji and Mulji, having realized that the Swami was, indeed, God incarnate, wanted to become renouncers in the service of the sect. Their parents protested to the Swami, who refused to accept them. They then castrated themselves, and began to serenade their guru at night. The Swami, who realized that they had, indeed, cut their ties to the world in a most decisive fashion, finally accepted them (Parekh 1936; 149-51). But instead of becoming individuals, they become servants of the guru.

TAKING STOCK

I am not providing, here, a complete list of ways and means to be an individual in Saurashtra. I have simply tried to show that, on the level of common sense, the individual can express his singularity in several ways. Such expression may have little to do with individualism as a conceptual framework embedded in South Asian culture. I have heard very little discourse linking the concrete person to a concept of individualism. There are indications, as when Ismail sees nothing wrong in paying his respect to the goddess, in spite of being a Muslim. What he says is not very explicit; rather he seems to take for granted that the individual has some room for manoeuvre with regard to whatever is determined for him by caste, religon, or other factors fixed by status or role. Such ideas, then, seem to be intrinsic to the individual and need not be explicit.

This attitude indicates a weak link, if any, to a culture-specific discourse on individualism. There is a disjunction between the common sense talk that individuals tend to in daily life, and the standardized discourse on philosophical matters. This should lead us to relativize the extent to which the individual expresses his culture. He also expresses something transculturally human: I suggest that, in any culture, he feels and acts upon a sense of relative singularity in relation to his role, and makes use of the room for manoeuvre that the norms governing the role may allow.

But the link may be less weak than it appears, since Indian tradition—at least as found in the *Bhagavad Gita*—enjoins precisely such a disjunction between a person's actions and his real self. In keeping action and philosophy distinct, practising a detachment from action, our persons here are in tune with that popular text. Indeed, they do not choose their actions freely, since much of their activity is enjoined by duty: but they try to do their duty well, to put their imprint on it. This they do in different ways and to different extents: some diverging from the role in minor matters, some going beyond it by infusing it with their own personality.

The idealized individual is a cultural frame like any other. Thus *any* cultural context—even the most individualist one—restrains individual expression. But, though the restraints are of the same kind, they are not identical. To realize oneself through action is surely different from detachment. What we have in our examples, however, are people who do both, though sometimes in different situations. The first frames and restrains expression as much as the second.

If we relate these findings to the emergence of the individual in South Asia and the West, we find a difference in mode and degree, rather than fundamental opposition. Historically, there may be an expansion of the room for manoeuvre, in India as in the West, which clearly increases with the frequency of change and social mobility. At present, the West may be favoured in these terms. The degree of individualism possible in a society, then, should be seen as contingent on historical circumstances, not in terms of some cultural essence.

MANAGING IDENTITIES

Detachment does seem to imply a capacity to view one's actions from the outside, as it were, and my friends often comment on the necessity of acting according to duty. 'What to do?' is a phrase that crops up incessantly in situations where duty or necessity enjoins action contrary to the wishes of the individual. My friend, the sociologist Haribhai Patel and I had decided to go together to the Indian Sociological Congress in Benares in 1974. Then came the great railway strike: there were no trains. 'We will find some way', said Haribhai, 'We must go'. He set himself to enquire about planes: all planes were full. He inquired about the possibility of going by bus, but this would take several days and the Congress would be over by the time we got to Benares. Then he came back. 'No problem' he said. 'There is no way to get there in time. What to do?' Then he laughed, shrugged his shoulders, and we went for a soda together. This simple statement does not indicate a choice to be made, but absence of choice. It exonerates the person from individual responsibility,[16] creating distance between the actor and his action. 'No problem', as those familiar with India must have realized, carries a similar meaning: there may indeed be a problem, but nothing much can be done about it.

If actors in Saurashtra are more conscious than we are of the changing requirements of situations, why should this be so? My answer relates to a point borrowed from Rex (1970) earlier. The complexity of Indian social life is such that communication requires an effort to achieve clarity. This is easier when actors conform to the stereotypic patterns of action associated with a category, and stick to the stereotype throughout the situation. But this very stiffness may lead to higher awareness than we have, that these limits are imposed by the situation, not chosen by the individual.

What I observe recalls Wikan's remarks with regard to Bali.

> What Westerners have perceived as an innate aesthetic mood, an ingrained disposition to be graceful and poised, I found instead to reflect a deliberate attitude, a willed response of 'not caring', 'forgetting' the bad that has come to pass, and 'letting bygones be bygones' if one is to thrive, or even to survive. (1990: xvi)

My point is that the Indian individual, too, struggles with the need to conform in widely different situations, and that the respect for people like Ismail or Dipak reflects other people's insight into the difficulty of conforming, yet remain simple or straight, to inspire confidence as individuals. Indians may indeed be more conscious of the distinction between their individuality and the pragmatics of role-play than Westerners are.

The dialectics of this proposition should be clear: the stricter the rules of role-play, the more the individual becomes conscious of them: the more the individual is allowed to influence the role, the more captivating the illusion (if that is what it is) that what he is expressing through his role-play is, in fact, his individuality. In India, then, the individual influences his role in three ways: by transcending it through his personal interpretation, by playing on difference in roles marginal to his social performance in general, or by using one of the culturally defined ways of opting out. These three modes all have their counterparts in the West. A fourth way, which is, I think, less present in today's India than in the West, is when social mobility and relatively free choice of roles makes of that choice itself an expression of individualism.

NOTES

1. In Radcliffe-Brown's terms (1952).
2. See Marriott and Inden 1974, Inden 1976, for their use of this linguistic concept.
3. There are also, of course, formal caste associations which in some cases become highly important.
4. Holi may, of course, be seen as the ritual which makes such transgressions legitimate. But its duration as well as its implications are limited.
5. This trend is obvious if we compare the caste-wise data of Enthoven (1920: 22) with the situation prevailing in Gujarat today.
6. Steed's fictive name.
7. The chief's MoBrSoDa. Marriage with the matrilateral cross-cousin is common among Rajputs (Virbhadra Singhji 1994: 159), so this is an extension of that custom.
8. It is interesting how closely the emic understanding here corresponds to structural functionalist thinking. Clearly, Indian villagers may think like Radcliffe-Brown, without ever having read him.
9. The *Sati* is best known as the wife who burns herself at the death of her husband, but the term has much wider connotations. It is derived from *sat* (truth, purity). A Sati's power derives from her pure or truthful life, so that anyone injuring her will suffer supernatural sanctions (Mallison 1973—introduction; Weinberger-Thomas 1990; Harlan 1991; Tambs-Lyche 1992: 515-23; Carrin and Tambs-Lyche 1993).
10. This very general statement must be qualified by the right, in many parts of India, of the wife to visit her natal family whenever she and for as long as she (Jacobson 1977). Moreover the mother, in many cases, went to her 'father's house' to give birth (Stephenson 1920).
11. N.N. Bhattacharya (1977) tends to see a matriarchal stage as the origin of the Goddess' dominant position in Hinduism. He refers to V. Ehrenfels (1941), who was a champion of this theory.
12. From a psychological point of view, the work of Carstairs and Kakar are important here. Among anthropologists Obeyesekere (1981 and 1984) is using a psychological approach to the problem. I have treated aspects of the theme elsewhere (Tambs-Lyche (1991,1992,1996; Carrin and Tambs-Lyche 1993).
13. In the Middle East, father-son dominance may imply that the father is kept 'ignorant' of his son's marriage (Barth 1971). Among Gujarati Brahmins, it is the groom's mother who is absent from parts of the wedding ceremony (Stephenson 1920).
14. There are two Khoja communities, Ismailis and orthodox Shi'as. Ismail was an Ismaili.
15. Conflict between Hindus and Muslims has increased since the 1970s.
17. When Pocock pointed out to an informant that several marriages in his family had been incestuous according to strict Brahminical norms, the man answers, precisely, 'what to do ?'.

CHAPTER 10

Public Transport: Dealing with the Other

A minute holds them, who have come to go:
The self-defined, astride the created will
They burst away; the towns they travel through
Are home for neither bird nor holiness,
For birds and saints complete their purposes.

THOM GUNN

Wilderness, we have seen, decontextualizes the person; so, to a lesser extent, do the fields. On the road, the decontextualized individual is re-contextualized, for his mode of transport reinserts him into another context, ruled by competition and hierarchy.

Travel is, of course, a mode of personal decontextualization known to us all. Yet every mode of travel confronts us with settings and rules over which we have no control. These are givens with which we have to deal, when finding our place among others, say, in the bus or in the train. Seasoned travellers know the rules, yet every meeting is different: we are constantly engaged in defining new situations. This is part of the excitement, as also sometimes the weariness of travelling. As a frequent traveller in Saurashtra, I tried to learn the rules, for I soon found them different from what I knew. As we shall see, rank is a constant presence, and the definition of the situation becomes, at least in part, a kind of ranking game. The word game is apt here, for the one general and outstanding quality of travel is that situations are ephemeral: we have, indeed, 'come to go', as Thom Gunn puts it.[1] What links situations, however, is not just the rules of the game, but the experience that remains as memory with the participants, becoming part of emergence. In Saurashtra, this experience is important, for people of all classes travel a lot. The game follows different rules on the buses and trains, and so these two settings provide us with further examples of that dialectic process of decontextualization and re-insertion which is, I think, fundamental to the construction of the individual.

BUSES

Bus transport is a state monopoly in Gujarat. Though there are problems in running this vast network, the general level of services is impressive.

There is usually a bus going where you want, without undue delay, and though they are crowded, capacity is constantly on the increase.

Let me describe, briefly, the character of bus services to Praj, some 40 km south of Bhavnagar. This is on the road to Mahuva, 60 km further south. Praj had some 3,000 inhabitants in the 1970s, a large village; yet no bus service had its terminus there. This is typical of Saurashtra's bus lines. Only very minor ones end in villages; most buses run from town to town. Lines criss-cross to a considerable extent. Then there are buses running short or long distances; as also standard, luxury or express services. The latter, more costly, tend to exclude the poorer sections of the population.

From Bhavnagar to Praj, one may take the Bhavnagar-Talaja local bus, running to the taluka centre some 20 km south of Praj; this is the slowest service. Then there is the Bhavnagar-Mahuva line, with some express or luxury coaches; the fastest buses, sometimes passing by night, run from places south of Mahuva to destinations beyond Bhavnagar. Though traffic from Praj to Bhavnagar is local the bus may be anything but. Conversely, long-distance travellers may choose, for some reason, to take the Talaja bus and change there for their destination, so even locals carry long-distance passengers. With the criss-crossing of routes there is no end of possibilities. Thus though Bhavnagar is the most important town in south-eastern Saurashtra, it need not occupy a central position in travel itineraries. From Mahuva, for example, people as or more often go to Ahmedabad, while for other purposes, Rajkot is the centre of Saurashtra.

The reason for stressing the point that people go from anywhere to anywhere will be clear if we compare social life aboard Gujarat State buses and the buses I knew from my childhood in Norway. In this rururban setting all buses went from town to village, branching out from the town centre. Since they travelled along two alternative routes, there was an important exchange of passengers at one place, where the atmosphere changed radically. Till then, it was marked by the reserve of strangers; later, there was a marked busriders' community of those going to the same village. They knew each other, and often met on the bus, going for work or shopping at the same time. Yet they might seldom meet in other settings. The bus was the main meeting-place of the local community, defining boundaries, so that those were part of the same community who used the same bus.

There may be buses running to isolated villages in Saurashtra, where a similar atmosphere is felt, but I did not travel on them, and most buses don't define community in this way. This is clearly because of the criss-crossing route patterns and variable travel itineraries. Busriders are strangers to each other, people come and go.

Gujarat buses have a crew of two; driver and conductor. The driver sits beyond a screen at front, and is not normally in contact with passengers. This contact is maintained by the conductor, who has a small seat near the rear entrance. But buses are usually full, sometimes extremely so, taking far more than the thirteen standing passengers officially allowed.[2] To find room, four or five passengers will climb the screen and sit in the drivers' cabin, often chatting with him. The conductor is busy with ticketing and other chores. When stops are less frequent, as on express or luxury buses, he has more leisure, but passengers belong to a class which does not chat with conductors. Seldom, therefore, is the conductor able to have more than brief and job-oriented interaction with passengers.

All towns have large bus terminals, important centres of social life, which usually attract hawkers and beggars as well as: a cafeteria, a newspaper kiosk, some grocery, tobacco, sweet and soft-drink stalls. Crowds are waiting for the buses, ranged on numbered platforms arranged in see-saw fashion along the building front. Whether local or long-distance, buses arrive at a platform a few minutes before departure, so there is always crowding as the bus backs into its platform. Some try to enter the bus before it enters, while it is refuelling or just parked. Inside information is then needed to identify the bus, and this is tricky, since conductors, drivers and officials try to keep passengers out. Those who succeed, generally put their luggage on the seat and leave. Strangely, luggage seldom seems to disappear when left on a bus seat, something which is certainly not the case if left on the platform.

As the bus backs into the stand, no quarter is given in the struggle to enter as quickly as possible. There is a great deal of pushing and pulling, with heavy luggage swung to advantage. If it gets stuck, however, one is sure to be bypassed. Women generally push harder than men, which surprised me at first. Traditional modesty is turned, here, to advantage. A man should, of course, never touch a woman in public and so the latter press against the men, often shouting phrases like 'don't touch me, you rascal' or even, 'Don't you dare touch my breasts!', using, in the latter case, these female protuberances as a kind of ram.

The door is the most strategic point, but whenever possible[3] passengers, and young men particularly, enter through the windows. This free-for-all fighting was present whenever I saw a bus entered or did so myself, worst at the big terminals. It is quite surprising that almost everybody—after the dog-fight—has found a seat. When I told the late I.P. Desai, the great Gujarati sociologist, of my surprise, he said: 'You must understand that what you are watching here is not scarcity itself; it is the ideology of scarcity'. No doubt he was right.

There is another rush for seats when boarding the bus. But the slow passage through the door—slower than necessary, because of the rush—helps to sort out things inside. Here, the situation is less chaotic. People do put markings on the seats to keep them for companions, and these are usually respected, as are efforts to keep neighbouring seats for friends and family. It is as if all agree that fighting is reserved for access: once inside, a rule of first come, first served is adhered to. I must stress that the rush does not exclude civility when appropriate. As a foreigner, I was in fact often offered somebody else's seat, while in other cases, people would press together to make room for me. But this was an exceptional gesture towards the foreigner. I seldom saw seats offered to old people or women.[4]

In two out of the three cases of conflict, the dispute is about seats. This is typical. The use of markings, for example, works best at intermediate stops where few new passengers, or none, join the bus. When starting from terminals, such markings work only to a limited extent. This is quite unlike their efficiency in trains, where they seem to be almost universally respected.

One day I find myself on a medium-distance bus, leaving an intermediate station. A woman of rural aspect—she is in skirt and blouse, not a sari—claims a seat occupied by an urban-looking, sari-clad woman and her child. The husband of the latter is seated in the next row to the front. He wears Western-style clothes and might be a bank clerk or somebody of a similar status.

The rural woman claims to have put her bag on the seat, a recognized marking. Her opponent denies that the bag was on the seat when she arrived. The claimant points to a man seated further forward. He is a big fellow, wearing a grey suit and a topi. 'Ask that Saheb', she says, 'Just ask him! Is it not true, Saheb, that one can leave something on one's seat and leave—it is one's own seat then? Is it not so, Saheb?' Turning to the other woman, she says: 'Just listen to what the Saheb says!' The Saheb speaks. 'Yes, yes'—he seems, in effect, to support the supplicant's claim—'but please calm down'. The latter, clearly, is his final message. But his attempt at mediation is not crowned with success. A short while later, the two women are fighting it out bodily, which seems to amuse other passengers, especially certain males. Four or five men finally have to grab the women, keeping them apart. They, however, continue to shout at each other until the rural woman reaches her destination.

The rural woman in this case is clearly appealing for protection in a difficult situation. What she offers in return is respect, and this offer is the essence of her use of the term 'Saheb'. Her offer of a transaction in these terms is, however, turned down; the Saheb does not interfere on her behalf.

The term Saheb, here, clearly does not refer to any particular position in society, or type of transaction outside the situation described. In using the term, the woman is bestowing superior rank upon somebody she does not know. He, indeed, might well be of untouchable origins (or perhaps, wearing a *topi*, Anglo-Indian). But in the context, he is certainly the person who looks most like a Saheb, and his dress, age, and general manner is such that, had he accepted the invitation, it is likely that other passengers would have accepted him as a Saheb, in the sense of somebody with status and authority.

The use of the term Saheb by the woman here is metaphorical rather than metonymical; while it does not stand for any particular transaction, it constitutes an invitation to act as if his superiority had such a base. In short, it is an invitation to transact in such a way that rank difference is created.

In this conflict, which the partners themselves are not able to solve, an appeal is made to a 'superior'. Such appeals will be recognized, I think, by anybody who has spent some time in India. It may seem trite to refer to rank for understanding interaction in an Indian context. I am, however, trying to attack the question from a slightly different angle, in that I try to locate the patterns of ranking in daily life transactions, and to reserve my reflections on a possible overall structure till the end.

On a bus heading for one of the larger towns in Saurashtra, a middle-aged, rather fat man in Western-style dress is seated. The bus is running about an hour late, as may happen on the long-distance routes. The fat man is constantly looking at his watch, and suddenly he shouts at the conductor: 'What is this? Almost an hour late! I shall miss my connection! Why can't you make these buses run on time? I require an explanation! You must make the other bus wait! It is the duty of the bus service to get me to my destintion in time! I have an important appointment ! Can't you make this bus go any faster?'

At the next stop, the conductor speaks to the driver. We do not hear the conversation, but there is no doubt—the driver is really trying to speed up. In fact, we are now going so fast along the bumpy roads that passengers have difficulty staying in their seats. One might have thought that the man would be satisfied at these efforts to get him to his destination on time. He has played the role of somebody in authority, a Saheb, and it has worked. But then we hear, 'What the hell is this? Is the driver mad? What kind of driving is this? Do you want to kill us all? You are going too fast!' shouts the fat man.

That does it: the other passengers giggle. The Saheb now inspires laughter. It is as if the mask of authority has fallen and we see the vain pomposity behind. The Saheb is just that ordinary nuisance, somebody trying to make himself important. And yet, with all these goings-on, the bus finally makes up about a quarter of an hour of the lost time.

The behaviour of the fat man is not specific to India. And yet, the way in which he claims authority, not referring to any specific status but shouting to demand respect, is rather typical of the way in which Sahebs, as a recognized interactional type, are supposed to behave. It is, in essence, exactly the manner in which the Saheb of our first case refused to act. But he was appealed to by an inferior; here it is the Saheb himself who puts himself forward, demanding deference from the bus crew.

The conductor has some authority, he may order a passenger to descend. Nobody without a certain self-assurance would command the conductor the way our Saheb is doing here. Ordinary people show deference to the conductor, as they do to anybody in uniform. Shouting to the conductor like our man does, constitutes a claim to high rank. By his very behaviour he demands to be treated like a Saheb.

Why is the claim accepted? In principle, no stranger should be important enough to order the bus crew about. The crew cannot know whether the man really is as important as he claims. But since the claim is for a general status, for no specific position, they have no means of knowing the limits to his power. This may, indeed, be why such claims are not specified. For a public employee, the corridors of power and influence may well be a closed book, but the institution of the 'complaint book' is ever present and well known. People have been known to lose their jobs because of a complaint lodged by somebody important. Probably, in our case, the bus crew simply chose to play safe.

The man succeeds in his bid for recognition by referring in his behaviour metaphorically to that general category of people to whom respect is due. In other words, he succeeds in his claim to be a Saheb, by initiating a transaction implying rank difference. But his success is spoilt by overdoing it, and when people giggle at his complaint of going too fast, they defrock the Saheb and deny him further deference.

THE COMPLAINT BOOK

The bus fills up at one of the larger bus stations in Saurashtra. The station is in the middle of this particular line, but due to some problem the bus was changed here. A group of three passengers now claim the seats corresponding to those they occupied in the original vehicle. But three newcomers already occupy these seats. A quarrel ensues.

The conductor tries to call the peace, hushing down the quarrelling groups and offering the passengers from the other bus alternative seats. He is not successful, however, and other passengers begin to take sides. The driver refuses to start as long as the quarrel is going on. A policeman tries to mediate through the window, but nobody listens to him and with a shrug he disappears. The passengers from the first bus are led by a middle-aged man in Western dress, of decidedly middle-class aspect. His opponents look much less formidable. After about half an hour, other passengers put pressure on the driver to start. At first he blankly refuses; but after about an hour—the quarrel is still going full swing—we leave for our destination.

The group from the first bus have now given up quarrelling. Instead the middle-aged man turns to the conductor, asking for the complaint book. The conductor asks him to lodge his complaint at the next station since his complaint book is not with him. This does not satisfy the passenger, saying that a complaint book should always be carried on the bus. The discussion now shifts to this new question, as passengers again take sides, for or against the question of complaint books in each and every bus. The middle-aged passenger now demands that the bus turn back, to enable him to lodge his complaint immediately. The bus stops, having run about five miles, then turns around. 'You just go and complain!' the conductor shouts. The discussion continues.

Back at the bus station, the driver leaves the bus. 'Bring me the complaint book—here!' shouts the passenger to the conductor. The conductor refuses this act of deference: 'You just go and complain', he says. 'The bus will wait.' But the passenger sticks to his seat, despite assurances by other passengers, that they will see that the bus does not leave without him. After some fifteen minutes, the driver returns, and the bus leaves—about an hour and a half late. No formal complaint has been made.

The behaviour of the complaining passenger in this case is rather similar to that of the Saheb who wanted the bus to speed up. By his commanding attitude and behaviour, he is 'hinting' metaphorically that he is somebody of considerable importance. Like the other Saheb, he is successful to a point, as far as the crew is concerned; they follow his command. But when he asks that the complaint book be brought, he is going too far. In fact, he may be asking the conductor to sign his own demission, for the complaint book is a real threat.

The demand that the complaint book be brought constitutes a demand for deference with no practical purpose, and this move loses, for the plaintiff, the sympathy of other passengers. Still, the Saheb has made his case: he has shown himself as somebody of consequence, who can give orders; he has established a ranked relationship with the crew, and is able to lecture the conductor about the rules of his work.

The question remains, however, why does he not lodge a complaint? By refusing to do so, his becomes an empty threat. The key lies, I think, in the logic of ranking transactions: once having demanded the complaint book, he cannot go himself without reversing the rank order, since he would then be acting at the request of the conductor. And it is in the nature of such transactions that, once inequality has been established, the rank order can be reversed only at the cost of spoiling the game.

The situation, with the quarrelling, chaos and delay which ensues, is not calculated to produce general respect for the saheb. What we see here is an example of a 'Saheb at bay'—though his demands may seem out of proportion to the original insult, he is determined that nobody should boss around with him. This is a type of situation I observed quite often in Saurashtra, and I also experienced, as many Westerners do, the frustrations of a 'Saheb at bay' myself.

In these situations, we see that the importance of rank is such that the actor is extremely conscious of any insult to his self-esteem. Reactions take forms that would be extreme in other, less rank-conscious societies. In this sense, ranking may be seen as part of emergence. But there are other, less psychological, aspects of the 'saheb at bay', which tie in with our earlier discussion.

We shall see below (Esser 1996) that any definition of the situation puts a penalty on the actor who wishes to change it. What is special, here, is the rigidity of positioning, or relativity in Mead's terms (1934), within the situation. There is, as noted, a key to be found in the concept of ranking transaction introduced by Marriott (1974, 1976). In such transactions the flow of prestations is, by definition, asymmetric, and this is why they create or maintain rank difference. Whatever descends from above has a value that follows, not from the quality of the prestation itself, but from its superior source.[5] This is the key to what either party gains; in Inden's terms (1976) the inferior gains superior substance while the superior enhances his superiority. The model is related to what both authors see as fundamental to the construction of the person in the Indian context; the substance of the person—like the *karma* af an individual—is the fruit of action and interaction in which he or she has been taking part. The concept of ranking transactions imply that if a superior position is claimed, one cannot honourably give it up. One must stick to it (Marriott and Inden 1977: 235). If challenged, the claim must be strengthened; to accept defeat, would mean losing face, become a comical figure.

I believe we may recognize this figure in a number of social situations in India. I shall call him the unsuccessful rank claimant. A typical example, here, is the comic figure of a popular play I watched in Bhavnagar in 1974. Wearing a *dhoti*[6] with his black jacket, he proudly introduced himself as an LL.B (AbF), where the suffix stood for 'appeared but failed'. The joke is a common one and needs no explanation. What needs to be stressed is the popularity of this figure in Indian imagery. The reason, I feel, is that such figures are particularly common in a society where rank is so important. The unsuccessful rank claimant is trying without success to establish himself in the superior position of a ranking transaction. The Saheb who complained of the bus being late becomes one the moment he protests that it is going too fast. A transaction of superior knowledge versus respect is apparently taking place, but once the superiority is seen by others as suspect, only mock respect is returned. It is a case of paying for bad goods in bad money. Since rank is so important, such mock response is devastating, and a real danger when claiming rank.

The figure of the unsuccessful rank claimant is part of emergence—the knowledge available to participants in social situations. Mock respect, or laughter, is one established negative response to a rank claim. And ridicule, in the Indian context, seems far more destructive than I am used to from Norway, where the proper answer might well be to laugh oneself, transforming the whole sequence into a kind of joke.

The two cases of Sahebs described here illustrate a schismogenetic pattern in Bateson's sense (1973: 35ff), typical of the 'Saheb at bay' and a logical implication of interaction structured according to ranked transactions. When such transactions work, both parties gain: and so their breakdown causes a schism, since both then stand to lose.

It is notable that urban middle-class people are involved in each of the three bus cases. They are Sahebs. There is a particular ambiguity about such persons. Their appearance is no guarantee of their status. Their nice dress only alludes to some unspecified, high position. For all we know, some of them might be untouchables! Western clothes make a person difficult to classify according to the diacritic marks of caste, and what they signal is something else: the person's general respectability in terms of dress. People used to deference do not easily adjust when it is absent, but in showing off their expectations they may hope to be identified as persons who normally obtain deference. Expectations may be taken for evidence, yet when signs of rank are diffuse, conflict may ensue.

The bus crew has a special position here, unlike the train conductor, whose rounds are infrequent and whose presence, therefore, is hardly felt. In relation to urban middle-class people, the crew are little better than peons. For rural people, however, they are persons of authority, since they belong to state bureaucracy and, on the bus itself, are in a position of authority *vis-à-vis* passengers. This authority, unquestioned by villagers, is challenged by urbanites who are able to ask for and use the 'complaint book'. Who knows, they may even know the supervisor—nobody knows what power they may wield, they may just be bank clerks or they may be the friends of a minister.

Thus uncertainty prevails. This uncertainty, then, may lead people to over-react—respect is such a difficult thing to obtain on the bus that disregard of somebody's status causes vehement reactions. In India generally, and no less on buses and trains, people are rank-conscious and sore when deference is not forthcoming. Uncertain definitions of rights, as in buses, must aggravate this situation.

Thus the bus as a scene is problematic in India. Nobody is able to put forward signs of rank that are immediately and automatically respected, and instead of the cool superiority affected in other situations—as when isolated by the exclusiveness of a first-class train compartment—the much more insistent allegations of superiority provoke conflict. For the bus as a scene is purportedly egalitarian. All have paid the same fare, and in principle have the same right to a seat. Such equal rights, uncommon in Indian social situations, pose problems. Insecurity forces everybody to fend for themselves as best they can and nothing is taken for granted. This insecurity is probably the main reason for the drama when people scramble for bus or train seats, and which, in its turn, reinforces the feeling.

THE INDIVIDUAL AND THE DEFINITION OF THE SITUATION

In his essay on immigrant trilogies,[4] a genre of literature which represents and possibly originated the three-generational model of immigrant assimilation, Boelhower characterizes the three phases not only as construction, deconstruction and reconstruction (an obvious contemporary transcription of their conventional content), but also, more interestingly, as vouloir-faire, pouvoir-faire, and savoir-faire. These latter terms, stressing the subjective dimension of adaptation, bring us back to the original definition of the situation, as W.I. Thomas conceived of it:

> Preliminary to any self-determined act of behaviour there is always a stage of examination and deliberation which we may call the definition of the situation. And actually not only concrete acts are dependent on the definition of the situation, but gradually a whole life-policy and the personality of the individual himself follow from a series of such definitions. (Thomas 1923: 42)

As Cappetti stresses, Thomas here 'courageously theorizes that personality—and even the whole life of an individual—is the product of choice' (1989: 128). He goes further than Barth (1966) in constructing from choice not only courses of action, but the double definition of situation and identity. The links between Thomas and Mead are obvious. But, Cappetti notes, there is a 'double nature' to Thomas' theory, for there are constraints on this level too:

> . . . the child is always born into a group of people among whom all the general types of situation which may arise have already been defined and corresponding rules of conduct developed, and where he has not the slightest chance of making his definitions and following his wishes without interference. . . . (Thomas 1923: 42)

Following this rather deterministic account, Thomas goes on to discourse on the opposition between the individual and the rules maintained by his community; an opposition which may have been framed by 'the narrative of how the old world declined and the modern world rose' (Cappetti 1989: 128) directing much of classical sciology. The idea that situations are pre-defined implies that there exists, for any actor, a certain number of type situations to which corresponding rules of conduct apply. We are led to the problem of decoding: to what type should we ascribe the situation in question?

The question is crucial, as Esser points out, for the answer defines the frames (Goffman 1974) that determine the meaning of whatever we choose, subsequently, to do in the situation (Esser 1996: 9). The choice, then, is also one of emotional mode, of rules of expression; we have to 'tune in' to the situation (1996: 12). Esser notes that the idea of unconditionally defined situations—ruled by predefined norms—has been fundamental to action theory, at least since Parsons (1936); I shall return to the possibilities of modifying these unconditional terms later.

Our efforts to tune into a defined situation implies two processes, empirically connected but theoretically distinct. We suppose the existence of an imagined *model* of the situation, defined by its *content*; and we imply that the model defines a modus of *interpretation* of any information received as the situation is acted out. Such a model is 'an image of a typical situation, culturally founded elaborated as tuning-in and associated with symbols' (Esser 1996: 12). It contains, Esser continues, certain elements: overarching goals, typical means of reaching them, typical sequences of action, typical and expected emotions, and, last but not least, the image of the self in the situation. Two conditions must be present for a given definition of the situation to result: a prototypical image of the situation in the mind of the actor, and a correspondence to the event that confronts him (1996: 12-13). The use of the term prototype is important. Cognitive psychologists such as Rosch (1978) use it for categories that are defined, not by their contrasts to other categories, but by their relation to a typical object. Thus objects are more or less typical, and applied to situations, we introduce a degree of play.[7] Not only is each situation different, but there may be more than one way of tackling it. This is why the unconditional definition of the situation, opposing the individual to a fixed pattern for behaviour, is less tenable than Thomas and other classical sociologists felt. This is where Esser, going beyond Mead (1934) and Bateson (1958), contributes most to develop the concept of definition of the situation.

THE RISKS OF DITHERING

There are always a number of prototypic models which may fit a given situation, says Esser; the choice implies risk, since nobody can know for sure whether a particular model fits the situation or not. Every valid model implies a particular overarching goal and so excludes others. He distinguishes the meaning of such models from their utility, stressing the presence of interest in human interaction (1996: 19-20). We are close, here, to Barth's models (1966), based on the interested actor. But Esser adds an emphasis on the cost of misinterpretation.[8] His particular point is the cost of changing the definition of a situation, once a particular model has been applied. The cost may be too great; which implies that when talking of change in the definition of the situation, we are dealing with a function which has a threshold level.[9]

This is precisely what I mean when I say that actors, in the situations I describe here, 'stick to their guns'. The cost of changing the definition of the situation has passed the threshold, and actors choose to avoid change. This implies that a small increase in cost may make the difference. If Sahebs, in the situations we described from Saurashtra buses, are slightly more afraid of ridicule than a Westerner would be, this is enough to make them act differently. We do not need to assume radical differences in norms or values: a modest difference can produce a radically different choice. What seems to be the case, is that Westerners have greater leeway in combining and modifying roles, before others react in such a way as to make the risk too great. Thus these modifications do not constitute a change in the definition of the situation, but are seen as relativizing our own position within it. Such differences clearly have their roots in emergence, in the way we perceive the social person.

We return, here, to problems of interpretation. How do we perceive situations and possible definitions of them? Classical sociology seldom saw a problem here (Esser 1996: 12). But we can no longer avoid it, and it leads at once to a dichotomy. We may conceive of one mode of interpretation as relatively direct and unconscious.[10] But Esser stresses the importance of what he calls the rational definition of the situation, where a choice has to be made (1996: 13). In other words, the decision has to be made, whether to act from habit or consider the matter consciously (1996: 21).

Such reflection always demands effort. We may see this exertion as a cost, which will be avoided unless there is some corresponding utility in the offing, as when the girl behind the baker's counter is so attractive that one would like to ask her out for dinner. We may define a function here, with a threshold value where it becomes interesting to depart from the habitual interpretation. If the hope of obtaining a gain, or that gain itself, is small, we choose the most obvious and least demanding model applicable to the situation in question (Esser 1996: 22-3). Moreover, the threshold value of the function indicates that there must be some important gain, and some real chance of obtaining it, if actors are to depart from the beaten track.

Such model building, which at first seems to lead to utilitarianism, ends up with a quite different realization. Utilitarian concerns must become very important indeed for an actor to change the definition of a situation entered into. We do not apply the rational mode of interpretation unless there are considerable gains to be had. It is only when the cognitive variables change, concludes Esser, that we approach the threshold value of these functions. He comments: 'So this is how that happens, which we so often observe: unrestrained living out of emotions and a complete blanking off of all reason—when only the model of the situation is sufficiently unchallenged' (1996: 24). But as we approach the threshold value, there may be increasing doubt, questioning of the rightness of unreflected action, which rises independently of the actual possibility of changing to the rational mode of interpretation, or of changing the definition of the situation. This is an insight which, I think, strikes most of us as true. Changing from the unreflected into the reflective mode, as a result of such doubts, always remains a possibility (1996: 25-6).

What Esser tries to achieve by this modelling, is no less than a solution to one of the oldest dilemmas of social science: should we conceive of action as rationally or irrationally motivated? Much of classical sociology took the latter view, while Barth and other proponents of choice imply some kind of rationality.[11] Esser tries to show that what appears as irrational and unreflected action is only a specific mode within a modellization built on the assumption of rationality. We chose the non-reflective mode of acting not from irrationality but the basically rational tendency to avoid the effort of rational interpretation (1996: 29-31).[12] If this is so, then a tendency to interpret the unknown, to arrive at what we recognize as a kind of rationality, is inherent in humans. What Esser has done, is to identify the tendency to repetition in human behaviour—what Bourdieu (1977) calls habitus—with a rationally attuned predisposition.

TRAINS

Just about everybody in Saurashtra travels by train. In the 1970s there were no broad-gauge trains; the lines built by the princely states were all of metre gauge, with a few narrow-gauge lines here and there. This meant that trains were slower and cheaper than buses. There is a dense network, since the princely states were eager, not just to link up with areas under British rule, but to use railways to unite their territory. Most lines were built between 1879 and 1922 (Tambs-Lyche 1997: 316, 325-6n.; Wilberforce-Bell 1916). Thus trains are fully integrated in the regional culture, even more than buses; and the rules of the game, when people interact in and about trains, are more firmly established.

This is not obvious when boarding a train, for the effort of entering a second class coach is comparable to the rush of getting on the bus. First-class passengers usually have reservations, billed on the side of each bogie.[13] In principle this is true of long-distance second-class travel too, but here there is always an admixture of passengers without reservation, and people are not so sure that their reservations will be honoured.[14]

At railheads, porters may be paid to deposit markings for the passenger before the train is backed up to the platform. These are respected even when they give one person sleeping room on a bench leaving all others to sit on the floor. First come, first served, is the rule, and sometimes it is necessary to insist if one holds a reservation to a seat already occupied. Porters, of course, know which wagons are unreserved and are thus able to find seats. For them, this is an important additional source of income. For local trains, reservations are seldom made, but even in the 1970s such trains felt the competition of buses and were not always full. Thus on the line south-east from Junagadh towards Mahuva, close to the Gir forest and through thinly populated territory, I have even experienced the unusual luxury of having a second-class compartment to myself.

Strictly speaking, only first-class bogies have closed compartments, and the possibility of locking the door is an advantage added to the padded seats distinguishing first from second-class travel.[15] Interaction in first class is limited to those sharing a compartment. They tend to stay together for a while, since few pay first-class fares for local travel. There is an implicit acknowledgement that first-class passengers generally are respectable people.[16] Thus interaction in first class follows different rules from those in second; perhaps paradoxically, the entry fee seemed to make for a more egalitarian mode, as if first-class passengers were more secure with a minimum of prestige already assured. Yet some ranking transactions as observed on the buses are found here too.

It is more revealing, however, to observe interaction in second class. Here, compartments are open; banks are arranged in facing pairs, with no wall towards the corridor. For social purposes, the facing pair of seats usually function as delimited space, but communication across the corridor or with standing passengers is always possible. Standing passengers is a term not to be taken literally, as most people find some way to arrange their luggage—suitcases, sacks of grain, baskets or whatever—to form some kind of seat. The fuller the train, the less the delimitation of each compartment is clear. Yet in the cases that follow, the facing seats define the space where interaction takes place.

I enter a second-class compartment. Five people are already seated, and one of them is talking to the others. He is denouncing the superstitions of the common people, the backwardness of their customs, and the advantages of modernity. Wearing Western-style clothes, the talker is clean-shaven, thirty to thirty-five years of age. The listeners, two men and two women, are older. They are dressed in the traditional manner. They do not speak, but confine themselves to grunts, nods and one-syllable assents.

'You are a student?' the talker asks, as I sit down. Answering that I am teaching at university, I am told that he, too, is a teacher. 'What is your qualification?' he asks. 'Ph. D.'. 'That is a very low standard', explains the teacher to the others. 'We do not recognize that in India'. I protest, but in vain. The authority of the teacher in relation to his listeners is already established. Clearly, what he says, they believe.

What is taking place between the talker and his audience? Looking at the communication as a ranking transaction, the gains of the teacher seem clear. He is gaining status or, at least situationally, respect. His defensive mood when I enter shows that he has, indeed, some gain to defend. But why do the others accept being talked down to? Norwegians or Americans, certainly, don't like that kind of behaviour at all.

But an observer from these would-be egalitarian cultures would find such one-way communication exceedingly common in Saurashtra, as elsewhere in India. If the speaker is a Brahmin, we put it down to caste-bound tradition; if he is old, to respect for age; if he is a university professor, for learning. Such references to established status reveal their inherent weakness in this case, for our man is a simple teacher, and even more, we like the others present have only his word for it. We must ask, then, not who or what is worthy of respect but rather how, by what course of action, respect is produced. This would suggest that the way to achieve superiority is to talk down to others, as if the arrogance with which things are said is proof of the quality of the statement. The parallel to our cases of Sahebs on the buses, then becomes clear.

Thus what the teacher in the railway compartment says, in his overbearing manner, is being claimed, by him, as superior wisdom (substance) and accepted by the others as such. He enjoys the privilege of a man of value; they, however, may claim to have received wisdom. They do indeed receive something of value from him—as long as they do not challenge his superiority. The reciprocity of the situation, therefore, depends on the lack of distinction between objects and partners in exchange that defines, for Marriott (1976), the concept of ranking transactions.

One may indeed refuse the inferior position in such a transaction, as we shall see. But the idea that the superior—any superior—has something to offer contrasts with an egalitarian viewpoint, where anybody else's superiority only underlines our own inferiority. The whole point is that the inferior, in a ranking transaction, stands to gain from his inferiority. He leaves the situation with an amount of value—say, wisdom—gained from the superior other. What kept me from accommodating to such thinking is clear; I saw rank as a zero-sum game. If we assume, instead, a chain of possible ranking transactions running through creation—from animals to God—then relative gains are always possible, and ranking becomes a non-zero sum game.[17] Put in simpler terms, it was in India I learnt to listen to the wisdom of old men.

The teacher's reactions, as I intrude on the scene, show that I am a threat. Claiming my educational standard to be lower than his, he disposes of the threat, leaving me in an unenviable position; to the others, I seem to have claimed a rank that I cannot sustain.

A DIVISION OF SPOILS

Entering another second-class compartment, I am offered a seat on an already well-filled bench. Somebody asks me if I am a Muslim. He may be looking at my beard—usually the sign of a Muslim or Parsi. I answer that I am a Pardeshi—a foreigner. The man tells me he is a Darbar; a third man in the compartment presents himself as a teacher.

The pattern of conversation which follows is very different from our last case, taking the form of a wide-ranging discussion of matters of custom and religion. The teacher is playing a well-defined part, representing the modern, educated view. The Darbar is commenting on the issues from a traditional viewpoint, while I am asked for a foreigner's angle. It is not a debate where each of us tries to gain the upper hand; rather an exchange of perspectives where each participant's statements are respected without criticism. No attempt is made to reach consensus. Others, surrounding us, accept the position of listeners, or as inferiors in the interaction that is taking place. Thus we are not equals discussing a single subject; each of us expound, in turn, our views to a respecting audience, one at a time and strictly in sequence. As one holds the superior position, the others are enriched by his exposition. The structure of each sequence—I talk—you listen—corresponds to our last case. Yet in a sense we are dividing the spoils, by assigning to each participant an area of expertise respected by the others.

ALTERNATIVE GAMES OF RANKING TRANSACTIONS

The contrast between these two cases suggest that there is an element of choice in the matter of each actor's projected identity. My own case is an obvious example. When I chose to be a teacher, I left my opponent limited choice; he must accept my superiority or denounce it. Since our area of expertise is the same, we become competitors in a single ranking game; a division of spoils is not possible. If I had chosen to be a foreigner, the situation might have developed differently.

When I did, the situation was defined so as to allow for complementary expertise, leading to a sequential equality where each takes precedence in turn. The division of spoils stems from the creation of three separate rank scales dividing the game in separate sequences. This way of defining the situation is, I think, not the result of coincidence but of an effort by all parties to create situational equality and avoid conflicting rank claims.

But even so, the structure of each interactional sequence seem predefined, as if this way of structuring interaction as ranking transactions is part of emergence in Mead's terms, the 'I speak—you listen' type being so much the accepted model for interaction that we find ourselves in what Esser calls the unreflective mood. Such a ranked transaction allows for only one superior at a time. In the first case, one person occupies this position to the exclusion of all others. In the other, the structure is repeated but its impact is modified by breaking the sequence down into three distinct parts.

IDENTITY IN PUBLIC SITUATIONS

As Berreman (1972) has shown, identity in public situations cannot easily be controlled. As we have seen they are also, viewed etically, nonexclusive and ambiguous. Just as I am both foreigner and teacher, so teachers have caste and ethnic backgrounds; they may belong to a religious sect; they may choose a broad varna identification; and so the actor has access to a large number of potential identities in any given situation.

This is true for all complex societies. Western sociology has long spoken of such identities as roles. In the West, however, one aspect of roles is that they may be mixed; as a Norwegian, living in France, who identifies with a number of anglo-saxon ideas, is an anthropologist and a teacher, etc., I present myself to others as a calculated blend of role images. By doing so, I have ample room of manoeuvre to project what I see as my individuality, and such a self-presentation often proceed by 'buts': 'I am a Norwegian, but I live in France; I am a university teacher, but I grew up in the countryside, etc. These 'buts' have a definite purpose; they modify the expectations that would follow from any single identification, so that my interlocutor will not identify me with, say, the rumbustiousness of the Norwegian or the arrogance of the intellectual.

In Saurashtra identities don't mix in this way. While the teacher certainly belongs to a caste, the expectations implied by being a teacher are not modified by reference to other identities. If our teacher is also a Rajput, the latter label carries quite different implications. As a teacher, one supports modernity; as a Rajput, one is quite often opposed to it. It would be quite conceivable, then, to present oneself as a teacher but a Rajput—producing a sort of conservative-modern mix—but what people in Saurashtra do, is rather to say: I am a Rajput and also a teacher. The implications of this formula is different. Semantically, roles are not mixed but added one to another, so that the role performances of the teacher and the Rajput may be kept separate and mutually intact.

The labels used may represent rank through references implicit in the labels, to specific ranking transactions outside the situation. Such is the case of the label professor, implying a ranking transaction with students. Labels may also, however, represent rank metaphorically, as in the case of the Saheb, where the behaviour of the actor hints at the existence of such transactions only in a general and unspecified manner.

THE DANGER OF INFERIOR SUBSTANCE

Communication is asymmetrical, and involves a transfer of coded substance. There is always a danger of absorbing inferior substance, even if listening to a fool on the train cannot be compared to the consequences of marriage, the ranking transaction most central in the South Asian context. To marry one's daughter to an inferior would indeed constitute a scandalous acceptation of inferior substance (Inden 1976; also van der Veen 1972, Pocock 1972). For in this particular transaction, the gift of a daughter to a superior is only one side of the coin; the acceptance of the spouse by the superior party constitutes a major amelioration of the coded substance of the wife's party.

The division of the spoils between the Darbar, the teacher and myself, then, corresponds structurally to the marriage circles which some Gujarat castes such as the Patidar[18] arrange to limit the cost of hypergamy (which may lead to exorbitant dowries) while at the same time guaranteeing against transfer of inferior substance.

THE SITUATIONAL FRAMEWORK

I have noted that individuals may gain some leeway in relation to caste norms by defining a private space where behaviour contrary to norm is allowed or at least tolerated. They create a separate situation to escape from the rules that pertain in more public settings. When Mr. Parekh is worshipping Shiva, he is not taking part in the deliberations of the temple committee. When Ismail is making his devotions to the goddess, he is not among Muslims. And when Arjun is paying respect to his guru, he is not accompanied by his pupils, for whom he himself should incarnate authority. Such disjunction between situations is, of course, familiar to us from Western society. In classical sociology, however, this disjunction is sometimes seen to distinguish modern from traditional societies, and there is a tendency to see India as traditional in this sense.

I have dealt with this problem above, but I shall resume briefly the conclusions. The categories used in Saurashtra are various: they may refer to caste, estates, ethnicity, religion or occupation. They fill the need for typifications, ideal types, or stereotypes, which Rex (1970: 139) sees as necessary correlates of any complex society, and which enable us to produce models for interaction and to orient conduct towards the other. Self-presentation in Saurashtra is made with reference to these categories, but actors have considerable choice as to which category they will refer for their situational identity. What is striking, however, is the degree to which they adhere to the implications for behaviour expected from each choice (Tambs-Lyche 1993: 169). To each category corresponds a stereotype of how members of that category are supposed to behave, and people in Saurashtra take care to act true to type as long as a given situation lasts. We now understand why: the categories are critical elements of emergence in the type situations Esser speaks of, as well as determinants of the flow of substance in the relativity constituted by ranking transactions. Given these implications, we understand why the choice is so important. It is difficult to prove that choices are made deliberately so as to define the situation in a particular way, but this is certainly what I learnt to do—and it worked. I can only assume that my Indian friends and acquaintances do the same.

Our problem with this, as Westerners, is the consistency that Emerson speaks about. How can one play different roles wholeheartedly, without mixing them, and still remain a single person? My answer is that people in Saurashtra get around this dilemma by commuting his demand for consistency from the domain of action to a meta-dimension behind action, the way of doing things rather than what to do. This is what we did when opposing the socially contextualized, Western image of the individual to the decontextualization implied by the Indian concept of *atman* as found in the *Bhagavad Gita*.

But the disjunction of the self, in Indian thought, from the social world parallels a disjunction between philosophy and common sense thought. Precisely since the *atman* is disjoined from social life, one cannot expect actors to put their ideas into practice—though one does hear, quite often, of the desirability of withdrawing from practical life to contemplate matters pertaining to *atman*. What we need here, however, is another kind of concept, capable not only of guiding practice but also of judging the acts of others.

THE ART OF BEING 'SIMPLE'

Maybe a clue here, is the term 'simple' or 'straight' (*siddho*). A 'simple' man is one who does not complicate the picture of his identity with 'buts' and reservations. Adding identities to another by an 'also' avoids the blurring of each identity. Thus the simple teacher conforms to the teacher stereotype, as the simple Rajput does to his. For the Westerner, this is not so simple, for the same individual may seem to hold different, and even opposed, opinions according to his self-identification in each situation. In Saurashtra, it is rather the person who introduces a complex, modified identity in any given situation who clutters it up and makes it hard to deal with. We may recall, here multiple senses of dharma: there is a dharma proper to each identity, to each role—not for the individual beyond or behind the roles.

In the West, the discourse concerning the singularity of the individual seems to be concerned with consistency in role-play across situations, between one situation and another. In Saurashtra, correct behaviour in each situation takes precedence. Yet while the simple man is willing and able to adjust to the situation, he is still recognized as the singular and unified actor who transcends these adjustments. Ismail and Dipak are examples of such straight or simple persons. It is their capacity for adjustment to any (sometimes not so simple) situation which earns them respect and opens the door for them anywhere. And this respect is *not* earned by the schemer who adjusts strategically to situations, not if he is unable to convince people of his sincerity. It is the individual then, who is recognized behind his multiple ways of acting out different situations, though the rules of the game are different from the West. Nobody would dream of accusing Mr. Parekh of hypocrisy, when he fails to make his personal ideas on religion relevant to the temple context.[19] If the ideal Westerner is a man for all seasons, the ideal in Saurashtra is an ability to deal with all kinds of situations on their own terms. Thus as Westerners we are tempted to construe the cross-situational affirmation of individuality as evidence of the existence of the individual, while we see the situational plasticity of the person, in Saurashtra, as a denial of individualism.

THE REPERTOIRE OF THE ACTOR

Barth, in an article too often ignored (1972b), has produced a simple paradigm of societal types based on the ways in which the situation is defined in interactional encounters. His classification is based on three elements: the inventory of social statuses as the total known to the society's members: the repertoire of statuses available to each actor, and the components used in defining the situation, which he defines as the relevant set of statuses, opportunities and tasks. Among other societies, he contrasts the encompassed systems of India with those of the West. Both have a large number of statuses in the system, and both have large individual repertoires. But in the Indian case, these repertoires tend to be combined in a limited number of standardized ways, a summation of statuses, a term he borrows from Weber (Barth 1960). This, he says, appears through elaborate structures of opportunities and tasks, signalled by complex idioms, which are manipulated to define particular situations—which is what I have tried to show here. In the West, the combination of statuses in the individual's repertoire are less standardized, and there is fluidity in the definition of situations, which may change in the course of a single encounter (1972b: 97). This, precisely, is not happening in the situations I have analyzed. The lack of fluidity in the definition of situation stems from the way statuses are clustered in them. This is interaction by category (Tambs-Lyche 1993), where reference to a category implies a stereotyped combination of elements.

Identities carry different rank implications. A Darbar and a teacher are labels indicating superiority in some ranking transaction contexts. A person describing himself as a shoemaker would not benefit from such associations, since his is an untouchable caste and the occupation is seen as the reason for its low status. The Darbar or teacher's superiority cannot be taken as given, as an accepted guru, for example, would command deference from everybody, including them. The label does not command deference; deference is due to a superior and superiority is by needs a relational concept. Clearly, however, the labels a person can use may be seen as resources towards achievement of superiority within any given situation, being the bases on which ranking transactions can be made, so as to carry the spoils in the situational game of rank.

I have tried to show how such a rank-conscious mood translates into regular ways of defining and maintaining social situations. When such encounters are interpreted in the exchange mode (Homans 1958, 1961; Barth 1966) the regularities are seen as resulting from strategies on the part of actors. Barth conceives of actors as exercising choice, based on a reasoned[20] appreciation of limitations and possibilities. There is a subjectivity involved here, as actors perceive similar situations differently, but in general, the determinants of social action rather lie with the conditions that constrain choice. In some situations, the choice seems obvious; in others, there are a limited number of possibilities that offer reasonable solutions to the problem the actor poses himself. For actors to apply such strategies in a regular fashion, however, they must have ways of distinguishing situations where a given type of strategy is appropriate. This is where Esser's type situations (1996) come in.

In any situation, there are objective factors which determine the situation, and subjective interpretations of it. I do try to assess objective factors when talking about scenes, but it is clearly difficult to isolate factors that are truly objective, independent of the actors' point of view. For Barth's models (1966) to work, external parameters must be clearly defined; the prisoner's choice is different from that of the Pathan chief. But constraints on choice are immutable only in a relative sense; the ecology of the prison does not survive an escape, as the winds that limit fishermen to boats that can be beached, become political restrictions once they demand that a breakwater should be built.

INDIVIDUALISM AND HIERARCHY

In Saurashtra, then, role-play follows stricter rules than in the West. Elements of other roles are, much less than in the West, allowed to intrude on the role one is playing. Individuals are less concerned with contradictions implicit in contrasting roles: one may express an opinion in one role, only to state a contradictory view in another. A Westerner, then, tends to feel Indians are constrained by their role in a way that undermines their individualism. But here we may be confusing person and individual—forgetting, perhaps, that the real individual is beyond each and all of the roles. Indeed, the individual may be more conscient of his non-identification with the role in India than in the West.

In so far as the link between philosophical discourse and everyday common sense is acted out, rather than talked about, we get no closer to an explicit ideology of individualism—or its negation—in Indian culture.

Is ideology to be defined as text, then, to be studied in and by itself, or as ideas that engender action? Whatever makes us act, may not be what we think we adhere to. While two castes may vie for primacy on the scale of purity and impurity, we might feel their members equally driven by material motives—the way Bailey (1959) saw Sanskritization as a corollary of competition.

Dumont's understanding of the cultural implies that a notion of hierarchy should manifest itself as a central part of emergence. It seems, indeed, clear that a persistent motive, when actors choose the category with which to identify, is to position themselves as high as possible in relation to relevant others. The categories used carry associations of rank, not surprising when they refer to caste. It is less obvious how to position, say, occupational and caste categories in relation to each other—who is highest then, the engineer or the Rajput? But in interactional terms, the answer is simple, for if the engineer wants to dominate the discourse he will try to steer it towards themes which an engineer is deemed qualified to talk about, and where the Rajput's high caste is of little importance. Such manoeuvres characterize my material. Categories imply rank, but actors establish a ranking pattern particular to each real situation, which depends on the choice of categorical identity in each case. Situations are defined so as to allocate rank differentially to participants. Even when participants aim at equality, this is done by a sequence of hierarchically structured definitions of situation, rather than a single, egalitarian one. It is striking how interaction reflects the concern with rank that we would expect from the texts of caste ideology. The dyads tend to take the form of ranking transactions (Marriott 1976, 1989). It may seem, indeed, as if actors are Homo hierarchicus (Dumont 1966a) whose implicits make them act the way they do. Insecurity in assessing the rank of unknown others may cause over-reaction, stressing rank beyond reasonable limits.

Rank consciousness and its implications, then, are central to social life in Saurashtra. But rank is not a cultural *ding an sich* which defies further analysis. The importance of rank stems from tradition; the competitive and conflictual nature of traditional society is central to present-day rank consciousness. What links relativity to emergence in Saurashtra, is the memory of a long history of war, struggle for land and dominance, and social conflict. It is a country where power has been all-important (Tambs-Lyche 1997). Just as I agree with Thoothi (1935: 119) that caste boundaries have been closed in defence against the dangerous world outside, so an assertive or defensive mood, with regard to rank, has become the individual's way of dealing with the complex and confusing encounters that life in this kind of society entails. No wonder, then, that elites or the hopelessly outcaste are the most eager to denounce caste or rank consciousness.

NOTES

1. I try, here, to go beyond the idea of 'transient people' (Clifford 1992), to indicate some of the complex ways in which the traveller belongs to the place he has left and that towards which he is going, as well as the settings determined by travel itself. See also Appadurai 1991.
2. On the most usual type of Ashok-Leyland bus.
3. More and more buses have barred windows.
4. In clear contrast to what I have experienced on Calcutta trams.
5. This was Mauss' point: the gift is cannot be dissociated from the status of the donor (1995: 161).
6. A loincloth.
7. Take 'bargaining' as a possible image; clearly there are cases of pure bargaining, typically limited to politics or the marketplace, and less typical cases, as when we are trying to obtain an object at a good price from an antique dealer who is also a friend.
8. An interpretative example: I am a painter needing money. I visit a friend. If I interpret his interest in my work as willingness to buy, I may gain a sale. If the interpretation is wrong, I may lose a friend. Esser's additional point is that I may calculate the risks: My friend will certainly not buy if I do not say the picture is for sale, while he may still remain a friend, even if I press the sale a little. . . .
9. The function has the form: Uj / Ui > (1-p) p , where U stands for risk, j and i are alternative models of the situation, p is the expectation that j is valid, while (1-p) stands for the expected validity of i. Uj is the value the actor is sure to retain even if j proves inappropriate, while Ui is the risk he runs by redefining a situation to which he has applied j (1996: 20-1). p will be small when the choice is uncertain: if obvious, its value would be 1 (1996: 19). If the fit of the model is good, p is high, and the definition of the situation will not change even if Uj is low; once an actor has chosen a particular model, it is unlikely that he will change it (1996: 21).
10. We go to the baker's counter to buy a loaf of bread, and the definition of the situation seems obvious.
11. The concept of rationality involved here is not the one used in economic theory, which depends on an extremely simple definition of the situation: rational market behaviour is a response to supply, demand, and resulting price fluctuations. Such situations turn up only in a narrowly defined context.
12. He adds that this is consistent with recent research into the functioning of the brain, citing Roth (1995: 207ff and 212ff): 'When something, in a given

situation, is perceived as important as well as unknown, the brain automatically focuses on consciously penetrating the situation, without any volontary decision on the part of the actor' (Esser 1996: 31).

13. This is the Indian term for a railway coach, reminding us that bogie coaches were introduced in India before they became at all general in Britain.
14. This description relates to the situation before computer reservations were introduced in the 1990s.
15. Here, too, things have changed, and padded seats are now found on second-class rolling stock. Even in the early 1990s such comfort was exceptional on the metre-gauge lines of Saurashtra, however.
16. The main exception being those Westerners who, in the 1970s, were regarded as 'hippies'.
17. Since rank is relative, the process of relativity may be seen as a game where the superior position constitutes the spoils. As such, it is a zero-sum game: only one party can win. But here the losers gain a transfer of coded substance (Marriott and Inden 1976) which partakes of the superiority of the winner. If the difference in rank is destroyed, the superior quality of the substance is spoilt. Nothing would be worse than to listen respectfully to an inferior, but when the fool listens to the sage, both parties gain.
18. Pocock 1972, Tambs-Lyche 1980.
19. In contrast to Christian concern with belief, which should not change from one situation to the next.
20. He uses the word rational which raises problems I wish to avoid here.

CHAPTER 11

Praj and its Social Life

And now in the night when the city, gentle with neon,
  Calls me from paper where love is an abstract perfection
To the village of friends who are gathered which nene ever leaves
  I must work out from the fragments of conversation
The total I answer for which is the total I am.

ANTHONY CRONIN

We have dealt, till now, with scenes where strangers meet, and social positions are improvised on the spot. In turning to the village, we might expect a major shift. The Indian village, indeed, has often been seen as the essence of time-honoured community, where everybody knows and keeps his place. I criticize this idea, as others have done (Inden 1990), but let us first see how relations are acted out in the village. In choosing a large village I may be cheating a little, for obviously the personnel are better known to each other when the village is small. Yet in Saurashtra, many villages are large, and it was in 'Praj'[1] that I had my first experience of village life during three months of field-work there in 1973-4. Due to circumstances explained in my preface, I could not make a survey of Praj. This sketch is presented as a contrast to the smaller villages described from other sources, but it is also the only village where I participated in a large number of scenes and situations.

I chose Praj for its complexity; I wanted to stay in a village where a large number of castes and religious viewpoints were present. It is not a community of insiders who know each other. It is closer to town life in a highly stratified society where one must distinguish between acquaintances and others, between inferiors, equals, and superiors.

With some 3,000 inhabitants at the time of my field-work, Praj serves as a centre for surrounding villages. In many ways it is more like a small town than a village. But the Census classifies both Praj and Talaja, the taluka headquarters to the south of it, as villages. It is situated on the main road between Bhavnagar and Mahuva, and in 1974 the narrow-gauge railway parallel to this road was still running; it has since been closed.

Praj is quite an old place. In 1764 it was one of a several villages recently acquired by Bhavnagar State, then in its major phase of expansion (BDG: 63). One may still see the remnants of the village walls, but Praj has outgrown its walls. Examples of this growth are two large buildings seen to the east on entering the village from the main road; schools, primary and secondary; and the Health Clinic.

The main street, running north to south from the bus stand, and the railway station to the tank, is lined with substantial two-storey houses. In the middle sector of this street, which forms the marketplace, these houses mostly belong to merchants. They have the large wooden balconies, beautifully carved and sometimes painted, typical of towns in Gujarat. They are a conspicuous sign of wealth since wood is imported from outside Saurashtra, and the elaborate carvings are expensive to make. Indeed, in towns most merchants now choose to decorate their houses with cheaper plaster reliefs that correspond to modern fashion. Some houses are empty, however: others are occupied by other communities. This is typical of a process seen throughout Saurashtra; village merchants move to town, often retaining their lands, becoming absentee landlords, and Praj's market is not dominated by these merchant families. Many of the shopkeepers come from other castes. In fact, the large merchant houses were not always shops; their owners were often Vanias in the strict sense—buyers of grain. Their economic role in the village may be unchanged, but it is simpler, today, to reside in the city and collect the grain through a representative or simply by sending a truck.

The largest shops in the main street do not belong to Vanias. One is the main soda/bidi shop in the village, situated centrally on a corner of the market street. This shop is owned by a Khoja Muslim family, of which Ismail is the second son. A little further to the south, marking more or less the boundary between traders and craftsmen, is the goldsmith's shop. He is a Jain, and the Jain temple is next to his shop. He, highest in rank of all craftsmen, has his shop close to the centre, while the *mochi* (shoemaker) is at the very end of this street, on the southern outskirts of the village. Most other craftsmen, washermen, tailors and barbers, have their shops between these two. But the carpenter, potter and others who need space for their activity, live in the north-western quarter, at the opposite end of the village.

The Jain *derasar* is the only religious institution on the main street. There are few Jains in the village, now that so many Vanias have left. Though the *derasar* is still active, and tended by a Shaivite Margi temple-servant, it is not a busy place. The only restaurant in the village is run by a Muslim and frequented mostly by that community. It is just a house or two from the main street, slightly to the south of the village centre. The Panchayat office, too, is on the main street, one block north of the soda shop. The side facing the main street is blank, the only sign of its importance being the loudspeaker mounted high under the roof. News and a few other programmes, mainly of interest to farmers, were broadcast to the village. The entry to the building, *via* a wrought-iron gate to its courtyard, is from a side street. The panchayat office is mainly used by the *mantri* and his secretary, who keep the land records (thus acting as *talati*) and runs the day-to-day business of the panchayat. The *mantri* is a Barot[2] by caste, while his secretary is a *darji* (tailor). The *mantri* lives in a village nearby, where some 500 Barots live.

I lived in the room used for meetings, behind the office. No meetings were held during my stay. It was comfortable, since I had access to one of the two latrines of the village. Obviously they were still seen, in Praj, as an item of dubious utility. Some time earlier, a social worker had built of a row of latrines in the south-west corner of the village, close to the shoemaker's

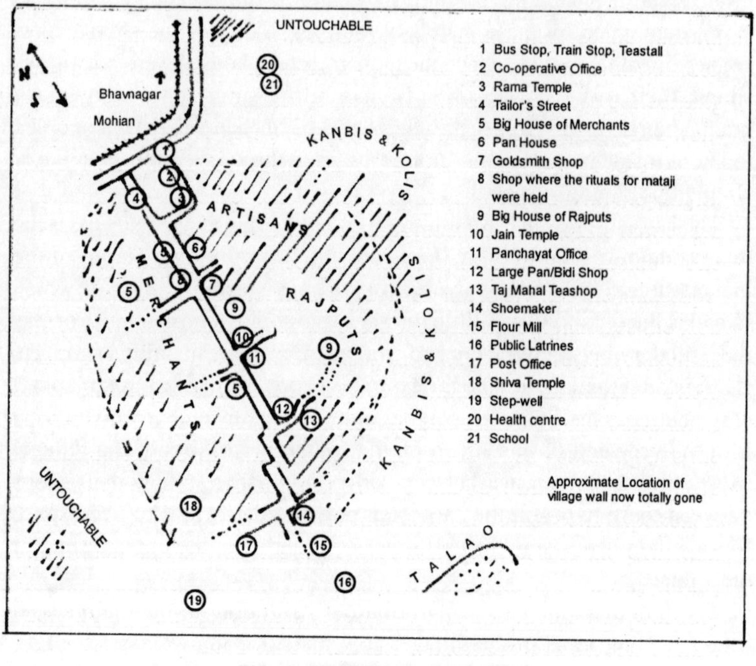

FIG. 3: SKETCH MAP OF PRAJ

shop. They were now locked up. Side streets are preferred for such purposes.

If we go up the side streets to the east of the bazaar we find the houses still large; but they are built of rough square stones and very different from those of the merchants. No merchant of substance live in houses presenting the naked, forbidding appearance of these dwellings. We are among the Darbars, known here as Garasia[3] Rajputs. This is to underline their local ancestry, as distinct from the Gohils, who belong to the clan of the royal house of Bhavnagar. From what I gathered, the Garasias here descend from the Koli chiefs and landlords of Praj, at the time of its annexation to Bhavnagar State. The biggest of these houses, two storeyed and large by any standards, belongs to the *pramukh* or village headman. The family has held this post for several generations, before and during the panchayati raj. This house, like others of its kind, has only one entrance—and no windows—on the ground floor. While not a fortress, it is easy to defend. It compares favourably in size to the 'palace' of Kalapi, the Gohil chief of Lathi, a recognized Rajput state.

Not all Rajput houses are as big or imposing as this one. Most of the important families live close to the main street. As we continue eastwards, Rajput dwellings become indistinguishable from those of Kanbis and Kolis, which lie beyond them. They are small, one-storey buildings with one or two rooms. The variation in Rajput housing is typical of the caste, where senior lineage members are substantial landowners, while quite a few are middle peasants, and some junior kin may have little or no land, subsisting as sharecroppers or farm labour. The Rajputs dominated the village co-operative society, which had some 200 members, from among about 400 farmers in the village. The secretary of the society, however, was a Shrimali Brahmin. 'Praj's best farmer' was a Garasia Rajput; he had some 150 *bighas* of land and owned a tractor. Several other Rajputs had properties of around 50 *bighas*, a large holding for the region, which coincides, incidentally, with the legal maximum.[4]

At the edge of the Rajput quarter, where it borders on that of Kolis and Kanbis, is the Rama temple, tended by a Brahmin. It is said to be 400 years old; if so, the so-called Kolis of Praj must have been Rajputized[5] before the area was annexed to Bhavnagar.[6] This is an important ritual centre on certain occasions, such as Dasahra,[7] and many Rajputs make a weekly visit there on Sundays. But it cannot be called a busy place, and it seems clear that, in 1973-4 at least, it belonged to the institutional rather than personal religious sphere for most Rajputs. The Brahmin is quite poor and not greatly respected. But there is another temple to Rama, beyond the railway tracks, and here old men of the village, especially Rajputs, gather in the evening to chat.

Kanbis and Kolis live in an extensive quarter next to the Rajputs, which forms the eastern edge of the village. They are small holders, sharecroppers and agricultural labour. They must have lived more densely when retained by the village walls, now nearly gone on this side. The unstructured appearance of this area, where no clear line seems to divide castes, may be a result of modern expansion.[8] Kolis are the near equals of Kanbis here, and they live side by side. The latter were hardly affected by the process that has made Patidars of many members of their caste. In Praj, they still paid bride-price at marriage,[9] and seemed unaware of the existence of dowry among their caste-fellows in towns.

North of the Rajput area, but to the south of the health clinic and the school, is an area inhabited by several craftsmen of middle status, such as the carpenters. They do not have shops on the main street. Among them live the *halvai* (sweetmaker), who is a Lohana, and some of the school-teachers. The *halvai* saw himself as superior to his neighbours, and was not very popular among them. They, probably, would rather have pointed to an elderly schoolmaster as a man of status in the quarter. He is a Gohil Rajput. There is no temple in this part of the village, with its mixture of castes. The *mistri* (carpenter) family that I knew in fact worshipped at a small Shiva shrine near the village tank, at the other extreme of the village. As so often in Saurashtra, there is no separate blacksmith's shop, even in this big village; whenever iron tools are repaired, it is done by the mistri. The craftsmen who lived in this north-western corner of the village tended to be of higher status than those in the south-west. Most clearly, of course, this is shown by the location of the shoemaker's shops in the extreme south-western corner.

Outside the village, to the south-west, is the largest living quarter for the low or 'untouchable' castes. On this side, the walls of the village are more intact, and so the separation of the untouchables is marked. Prominent among them are the Dheds (originally weavers), often called Harijans here, and the so-called 'untouchable Kolis', a designation which remains enigmatic. Dogs keep unwelcome visitors away from this quarter, which is distinguished by its low and poor dwellings made of twigs, reaching only to shoulder height, and covered with sackcloth. The poorest dwellings belong to Waghris.[10] There is another, smaller, Waghri settlement north of the railway tracks, equally poor. Waghris are conspicuous in this area by the pigtails worn by males, which the higher castes do not allow them to remove.

Apart from the two, quite substantial, religious buildings mentioned, there are several small shrines in the village, mostly for a Mata. The most elaborate goddess shrine is in the south-west corner of the village. South-west of the village, at the far side of the tank, are the *palios* or memorial stones dedicated to those men and women who died in a heroic manner. Most are Rajput males, but women and members of the Kanbi caste are also represented. Not all the deaths recorded are equally heroic, however; one stone is dedicated to a man who died of snake-bite and another to a man whose house collapsed on him. The ruin still occupies a large site in the centre of the Rajput quarter. Clearly he was a man of substance; there must be a story here, but I did not get it. Among the *palios* there are a few trees or stones dedicated to Matas, apparently nameless. There is no important temple to the goddess in the village, but there is one—to Ambaji or a form of her—on a hilltop within walking distance, like many such temples in the *jangal*. At that time there was little animosity between Muslims and Hindus in the village, and it was to this temple that Ismail accompanied me.

News, we have seen, often enters the village through a small teashop on the main road, close to the bus stop. Here, newspapers are read by literate men, as others gather around. The latest developments in the groundnut price is the item which interests everybody, but other news is also digested here on the way to the village at large. I found that news travels quickly and, in spite of considerable illiteracy, people were remarkably well informed about recent events in town.

I was in Praj when India's first 'nuclear device' was sprung, and there was a lot of enthusiasm for this event. News of the disturbances in the state (1974) reached us quickly and my decision to leave for a couple of weeks was made—I think wisely—on the basis of oral information which proved to be accurate. Locals, however, stressed that there was likely to be no trouble in the village, and this, too, proved to be the case. The disturbances, inspired by J.P. Narayan, which ultimately led to the Janata victory at the polls, were largely an urban phenomenon in Gujarat.

Groundnut is the most important crop in Praj, with onions a close second. A large part of the fields are irrigated, and artificial manure is known and used. I was struck by an apparent opposition which proved to be fairly general in Saurashtra, between the high standard and productivity of agriculture and the traditional outlook of the dominant caste, as well as the rigidity of class. In 1973-4, wages of farm labourers were among the lowest in the country, contrasting sharply with the relatively high income among farmers. Minor villages depending on Praj for certain goods and services include the Barot village mentioned; a village of Kanbis; a smaller multi-caste village; another where Rajputs are dominant, but where tenants are mainly Palleva or Palival Brahmins,[11] and a village of the latter community only. These 'Brahmins' are somewhat enigmatic. As a local Shrimali Brahmin said: 'They are not real (pakka) Brahmins, but they are descended from Brahmins and have taken to farming.' I rather think they are Sanskritized Kolis.

This brief description of surrounding villages shows the variety of settlements to be found in any single region. To get a picture of social complexity in Saurashtra, one cannot stop at the village, even when it is big and multi-caste. Towns or large villages are at the centre of micro-regions containing a diversity of settlement types, and their social fabric is variable, changing from one region of the peninsula to another.

MAIN STREET

For social settings, we may start where I myself did, in the main and market street. The day after I arrived in Praj, I went for a walk through the village. Leaning on experience in rural Norway and Europe, I greeted everybody by a nod or a raised hand. But this, it soon became clear, was not the thing to do: people were laughing, and even those who answered my greeting, evidently found my behaviour funny. Exceptions were only those to whom I had already been introduced. Thus I had to change my ways. I now greeted only those I already knew. This seemed all right; evidently this behaviour, associated for me with urban life, was much closer to the mark. Indeed, the main street of a large village like Praj did not show a quality of interactive style different from what I found in the towns. It was only, I found later, in small one-caste settlements, as well as in the back streets of village or city, that one was supposed to greet everybody, or almost.

Then another dimension, which should perhaps have been obvious, became evident. As I was associated with relatively high status I was not supposed even to greet all I knew. Rather, people of lower status were to greet me first, and to indicate, by the manner of greeting, the rank differential. We now see why my initial sortie, greeting landowner and sweeper with the same joyful enthusiasm, was met with universal glee.

One should return the greeting of an inferior in measured, though not unfriendly terms. His greeting, however, may be enthusiastic—especially if he is going to ask a favour. Enthusiasm should be retained for equals or superiors. As for those whose rank is unknown, no need to greet them at all. The conditions that lead fellow travellers to communicate are absent here. This evidently saves trouble, as one does not run the risk of expressing inferiority to an inferior, or vice versa. Yet schoolboys shouted 'good morning' or even 'what is your name' at the sight of me—as they do to Western tourists all over northern India—and the implication is not all that flattering. For, while there is nothing disrespectful in the greeting, the peel of laughter which follows is ironic. Indeed, ostensibly respectful forms of behaviour mimicked in such a way as to negate their referential connotation, is a common form of humour in Gujarat and other parts of northern India, and the term 'Maharaj' is used to address both the Brahmin and the sweeper.

The village main street is clearly public space. Thus while most village shops are open to the street, one cannot look into any private dwelling from main street level in Praj. Most dwellings here are two-storeyed. The merchants live on top of their shops, in houses easily recognized by their wooden verandahs. Other houses, massive-looking, are without shops or window openings at ground level. They belong to Rajputs. In this the main street of Praj differs from that of a town; there, almost all main street houses are of the merchant type, even when inhabited by members of other castes.

The main street in Praj is also the shopping mall. Not only are most shops found here, but traders using a stand or a cart have their particular positions along this street. In the morning, and after the afternoon nap, almost everybody comes here. Men predominate, but quite a few women are seen; only among the very few does purdah imply complete absence from the street. But women spend time in the street only for explicit and definite purposes, such as shopping. Roofs in Praj are not flat, so women cannot move along them, as they do in northern and eastern India; instead, they prefer the back streets and alleys whenever paying calls of a less definite nature. This is not due to suspicions of meeting males; witchcraft or simple female scheming are as important. Women should have a definite purpose when visiting—but there are many excuses for a chat.

Exceptions to this rule are the women of the pastoral (*maldhari*) castes, and lower-caste female labourers. The contrast is obvious when one enters the side streets and back lanes, for here more women are seen. Thus it is men who use the main street as a forum for informal gatherings, leisure, or simply chatting. Mostly, however, they do not stay talking on the street itself but at specific locations, such as the large soda shop of Ismail's father. Here, at most times of the day, a group of men were talking eagerly. They also gather at the small café known as the 'Taj Mahal', and at certain other shops.

The main street is certainly where most men meet, but not the centre of everybody's life. Respectable women spend little time there; they stay in their houses or visit others, avoiding main thoroughfares. Viewed as a whole, the village has not really a centre-periphery structure, but rather a multi-centred character where each quarter is associated with particular groups, identified by caste categories.

Of the temples only the Jain *derasar*, located beside the goldsmith's shop, adjoins the main street. The goldsmith, like some of the present but many of the former merchants of the village, is a Jain. Their temple, then, is in the merchant's quarter as much as it is on the main street. Thus there is no village temple, as in southern India. This is typical of northern India and almost universal in Gujarat. The sanctuary which, socially and politically, comes closest to serve the whole village is the Rama temple, well off the main street, where the Rajput quarter fades into that of the Kolis and Kanbis on one side, and of the artisans on the other. Rama is central to Rajput identity and prestige, but popular with Kolis and Kanbis too, at least to the extent they still copy Rajput custom. They did so for a long time, until Rajput prestige started to suffer from post-Independence changes. Other temples, too, are located in the area inhabited by their devotees. In Saurashtra, generally speaking, deities are tied to people, not territory.

Politically, several locations may be thought of as central. As noted the main venue for political discussion, in 1973-4, was a small tea-shop close to the bus-stand and outside the old village walls. The panchayat office, however, is at the very centre of the village, at a side street which runs between the Rajput quarter to the south, and the quarter where most pure artisans live, to the north. Following it towards the north-east, one ends up in the Kanbi and Koli quarter. Panchayat meetings are of course held there, and the secretary, who deals with the land register, is present here during office hours. But these functions hardly made the office a central meeting-place; the Panchayat saw little inconvenience in housing me there, and I do not think it bothered them much. A third centre is the house of the village headman, on the main street and close to the *derasar*. His was the most powerful Rajput family in Praj, and they held this position well before the modern panchayat was formed. Thus he had both formal and traditional legitimacy, and was obviously in control of the village. People turned to him for protection and support, whenever the panchayat secretary could or would not help.

While one may meet anybody in the main street, it is not a meeting-place for all. It is the marketplace, and so traditionally the merchant's quarter. The situation in Praj recalls the definition of plural society by Furnivall (1949): a society constituted by a certain number of culturally distinct groups which meet in the marketplace. As a public place, the main street conforms to our ideas of urban, rather than rural, life, and while most people may know about each other, they do not necessarily exchange greetings. Their presumed knowledge of each other's identity is far from obvious to the casual observer.

BACK ALLEYS

Villages differ in form, size and social complexity. Still, the general traits of Praj's main street as a social scene are reflected in other villages. While size makes a difference, this remains a matter of degree. To get into bounded space we have to enter areas that form essentially the spatial domain of a single community.

Unlike the main street, the back streets and alleyways are not fully part of a public domain. Both in villages and towns (Desai 1964; Doshi 1974), castes and communities cluster in separate wards. These may be well demarcated, or fade gradually into one another; but the feature of residential segregation is general of all large, multi-caste settlements. Exceptions are only the single-caste hamlet and the modern multi-caste suburb, where class to a degree replaces caste as a criterion for segregation.

Thus the back streets and alleys form the spatial domain of a single community. This does not mean that they are closed to outsiders; only rarely there is some physical demarcation in the form of a gate or other boundary marks. Yet life here takes on a different character from the main street. Groups are seen to gather without the reference point of a shop. Women are often seen and less conspicuously veiled. They often gather at wells and water taps, much as they did in older European settlements. It is significant that water posts are seldom found in the main street, and then they are used by men.

Thus when you come to a water tap surrounded by women washing clothes or fetching water for household purposes, you know you are entering community space. This also applies to spots on the river where women gather for such purposes, and, of course, even more so if women are bathing. It is true that one does see men watching from a distance; but going close is considered an intrusion. It is easy to see why romantic stories—and paintings—so often illustrate men happening unawares (?) upon women bathing.

In side streets and alleys, houses are more accessible and open to view than on the main street. Exceptions are the better houses of high-caste wards; only poor Rajputs, for example, have houses open towards the street. In Praj, the Brahmin tending the Rama temple has such a small and open house, similar to his Rajputs neighbours, with two rooms and a semi-open cooking hut in a corner of the yard. His house is surrounded by a wall, but it is too low to shield the inhabitants from view. To some extent, this wall marks the exclusiveness of his caste; there is no Brahmin quarter in the village. There are other Brahmins, some of whom have substantial houses, but they are not priests.[12]

Shielding the dwelling from public view is one of the most obvious status symbols in Saurashtra; but high blank walls are much less common than in northern India (Wiser and Wiser 1936). Indeed, Pramar notes that 'the women of Saurashtra were far freer and were apparently able to take care of themselves better . . .' (1989: 124) than in north or central Gujarat. He feels that the feudal structure of Saurashtra, where the chief and his men were responsible for defending everybody within the village walls, explains why community quarters were seldom demarcated by gates and walls. In side streets and alleys, daily tasks such as cooking may be observed, and there are more animals, which one quickly learns to see as an indicator of community. Muslim quarters abound with goats, while low-caste and untouchable areas have pigs.

For the outsider, there is an important change as he turns from the main street into the alleys: he becomes a visitor. The greetings superfluous in the main street are proper conduct here. Similarly, it is not impolite for inhabitants to ask the stranger his purpose in entering their area. Still, the transition from by side streets into the back alleys, is gradual. Even the transition from alleyway to courtyard may not be visibly marked, though again there are differences related to the caste or community occupying the area.

Among Rajputs there is considerable variation in this respect. The *pramukh's* house presents a forbidding aspect. His courtyard, too, is enclosed, and the walls are high. Similarly, other important landowners have their courtyards well screened from the public eye. These families practise a degree of purdah. As we move towards the poorer end of the Rajput area, however, houses become single-storeyed and their courtyard walls lower and less prominent, till they disappear altogether, and the dwellings become indistinguishable from those of Kanbi and Koli peasants. The kitchen moves to a shelter on the verandah, and women can be seen cooking. Having a kitchen sheltered from view is an important status symbol. As Rajput houses mingle with those of Kanbis, and these again with those of Kolis farther out, even the cooking hut disappears, and women cook in front of their house, as do untouchable women in front of their small dwellings.

Only the main street is public space in Praj; back streets are associated with a community. Whether from the same town or village, or a complete stranger, the visitor is conceived as an outsider. If visiting in a particular and recognized capacity, he is treated in accordance with the role. If not, he is asked why he has come.[13] In all cases, the greeting follows a certain rank pattern. If seen as a person of higher rank than the locals, the outsider is spoken to and treated more politely. But even so, he will be given to understand that he is in somebody else's area.

Thus what is seen as rights in territory modify, to some extent, the rank differential that might otherwise be brought into play. Among locals, relative rank is of course known. But familiarity between neighbours make the marking of rank difference less obvious. As within the caste, standing (Pocock 1972) may be more central than status, and individual qualities may modify criteria of rank defined by caste. Old servants, for example, may here receive an amount of deference which would not be due to them in the main street or another public setting.

COURTYARDS

The larger and more enclosed the yard, the higher the status of the Rajput family. Rich merchants including the *soni* (goldsmith)[14]—have well demarcated courtyards, usually at the back of their house since this often faces the main street. In their case, the military aspect of the Rajput house is lacking, though their living quarters are on the first floor. Merchants' courtyards are mostly sheltered not by separate walls but by their own out-houses and the backs of other houses, since they live in the centre of the village. Their shops face the street, but there are always lockable shutters. They are closed, routinely, at any sign of disturbance, or even when the buffaloes come home from the fields, when everybody seeks shelter from this host of heavy animals galloping down the streets.

In Praj, it is not easy to see which houses belong to Muslims. In general, and apart from old Islamic states such as Junagadh, there are few examples of specifically Muslim architecture in Saurashtra. Indeed, Muslim housing depends on caste as much as that of Hindus; craftsmen and peasants' houses are more or less identical to those of their Hindu counterparts. If there is a tendency, among richer Muslims, to shield their courtyards and women more conspicuously than Hindus do, this is not really noticeable among the poor. Ismail's Khoja family had a house more typically Muslim; it had a large, well-sheltered courtyard and the women only very occasionally went outside. The house was on the main street, but on its north-eastern side, facing the merchant houses; and it did not have a verandah. Khojas and Voras in town, however, have houses indistinguishable from Jain or Hindu merchants, except, to an extent, for the motifs of the woodcarvings. But they do not always adhere to the Islamic rule of avoiding human or animal figures.

The pure craftsman castes have houses similar to those of the Brahmin and peasant. In the north-eastern corner of the village, some have large courtyards; thus the *mistri* (carpenter) and the *kumbhar* (potter), whose yards serve as working space. This is less the case of the halvai who comes from the large Lohana caste of small traders; his large yard rather indicates his sound economy. It is well walled; his wife does, in fact, do a lot of cooking in the yard, and I should add that she (unlike her husband) is extremely attractive. It is probably as well, for her reputation, that the milk needed by the halvai is always sold by women. The yards of the carpenter and the potter, however, are not so well walled; in the first case, mostly men work there; in the second case, the family is not well off, since the competition of factory-made goods is heavily felt by them.

Unlike these craftsmen, the shoemaker is impure, and lives on the extreme south-eastern fringe of the village. It is hard to say whether his house is inside or outside the walls, since they are gone at this point.[15] Still, it is of solid stone, and so far as I know, he was the only untouchable to live so well. His workshop is in the house. His income, like that of the potters, has fallen because of factory competition. He still furnished Rajputs and other traditionally dressed men with the heavy leather shoes typical of Saurashtra in 1974. Yet his house may well have been a vestige of former prosperity.

We have said little about private space, for the perhaps obvious reason that much of it is sheltered from observation. Private space begins at the courtyard, and we have seen how the courtyard of rich and powerful people is sheltered from view. Thus one of the most obvious differences between high-caste people in general and those who are poor or of low caste is exactly the degree of privacy that they can afford. Purdah requires a large house with a sheltered, courtyard, otherwise veiled woman can be watched by outsiders going about her tasks. Some groups, notably

Muslims, try to practice purdah anyhow, but this is not very common in Gujarat and less so in Saurashtra.

INSIDE THE HOUSE

Privacy in Saurashtra can in general be seen as a function of power. In Praj, the main modification to this trend was the Brahmin priest of the Rama temple, whose courtyard was better walled than those of his lower-caste neighbours; but it should be noted that this did not mean that the courtyard was not open to view from the outside. The partition was symbolic rather than constructive of visual privacy.

Inside the walls, in courtyard or house, the family prevails. Here age and sex largely define the attribution of roles, with servants placed below the family proper. While men predominate when visitors are received, and women appear to serve them, this gender-based hierarchy becomes far less obvious when the visitor is well known to the family. The power of older women then becomes more obvious. It should also be noted that, while I have seen Bengali women ordered about by their husbands, Gujarati women are seldom given orders in this sense. The role-taking in front of visitors appears spontaneous and voluntary on the part of the women. Typically, I have heard Gujarati men suggesting that their wife should serve food, while she decides, on her own, that tea will suffice. Men could only protest mildly. Briefly, Gujarati women give an impression of controlling the house, of being independent enough to decide themselves what is required of them. The pastoral women are different again; it is they who welcome the visitor, while the men may well retire into the background.[16]

THE 'TAJ MAHAL'

The 'Taj Mahal' is a small place, and its unofficial name is a joke shared by the owner. Unlike the shops, it is located inside a building. Most customers take tea only, but light meals such as *poris* are available. I never saw a hot meal served there. It is dark, and peeping through the low door, it is not easy to see who is inside. Certainly, there are no women, nor did I ever see the Brahmin priest here. The important landlords were seldom seen, either, nor the Waghris—lowest of the untouchable groups. In fact, those who took their tea here, were mainly artisans from the middle layers of the community, and many were Muslims. Perhaps this was one reason for the egalitarian atmosphere of the place—the men were joking and talking informally, and the main deference shown was to age. Of course, when one of the important landlords entered, the respect shown him was noticeable. But why should he enter?

The Taj seemed to serve a function common to many Muslim cafés in Gujarat; it was the local labour exchange. The habituees were artisans for a good reason; they knew their potential customers would look for them here. A few small farmers or tenants also came, and I think this was where they sometimes got some extra work to beef up their scanty incomes. Typically, one man would pay for a round of tea for the others, while next day it would be another's turn. Some poor men, of course, seldom paid. But the atmosphere of cameraderie or brotherhood was not only a function of equality; it was, I think, modelled on the Muslim cafés of bigger places, where an egalitarian mode bears witness to the ideals of Muslim brotherhood, in opposition to Hindu hierarchy. In this sense, the Taj offered a refuge from the rank implications of most venues in the village, a refuge which, in the seventies at least, seemed not unwelcome even to Hindus.

GATHERINGS OF MEN

The men gathering at the Taj form but one of many groups in the village. While such groups may gather in or by the public arena of the street, the gathering itself constitutes a semi-public arena, visible to all and sundry but not equally open to all. Thus there is a separate *pan/bidi* stall outside the old village, near the bus and railway stops, which is frequented by Waghris and other untouchable groups. At the large Khoja shop, one did meet untouchables of other castes, but I never saw a Waghri there—it is hard to say whether they were actively discouraged or just did not feel comfortable there. The former explanation is quite likely, for they are the lowest of all castes in Praj, and so treated.

Another tea-stall in the bus stop area is said to be the locus for political discussion in the village. This is also where the daily newspaper was read aloud. Men of importance would be present for the news, of which the groundnut prices, with the prices of some other cash crops, were probably the most important. Those who gathered here were supporters of the Congress party, which then controlled the village panchayat. The opposition gathered in another stall; as I was introduced to the village through its Congress leaders, the opposition did not like my presence and I never got close to them. The tea-shops of the untouchables and the Congress group do not face the main street. This may well be significant. The main street Khoja shop was frequented by most castes and groups, and certainly not the place for discussions meant for the ears of just a few.

WELCOME TO THE VILLAGE: A SERIES OF INVITATIONS

I had barely arrived in the village when I began to receive invitations. In fact, during the first two or three days I was invited to dine by five or six people, so that I had to refuse some, since I soon found that nobody would accept moving their invitation to a later date. I must also have made several *faux-pas*, since the host usually sent a boy or a servant who would say, simply, 'the Saheb asks you to come and eat', without ever telling me who the Saheb in question was. Thus I had no way of choosing rationally, and dealt with the invitations on a first come-first served basis. Another *faux-pas*, for it soon became clear that not only was I supposed to favour the most prestigious people with my visit, but also to see them in proper order of rank—the most important ones first. Luckily, perhaps, there was no universal agreement on what the proper order was—the *pramukh* did not invite me, otherwise that priority at least would have been clear.

In other words, my presence set moving a whole process of competition for rank, which faded away, however, as I think the word spread that I was neither important nor very interesting. The visits as such were not very interesting either. Usually, I would arrive in good time, to be seated in the front room. Water or tea, sometimes with a simple snack, was then served, but the host would only appear later, if at all (some hosts were absent), to invite me to eat. A few polite remarks were exchanged, then the meal was served, and then it was more or less indicated that I was supposed to leave. Thus while I ate well, I learnt little from these visits, except what was obvious: it was important to have invited me, and if possible to have been the first to do so, but the importance of this move stemmed from the rivalry between prominent people in the village, and had very little to do with me. The main interest of the visits, then, lay in showing the permanent state of rivalry between village leaders.

A TALE OF TWO COOKS

The *mantri* of the panchayat, no doubt from the best intentions, had made arrangements not only for me to stay in the panchayat meeting room, but also to take my meals with the Brahmin family responsible for the Rama temple. This of course neatly avoided any considerations of purity or rank I might have had, and probably also was intended to help the rather strained economy of the temple priest. It might in fact have worked well—the sum I paid was quite reasonable for me yet not inconsiderable in the village context. But it did not work well. I must say that the Brahmin was never present when I came to eat there, when I met him elsewhere he was not very friendly, and his wife clearly wanted to keep communication with the foreigner to an absolute minimum. Since I was not a Brahmin, I was served in the courtyard, and had no company save for the village youth watching me from beyond the courtyard walls. But what I found hard to stomach was the lack of cleanliness: I always seemed to eat from a plate covered with flies. By this time I had left Western standards of cleanliness well behind, so I did not feel it was I who was too finicky: briefly, I never ate dirtier food in a dirtier place. After two or three meals I gave up and tried to do some cooking myself. It was not a success. Very few vegetables were available in the market, eggs were seldom seen, and I simply did not have the training, time or equipment to cook in the village manner. After a couple of days I put the problem to Ismail, who at once proposed a solution.

'Can you eat food made by a Jogi?', he asked, explaining that the caste in question was of very low rank. I assured him this did not bother me in the least, and so Bharu, who worked for the family making bidis, became my cook. Or rather, his wife cooked and Bharu brought my meals to the Panchayat office. The arrangement was simple: I paid for their provisions and they cooked for me. It worked out much cheaper than the Brahmin's rate, the meals were tasty, and last but not least, they were scrupulously clean. Bharu was an intelligent and quite progressive man, though illiterate. He and his wife subscribed to the view that 'a small family is a happy family', as the family planning posters beamed to us from many a lamp-post, and it was with some pride that Bharu showed me a rather technical manual of human procreation and family planning, the illustrations of which he had studied scrupulously.

Bharu also proved a great help in my work, always smiling and ready with a solution to any practical problem. But I was aware that taking food from a Jogi might pose problems. Certainly, the invitations from prominent people ceased coming in, whether for this reason or simply because they had served their purpose, I never knew. I did not miss them. Nobody criticized me openly, but it is true that from then on, I had little contact with Brahmins and Vanias in Praj. Rajputs did not seem to mind, nor did the members of various middle-range castes I frequented. And since Ismail, son of Bharu's employer, was after all a Muslim, my contacts with them were excellent.[17]

THE GODDESS POSSESSES A KANBI MERCHANT

One Sunday evening (Christmas Eve, incidentally), I was walking down the main street of Praj after witnessing *arti* in one of the temples—it was sunset. I was called to join quite a large gathering, seated in front of one of the main street shops. This was a mixed-goods shop run by Bhagatbhai Patel, a Kanbi. Inside his shop, two men were brandishing large wind instruments—about a metre and a half long, made from a single, straight tube—then they were blowing a deep, hoarse note, directing their instruments at a row of pictures depicting several different goddesses. When I joined the audience, one of these horn-blowers—the Kanbi owner of the shop—expressed his scepticism: these foreigners, he said, had no real respect for anybody but Ishvi (Jesus) and ought therefore to be kept away from Hindu rituals. I tried to defend my presence, claiming that all Gods are one, and this was gruntingly assented to.

The audience now started to increase, as if called by the horns; a number of men arrived. Some were Rajput: almost all were wearing traditional village dress, and I think they were mostly Kanbis and Kolis, members of the 'thirteen castes'. The time was now about half past nine, and the new arrivals began to sing, accompanied by 'Jhang' (two half-cups of brass joined by a string) for rhythm, as well as tabla and harmonium. The latter was handled by the chief singer, whose lines were repeated or answered by the rest of the group. The chief singer was a middle-aged man, wearing a long beard and long hair. By caste he was an Atit, a small community often serving part-time as 'low-caste priests', chiefly serving in ceremonies concerning the goddesses. The Atit had an excellent voice, and his singing was loud and enthusiastic, creating an effect very different from the bhajan-singing I knew from Krishna-worship. Indeed, I later realized that the singer was close to, or had passed into, the trance usually associated with goddess-worship.[18] At intervals, the singing was interrupted by, or accompanied by, the blowing of the large horns in honour of the goddess. She was called by several of her names, indicating the conflation of the different deities into the 'one' goddess. Thus while the chief object of devotion seemed to be Ambaji, Khodiyar was addressed in at least one of the songs, while a number of them simply referred to 'Mataji', without further qualification.[19] Around ten fifty the shopkeeper, acting as host to the group of singers, served them milk, whereupon he performed *arti* before the images of the goddess. He then closed his shop and went home.

But the singers, now in a great mood, continued enjoying themselves, and a small part of the crowd remained. Singing solo, one after the other, the singers now enjoyed themselves greatly. Then, after a while, one of them began to dance. He did so in a semi-sitting position, hands and upper body moving ecstatically to the rhythm: his movements clearly symbolized riding, and his hands were often in the position known to us from the horsemen depicted on the memorial stones. He did not dance alone for long: as others joined in, they danced in pairs, advancing against each other in mock fights. No longer were we singing for Mataji: these were the songs of the rider-heroes of the past, celebrating a martial tradition.

In between two dances, one old man declaimed a poem—in a rather uncertain voice. But, 'this was good!' the Atit singer assured us, as some of the younger members of the group smiled in disdain. I had to dance too, of course, trying to remember the most martial elements of badly learned Norwegian folk-dancing. After that—it was now one o'clock, very late indeed for an Indian village—everybody seemed happy: it was then only I realized that this extra performance, continuing after the shopkeeper's ritual, was in honour of myself. In fact, this was the way the traditional core of the village—the 'thirteen castes' traditionally allied to the Rajputs—welcomed me to their village.

Although this session of late-night dancing had nothing to do with Bhagatbhai's ritual as such, yet it was striking how the one followed the other. The goddess ritual and the martial dancing may not be linked but they unite the same core group of men. Moreover, the style of performance is similar, and the values clearly related: we are here, I think, close to the node of Darbar culture in Saurashtra, the link between devotion and the celebration of power made explicit through the continuity of the proceedings.

A week later, Bhagatbhai's ritual was repeated. Sunday is, indeed, the 'day of Mataji', and her devotees take but a single hot meal that day. This time—perhaps because it was New Year's eve by the Western calendar—the singers were not only offered milk, but tea and *prasad*, too, by their host. He also gave them one rupee each. Again, only men were present, some Rajputs, some Kanbi, and some Koli, while some apparently belonged to other castes from the group of thirteen, to judge from their appearance, language and behaviour. Ismail was there, listening with respect and interest, and there were some other Muslims too—but no Brahmin or Vania. The Atit was again lead singer, and clearly these performances formed part of the 'semi-priestly' tasks associated with his caste.

This time, I taped the performance. But unhappily this time the singing was less successful. The Atit was not satisfied, and at no time seemed to achieve the trance-like state of the first occasion. He simply did not seem to be carried away by his own singing. Everybody seemed to feel the difference, and when they asked me to replay my recording, they were unanimous. This time the singing was not good. The Atit, laughing but somewhat embarrassed, withdrew to the periphery of the group, smoking his pipe.

My efforts to tape the performance may have spoilt it. But I did learn, here, that such sessions of ritual are unique events: one is not like another. They are performances in the sense of an artistic production, not simply the acting out of a pre-existing schedule. The Atit's pleasure in achieving what he wants, and his disappointment when inspiration fails to materialize, are the reactions of an artist, not a 'ritual technician'.[20] The essence of the art is the creation of an atmosphere in which the singer, and then the devotees and the audience, are carried away. In this particular ritual, the art of letting oneself be carried away borders on trance, underpinning personal devotion and enthusiasm for the cult and its object. This, then, are qualities that Mataji—the goddess—is deemed to inspire, and which in turn are brought forth in her honour.[21]

A few months later I attended the ritual again. The Atit was no longer there, and there was no longer a group of singers. This time, however, Bhagatbhai himself was possessed by the goddess. His trance was signalled by shivering and convulsions. He did not, however, relay to us any significant message from the goddess: he simply stayed, mute but shivering, facing her image. He seemed satisfied to have reached this state, but the possession was not a success with the audience, who remained lukewarm. They did not tease Bhagatbhai, but they were unimpressed and rather bored. Clearly, the spirited, trance-like singing of the Atit had appealed far more.

The juxtapposition or replacement of one element by another seems, however, to justify the view that the Atit's first performance was seen as 'a kind of' trance. Again, the reaction's to Bhagatbhai's possession underlines the uniqueness of each performance as an event in itself: I would like to characterize it as an experiment. Apparently, this was the second time that Bhagatbhai had achieved trance, and so the news had spread. To him, it was a significant stage in his progress towards a closer relationship to the goddess. To the others, it may have been a religious move worthy of respect, but Bhagatbhai's efforts apparently did not inspire or fascinate them.

Among the spectators we may distinguish at least three categories. For Rajputs and other members of the 'thirteen castes', possession is an acknowledged and generally respected phenomenon. Individuals may, of course, differ with regard to the meaning or importance it has for them, and in their criteria for judging any particular instance of possession. It is clear, however, that there are degrees of involvement, enthusiasm, 'being carried away', without any clear line being drawn between trance and other forms of emotional involvement. These degrees apply both to the performance itself and the criticism others make of it. As long as we stay within this category of people, however, possession as such is a phenomenon taken for granted: within this frame, it may be judged more or less 'good' or 'genuine'.

The second category of personnel includes the Muslims, who probably did not share this belief in possession, but were watching the spectacle with interest. Some smiled a little, at these antics of the 'superstitious' Hindus, but they certainly did not make fun of it or criticize it openly then and there. The characterization of a belief in possession as 'superstitious' was worded in other contexts, where it was sure not to offend anybody.[22]

The third category is important: these were the conspicuously absent Vanias and Brahmins. Though individuals might differ in their answers when asked why they did not watch Bhagatbhai's ritual, I have no doubt that the basic reason was that no Brahmin or Vania, in general, would like to be associated with such unorthodox, non-Sanskritic, or popular ritual. To maintain the difference between true Hindus (or Jains) and these popular practices is an important symbolic strategy, underlining the distinction between the pure and less pure religious forms. Unlike the Muslims, then, Brahmins and Vanias needed to mark their difference from popular religion since, in another idiom, they were all Hindus.[23]

Bhagatbhai's ritual may usefully be compared to the examples of possession in goddess-worship that Pocock describes from the Gujarat mainland. They clearly relate to similar cults, but we may note some variations. In the least Sanskritized of Pocock's three examples, Shivabhai, a Kanbi of relatively low standing within the caste, is possessed by Mataji (1973: 43-7). This is what Bhagatbhai tried to do. Shivabhai is already recognized, however, as a *bhuvo* or spirit medium of Mataji. I am doubtful, however, that Bhagatbhai would like to be categorized as a simple *bhuvo*, for this position is socially ambiguous among Kanbis, and Bhagatbhai, owning a reasonable shop, has a certain standing in the local caste group.

Typically, in Pocock's second example (1973: 48-50), the host, who belongs to the medium levels of his caste, has invited a *bhuvo* from the low Patanwadia (Koli) caste who acts as the medium of the goddess. Moreover, the questions are put to the medium by a member of the Raval caste, also relatively low in the hierarchy, specially hired for the occasion.

Thus the host (*jajman*) avoids the ambiguity inherent in Bhagatbhai's role when he acts as medium and host at the same time. When Bhagatbhai invites the Atit and his group of singers, however, there is a parallel to Pocock's second example. Yet the Atit does not act as a *bhuvo*, and the forms of performance and possession are quite different. Pocock's third example might have satisfied our absent Vanias and Brahmins, since there is no possession, and worship is directed to the pure form of the goddess.

What I wish to stress is that Bhagatbhai's ritual situates itself and is situated by others within the social order of the village. In religious terms, Bhagatbhai is seeking a closer lien to the goddess. In social terms, the forms he chooses place him as what, indeed, he is: a rising entrepreneur from a peasant caste, still striving for prominence within the traditional religious horizons of his caste, and not yet attempting (as do the leading Patidar entrepreneurs) to approach his religious practice to Vania standards. As such, his ritual draws people from the traditional, Kathiawari-speaking milieu of Rajputs and peasants—the thirteen castes—but are shunned by the more Sanskritized communities of Vanias and Brahmins.

THE *CHORA*

Like all Rajput villages, Praj has a men's house or *chora*, which is still a significant social scene. The *chora* is a roofed platform enclosed on three sides but open on the fourth: everybody can see who is inside. It is the meeting-place of village Rajputs and their clients belonging to the *ter tansali*, and it is here that Panchayat meetings were held, before the introduction of the statutory, elected Panchayat. I was in Praj when the village Barot came from Sayla[24] on his annual round. He stayed about two days, and most heads of Rajput families came to see him at the *chora*, to report on births, deaths and other important events in the family. Only a small number, however (perhaps a dozen) stayed long enough to listen to the Barot's recitals. They were mostly older men, regretting the absence of the youth and commenting on the decline of custom. Moreover, not all the old men present were Rajputs, though they all belonged to the *ter tansali*.

Listening to the bard, we smoked the *hookah*. This was passed round, following a strict order. The Barot had the first smoke, followed by the most prestigious among the older men. Others followed in turn, and all Rajputs smoked before the client castes had their puff. As a kind of non-Rajput guest, I was placed between the last Rajput and the first client. This rank order generally corresponds to what we hear from myth and story: the bard smokes first, then the chief, and then the chief's men in descending rank order. In such stories, jealousy often expresses itself through this smoking order.[25] There was no apparent conflict during these sessions in Praj, however, and in spite of the rank order, the tone was friendly and relaxed. The difference stressed was that between the bard and his audience.

This example shows that the old ideas of rank order are far from dead. Yet the relaxed atmosphere perhaps indicates that the *chora* is, today, a scene of secondary importance. In the old days, it was the venue of political discussion and the atmosphere may well have been different. Today, real politics are discussed elsewhere, and the pleasure of gathering to hear the Barot was rather a nostalgic celebration of a tradition shorn of its former, sometimes conflictual, implications.

A MUSLIM GATHERING

One night I was sitting by the Pir's grave in Praj listening to Bapuji, the keeper of the grave, reading from Muhammed's own commentary on the Koran. He had planned to read systematically for a month, but this evening he stopped quite soon. 'Finished', he said, closing the book. He was reading to a gathering of four or five men, all Muslims of the village but myself; he translated and explained. One man, dressed like a Rajput, put a number of questions, clearly from interest in the subject-matter. But the others soon got tired, asking Bapuji if he was not going to finish soon. Bapuji took it nicely. Still, he gradually became a little irritated, indicating that either they should listen, or they should leave. At length he gave in. Most of the commentary read by him, after all, was to the effect that a wise man should never get angry.

What was striking was the informal nature of the gathering. Whatever the Koran might say, my Muslim friends in Praj were eager to stress that they were subject to none of the religious taboos of Hindus. They could drink or smoke. Bapuji's readings were screened by a thick smoke from our pipes and bidis, even if he himself never smoked when reading the holy book. More than a religious occasion, it was a friendly gathering; when the reading was finished, we chatted about a large number of other themes till far into the night. This gathering is but one example of how men in the village gather at different venues, informally and friendly, and of how this social purpose may well dominate any apparently ideological or religious purpose of the gathering. In spirit, the evening described here is close to that of an urban phenomenon, the club.

WHEN OTHERS ARE KNOWN

In Praj, the size of the village precludes knowledge of the whole population, but we might expect the transparence of caste status to produce a situation where the rank of others is usually known. Ranked interaction, then, should take on a standardized and consistent form, where everybody greets each other according to relative rank.

This is not borne out by my observations. True, inferiors are supposed to greet superiors first—and not vice versa. But inferiors do so when they deem it proper, and superiors answer, similarly, when they wish. These greetings, moreover, remain dyadic; they are not generalized so that an observer, watching the scene, can construct a clear pecking order. The reason is simple: in Praj, as in other large villages and in town, most people do not greet each other at all. But since they know about each other—even when there is no particular relation—the avoidance of greetings must be deliberate. Inferiors greet superiors when sufficiently bound to them, and superiority can manifest itself only when a ranked transaction is already in existence. Thus the main village street, as a public scene, offers the possibility of avoiding ranked interaction. The need to show one's inferiority only arises in established relations.

In smaller villages, where one servant may serve all landowners, such avoidance may be impossible (Berreman 1973). There is reason, in Saurashtra as in Europe, to move to a bigger place to avoid an identification that carries stigma. But there is no need for the anonymity of the city, provided the place is big enough for interaction to take place in the public mode of the main street, rather than of the back alleys or the small village.

In Praj as in other large settlements, the big soda/*bidi* shop creates an opportunity for temporary community between customers. Here, two tendencies are at work simultaneously: acknowledgement of pre-established hierarchy and a certain equality in the constitution of the group. A full analysis of rank here would be quite complex. What seems clear, however, is that between customers of relatively equal rank—say, members of the *ter tansali*—equality prevails. When joined by persons of markedly lower rank, the difference becomes explicit, for example in the form of greeting. Still, the gathering at the shop may be seen as an instance of constructing equality within a hierarchical context.[26]

So what happens when a landowner and his labourer arrive at the shop together? They may well act out the situation on a quasi-egalitarian basis. While everybody knows that one works for the other, he will avoid giving orders at the shop so as not to spoil the definition of the situation. By doing so, he may hope to gain loyalty from his employee. If, however, the boss emphasizes his superiority too much in this setting, he may find that his labourer simply goes elsewhere for his *pan*-or-soda break next time.

The quasi-equality that may emerge at the *pan*/soda shop, then, is close to that found in the field, or in the club. I would assume that women construct similar near-equality situations when gathering at the well or at the river for washing clothes or for a bath. In these latter situations, however, those of highest rank are often excluded.

I have noted some of the ways in which housing corresponds with caste, community and class. These examples illustrate general trends. The demarcation between courtyard and back street or alleyway varies, basically, with wealth and rank. The richest and more powerful groups shelter themselves more fully from public view; among poor people the line between alleyway and courtyard is blurred.

The quarters of untouchables are outside the village walls, and their poverty is indicated by the building material, sticks and branches, as well as the size of their huts, which are usually lower than a standing adult. Moreover, their quarters are fenced by thorny hedges, and guarded by ferocious dogs, and while people walk freely in the back streets and alleys of the 'pure' communities, the 'untouchable' areas are avoided by all above the pollution line, except during punitive expeditions. For violent attacks on untouchable quarters, including rape, burning and sometimes even killing, was a recurrent feature in disputes over wages and other issues in the seventies.[27] The culprits were normally Rajputs or representatives of landlord interests.

To sum up, the physical map of town or village represents a graduation from public to private space. Individual privacy, as we cherish it in the West, is hard to find. To write my notes I used to say I was tired and needed a nap. But the doors and windows of the panchayat office were closed only by bars; I was visible to those who climbed the plinth along the wall to look in. 'Ah, you are not sleeping', they would say, cheerfully, and enter. . . . Yet there are degrees of privacy, especially concerning the areas where women are or may be present. According to the community inhabiting a given quarter, the transitions from space that is public, or relatively private, is relatively continuous or highly demarcated. The higher castes lead more sheltered lives, so that the demarcation may be seen as defensive, in a wide sense of that term. Privacy is a function of power, and marks of privacy, whether physical or symbolic, signify the power they imply.

URBAN OR RURAL?

It is not easy to determine what distinguishes a large village like Praj from a town. Perhaps the political structure provides the best clue. In Praj, an agricultural caste is dominant, and urban castes such as the merchants play only a minor role. In this sense Praj is a village. Where the dominant caste was headed by a ruler, and/or the merchant community played an important part in community affairs, I prefer to speak of a town.

Praj's chiefs do seem to have been rulers in their own right in the early eighteenth century, until the area became part of Bhavnagar State. They were then regarded as Kolis, the politically dominant community of the region between Gogha and Mahuva at the time. This probably means that they had not yet adopted the symbolic embellishments of dominance that characterizes Rajput culture. Thus, when incorporated into the larger state, the Koli chiefs became Rajputs and aristocrats, but never princes, and Praj, though important, never became a capital, to benefit from that status during British suzerainty. This, I feel, is why it never became urban, unlike some settlements of similar size. Though urban and rural may be seen as a fundamental opposition in Saurashtra (Spodek 1976), there is no hard and fast dividing line. Praj today would have been more urban had the merchants not moved to town, or if its chief had retained a degree of independence. Throughout history, then, large villages such as Praj have had urban potential, while the seats of former rulers could well be reduced to village status.

NOTES

1. Synonym for a village situated about forty kilometres south of Bhavnagar.
2. Genealogist and poet. For the distinction between Barot and Charan, see Virbhadra Singhji (1994).
3. Garasia means those who hold land in *giras* or *gras*, roughly comparable to *jagir* elsewhere in Rajput India. In Saurashtra, however, there may well be several such landholders to a village.
4. When a family has more land than the legal limit, this usually means that the land is officially divided (say, between brothers), but is actually managed as a single holding.
5. I have elsewhere (1997: 84-7) noted the role of the Rama cult in building the Rajput Great Tradition (Kolff 1990). The date given for the temple fits the spread of the cult among Saurashtra's Rajputs. The Praj Kolis may have adopted the cult at roughly the same time as their Rajput neighbours.
6. People in Praj told me, 'when a Rama temple is old, it is called a Thakormandir; when it is new, it is a Rammandir'. Explaining the term Thakor, in this context,

I was told that Rama, Krishna, all *avatars* of Vishnu are called Thakor. Shiva temples are named from Shankar; my informants seemed to imply that their temple had always been Vaishnavite. This is contrary to Ghurye's (1962: 198-9) view that most Rama temples are old sanctuaries to Shiva. But note that in Bengal, Thakor is used for Shiva.

7. Dasahra is the 'tenth night' following the nine nights (*navaratri*) dedicated to the goddess. It was the day of the traditional buffalo sacrifice held by the chief or king, and often included a procession marking the village boundaries. As may be inferred from these allusions to authority and territory, it was above all a festival of the Rajputs and other Darbars.
8. These Kolis are not untouchable, though it was in Praj that I was told of the existence of such Kolis.
9. Patidars pay dowry, or else practice brother-sister exchange, mainly in north Gujarat (H. Patel 1961).
10. This community is described by P.G. Shah, 1967. Their position in Gujarat is generally very low. But in Ahmedabad, Waghris have become entrepreneurs in the embroidery trade (Tarlo 1997).
11. It is this latter community which I have mentioned elsewhere (1997: 203).
12. In Praj, these were mainly Shrimali Brahmin merchants.
13. The Western response, 'just looking around', is at best seen as quaint and at worst as an intrusion.
14. The goldsmith is seen as a Vania in Saurashtra, rather than as a craftsman.
15. Though vestiges of old walls between his house and the others may indicate that he lives outside the walls, it is not easy to say whether they crumbled before or after he built his house.
16. See Tambs-Lyche 1997: 158-9, Westphal-Hellbosch 1976.
17. These experiences may usefully be compared with Berreman's (1962).
18. In Gujarat variations of trance have been little studied. More conventional forms, as when Bhagatbhai enters into shivering, are obvious examples, but I did feel that the Atit, here, also represents a form of trance.
19. The Atit was addressed as *bapuji* (dear father), Bhagatbhai, as jajman, *dadaji* (dear grandfather).
20. Without going further into the question, let me note that the performance aspect is very strong here. The daily *arti* in the temples, for example, does not have the character of an artistic performance.
21. This is how I experience and interpret it; there is clearly scope here for further analysis.
22. Some of the Muslims, familiar with Sufi tradition, may indeed believe in possession: what I say reflects what some of them said. They may have preferred me to associate superstition with Hinduism.
23. There was little Hindu-Muslim animosity in Praj in the 1970s, and little fundamentalist pressure, so Muslims did not need to mark their difference by abstaining from watching Hindu ritual. There may have been some who would not be seen watching, but if so I never got to know them.

24. There are two castes of genealogists and bards in Saurashtra: Charan and Barot. Most aristocratic Rajput lineages have Charan bards. That the Garasia Rajputs of Praj are served by a Barot may be a sign of their late accession to Rajputhood. Many Barots themselves like to assimilate themselves to Brahmins, and claim to be superior to Charans. This is not generally accepted, certainly not by Charans. Sayla is an important Barot centre, but the Barots there are not all genealogists. Some are wandering minstrels.
25. Often, in fact, such conflicts relate to the drinking of opium water (*kasumba*) rather than smoking the *hookah*, but it seems clear that the rank order used was the same.
26. This recalls, of course, Dumont's remarks on the sect (1966: 237-42). But for him, such manifest equality framed by caste hierarchy gradually transforms the sect into a caste. Here, equality is only established as part of a particular situation, and this situational equality does not affect the ranking of castes in a holistic idiom.
27. This was clear from press reports, and confirmed by informants. I did not observe such incidents.

CHAPTER 12

Rural Settlements: Hamlet and Village

Lo! where the heath, with withering brake grown o'er,
  Lends the light turf that warms the neighbouring poor;
From thence a length of burning sand appears,
  Where the thin harvest waves its withered ears

GEORGE CRABBE

THE HAMLET

This survey of the settlements in Saurashtra, on which studies are available,[1] moves from the simple to the complex, to identify the processes that lie behind increasing complexity. I shall then present a typology of settlements, using a a common model of how such settlements are formed. Such a model is not history; but an abstraction of process from real time, where the sequences modelled may, on occasion, be altered or reversed. Hamlets exist today on the ruins of older and more complex settlements.

RABARI HAMLETS

Pacchatardi is a pastoral hamlet, close to the village of Pacchatar near the ruins of the old Jethwa capital of Ghumli,[2] destroyed between the twelfth and fifteenth centuries. The name Pacchatardi is a diminutive of Pacchatar.[3] The hamlet seems to have been there for a long time, but there is no story of its origins, apart from the idea that it was already there when Ghumli was flourishing. Have the itinerant herdsmen stayed here all the time, while settled society crumbled around them? What we see may be a case of regression; with the fall of the capital an area close by has become peripheral. This is the opposite of some cases to follow, where a pastoralist hamlet formed the original core of what later became a village, as new lands were brought under the plough.

Pacchatardi may serve as an example of a pastoral community living apart. It has only 246 inhabitants, in 36 households. 32 of them belong to the Rabari caste. Thus it is practically a one-caste community. There are two Sagar households, and one each from the Bava-Sadhu and Lohar castes. The Rabaris of Pacchatardi consider themselves part of the *ter tansali*, though they are peripheral to village society. Both Trivedi (1961) and Westphal-Hellbosch (1974) stress the alliance between the Porbandar royal house and the Rabaris, who served to defend the state and its northern boundaries in particular. The Barda hills, on whose edge the hamlet is situated, for a long time formed the boundary between the Porbandar and Navanagar/Jamnagar states.[4]

Until the early 1950s this hamlet lay in an area that was peripheral, economically and otherwise. In emic terms, Pacchatardi is in the *jangal*, the type of area where most single-caste communities are found. It is typical that Maldhari castes are found in such areas, unsuitable for serious agriculture but, especially when forested in earlier times, quite suitable for grazing. Seen in this context, the hamlet is small, but there are many that are smaller.

Thus in 1990, I visited an even smaller Rabari settlement in the Gir forest. We were coming by motorcycle from Visavadar (the administrative centre of the forest area) when we came upon a cluster of compounds by the side of the road. There were about five compounds, consisting each of a couple of huts and an enclosure for the animals, and according to the women who—quite typically for the pastoralist comunities—received us and served us sour milk, they were about forty all told. The first family had settled here some three years ago, others following as the word spread that there was ample water and grazing for their cows. Water was available from the brook that ran in a deep ravine below the hamlet, pasture in the deciduous forest around. The households settled here were all related by descent or alliance, though they had come from different parts of the peninsula. In this sense they were not isolated: the woman who received us came from Marwar, and had married her husband at the large, annual marriage fair of the Rabaris, at Jalor (Jellore) in western Rajasthan.

Though they were happy to stay here, the Rabaris feared they would have to move: the Forest Department is not happy to see pastoralists settle in the Gir area, since they claim that the animals of the settlers contribute to the already serious degradation of the forest.[5] Though this settlement may be seen as a product of the ecological crisis that threatens pastoralists,[6] such pastoralist hamlets have existed in the Gir, as well as in areas where the forest has now disappeared, for a long time. We assume that such settlements have been established, maintained or abandoned as part of regional processes, as agriculture has been extended or as farmers have left their lands for different reasons. At present, increased irrigation and intensification of agriculture tends to drive the Rabaris farther into the *jangal*, into more and more peripheral locations, rendered less and less viable as the forest cover degenerates and grazing conditions get worse. Rabaris are the group worst hit by these circumstances, for the Bharwad shepherds tend rather to develop their symbiotic ties with villagers. Typically, they are numerous in the Gir area, but apparently have not established separate hamlets in the forest. Rabaris, preferring to keep their independence, retreat farther into the *jangal*. Clearly, then, their hamlets cannot be seen in isolation; that isolation is itself part of a larger process.

OTHER HAMLETS IN THE GIR FOREST

Jambur is a characterized by the Census as a tribal hamlet. Tribal but not aboriginal, for its inhabitants the Siddis are of African descent. They are Muslims, and came to Saurashtra in connection with trade on East Africa, probably as slaves. Some Siddis rose to prominence under the Moguls, however, and in British times they even retained control of Janjira state south of Bombay, which also controlled Jafrabad in Saurashtra.[7] Some Siddis are seamen, and I met one who was quite well off. Their presence in the Gir forest involves, badly as we know it, the history of how they came to seek refuge in the *jangal*, on the fringe of caste society (Basu 1995; Tambs-Lyche 1996b). It is clear that they are a stigmatized group. Classified as a scheduled tribe, they are peripheral to Saurashtra society. No other group is found in the hamlet.

Jambur is situated across the river from the village Madhupur, established around 1930 'with a view to control and recover Government dues from the recalcitrant Siddis inhabiting Jambur' (CVM 10: 1). The Gir forest was under the authority of Junagadh State. It was often a refuge for outlaws.[8] Jambur itself is said to have been settled some 300 years ago. The Siddis, believed to be mainly hunters at the time,[9] had founded a shrine of Nagarsha Pir in the village. 'Siddis scattered over the surrounding forest region', states the village monograph, 'have migrated to Jambur with a view to live in unity' (CVM 10: 1).

Like other peripheral groups, the Siddis 'used to plunder and harass the people and stealthily reap their harvests at night' (CVM 10: 6). The village monograph, however, is quick to point out that such activity ended on independence. They subsist today on agriculture and farm labour, often combined with animal husbandry. But the means of livelihood most typical of the Siddis is the exploitation of agate (*akik*), semi-precious stone excavated in the forest. These stones are said to have been first exploited by Bava Ghor, an elder brother of Nagarsha Pir. This myth may indicate that the Siddis, in fact, did not start off as hunters, but that their settlements in the forest were associated with the agate industry from the start. Thus we must look askance at the term tribal used here. As agate miners and sellers, the Siddis find their place in the pre-industrial craft economy of Gujarat.[10] They are specialists rather than survivors of an archaic social order. Here, I see them as a special case of the one-caste, specialist hamlet. Like other communities, the Siddis have their own caste *panch* which is stated by the village monograph to be quite effective (CVM 10: 38).

Westphal-Hellbosch (1976: 133-6) describes a Charan hamlet in the same area. She is mostly concerned with the buffalo sacrifice. This community of Charans are still buffalo pastoralists, unlike most of their caste-fellows today,[11] and though their hamlet is larger, they ressemble in this sense the Rabaris of the Gir. But in addition to the grazing and water available for their buffaloes, there may be another reason for their retreat into the forest: the practice of animal sacrifice, which is today forbidden in Gujarat.

KAJARDA: FREEBOOTERS ON THE RANN COAST

The hamlet of Kajarda is yet another example of a peripheral community (CVM 16). A 'freebooters' village' on the Rann of Kacch, it is truly isolated, its Miana inhabitants having lived largely outside the control of traditional states. Here, the historical context is clear: they were invited to the area by the chiefs of neighbouring Malia,[12] since these unruly robbers, feared by neighbouring peoples, might help little Malia in its fight against stronger states. Certainly, they have been there since the eighteenth century; the first time we hear of them—as dacoits—is in 1771. Kincaid traces their origin to Sindh, where '. . . their brethren may still be found earning their livelihood by fishing, snaring duck and coot, and acting as beaters to district officers of sporting tastes; and in former days I have often availed myself of their services on the wide lakes formed in the talukas of Mehar and Larkana by the Indus . . .' (1905: x).

British writers are unanimous in treating them as outlaws. Like other such groups, they ranged far and wide over northern Saurashtra and even into Ahmedabad district. From such expeditions they withdrew to their inaccessible hamlets with their booty. A rather full account of the sources dealing with them is given in the village monograph (CVM 16). Watson describes their settlement in Malia:

It appears that the Mianas had settled in Cutch for many generations, when about 150 years ago [AD 1780] the first Chief of Malia . . . invited a number of them to aid him in his dispute with his brother, the Chief of Morvi. They came to Malia, had lands assigned to them and aided Morji in acquiring villages from Morvi and becoming independent. Morji's descendants have had to pay dearly for this step, for . . . the Mianas have been pre-eminent for their depredations and their contempt of authority, and the Chiefs of Malia have been unable to keep them in order. . . . During a great part of the year they live in the open country and meet in groups of a few families in temporary houses . . . being called a Vandh. From these Vandhs they start their forays and after they return from an expedition display great skill in burying and hiding all stolen property. Many attempts have been made to bring their tribe to order. . . . (Watson 1884: 1966-7)

By 1903, however, a concerted drive against outlawry by various states had succeeded in reducing the last Miana band of 'any consequence' (CVM 16: 10). While they were described by Watson as 'bad husbandmen' the monograph asserts that they were no longer idle, nor bad husbandmen. They toiled with 'an inhospitable soil' (CVM 16: 11). Today they are dependent on agriculture, fishing, livestock rearing and the production of charcoal (CVM 16: 20, 23). The Mianas are quite poor, and practically no service castes reside in Kajarda, making it a typical hamlet by our definition. Only two households each of the Saiyad and Fakir castes reside in Kajarda. Like most peripheral populations, they hardly attract specialists to their settlements.

The hamlet, then, is not a simple form of community that can be understood in isolation from its neighbours. Whenever people live in hamlets, our first question is why they do not stay elsewhere, and with others. There are two answers: hamlet dwellers have no need of the larger community, or they are those for whom other communities have no place. These two factors may be combined in various ways. Fishermen, who follow an occupation seen as impure, are probably more often pushed out by others than pulling away from them. Pastoralists, on the other hand, may be better off away from the farming communities. Siddis are rejected by others, while the Mianas of Kajarda, when still robbers, had good reasons to put some distance between themselves and their prey. That the isolation of part of the population in hamlets is a product of relations with villagers and townsmen, in a complex social system, is stating the obvious.

SUTRAPADA: A FISHING HAMLET ON THE SOUTH COAST

Not all hamlets are small: population and complexity are not directly related (see Table 1). Sutrapada is as populous as a village, yet four of its seven castes are fishermen. Only the fishermen's hamlet is dealt with in the monograph (CVM 9); the main village of the same name lies farther inland. Should it be seen as the separate fisherman's quarter of a larger settlement or as a community in itself? In any case, it is another piece in the puzzle of settlement forms. The hamlet is quite recent. The main body of its inhabitants fled here from the then Portuguese island of Diu, during the 1950s. Before they came, only a small community of Muslim fishermen (Machhiyara) lived here. The Hindu fishermen belong to four different castes: Vanakiya, Koli, Ghedia and Ghoghalia. Two Sindhi Lohana traders and a Muslim *hajam* (barber) are settled in the hamlet.

Of the four Hindu fishermen castes, three are subsumed under the generic term Kharvas, used for seamen or fishermen. The Ghoghalia Kharvas are named after their village Gogolo in Diu, from where they migrated around 1945. They were fishermen there. They number 399 or 41.82 per cent of the village population. Koli Kharvas are originally Ghedia Kolis who have taken to fishing. They came to Sutrapada from Vanakbara in Diu. Numbering 366 they form 38.68 per cent of the population. Vanakiya Kharvas also came from Vanakbara, but are fishermen by tradition. They were also known as Moilas. The 82 Moilas form 8.6 per cent of the population. Finally, Ghedia Kolis are originally of the same caste as the Koli Kharvas but came from Ghed, a waterlogged coastal area stretching from Mangrol to Porbandar, where they were agriculturalists. They are not fishermen, but carry baskets of fish and selling it. They number 56, or 5.56 per cent of the population. Muslim Macchiyaras, the original inhabitants of the hamlet, are now a minority of 40 persons, or 4.19 per cent.

The overlap between the generic categories 'Koli' and 'Kharva', as well as the distinction between the two branches of Ghedia Kolis due to their different history and occupation, indicates the fluidity of caste boundaries among lower ranking groups. At the same time, we see how fishing brings different groups to live together, regardless of their diverse origins, and how even a large fishing community seems unable to attract a significant population of specialists not connected with fishing.

HAMLETS: AN OVERVIEW

As these examples show, one salient feature of hamlets is that they are peripheral. Sometimes, as with Jambur and Kajarda—and to some extent Pacchatardi—this is a geographical fact. For Sutrapada, and, perhaps, for Pacchatardi when Ghumli was still a capital, this peripheral position is couched in social terms; though spatially close, they form a separate community from the neighbouring town or village. This blend of social and geographical factors is central to the term 'periphery' as used here. Hamlets harbour people who are, for various reasons, outsiders to village society. Their ecological adaption is a factor; pastoralists need space for grazing, fishermen must stay by the beach. Robbers like the Mianas need to distance themselves from their victims. But the main factor in forming hamlets is social; pastoralists are seen as savages, Siddis are stigmatized, fishermen are impure, and robbers have opted out of village society. Hamlets, therefore, cannot be seen as examples of a separate ecological adaptation; they must be understood as complementary to villages, as part of a regional system.

The hamlet is socially egalitarian, at least relatively speaking: it consists mainly of a single caste, or of a cluster of castes whose statuses are reasonably equal. But this egalitarian appearance is spurious, for the social position of the caste is one of the reasons for the hamlet's existence. The hamlet is characterized by its small size, and by a lack of complexity in its division of labour, being the home of primary producers. A hamlet of agriculturists is often a 'colony' of a larger village, and not too distant from it. Such a hamlet might contain a mixture of agriculturists and

TABLE 1: POPULATION AND CASTE COMPOSITION OF VILLAGES IN SAURASHTRA

Name	Population	No. of castes	Average size of caste group
Pacchatardi	246	4	61.5
Jambur	468	1	468.0
Kajarda	499	3	166.3
Velavadar	522	15	34.8
Ranawaton-ki-Sadri+	640	23	27.8
Ratadi	755	8?	94.4
Chichod	809	12	67.4
Sutrapada	954	7	136.3
Praj	3,000*	27.5*	109.1

Notes: +Ranawaton-ki-Sadri is included for comparative purposes.

*Estimates. The number 27.5 is a result of a relative consensus in describing the village as having between 25 and 30 castes. Data lacking for Khistri and Luvarsal. Of Ratadi the population is precise, but the number of castes is only those mentioned in Fischer and Shah's work, and is likely to be slightly higher.

husbandmen—and a population divided among at least two castes—without materially affecting the character of the settlement. Other typical examples of the hamlet that functions as an oulying ward of a larger village are populated by pastoralists or fishermen. Such settlements, not directly involved in the competition for land, might be independent rather than 'colonies', in the sense that they see themselves as a distinct unit in cultural and political terms. The relationship of hamlet to village is clarified in Table 1, where the population of each settlement is compared to the number of castes found in it.

There is another point that these communities have in common, which brings us back to the theme of historicity with which I began. Pacchatardi has been there for very long. Kajarda owes its existence to a single event: the chief of Malia's invitation. Jambur's settlement may have taken longer, but as far as we know, the families that settled there were part of the same, single process of concentrating Siddis in the periphery. And while several different communities of fishermen have gathered at Sutrapada, we do not get the impression that each new community made a difference: the coming of new groups stand as relatively insignificant events in the collective memory. Thus, the simple structure of the hamlet is because of processes before, during and after its foundation. This is the kind of temporal consciousness we associate with myth, rather than history.

FROM HAMLET TO VILLAGE

Temporal consciousness changes as we turn to villages, as we shall see. The more complex village structure always refers to a narrative of how this complexity came about. Thus historicity turns on a series of events, rather than a single one.

We get a clearer view of the relationship between complexity and size by considering Table 2, listing the proportion of villagers who belong to the 'dominant' caste. Hamlets have more than 80 per cent of their population coming from the dominant group.

A settlement, then, remains a hamlet as long as it lacks a substantial population in secondary niches, i.e. serving the community as such rather than exploiting the natural resources directly. The story of how these people came may be the best, a well as I think the indigenous, way of visualizing the village as a social formation. Ranawaton-ki-Sadri, a village in Mewar (Chauhan 1967) was served at first by craftsmen and specialists settled in nearby villages. Its evolution from hamlet to village depended, Chauhan stresses, on the settlement's capacity to attract such personnel

TABLE 2: DOMINANT CASTE AS A PROPORTION OF VILLAGE POPULATION

Jambur	100%	Luvarsal	60%
Kajarda	94.2%	Chichod	56.4% *
Sutrapada	89.1% #	Ratadi	'majority'
Pacchatardi	83.7%	Praj no data; probably ca.	20%
Velavadar	65.2% +	Ranawaton-ki-Sadri	19.2%

Notes: # Denotes the three Hindu fishing communities; no clear dominance pattern.
+ Kolis (43.8 per cent) and Kanbis (21.35 per cent) are together dominant in this village.
* Denotes Kanbis, now dominant; originally the village was held by Mahia Rajputs, now forming 19.4 per cent of the population.

as permanent settlers. Such additions to a hamlet, beyond a certain point, is what in my definition turns it into a village. In spite of several castes, Ranawaton-ki-Sadri is not 'self-sufficient' in such services. Such self-sufficiency, in the last resort, can never be absolute, it is a matter of degree. The distinction between 'hamlet' and 'village' must allow for intermediate stages.

The capacity to attract service castes does not depend only on size or surplus production. In Saurashtra, large regions are dominated by cash-cropping, and money has long pervaded the local economy. In other areas, poor and peripheral, specialists hardly reside in the villages. Thus the potential for 'jajmani' is limited, and I found examples of the latter to be few and scattered. This is not, however, what Daniel Thorner found in the 1950s, when he spoke of Saurashtra as one of the regions where such arrangements were still common.

Looking again at Table 2, we see another, clear distinction among the agricultural villages. While Ranawaton-ki-Sadri and Praj have Rajput populations of around 20 per cent dominating the village, Chichod and Velavadar, dominated by Kanbis alone or in league with Kolis, have in fact a majority of their population coming from these castes. The same is true of the Mer village Ratadi. If we note, moreover, that Chichod's Rajputs still number about 20 per cent of the population but have lost their dominance, a certain pattern becomes clear. Agricultural villages, in short, seem either to be dominated by a minority of Darbars, who must have, or have had, access to power to maintain their dominance. In Sadri they are the 'kinsmen' of the jagirdar; in Praj they form part of the aristocracy of Bhavnagar state.

The Mahia Rajputs of Chichod appear as an exception, and their dominated status stems, essentially, from the fact that the state (Gondal, in this case) does not support them, but instead encourages Kanbis to settle in their village. The Mers of Ratadi are also Darbars, however, and there may well be other villages—normally small—where Darbars are in a majority. But Mer villages were not normally held in jagir; they were held 'in common' by the members of the local lineage, or the lineage which claimed local pre-eminence. There would seem to be examples of a similar type from the Kathi areas, and perhaps some Rajput groups, too, were in this position.

Thus we may say that the proportion of dominant Darbars to the whole village population generally would range between some 20 and 50 per cent. When the proportion becomes lower than 20 per cent, we approach what I shall call the zamindari village; the dominant caste members are too few to exert their power without hirelings to bolster it.

Zamindari villages in Junagadh were examples of this type. The zamindar's residence was fortified as against the village and defended by mercenaries. I visited one such village, some fifteen kilometres south of Junagadh, in 1973. The castle towered over the village much in the manner we recognize from feudal villages in Europe. Perhaps typically, too, as I entered the village on my bicycle, a small girl at once ran towards the castle, crying 'Malik! Malik!'—thus expecting that the chief would want to see me. He did not appear, however, and as I spoke to the teachers at the village school (where the children that day got an impromptu lesson in bad Gujarati on Europe and Norway), it was clear that the influence of the former zamindar in village affairs was limited. Yet he was the owner of the stone quarry nearby, where many of the village men worked. As far as I understood, however, his powers sere now strictly those of a capitalist employer while the Panchayat, dominated by the Ahir caste, ran public affairs. I sensed, too, from the teachers' explanations, that the relations between these 'public authorities' and the former zamindar's 'private enterprise' were not without conflict. I could not pursue the matter since I was asked to abstain from field-work in the Junagadh area.[13]

I know of very few examples of such villages in the Rajput states, however; here, the village as a whole was fortified by walls and the landowners must have counted on their tenants for its defence.[14] But let us now turn to a typical Rajput village—though our example is not from Saurashtra, but from Mewar.

RANAWATON-KI-SADRI: A VILLAGE IN MEWAR

The best account that we have from western India, of the transition from hamlet to village, as embedded in local history, is Chauhan's monograph on Ranawaton-ki-Sadri, a village in Mewar, western Rajastan (Chauhan 1967). Chauhan shows us the process which, over a period of some one hundred years, has formed the present village. This process corresponds to the process of village formation that V. Singhji holds to be typical of Saurashtra: 'A considerable number of villages were gifts to younger brothers of the rulers or more rarely to some dependents who served the ruler for a long time' (1994: 19). Sadri is an example of the latter case. Since its foundation in the first quarter of the nineteenth century, 'its *jagir* chief planned the growth of the settlement to provide it the necessary degree of heterogeneity for its functioning as a village community. By 1910, the village had attained the status of a matured community' (Chauhan 1967: v).

Thus Sadri was the result of planned development, and its growth was both recent and relatively quick. This development works towards a clearly defined goal, and we may assume that the 'model' of a full-grown or complete village that the jagirdar had in mind was a common type. Let us note, here, that cases of landowners taking an active role in shaping the community under their control, are not unusual.

The war-ridden past is still present in the form and structure of village society. Chauhan talks of a society 'almost permanently on a war-footing economy where barter played an important role' (1967: 3). This manifestation of history through social form underlies the martial identity of Rajputs even when modern administration and police have made superfluous the actual conflicts around which the village was organized. The history of Ranawaton-ki-Sadri runs through several stages, implicitly introducing a generative model (Barth 1966) of village development:

> The initial stage provides the background of a hamlet that lay in an outlying forested area of the *jagir* of Sanwad.[15] In the first decade of the nineteenth century, the hamlet hardly provided any sign of growing into a village community. It had nineteen families of five castes without anyone to take the responsibilities of guaranteeing security or for increasing agricultural production in that wilderness. A big push was given to the growth of the hamlet with the arrival of Thakur Zorawar Singh in the second decade of the nineteenth century. (Chauhan 1967: 10)

In many ways, this outlying hamlet resembles Pacchatardi. Though the Sadri hamlet is multi-caste, its five castes provide for only a low degree of social complexity. Chauhan reflects on the outlying hamlets, and their relation to existing villages:

> When a small settlement springs from a large neighbouring village, the latter acts as 'home country' in relation to the new 'colony'. The distance between Sanwad and

> Sadri is four miles, and migration . . . took place in several stages. In the earlier period some of the artisans and service groups treated Ranawaton-ki-Sadri as a place to visit for work. . . . Gradually some of them hired a house in Sadri and started living there for a few days in a month. In such cases, the *jagirdar* provided cooked food to the artisan on the days of work. . . . Finally, the artisans found a sufficient number of *Jojmans* to serve in the new settlement and came over to it as residents. (1967: 11)

Thus while the jagirdar strove to build an agricultural village, he took care to invite specialists from the beginning.

Let us define more closely the type of hamlet involved and its gradual transition from hamlet to village. Sadri was an agricultural hamlet, which began as an extension of the neighbouring village of Sanwad. We may assume that land became scarce in the village, so the distance to the fields increased. Four miles would be an hour's walk, and so some farmers moved to lands known—or already tilled—by them. In social and political terms, they would still be seen as belonging to the original village, and so served by its specialists, through the intermediate arrangements Chauhan describe.

In Sadri, pastoralists were also a significant factor. Apparently, the Gadris were among the oldest inhabitants of the village, which was originally known as 'Barah Bhaiyon-ki Sadri' after a group of twelve Gadri brothers, said to be its original founders. The Gadri are traditionally shepherds, but in Sadri they also farm (Chauhan 1967: 44). They may be compared with the Bharwad of Saurashtra, or possibly with the Rabari and Ahir. Thus in Sadri, the better-known Ahir caste, which merges with the Gujar in other parts of Rajasthan, is seen as a clan of the Gadri. It seems, therefore, that the settlers from the main village were in fact clustering around an existing core of pastoral settlement. The arrangements made when a village or hamlet is too small or poor to provide a permanent base for the specialist, recall similar forms noted by Beidelman (1961) in his discussion of the jajmani system. He also notes the travelling artisan castes, whose adaptation is based on the inability of small settlements to provide all the services they need. Similar arrangements are, of course, known in other countries.

We may distinguish, then, agricultural hamlets from peasant villages by the degree of self-sufficiency in specialist services. It is with reference to this dimension that Saurashtrians distinguish between 'large' and 'good' villages—terms they tend to use synonymously—and 'small' villages or hamlets, which by implication are 'not so good'. In Sadri—and here the contrast with Chichod is quite clear—the impact of the jagirdar lies precisely in creating the infrastructure of services needed to make the village 'good'.

The implication is that where specialists are few, members of high castes may have to do 'low-status' work themselves. This affects their 'standing' (Pocock 1972) in relation to their caste-mates from larger and 'better' villages. Such ranking criteria inform the internal rank system and the differentiated marriage patterns of the Patidar caste of mainland Gujarat. Similar associations between rank and village size are common in Saurashtra. This, then, is the standard by which villages are ranked.

In the second stage, the jagirdar invited 'agricultural castes who could improve the yields from the land both for themselves and for the *jagir*. . . . During the second phase the Thakur encouraged the farmers to get new wells dug up or the old ones repaired' (Chauhan 1967: 11-12). Thus, having made his hamlet into a village through the provision of services, the landlord worked systematically to improve his domain and the yield from it. Sadri's links to the parent village were now weakening, as the jagir established itself; settlers now came from the surrounding region, until, at a certain point, immigration diminished. From 1910 onwards, there was out-migration (1967: 12-14). With the deliberate increase in agricultural population—and revenue—to a certain level, the goal of the landowner was attained. Sadri had 'matured' as a Rajput village.

From the account of Ranawaton-ki-Sadri we distinguish a certain point at which the supply of services outgrow the economic base. The landlord's eagerness to create a real village results in a relatively uneconomic situation, the cost of which he bears. This strategy was successful, however, and the next stage is characterized by an expansion of agricultural production, providing the base for the service castes as well as enhanced revenue.

It is an instance of planned investment for economic expansion. Such a sequence may not be typical; in many cases, the inflow of specialists may have followed the expansion of the economic base. Yet we shall see other examples of such deliberate policies, both in Velavadar—a village created by Bhavnagar state—and in Chichod's later history, when that village came under Gondal. Bhavnagar and Gondal were among the Saurashtra states following such a policy systematically (Spodek 1976: 37, 101). But the example of Ranawaton-ki-Sadri is significant in marking the dialectical nature (initiatives and response) of such expansion. Here is an excellent example of how the structure of a village is explained by its history, or vice versa, pointing to the kind of historicity which, I feel, is a central part of social consciousness in Saurashtra. It also shows that 'traditional' Indians knew perfectly well the option of planned development.

VILLAGE GROWTH AND VILLAGE DOMINANCE

The function of the landowner is not just economic. As a Rajput he is the archetypal regional jajman or patron, making service for him attractive to the traditional service castes. To serve Bhils or Gadris is however more problematic for specialists, and the relative position of the jajman, may be as important for attracting service castes as the ability to pay them. Thus fishing and pastoral settlements often remain hamlets, whereas agricultural settlements often grow into villages. When the dominant caste exceeds half the village population, however, they clearly are no longer a local aristocracy. They may still be counted among the Darbars, but can hardly maintain the pattern of local transactions that accompany the title. In little more than name, then, do they differ from peasants such as Kolis and Kanbis, who numerically dominate their villages.

This is why I call Sadri and Praj 'full-fledged' Rajput villages. The relative lack of complexity in Velavadar and Chichod corresponds with their caste composition, dominated by peasant castes. They have very few members of the 'pure' service castes. Because of the lower status, such groups do not attract specialists in the way the Rajput village does. Neither do they have the same need for servants to bolster their status.

Now, we may assume that conquest or acquisition by high-caste landowners depends on the quality of the productive resources. Thus we find that most Rajputs have settled in agricultural villages, and that they are few in the areas where agriculture is poor. This is precisely where we find Kolis in a dominant or, rather, independent position. Thus around Ghela Somnath, a barren and hilly area in the centre of the peninsula, the Kolis used to be ruled by a single Parmar Rajput family, who did not have the support of a localized Rajput group. With the disappearance of jagirdari rights, the Parmar, too, has gone. The poor villages of this area have few specialists. Similar factors are at work in Velavadar, a village created by the ruler of Bhavnagar state for peasant settlement, and at Kajarda, too far and too poor to interest even an adventurous conqueror.

The situation was different in a couple of villages close to the Rann, dominated by the Ahirs. This ex-pastoral caste had attracted a rather complete set of village servants, in the larger of the two villages they held. But when I visited them, they maintained that their little domain had formed a separate state in British times. I later put this to a descendant of the rulers of Malia, however, and he did not agree: 'These villages belonged to me', he said. Perhaps both versions are partly true, for while the two villages may have belonged officially to Malia,[16] they must have been remote and difficult to control, so perhaps they remained 'independent' in practice if not in form.

The villages I present show the range of settlement types in the countryside of Saurashtra, but each also has its individual history, and we shall see that the latter is the simplest way of explaining their particular form. It also links each village into the political history of the region. A typology of villages must rest, then, on the historical processes we can discover. Thus I describe the historical and geographical circumstances of their formation, so as to discern elements of a typology till we get a picture of the forms rural settlements may take within the varying constraints and possibilities of the regional structure.

VELAVADAR: AN AGRICULTURAL VILLAGE OF THE BHAL AREA

The village monograph on Velavadar (CVM 13), describes a settlement of the saline coastal plains known as the Bhal, along the coast of the Gulf of Cambay and close to the eastern boundary of Saurashtra. The village actually borders on Ahmedabad district. As for its ecological setting, the village has something in common with Kajarda; both settlements are in saline flats close to the sea, areas which have traditionally been shunned by cultivators. But the history of Velavadar is quite different from that of Kajarda. Around 1760 the ruler of the Bhavnagar invited Kanbi and Koli cultivators to settle there. This has lent to the village its special characteristics. But the invited agriculturists were not the first inhabitants: those were Bharwad pastoralists, who wintered here while migrating to the Gujarat mainland or other parts of Bhavnagar district for the summer. Their descendants are still found in the village. Like Sadri, then, Velavadar grew around a pastoral hamlet.

Geographically, this area is peripheral, due to its special ecological conditions. Waterlogging during and after the monsoon still blocked all vehicular traffic in the months of December to March 1961. Because of the saline conditions, drinking water has been a problem. In spite of plans by the then Bhavnagar State to supply the village by pipe-line, water still had to be brought from eight miles away until Independence. By 1961, however, the pipe-line had been built.

In spite of its peripheral situation and special history, Velavadar has become a multi-caste community. Kolis and Kanbis, the cultivator groups originally settled on the land by the Bhavnagar Darbar, remain the largest groups. Numbering 219 (43.83 per cent) and 141 (21.35 per cent) respectively, these two groups form the core of the settlement. None of the two castes seem to be dominant; the village Panchayat had 5 Koli and 3 Kanbi members out of a total of 13 in 1961. To this may be added the statutory female member, who was a Koli. Together, then, these two castes formed a dominant bloc. Of the two, Kanbis have the higher rank. It is perhaps significant, in this community dominated by castes of medium rank, that the Sarpanch is a Vania. Thus a person of good social and economic standing, rather than representative of a large caste group, has been chosen for this office. Since the village was established by direct grants from the state (ryotwari), no 'feudal' ties complicate the picture. The Bharwads, the original inhabitants, form the third largest caste with 47 members (9 per cent). There are 24 Muslim Baluch—a community which is relatively strong in the nearby area around Dholka to the west—whereas a number of castes are present with 15 members or less. They are the Brahmin, Rajput, Babar, Sadhu, Kumbhar, Vaghri, Bhangi, Chamar, and the family of Jain Vanias from which the Sarpanch is recruited. Thus there are 15 castes in a community of 522 inhabitants. This is a large number for such a small and peripheral community, though diversification by caste remains less pronounced than in Sadri. The latter village was owned by a Rajput; Velavadar is dominated by agriculturalists of the lower-to-middle castes. We have noted the importance of this factor.

In both cases, political stability may have aided the process of diversification. Sadri had a benevolent and forward-looking jagirdar; Velavadar was created by the policy of the progressive and stable state of Bhavnagar. The settlement history of Velavadar confirms this supposition. Five generations ago the only families with present-day descendants in the village were two Koli and one Bhangi household. Four generations back, the situation changed dramatically: by then 17 households of Kolis, 7 Kanbi households, 8 Bharwad households, 5 households of Baluch and one household each of Vaghri and Chamar had been added. Thus the hamlet was becoming a village.[17]

Four generations back, the village would seem to have been dominated by Kolis. Kanbis came later, and this may explain why, in spite of their higher status, they never became dominant. Two to three generations ago 13 Koli, 9 Kanbi, and one each of Baluch, Sadhu, Kumbhar and Vania households were added. Thus by the beginning of the present century, the village had found its present form. The numerical proportion of Koli vs. Kanbi had come to be about the same as today. The settlement of a Kumbhar and a Vania during this period would seem to indicate that the village was 'coming of age' in terms of specialists.

One generation ago some 6 Koli households and one each of the Kanbi, Khoja and Brahmin castes came to the village. Further, one Koli household, 2 Kanbi households, 3 households each of the Brahmin and Rajput castes, 2 households of the Babar caste and a household of Sandhi have settled here during the present generation.[18]

It is probably significant that castes higher than Kanbi and Koli (Brahmin, Rajput) are recent settlers, whereas the lowest-ranking village servants came early. Service castes are not really numerous, even if we add that one Kanbi household work as tailors. Thus, if we assume that the relative absence of higher-ranking specialists is due partly to the low rank of the dominant castes and partly to the lack of the particular initiative of Sadri's jagirdar, the development of Velavadar is not unlike that of the former village. Rather surprisingly there are four Brahmin households in Velavadar, while Sadri has no resident Brahmin! One is the teacher's, so we may exclude it. There is a Rama temple, and we may perhaps assume that this is the responsibility of one Brahmin household.

The original occupation of the teacher's household, however, is listed as agriculture. The religion of the village seems to be oriented towards *bhuvas* (spirit mediums) rather than temples and their priests, so it is unlikely that the remaining Brahmins are religious functionaries. Most probably, they are farmers or even agricultural labour. There are, as I have noted elsewhere, cultivating castes in Bhavnagar District who claim to be 'Brahmins' but who are, socio-economically speaking, little different from Kolis. Living mostly in peripheral villages, their 'Brahminhood' may be the fruit of recent Sanskritization. They may form part of Velavadar's Brahmin population.

The holdings, in this area of poor lands, are relatively large. Kolis hold 56.6 per cent of the land, Kanbis 32.08 per cent. Thus the Kanbis are, on the average, slightly better off than the Kolis. But there is considerable variation among individual landholders. 58.21 per cent of them have more than 25 acres of land and cultivate 82.78 per cent of the total area (CVM 13: 17). Thus economic stratification, in this village of relatively low-caste dominance, is prevalent within the landowning castes themselves.

As befits a well-planned village from the time of the states, the different castes live in well demarcated areas of the village, of square shape and separated by straight roads. The village has a *chora* with a Rama temple attached, just like a Rajput village. According to the monograph, all Hindus worship at the temple (CVM 13: 4). This is unusual, if we compare the larger villages. But Velavadar's population is concentrated in the middle range of the caste system: if the Rajputs, traditionally the champions of

Rama, are absent, so are the untouchables. In this perspective it is not surprising that Kanbis, Kolis and craftsman castes worship, together, a deity whose social connotation is superior to all of them.

Velavadar was built as part of a policy to settle the periphery of Bhavnagar state. Without this political initiative, the village could not have come into being.

RATADI: A MER VILLAGE IN PORBANDAR

Ratadi is an agricultural village dominated by Mers situated inland of the port of Porbandar. The Mers were the community on which the authority of the Jethwas of Porbandar rested: the Jethwas themselves were a very small group. I have elsewhere described this state as the last survivor of the tribe-king alliance which preceded the fully developed Rajput political order in Saurashtra (1997). Its form must be seen in relation to this political context. I have not been able to find the census village monograph, but Fischer and Shah describe the village in their study of traditional crafts (1970).

Ratadi is at the heart of the Mer area. It was, however, formerly owned by one landowner, residing in the nearby village of Baradia. Streets in the village were originally allocated to one '*falian*' or patrilineal segment, formerly constituting a defence unit in wartime. The Mers constitute the majority in the village. Thus, at the abolition of zamindari, they became a dominant caste in the full sense of the term.

Among the Mers in Ratadi, the Keshwara lineage form the bulk of the population. Membership involves special rites and ritual duties, for it was by this lineage that the relationship between the caste and the Porbandar raja passed (Trivedi 1961). The village headman is also a member of this lineage, and his office is hereditary. All Mer are farmers in Ratadi. They also keep cattle, milk and milk products being important in the local diet. Rabari shepherds of the village keep sheep and goats. Thus the Mers of Ratadi are typical of dominant castes in Saurashtra villages. Though they differ culturally from Rajputs and Kathis, their structural position is the same.

The village has only a few craftsmen: three carpenters and two cobblers. Other crafts are found in the nearby village of Baradia. As in Ranawaton-ki-Sadri, we see the power of the landlord to attracting the service castes, and their general unwillingess to settle in small villages dominated by a caste of medium status.

CHICHOD: AN AGRICULTURAL VILLAGE OF CENTRAL SAURASHTRA

Chichod grew in a peripheral situation, though in the centre of the peninsula, and its foundation did not depend on any established state. The name is given as Sinh Chhod, 'where lions were made to quit', indicating that it was cleared from the wilderness. It is in a hilly area, formerly forested, and was unirrigated in 1961. Rainfall is very uneven. The forest is said to have been the abode of the demoness Hidamba, subdued by Bhima, the hero from the *Mahabharata*, who married her. Perhaps it is no coincidence that the leader of the original settlers was also known as Bhima, a Mahia Rajput. He and his followers arrived—according to the village monograph—to establish the present village at the beginning of the nineteenth century.[19]

Before that, however, there had been a village here established by Parmar Rajputs in the sixteenth century. These clearly were a band of migrants seeking to establish themselves beyond the reach of the then authorities. At this time Jam Raval of Navanagar drove several groups southwards; directly or indirectly, the Parmars may have been affected by these moves.[20] They are said to have subsisted by husbandry and were sporadically raiding the surrounding areas. A Hanuman temple, dating from this period, as well as the *palio* of one Pingalji Parmar, testifies to the truth of this tradition.

In the eighteenth century, a period of war and unrest, the Rajputs left, but Rabaris and Sumara Sandhis continued to live there. The Rabaris grazed their animals in the nearby forest. The Muslim Sandhis have left two cemeteries in the village, while several *palios* bear testimony to the presence of the Rabaris. Perhaps the first settlement was, again, a pastoralist hamlet, around which the Parmar Rajputs established their village. Without archaeological evidence we cannot know much more, but the presence of the Rajputs would normally indicate some agriculture at this stage.[21] The Mahia Rajputs who re-established the village in the nineteenth century were again a band of migrants.[22] Originally hailing from Marwar, where they were known as the Mena Rajput,[23] they had first established the village (later town) of Wankaner in north-eastern Saurashtra,[24] before settling in twelve villages of Junagadh State, which were later conquered by Gondal.

Now, the village is less peripheral. 'Though the early settlers', says the village monograph, 'had little knowledge of village planning, the effect of the meticulous care of Shri Bhagvat Sinhjee the former ruler of Gondal for village development are evident in its later growth'. Improvements to agriculture and the countryside in general was a feature of Bhagvatsinhji's rule; and Spodek contrasts his progressive agricultural policies with the sporadic efforts of the neighbouring state of Rajkot (1976: 101-2).

As befits a Rajput village, there is a *chora* and a Rama temple. But today, the Mahia Rajputs are no longer dominant. This position has been taken over by the Kanbis, who form 56.37 per cent of the population of the village. Mahias are now only 19.41 per cent; the Kolis, also agriculturalists, 10.41 per cent. Thus these three agricultural castes together form 86.29 per cent of the population. With another 5.81 per cent taken up by the Bharwads, we see there is little room for the service castes. Other castes present are Valand, Darjee, Brahmin, Sadhu (Margi), Suthar, Mochi, Meghwal and Jain Vania—a total of twelve.

Of the present population, 27 Mahia households claim to have been established here for 'more than 5 generations'. Only 9 households of Kanbis make the same claim, together with 9 Koli and 4 Bharwad households. Thus, by around 1815-35,[25] the village was well established; though we have no evidence, as yet, of specialist castes. The village was peripheral, but not quite a hamlet.[26] I tend, therefore, to think that the Mahias did not arrive in the early nineteenth century, as the village monograph states, but in the late eighteenth century. During these years, Junagadh's frontiers were fluid and state control weak after the death of the powerful Dewan Amarji in 1784. This period was one in which immigrant settlements such as those of the Mahia seem possible and probable.[27] In 1821-4, the 'Junagadh militia began to plunder and lay waste the adjacent territory, and especially made a dreadful havoc in the district of Dhoraji' (Mehta and Mehta 1896: 658). But Chandrasinhji of Gondal got the British to intervene, and Junagadh had to restore the booty to Gondal, as well as paying a handsome compensation to the British. There followed a short war between Navanagar and Gondal.

In 1815-35, Chichod was still dominated by the Mahias. From 1824 Gondal was left in peace, and it was probably Chandrasinhji, who died in 1841, who was responsible for inviting a large number of Kanbis to settle in Chichod. The settlement history reflects the shift from Rajput to Kanbi dominance. 'Between 4 and 5 generations ago', bringing us up to around 1845-60, the change seems to have been in full swing. Of Mahias, only 5 new households had arrived, as against 26 households of Kanbis. 2 Koli, 6 Bharwad and 1 Valand household date their history in the village from this period. Thus we find that by 1845-60, the two major castes are more or less evenly balanced in Chichod, with 34 Kanbi as against 32 Mahia households. Since the Mahias were established earlier as the highest-ranking caste, this does not necessarily represent a shift in dominance. But the relative position of the Mahia Rajputs must have weakened considerably by this time.

The next period brings us to 1900-10. 28 households of Kanbis date their settlement in the village from this period, as against only one household of Mahias. The numerical balance has been upset, and Kanbis are gaining dominance. 5 Koli, 1 Bharwad, 2 Valand, 2 Vania, 1 Brahmin and 1 Meghwal household came to the village during this period. The increase in Koli households may have weakened the Mahias' position further. The presence of Vanias, as well as the Brahmin, indicate that the village was becoming more 'civilized' and less peripheral. In the next period, only the addition of craftsmen (2 *darji*, 1 *suthar* family) is significant; this further strengthens the trend. The village was clearly becoming more prosperous. Still, we see that Chichod has a much smaller admixture of service castes than the smaller village of Sadri. It is reasonable to relate this fact to the dominance of a relatively low agricultural caste, the Kanbis.

Between 1835 and 1910, dominance of the village passed to the Kanbis. Why did this happen? Two factors must be considered. First, the Mahias suffered a loss of relative independence after a conflict with Junagadh, of which more below. Second, the progressive policies of Bhagvatsinhji drew the village closer to the market economy and favoured the Kanbis. He came to the *gadi* of Gondal in 1870 as a minor, and took over the administration from 1883 (Mehta and Mehta 1896: 658). The two factors may be related. Kanbi settlement might serve to neutralize an unruly element, as the Mahias undoubtedly were. Then, the conflict with Junagadh may be seen as a last attempt by the Mahias to escape the integration of their peripheral area into the states. We know little of the rulers from Chandrasinhji to Bhagvatsinhji, who seem to have been relatively insignificant, yet in this period numbers of Kanbis had arrived at Chichod.[28] Were they invited by the rulers of Gondal? Certainly, there was a real change with the accession of Bhagvatsinhji to full powers.[29] The priority of one or the other of our two factors, and their interrelation, cannot be safely established.

The Mahias responded by an adventurous policy of conquest.[30] But such a policy was no longer workable. Instead their dominion was swamped by the growth of the neighbouring states. They were defeated and re-absorbed into their former village as peasants.[31] These conflicts were only the last in a long line. The Mahias, like their Parmar predecessors, had certainly been 'taxing' the surrounding peripheries of larger states. Like many Rajputs of dubious repute,[32] they were often seen as Kolis.[33]

Pacification of the Mahias may be one reason why the Kanbis were allowed to settle in the village, but Bhagvatsinhji's agricultural policies must also have been important. When cash assessment was introduced in Gondal in 1887,[34] all tenants on *khalsa* (state) land were given security of tenure. The Mahias, who were Garasias (held their land by permanent feudal rights) were bitterly opposed to this move (CVM 8). Only gradually were they persuaded to adopt the new system. This opposition may have been strengthened by a conservative attitude to agriculture. Though groundnut, the main cash crop today, really started in 1929, we may assume that Kanbis, here as elsewhere, were the pioneers of cash-cropping. Today they are not only numerically and politically dominant in the village, they also have much bigger landholdings than the Mahias—15 acres 4 gunthas as against 8 acres 36 gunthas (CVM 8: 28). In terms of average per capita income, the Kanbis, with Rs. 400, by far surpass the Mahias' Rs. 285. Kolis were only marginally worse off than Mahias in both respects.

In spite of the orientation of the village economy towards cash crops, jajmani relationships are said to persist. Thus the suthar, the valand (barber) and *darji* all subsist partly by traditional annual payments in kind, made from each of the households that they serve. For the suthar and *darji*, these payments cover only repairs; new utensils or clothes are paid for individually in cash (CVM 8: 59-60). In other words, there is a difference between the ongoing maintenance of productive capacity, where the mode of payment recalls the 'jajmani system' popular with an earlier generation of anthropologists (Beidelman 1961)—and new investment, which is part of the cash economy. Such distinctions seem common in Saurashtra, and may well be old.

Chichod, then, has a very different history from Velavadar or Ratadi. Up to its incorporation in Gondal State, it rather recalls the 'freebooters' hamlet' of Kajarda. Incorporation changes its structure profoundly, but not without conflict.

HISTORICITY AND VILLAGE FORM

I wish to stress the importance of local history in explaining the form each of these villages has taken. This brief survey confirms Singhji's assertion that villages grow at the instance of their owner or ruler,[35] but only partially. There are other political processes at work, such as conquest or foundation by a group that, at least for a while, avoids integration into the rulers' network of power relations. Such relative independence tended to reflect negatively on the village's prestige, however. In all cases, community formation was a political process possessing a historical specificity of its own—there is no 'organic village community' unchanged since a distant past.[36]

On an etic level, then, historical analysis is needed to explain the particular form each village has taken. On an emic level, the memory of historical events serve to explain each caste's position in the village. Village form lends to historicity a central place in the villager's understanding of his own life-world. The historical perspective is no longer that of the hamlet, focusing on the single event or process that gave birth to the settlement. The complexity of the village can only be exlained by a sequence of distinct events, so we move to a conception of development of form over time. From the triple perspective of 'before, during and after' that frames the founding event of the hamlet and lends a mythical form to the narrative of its past, we move to another kind of historicity, where the multiplicity of communities each claiming their past, demands numerous events of explanation. Thence we are led to an awareness of ongoing process as the most satisfactory way of constructing a single narrative to include these events. Put more simply, the social complexity of the village demands explaining, and the simplest way to do so is to construct a historical narrative.[37] Indian tradition is historicist, I hold, because of the complexity of the life-world to be explained, and this is certainly so in Saurashtra. The village is not a timeless entity but its very opposite: it incarnates in its form the very concept of time and history found with its people. It is, indeed, the past in the present.

NOTES

1. The census of India provides data on several settlements of different types. Trivedi's monographs on the Mers (1961, 1985), and Fischer and Shah's study of craftsmen (1970) help, as does Strandberg (1976).
2. A ruined city north-east of Porbandar (Burgess 1971: 178-86).
3. Something situated at the rear or the back.
4. I have noted (1997: 224) that Gandhi's grandfather lost several villages to Jamnagar when he was Diwan of Porbandar. (See also Sharpe 1931: 17-18.)
5. For an ecologist's view, differing from that of the forest department, see Berwick 1976.
6. There is considerable desertification and deterioration of vegetation in Saurashtra, as in Rajasthan and Kacch. Tubewell irrigation may be partly responsible for the crisis, causing the level of ground water to sink. The grazing area is reduced both by desertification, and by intensification of agriculture—since less land is left as fallow—so that the pastoral adaptation is gravely menaced.

7. Mehta and Mehta 1896, Ib: 858-66; II-III: 129-30. There was also a minor state controlled by the Siddis near Surat. These states were basically tied to the history of the Mogul navy as the empire declined.
8. See Kincaid 1908, and also Tambs-Lyche, forthcoming.
9. This is the opinion of the author of the census monograph. Personally, I am more inclined to think that the Siddis became 'tribalized' either by fleeing from slavery or fleeing the centre to escape stigmatization when they became free.
10. For this point and the Siddis of Gujarat in general, see Basu 1997.
11. All Charans are believed, at one time, to have been buffalo herders.
12. Unless the coastal area south of the Rann is in fact their ancestral home (Kennedy 1908).
13. It was the Ministry of the Interior in Delhi who asked me to stay away from Junagadh, as it was 'too close to Pakistan'. This closeness was clearly seen in terms of history, not geography.
14. This is a very different situation from that found in Marwar, for example, where the residence of the jagirdar is often an obvious presence. The few examples of similar situations in Saurashtra would include several where the residence has long been a ruin, or else 'villages' which were in fact capitals of diminutive states.
15. We may note that this period also saw the arrival, in Mewar, of James Tod.
16. I certainly have not been able to identify them as states according to Mehta and Mehta's (1896) catalogue of princely states, which includes a large number of truly minuscule entities.
17. By these indications, one would deduce that the establishment of the village took place between 1815 and 1835, rather than around 1760, as the latter date would imply 'generations' of 40 years each. 25-30 years sounds more applicable to Indian conditions.
18. At the time of the study, about 1961.
19. I think they must have arrived somewhat earlier, as I shall argue below.
20. Their settlement in the village thus appears to correspond to stage one of Fox' model (1971: 69ff).
21. The village may have been destroyed by some neighbours, or the marginal conditions might have led the Parmars to seek better lands elsewhere. It is notable that the Rabaris also left.
22. Like the Parmars, their settlement in the village corresponds to stage one of Fox's model (1971: 69ff).
23. The Menas (Minas) are now considered a tribal group in Marwar (M.H. Singh (1894) 1990: 51-6). The use of the term Rajput here may be a way for the Mahias to embellish their ancestry.
24. The story of how they came to leave Wankaner is indicative of state-hinterland relations at the time. It shows, too, how Bhima, the founding hero of the Mahia community, is cast in the mold of the chivalrous, gift-giving chief or king:

> It is said that one day a Rajput woman with a child came for protection to Wankaner and told Bhima Mahia that she was a wife of the neighbouring Jadeja king but was under the disfavour of the king, and her child being the *tilak kumar*, i.e. the eldest son, her *sokya* or a co-wife was trying to kill him. Bhima Mahia gave her protection. On hearing this, the Jadeja king came to invade Wankaner, but he was kidnapped at night by the young Mahia. When he awoke he knew that he was in the hands of enemies. Bhima Mahia told him: 'Your wife is my sister and I will not surrender her', and further told him that he would give Wankaner which was then a village to the child. Thus Mahias after giving Wankaner as *kapada* migrated in search of other settlements. . . . One of these Mahias, Kala Mahia, established village Chichod as Mahias were capable and willing to tackle the menace of wild animals. (Village Monograph no. 8; 2)

Wankaner became a separate state under the Jhala prince Sultanjee in the seventeenth century, and he is said to have driven the Mahias and the Babrias from the area (Mayne 1921; 91). The episode as told here, must be earlier, since the reference is to a Jadeja, not a Jhala, ruler—nobody, in Saurashtra, would confuse these two clans. If we accept the village monograph's date for the re-establishment of Chichod by the Mahias, about 200 years had passed since they left Wankaner.

25. Counting each generation as 25-30 years.
26. If we assume that the village would have needed two generations to grow to the stature it seems to have attained by 1815-35, we arrive at a date around 1755-85 for the re-establishment of the village.
27. During 1782-4, Junagadh fought almost continuously with Gondal, Porbandar and Navanagar (Mehta and Mehta 1896: 655-6), and there were clashes with Bhavnagar, the last and conclusive one in 1796.
28. Dave says that the history of this period is 'lays bare the general weakness of the administration and the want of proper check on irresponsible managers expert in the art of peculation' (1889; 99).
29. Dave stresses this point. We may remark that he wrote his history in the reign of that ruler and very probably at his inspiration. Yet Bhagvatsinhji was also highly regarded by the British.
30. This is what Fox, writing of the 'development cycle' of the Rajput lineage, calls a 'stage one' situation (1971; 69ff). At this stage dominance is established.
31. Wilberforce-Bell gives the following account:

> A small tribe known as Mayas . . . who hold land in twelve villages of Junagadh State, had endeavoured in AD 1872 to attack the town of Junagadh with the idea of restoring the dynasty of Chudasama Ras (who had been dethroned by the Muslim conquest of the state in 1470-72). In consequence . . . they were then deprived of their arms, with the result that they went into outlawry. . . . Subsequently their holdings were demarcated and their rights defined, and they were ordered to pay a moderate assessment in lieu of military service. . . . They refused positively to pay such assessment, and when their appeal . . . suffered rejection they deserted their villages in December AD 1882, and taking up a position on a hill in neutral territory, defied all attempts at mediation. . . . The

> result was a fight in which both the Mayas and the police lost considerably. A commission . . . was now appointed to inquire into the Maya grievances . . . against the Junagadh State and its police. The disputes dragged on, and it was not until six years later that a satisfactory conclusion was arrived at, and peace was finally restored. (Wilberforce-Bell 1915; 238-39)

32. Virbhadra Singhji (1994) uses the term Rajput for such groups.
33. This is clear, for example, in the following account:

> [The Mahias] . . . are generally included under the name Koli. They are a turbulent, excitable tribe, and at times have given much trouble. In 1867 they were in open revolt, and established themselves in the Gir hills. Afterwards on being recalled, certain lands were made over to them on service tenure. They were disarmed in 1873 and since then they have quietened down. (Watson 1884; 139)

34. First actual assessment in 1893-4.
35. Le Grand Jacob stressed the same point in a report written in 1842 (Selections, XXXVII: 12-13).
36. This is also the view of Virbhadra Singhji (1994: 18-26).
37. It is striking that Chauhan and the authors of the village monographs, all Indian scholars, proceed directly to explain village form by its history. Western anthropologists, however, have tended to explain the form *per se*, no doubt alerted by Radcliffe-Brown and other functionalists to avoid historical explanations. An early but perhaps extreme example is Lewis 1954.

CHAPTER 13

Rural Settlements: Process and Power

Beneath those rugged elms, that yew tree's shade,
    Where heaves the turf in many a mouldering heap,
Each in his narrow cell for ever laid,
    The rude forefathers of the hamlet sleep.

THOMAS GRAY

A MATURE RAJPUT VILLAGE

We may well insist that each village has been formed by its particular history, but it would indeed be strange if these histories have nothing in common. In order to retain the specificity yet achieve a more integrated perspective, I shall adopt Barth's idea of generative models, capable of producing a variety of forms from a limited set of factors. To identify these factors, I shall look more closely at a village which, though not in Saurashtra, has been analysed better in terms of its history than any other in the literature of western India. This is Ranawaton-ki-Sadri in Mewar (Chauhan 1967). I hope to show that Mewar and Saurashtra have enough social and cultural elements in common to render the example useful, in spite of some differences.

In Sadri, we see a small Rajput village reaching a degree of social complexity unmatched by our examples from Saurashtra. At the time of Chauhan's study, the following castes were found in the village, distributed according to geographical sectors: Rajputs in the north-west, Gadris in the south-west and south, and Jats in the middle to north-eastern parts; while to the east and south-east were found the lower castes; Bhil, Sadhu, and Chamar (Chauhan 1967: 25). Gadris remained the biggest group, constituting19.7 per cent of a total population of 640. Rajputs were 19.2 per cent of the total, while 17.3 per cent of the population were Bhil. Other groups present in some number are the Jat (9.0 per cent) and Chamar (6.7 per cent). No other groups had more than 5 per cent of the population, though the number of castes present run into 23.[1] Thus the village, though complete in structure, remains small compared to most villages in Saurashtra, and it is evident that such a structure presupposes rather wide-ranging marriage networks for most castes.

We note that no Brahmin family is permanently settled in Sadri. The Rajputs employ a Brahmin from Sanwad for family rites; village rituals are taken care of by a Brahmin from nearby Patolia village. The village temple is attended to by a member of the Sadhu caste, a lower caste fulfilling some ritual functions (1967:16).[2] The absence of Brahmins is not unusual in smaller villages, in Saurashtra as in Rajasthan. A certain economic base is needed for any specialist, and the Brahmin's services are not the cheapest. But if one family could have served both village and family functions, as well as tending the temple, the size of the village might well have allowed them to settle there. The division of ritual functions between two Brahmins and a Sadhu clearly prevents this, and no further explanation of this ritual division of labour is given by Chauhan.

The caste ranking is clear. At the top are the Rajput, closely followed and sometimes challenged by the Mahajan—corresponding to the Vania of Gujarat. There follow the medium-ranking castes of Jat and Gadri. Below them are a number of specialists: Suthar, Nai, Kumhar, Darzi, Sadhu, Kharol, Luhar, Teli and Daroga. Below these again, and regarded as lower castes, Chauhan places the Bhil, and the low-ranking specialists of Rawat, Khateek and Khalal. And then follow the Balai, and last, untouchables: Chamar, Regar, Meghwal, Doli, and, lowest of all, the Bhangi (Chauhan 1967: 16).

Thus in Sadri, Rajputs are not only dominant, but also the highest-ranking caste. This rank is contested, however, by the Mahajan or merchant family (1967: 16, 87). In terms of power, their relationship is clear; it was the policy of the jagirdar to allow no more than one merchant family in the village, for fear that 'the feudal power would be diluted'. Indeed, he is said to have used 'threats' to avoid further immigration of merchants. He also lent money himself to the agriculturalists (Chauhan 1967: 16-17).

This did not prevent the Mahajan from claiming a rank equal to, or even superior to, the Rajputs.[3] The Rajputs of Sadri are dominant, as a function of the *jagir* system, not as the result of conquest by a band of adventurers.[4] The jagirdar is agnatically related to the royal house of Mewar. The largest caste, the Gadris, were, as is often the case, among the first settlers. The Jats are recognized, here as elsewhere in Rajasthan, as excellent cultivators. They came with the growth from hamlet to village, and their role is similar to that of the Kanbi in Saurashtra (Chauhan 1967: 45). Bhils have a special position in the constitution of Mewar (Tambs-Lyche 1997: 39-41; Stern

1976). They are regarded as tribals, though in Sadri they are farm workers or smallholders. They are also seen as the original inhabitants, though in fact they migrate more frequently, both in and out of the village, than other castes. The *bhopa*—spirit medium—of Sadri is a Bhil, representing Lal Mata, a local goddess. Chauhan calls him a 'magician' and a 'medicine-man' (1967: 47, 60-1).

Other caste groups are small. We note the Sadhu tending the temple and thus occupying a position usually associated with Brahmins. The bardic castes are absent in the village. A craft now seldom found in Gujarat villages is the butcher—Khateek—catering for the non-vegetarian dominant caste (1967: 48-9). I did not find any in Saurashtra villages, not surprising given the strong pressure towards vegetarianism. Even in Sadri, and in spite of continuing demand for meat, several Khateeks have turned to agriculture. With better communications, this craft probably tends to be centralized in towns. Butchers hardly add to a village's prestige these days; in town they may be better able to defend their interests.

Chauhan's description of the traditional economy is better than any data from Saurashtra, where in any case cash-cropping (groundnut, tobacco, onions) has made such examples hard to find, in spite of some writers having seen Saurashtra as a region where 'jajmani' relations lasted till recently. Chauhan divides the village population into three categories. These are the agriculturalists; the artisans and service-groups; and business and miscellaneous groups (1967: 90). Like other writers of the period, he tries to define the nature and extent of the 'jajmani system', and gives us a list of specialist services: the Luhar, Suthar and Chamar provide items used in the production process; the Kumhar and Teli produce consumer items; and the Nai, Bhil (messenger) and Dholi (drummer) provide services (1967: 91).

Chauhan stresses that the village is far from self-sufficient; several kinds of goods and services are brought in from outside. The village does, to an extent, depend on the market economy. Still, the Suthar and the Luhar were paid in grain. 'A study of such relations', he says, 'showed that traditional services were obtained in lieu of grains and cash payments made for other work.' Thus Chamars in Sadri were paid cash for the leather vessels used in drawing water, but these were sometimes paid by traditional emoluments in other villages of the region. Other service castes are paid by a mixture of daily payment on the rendering of the service, and traditional quantities at harvest time (1967: 92-5). Thus while some payment in kind remained at the time of Chauhan's study, there was no complete jajmani system.

A GENERATIVE MODEL OF RURAL SETTLEMENTS

No village can be typical of Saurashtra. Rural settlements range from hamlets to what might be called small towns, but there is no single continuum of forms ranging from small to large, from simple to complex, and the variation cannot be reduced to a small number of types. Yet I shall show that the various forms may be seen as produced by a limited number of processes, using what Barth (1966: v) calls a generative model.

Let us review the types observed. What is typical of the hamlet is its lack of complexity; it lacks the division of labour and multiplication of castes typical of the village. To become villages, these communities need specialists. We have seen, from in, how such specialists may be called to the village as a conscious policy. In all cases, such additions imply a power relation; the specialists are invited or allowed to settle by the community. Thus they really are its servants, whether Brahmins or sweepers. The addition of servants is one of the processes that makes the hamlet a village.

Another such process I call amalgamation. In this case, newcomers to the community are near equals of the original inhabitants. They may be pastoralists settling near agriculturists. If land is plentiful, one caste of farmers may join another, as in Sadri, Velavadar, and Chichod, though under different political auspices. There is ground for scepticism whether an agricultural community would want to share its land if there was no outside pressure: in all three cases, landlord or state sponsor such amalgamation. The fishermen of Sutrapada, on the other hand, seem to have accepted the immigration of other fishing communities. But fishermen do not make the kind of territorial claims that agriculturalists do.[5] Their attitude to newcomers may depend on whether fish is abundant, and market demand adequate. Amalgamation, then, is defined by the relatively egalitarian relationship between the newcomers and the established group. This process does not in itself make a village of the hamlet, but may extend the base for inviting servants, thus raising the status of the village. This might help in making an established group accept the immigrants.

Finally, there is a third process: conquest. An existing community is taken over by outsiders, typically a band of Rajput adventurers establishing their dominance. But this is not the only way to produce similar effects. When Sadri was given in *jagir*, the new lord introduced his caste-fellows to the village, and they became, by his power and theirs, the dominant group. Similarly, in Chichod the support given by the state to the Kanbi

(A) One-caste communities (Hamlets)

A1	A2	A3
One-caste farming	Pastoral hamlets	Fishing hamlets

(B) Several-caste communities

B1a	B2a	B3a
A1 plus servants	A2 plus servants	A3 plus servants
B1b		B3b
Two-caste farming (e.g. Koli and Kanbi)		Several-caste fishing (several castes of fishermen
	B4c	
	Mixed pastoral and farming (e.g. Bharwad and Kanbi)	
B1d		
A1 conquered by high-caste farmers (e.g. Kathi and Koli)		

(C) Complex and Multi-caste Villages

C1e	C2f	C3e
A1 with multiple servants and low-caste immigrants	A2 taken over by farmers or B1 a/b with immigrant pastoralists	B3b with service castes or B3a with additional fishermen
C1b		
B1b with servants		
C4f	C5e	C5f
B4c taken over by higher-caste farmers	B1d with multiple servants and low-caste immigrants	B1d reconquered by a third farming caste

(D) Small towns

To C, add either (g) ruler or (h) sizeable merchant community

FIG. 4: TYPES OF VILLAGES IN SAURASHTRA

immigrants was instrumental in reducing the Mahias to dominated status. The definition of 'conquest', in this context, rests on the superior power of the newcomers.

The three processes identified here are capable of generating patterns that correspond to a great deal of the variety of form. Our simple model does, however, indicate that power relations constitute the most important variable for explaining the varied forms of rural settlement found in Saurashtra, as I have tried to show in Fig. 4.

Of the villages mentioned in this section, Pacchatardi is basically a pastoral hamlet (type A2). Kajarda is basically an agricultural hamlet (A1), but may be seen also as a primitive stage of the agricultural village with a few servants (B1a). Ratadi, with its clear Mer dominance but several service castes, is a fully developed agricultural community with a single farming caste (B1a), or possibly—but here we lack the necessary information—supplemented by low-caste immigrant labour (type C1e). The distinction would depend on the number of immigrant low-caste tenants and laboureres.

Chichod, too, would seem at one stage to have been an agricultural hamlet (A1) developing into a village of single-caste farmers with a few servants (B1a). This assumes that the pastoralists left the place when the Mahias established themselves. With the immigration of Kanbis it has grown into the twin farming-caste type with servants—type B1b or C1b, remaining perhaps closer to the former in that the servants are few.

Velavadar, starting as a pastoral hamlet (A2), was settled by the Bhavnagar *raj* as a twin farming-caste community (B1b), thus becoming a mixture of this latter type with a sizeable pastoral community (B4c). It has since grown to a multi-caste farming community with servants (C1b), however, as the pastoralists have taken to farming.

Sutrapada is a several-caste fishing community (B3b) or possibly, taking the specialists into account, our type C3e. The specialists remain few, however. For Praj we have no proper history, but it is certainly on stage C now, which implies a farming community with multiple castes engaged in farming, as well as specialist castes. It may probably best be seen as C5e or C5f according to what we might be able to learn about its actual history. Praj is even bordering on stage D—a small town but for the fact that its leading merchant families left the place. Sadri started off as a mixed hamlet (B4c), its particular composition due to its position as a peripheral hamlet belonging to another village. It then acquired servants and landowner(s) through the same development process, ending up as a multiple-caste farming community of type C4f.

The ambiguities in placing some of the villages show how the typology is based, not on fixed states, but on processes. It is a question of judgement whether a village should be seen as A1 (single-caste farming) or B1a (A1 with servants). Should we draw the line at the first or the fourth family of service castes to arrive? Similarly, whether Chichod is seen as a B1a village (as the Mahias may have preferred it to remain) or a B1b village (as it became when Kanbi influence gained them equal rights with Mahias) is not just a question of stages in its history, but also whose point of view we adopt.

The typology, then, makes no claim to accuracy for the classification of particular villages. What I claim, is that it produces an etic perspective which corresponds, on the emic level, to the historicity of village dwellers. On the etic level, this explanation of village form in terms of processes based on power relations, offers a model by which we may generate a great variety of village types. On an emic level, each of the processes subsumes a number of singular and local events which informants—while they never construct this model—would recognize as similar.

POWER RELATIONS: THE FIELD OF RAJPUT KINSHIP AND POLITICS

In an earlier analysis (1997) I used the concept of fields, in Grönhaug's sense (1974: 3ff; 1978). Five fields were identified, which I shall use again here to specify the dynamics that link local communities to general, social processes in the region.

First is the field of kinship and lineage politics of the Rajputs, where we are particularly concerned with the state-building clans, identified, above, as martial immigrants. The dynamics of this field accounts for the transformation, by what I have called conquest, of type A1, B1a or B1b communities to types B1d, C5e, or C4f. The newcomers here superimpose themselves on the existing structure, reducing the formerly free farmers to peasants of tenant status. Somewhat less common would have been the transformation of B1d type communities—where the original farmers are already reduced to tenants by later arrivals—into type C5f, which implies a second conquest and a three-tier structure of the farming community.

The impact of the kinship-political field is regional. Conflict and conquest created, for large areas, the kind of political instability which, in its turn, lead merchants to seek protection in cities, or certain communities (A1, A2, possibly even A3) to withdraw further towards the periphery. This impact also created the need for the fortifications we see all over Saurashtra, and prevented the formation of small, undefended agricultural hamlets in the space between larger, fortified villages.

The only chance for such small, non-defensible settlements would be the protection of a strong state—the Bhavnagar village of Velavadar is a case in point. Alternatively, there was the no-man's land between states, such as where the Mahias founded Chichod. That case also shows how ephemeral such a position might be. Then, beyond the pale of a conqueror's interest, we find hamlets like Jambur or Kajarda, or Pacchatardi, of interest only to pastoralists. Otherwise, only Rajput protection (or that of their rivals) could provide conditions for growth, as at Sadri.

Most important villages would become subject to a chief and his followers during this period, when the field of Rajput kinship and politics came to dominate the countryside. In spite of exceptions they are the closest we can get to a typical village of Saurashtra. Such a village would tend towards a certain stability, for of its own it could not become a town. Only by the dynamics of the second field, where the merchant enters the scene, might it rise above village status and its ruler to more than a chief.

THE FIELD OF MERCHANT NETWORKS IN THE POWER GAME

The second field becomes of paramount importance for the rise of D communities from C. Only by trade could villages become towns. But, once this transformation has been achieved, the proper dynamics of the second field come into play and influence power relations. While Junagadh was but slightly affected by such dynamics (a factor which, indeed, may have contributed to its decline towards the end of the eighteenth century), Jamnagar and Bhavnagar seem to have depended almost completely on them. The rise of Bhavnagar and the decline of Gogha, as an example of competition for trade, shows how such competition was closely tied to power. Military force was important, as Bhavnagar's efforts to suppress piracy show. Jamnagar's contemporary policy, of coming to terms with the pirates (Spodek 1976: 12), may have worked, but hardly inspired confidence with the British!

Trading towns depended on their geographical position. Jamnagar, Bhavnagar and Ghogha were ports: Junagadh was not, and trade may have suffered from that fact. But equally important was the ability of the ruler to gain the confidence of the trading community. Some such communities grew locally, some were attracted from outside. In Jamnagar, the Bhatias were apparently local fishermen and small traders taking on more ambitious projects, while the Jains came as the town grew (Tambs-Lyche 1997; Banks 1992). Bhatias were probably the main architects of the network that built Jamnagar's position, the links to Oman and Zanzibar. Their mainly western and south-western orientation contrasted with the links that Bhavnagar maintained.

Each trading city had its own network based on the interests of its own trading communities; these of course overlapped and forged ties between the cities. Merchants made a city's fortune, but this did not prevent their interests from clashing with those of the rulers. This conflict became stronger from the eighteenth century onwards as rulers, in a mercantilist policy, wanted to control and participate in trade (Spodek 1974, 1976). At the same time, the wide-ranging interests of the merchants collided with the more parochial concerns of the states. This conflict did not prevent a certain commonality of interest. Next to Nagar Brahmins, Vanias were the most common caste to be found as dewans. Qanungo gives several examples of how Vania dewans in Rajasthan used diplomacy to avert disaster at the hands of a strong opponent (1969: 50-5). She also notes that the choice of a caste ousider as dewan had other advantages: 'On an expedition not commanded in person by the chief or his heir-apparent, different septs of the same clan even would rather submit to the command of a non-Rajput *Pradhan* (dewan) than agree to have the head of a rival family as their "Commander-in-Chief"' (1969: 51). He was filling the role of neutral intermediary in conjunction with the inherently conflict-ridden segmentary lineage system. Obviously, for this purpose, a Khawas ('slave')[6] or a Nagar Brahmin might serve equally well.[7] The Nagar, too, was an outsider belonging to the city, rather than to the land-based feudal system of the Rajput clans. And he, too, would have to be paid. The role of finance must not be underestimated, as shown by the role of Sheth Jorwarmal Baphna in turning the finances of Mewar state around—at the instance of Tod (Qanungo 1969: 54).

These two fields have important implications for the regional organization in traditional Saurashtra. As such, they also influence the form of local settlements. But to understand the role of power internally in such settlements, we need to look at the next three fields identified in my analysis of traditional Saurashtra (1997).

POWER AND AGRICULTURAL PRODUCTION

How is the relationship between peasant and landlord affected by the specific characters of the above two fields? One indication is that, in spite of the frequent migration of peasants, Spodek notes that even after the reforms of 1952 agricultural taxation in the peninsula was three times that of neighbouring Bombay State (1976: 80). The princely states merged with Bombay had a much higher level of agricultural taxation than the areas under British rule (Pathak and Patel 1970: 39). Still, the situation was more difficult to judge in Saurashtra; it was found, in 1948, that 2,200 villages had never been properly surveyed and had been assessed on an ad hoc basis. In some of these areas, 'crop sharing was still prevalent' (1970: 42). As an example, the total land revenue paid by the Rabari hamlet of

Pacchatardi to the Jamnagar State government was Rs. 1251-1-0; by 1961 this had fallen to Rs. 787,62 though the value of the rupee had fallen considerably. Yet cash assessment, when proposed, seems to have met as much opposition from the Khedut as from the Darbar (Ray 1978: 219ff). Why should the tax burden on agriculturists be higher in the princely states, and why particularly high in Saurashtra? Shortage of land cannot be the historical reason (Spodek 1976: 27). Migration of peasants has already been mentioned as a factor restraining rajas and landlords from putting too heavy a burden on the cultivator. We have indicated how the defensive arrangements of villages attest to the importance of power relations for their continued existence. The need for defence of the village, of course, also implies the need for security on the part of the individual.

The old Junagadh state was built on zamindari tenure, so the landlord of each village held his fief by the power of the centre rather than of his kinsmen. His fortress was defended against the locals by hired men, just as Junagadh, founded by a vassal of the Moguls, had used hired troops. The contradictions in the village power system are visible even today and Tod's description of Junagadh implies that he, at least, thought such an arrangement highly counter-productive (1971: 360). But even when the whole village was walled in, as in most Rajput villages, the defences were clearly those of the Rajputs rather than their subjects. And yet, peasants may have preferred present and known masters to unknown outsiders. The Mulukgiri—tax-collecting—expeditions of the Marathas were as much a threat to the peasant as to his lord.

Some of these threats were from people who were themselves peasants. Thus the Miana of Malia, whom we have met at their hamlet Kajarda, seem hardly to have been taxed at all by the Malia chiefs. Instead, they themselves left their village for dacoity. Here, it was the independent, peripheral peasant who taxed the surrounding area, at a radius of 40 to 60 miles, with certain raids extending to 100 miles from home (CVM 16, Watson 1884, Kincaid 1905, Kennedy 1908). Gradually, however, the paramount power managed to curb their activities. In 1903 'the last Miana gang of any consequence was wiped out and a stable peace returned at last to the region' (CVM 16: 10), and in 1904 severe regulations were imposed specifically on the Mianas.

The origins of Chichod were, as we have seen, not too different from those of Kajarda. The Mahias (apparently not yet called Rajputs) were peripheral peasants with a certain notoriety in regard to robbery or dacoitry. But these conditions were changed by the policies of Gondal state, when

Bhagvatsinhji introduced cash assessment in 1887. At the same time, tenants on state land gained effective ownership of it (CVM 8: 23-4), so a number of feudal intermediaries disappeared. This move on the part of the state met determined opposition from the feudal lords as it practically annulled their old 'rights by conquest' over their tenants. They '... insisted upon retaining the old system as far as their estates were concerned. Under the circumstances, the ruler could not compel the landlords to give their tenants the benefit of the new system. They were, however, induced to adopt the new system which they gradually did' (CVM 8: 24). It was the beginning of the end of feudal tenure in Gondal, marking the transformation from the widely distributed powers of the feudal order to the centralization characteristic of the modern state.

Such a move could not have been made in the eighteenth century and depended on the backing of the British. Similar moves were made in Bhavnagar. In Chichod, the results were far-reaching, even if its Rajputs were themselves but peasants. It made possible the incursion of Kanbis, with no links to the former lords, who became dominant in the village. The reforms led to the apparently anomalous situation where the dominant caste is of lower rank than the village's former owners. In this, it preceded the land reforms of the 1950s, which had similar effects on a much larger scale.

Velavadar was from the start a ryotwari village, where taxes were paid directly to the state of Bhavnagar. Thus, while the Kanbis outrank Kolis, there is no hierarchical relation between the two castes with regard to land or power. Praj is a more problematic case, but probably its Garasia Rajputs are but its old lords, in a Koli tenure system which at present we do not know, rajputized into the frameworks of Bhavnagar state.

In all cases, power and land rights were intrinsically connected. The rights of first settlers might be alienated by conquerors; the land belonged to those strong enough to hold it. The link between power and landholding was broken only when the centralized power became able to legislate over the heads of even the most powerful villagers.

POWER AND THE PASTORALISTS

Though Pacchatardi is a hamlet of pastoralists, we should note that the inhabitants do not rely, for their livelihood, on their animals alone. They also farm. 'The insufficiency of either would adversely affect and impair the village economy. Both are complementary and help promote each other' (CVM 1: 25). Thus the relative independence of pastoralists in modern times depends on exploiting both niches, or indeed, on retreating further into the periphery, like the communities of the Gir forest. In modern times the pastoralists have been at the mercy of the settled population. They may retain a bargaining position, as we know from a number of mutual agreements (Tambs-Lyche 1992: 238-40). But their general position in the power equation of rural Saurashtra veers between exclusion on the one hand, and inclusion on the agriculturalists' terms. The pastoralists in Velavadar have become part of the village community, paying their part in maintaining village services. But here they were the original settlers, and the (relatively low) castes of agriculturalists were settled on the land by the princely government, rather than by their own power. It would seem to remain true, when regarding modern settlements, that the political role of pastoralists has been peripheral, and subsidiary to that of agriculturists. I exclude, here, the very special influence constituted by the ritual position of Charans.

POWER AND THE SPECIALISTS

Hamlets lack the resources to attract service castes to any significant degree. But villages have specialists, and we shall look briefly at the arrangements used in maintaining them.

In Velavadar, jajmani relationships are still found. Perhaps, however, they are closer to what has been called the 'baluta' system (Fuller 1990: 36-8), as it is the community, rather than individual patrons, who pay for specialist services. The specialists like barbers are paid according to the employer's status.

> The agriculturists pay Re. 1 per year per adult male member in the family requiring the services of a barber and 4 *manas* equal to 18 *kutcha* seers of grain like *jowar*, *bajri* or wheat and some cooked food on every alternate day. Besides the above payment a barber receives *gur*, chillies and other spices from cultivators. The cattle breeders also pay the barber Re. 1 per year per adult male of family and a quarter or two lb. of milk once a day. Others pay Rs. 10 per year for every adult male member of the family. The *pujari* or person in charge of services at the Ramji Mandir is paid in cash as well as in kind. On religious days like Navratri or Ramnavmi, they raise money by voluntary subscriptions and make over the collection to *pujari* as remuneration for his service. If the *pujari* feels that the amount is not enough to maintain him all year round he requests for further donations. Besides enjoying all the income offered to the deity, he receives from the agriculturalists 2-4 *mana* of *jowar* or *bajri* or wheat during the harvesting season. (CVM 13: 37)

In this rather egalitarian village, the burden of maintaining the specialists is shared by the core producers, the agriculturalists. The share paid by the pastoralists indicates that they, too, are seen as part of the community. The effort of attracting specialists, then, is best seen as a common project of community improvement. This cooperation with regard to village services contrasts, in Velavadar, with the village co-operative's lack of success: the latter is described as 'defunct' (Ibid.).

Similarly, in Chichod, all payments to specialists are fixed at village level. The specialists present in Chichod are the *suthar*, the *darji*, and three families of Valand (barbers).

> The Suthar has a fixed number of peasant households whom he serves. He repairs agricultural implements for which he is paid annually in kind at the harvest time, at the rate of one B.md. of foodgrains and half a B.md. of groundnut per pair of bullocks. For manufacture of new tools and implements full price is charged in cash. Similarly the Darjee renders his services to the peasant households on customary basis, for which he is paid at the rate of 0.25 B.md. of cereals per person and 0.25 B.md. of groundnut per family. The services rendered by him are confined to repairs of clothes and they do not include stitching of new garments for which he charges at full rates in cash. There are three Valand families in the village who also have a fixed number of households for services as barber. The amount paid is fixed at the rate of 0.62 B.md. per adult male member and 0.50 B.md. of groundnut per household.
>
> The unit of payment in kind fixed per pair of bullocks or per person, etc., is locally known as *map* or measure. The payment in kind of cash crops . . . is customary and all the peasant households abide by it, it is voluntary and artisans have no claim as it is given at the pleasure of cultivators. As there is no Luhar or Kumbhar family in the village, they come from the nearby villages, and cash payments are charged for their products and services. For services of Soni people go to Patan vav and Dhoraji. (CVM 8: 60)

Chichod's shoemaker and Brahmin are not included in such arrangements. As in Velavadar, the agriculturalists form the core of the community and are the main source of income for the specialists, but they are less united in Chichod. Contrasts in lifestyle and patterns of expenditure between the Mahias and Kanbis in Chichod, are much stronger than between Velavadar's Kanbis and Kolis. Typically, Chichod forms part of the area of a very active cooperative society, but the Kanbis dominate it. 40 out of 63 Kanbi households are members, as against 7 of the 27 Mahia households. No Bharwads are members; two Koli households and a single Brahmin family complete the membership.

United or not, one thing is clear from both these cases. The maintenance of service castes is organized through the community of agriculturalists, and regulated through their domination. While such arrangements may be customary or traditional, there is little to indicate that they are ritual. Cash and kind payments are mixed in various ways, and the function of payments in kind seems to be to secure the amenity of a service beyond the fluctuation of cash income which such services may bring. While the word jajmani is employed by the authors of the village monographs, this term does not seem to be used by the villagers themselves. As Fuller puts it, in many Indian villages we find relationships '. . . of the type labelled "jajmani" or "baluta", in which customary payments in kind are made. However, these relationships and payments cannot all be subsumed within a single analytical category and they do not, even when taken together, define or constitute an integrated *system*' (Fuller 1990: 41).

What we do have, I suggest, is a demand for specialist services at village level. This can be satisfied if a rich landlord (typically a jagirdar) is willing to provide for them out of his revenue, as was the case in Sadri; which implies power to extract such surplus. Alternatively, the community of agriculturalists, as the dominant power at village level, share the burden themselves, which can be done in a number of different ways. In either case, the form taken by these relationships, integrating the specialists with the village community, is a function of the type of power relations that underlie village organization.

THE BASES OF POWER IN SAURASHTRA

The concept of 'power' is ambiguous. I use it here in the Weberian sense: '. . . the chance of a man or a number of men to realize their own will in a communal action even against the resistance of others who are participating in the action' (Weber 1961: 180).

I am aware, of course, of the criticism this position has attracted. The moot point is the independence we ascribe to actors in our model. Since Weber distinguished between power and authority (or legitimation), he wished to dissociate factors immanent in the actors (respect for traditional authority) from what is going on between actors. The actor's will is clearly a problematic concept: feminist authors stress how women have come to accept male authority; Habermas and others of the Frankfurt school have underlined how alienation and false consciousness grant authority to a social order.

Here, I prefer to use emergence to describe the effects of socialization. In thus coupling Mead's approach with Weber's[8] I wish to maintain the distinction between the subject and the actor: the former is restrained and shaped by the ideas current in his life-world, while the latter acts from that subjective base. Clearly, the two influence each other: but I maintain that the dynamics of thought and consciousness differ from those of resources and practical limitations.[9] In these terms, power is part of relativity, not emergence. Thus, power may be based on any resource providing a group with the means to impose its will over others. In Saurashtra, we find several such sources of power, but the most important are control over land and trade.

Control over land is basic for the feudal order of the Darbars; control over trade founds the mercantile organization of the Vanias. Merchants never achieved, in Saurashtra, the independence that made European merchant republics possible, and never wielded military power in their own right. Ultimately, therefore, the merchant communities were dependent on the princes for military protection.[10]

Similarly, the acknowledged military prowess of certain pastoral communities did not make them independent players in the political arena. When employed as a military force, they might gain influence, and they were difficult to control, a trait they shared with some peripheral farming communities. But from the middle ages onward, no pastoralist group controlled territory so that significant populations depended on them.[11] Among Brahmins, only the Nagars wielded power locally, through their landholdings and their influence at the court; but there is no hint that Brahmins might use priesthood as a power base; at most they wielded a certain influence over the ruler.[12] In general, the question of power, till independence, can be reduced to control over land.[13]

Vallabhi, last of the kingdoms of classical India in this region, had an urban power base. With the emergence of Rajputs power came to be relocated in the countryside. This new balance between centre and periphery introduces the Middle Ages to the region, as the peripheral forces grew gradually into Rajput chiefdoms. The earliest form of this new order was an alliance between tribe and king: the chief's power rested on tribal leaders who already controlled a certain territory (Tambs-Lyche 1997). Tribal settlements might still be hamlets, at stage A1 or A2 of our typology. This structure, seen in the Chudasama state of Junagadh as well as Mewar on the mainland, remained at the core of Porbandar state till its dissolution after 1947, and we still see its effects in Ratadi. As tribal chiefs became middlemen between the community and the king we move to a stage intermediate between feudalism from above and from below (Kosambi 1975). With gradual stabilization of the king-tribe alliance, the village types B1,

B2a and B4a would represent a natural growth of such communities.

This form resembles the situation in parts of eastern India until 1947, such as upper Orissa, where the Hindu king's power rested on an alliance with tribes (Eschmann, Kulke and Tripathi 1978; Sinha (ed.) 1987). Fishermen's communities (A3, B3a, B3b) would easily fit into a similar process. Other communities were closer to the king. In Junagadh, estates continued to be held by Nagar Brahmins,[14] a group which had received many land grants from the Vallabhi kings (Enthoven, 1920, and Tambs-Lyche 1997). The city was taken by Mahmud Begada in 1470, but Nagars retained their position, and continued to hold land there till the land reforms of the 1950s. Then there are the merchants; Jain literature testifies to their continuous presence. We may assume that some artisan communities, too, survived through the middle ages.

In eastern Saurashtra, the Kolis were independent peasant populations with their own chiefs by the fifteenth century, and remained so till the eighteenth. Other Kolis became subject to Rajput rule, like other peasant populations. By the eighteenth century, Rajputs became what we would call, today, a dominant caste (Tambs-Lyche 1997). Their rise changed the form of a large number of peasant communities (the A1/B1a/B1b types) into villages built on feudal tenure (B1d), and then gradually, as lower castes came as labourers and artisans settled in the village, to mature feudal villages (C5e). Sometimes, Rajput conquest of villages earlier taken over by, say, Kathis produced a village of the C5f type. The form of land control created by the state-building Rajput clans does not depend on numerical majority at the village level.[15] They must co-opt other sections of the population in an alliance. This perhaps explain the institution of the *ter tansali*, corresponding to Mayer's allied castes in Malwa (1958,1960).

A community of farmers might succeed in becoming the protectors of merchants,[16] and so their leader would become a chief. Such processes replicate, on a small-scale, what happened when Jam Raval founded Nawanagar (Jamnagar) in 1540. The merchants made a village into a town, and at their departure, we have seen, the town reverted to a village.

'Traditional' Saurashtra, such as it is still remembered, may be identified with the emergence of the Rajput state, paralleled by less centralized polities such as that of the Kathis. In both cases, control over land is the main power base. To evolve from chiefdom to state, however, control of trade was necessary, and this need became more acute as guns and mercenaries became available from the sixteenth century onwards. The cannon emerged as the superlative weapon of the age, and only chiefs who had access to money could afford it. Thus control over trade took on a new importance.

Competition between chiefs, however, also led merchants to shelter under the fortress walls, and the ruler-merchant symbiosis was established.

The types resulting from our generative model of settlement types thus correspond to the trends we observe in the history of Saurashtra. This history is shaped by the development of power relations. Independence, the abolition of feudal tenure, and the development of trade and industry all tended to weaken the importance of land as the base of power, and the control of important positions in the money economy became more and more critical. It is with these developments that modernity enters Saurashtra.

NOTES

1. All numbers refer to the 1958 census made by Chauhan himself (1967: 17).
2. Chauhan finds the absence of a Brahmin 'difficult to explain' (1967: 16).
3. We have referred to this rivalry, on a more general level, earlier.
4. Thus the village is a 'secondary growth' in the terms of Fox (1970).
5. We might pose the question of exclusive fishing rights here, but this seems more apt in parts of India where one section of fishermen is in fact a locally dominant caste, as I have observed in the region of Balasore, Orissa. Such internal stratification among fishermen seems to be unknown in Saurashtra.
6. A recent and useful discussion of this group is found in Virbhadra Singhji 1994: 227-37.
7. The most famous case being Meraman Khawas of Jamnagar.
8. For South Asia, similar approaches are used by Barth (1959) and Bailey (1959, 1961) among others.
9. I have noted earlier how this distinction is, in itself, subjective as well as objective: what influences the actor's choice of action is what he or she feels or believes to be real.
10. Tambs-Lyche 1997, 1998: see also Spodek, 1976.
11. In the intermediary period—ninth to twelfth century—states were based on an alliance between the king and a tribal, probably pastoral, population (1997: 36-42), which dominated the city politically. We may assume that this order had to come to terms with established landholders, such as the Nagars of Junagadh (Girinagara). In what later became Porbandar state the Mers, allied to the king, took over most of the land.
12. The Nagars were landholders under the Vallabhi kings (fifth to eighth century), but apparently lost much of their land during the middle ages—except in Junagadh (Tambs-Lyche 1997: 209-13).
13. This may have been different under the Vallabhi kingdom. Land cannot then have been scarce, and it must have been more important, strategically, to control the workforce. But above all, the control of trade was crucial to the Vallabhi kingdom. Possibly this gave access to other scarce resources which in their turn made control over labour possible.

14. This is at least implicit in the description of Junagadh state by Ranchodji Amarji (1882).
15. Unlike, for example, the dominance of Jats in the Punjab (Mayer 1958, Pradhan 1966).
16. As in the example of Chital, mentioned above—also Tambs-Lyche 1997: 68-9.

CHAPTER 14

Hierarchical Discourse and the Image of Society

Reaching for the world, as our lives do,
As all lives do, reaching that we may give
The best of what we are and hold as true:
Always it is by bridges that we live.

PHILIP LARKIN

In explaining variations in village form, I have kept to factors inherent in the dynamics of power. These processes take place in a context, however, which is defined by concepts such as conquest, control of land, contracts of land tenure or specialist service, which are part of the way people in Saurashtra construct their social relations. We have seen, too, how an image of traditional Kathiawar informs the present. Traditional society was not held together by a religiously inspired hierarchical order, but by the culturally recognized, unifying power of the king. I have shown, both for traditional (1997) and modern Saurashtra, that the conflicting interests of merchants and warriors contribute to a single social formation. What remains is to show that the conflicting arguments as to what kind of society Saurashtra is or should be, are subsumed by rules that govern the resulting discourse. They define a common ground, not by the content of arguments but by the nature of the argumentation.

COMMUNITY AND HIERARCHY

Relationships between castes in Saurashtra are generally assymetric, in spite of the relative egalitarianism among the thirteen castes. But they are also highly competitive, and there is no indication that they were less so in earlier times (Tambs-Lyche 1997). Nor are the implications of a scripture-predicated, traditional ranking evident. Sometimes, a Brahmin is in charge of the temple; paid and installed by the landowners, he is the most prestigious of their servants, but his prestige is nominal and does not have many social implications. He, like the *purohit* in Heesterman's view (1985: 155), cannot transcend the status of those that pay him. In the village, as at the level of the traditional state, the place of the Brahmin is not remarkable.[1]

Thus the settled, agricultural village has a rank order, but its focus is the dominant caste.[2] The hamlet has only a hierarchy of reference. The region, more complex, is focused on the dominant, landowning community that more often than not is its defining factor; but its hierarchy is of a mixed and rather muddled character. People are aware of this: the regional caste configuration is not the point of reference needed to sustain a Dumontian view of hierarchy. And traditional society, like the social wholes that the villager knows at first hand, have to him a quality of historicity, a history of conquest and migration, alliance and conflict, that derives from his recognition of equations of power rather than from an ideal order of society.

In short, in so far as the social whole to which hierarchy must be referred is an active factor in the organization of social life in Saurashtra, it is a point of reference, an ideal, rather than a principle inherent in the social organization itself. This ideal conforms neither to any known caste constellation of the present, nor to traditional society. Its most obvious form is precisely the classical, four-varna model which serves as the base for Dumont's ideas. Yet the ideal, though distant from social reality, has its effect. The idea that social relationships are of an asymmetric nature, that lord and servant are natural categories of society, pervades social consciousness and, thereby, social relations. In this sense, Saurashtra society is not only hierarchical, but strongly so, with social differences greater than in many parts of India. Yet on the local level, these differences are ascribed to power differentials, to the sometimes unjust course of history and of fate, but not to the four-varna model of the ideal state.

On a more general level of discourse, however, the varnas may be referred to in any way one wishes. We have seen that such references may produce highly unorthodox classifications, as the speaker tries to turn the model to the advantage of his own caste. Such references to a properly hierarchical order may indeed be seen as englobing or encompassing local rank orders, and Brahmins certainly see an advantage in making reference to it. Yet even if the ideal order may offer them advantages in terms of discourse, we have seen that these advantages may be difficult to convert into more tangible gains. As we saw at Rambhai's guest-house, the Brahmin may emerge victorious in public discourse only to find himself contradicted and his pre-eminence denied when he is no longer present. This, however, does not concern the rules of discourse, but serves to underline the limited relevance of its hierarchizing effect beyond the limits of the discursive situation.

INTERPERSONAL RELATIONS

The regional caste system may serve actors as a map of the social landscape, but important directions of the map derive from the generalized discourse in which the ordered, hierarchical model is the reference. These directions (and this to me is where Dumont's insights remain crucial) transcend caste boundaries. Interpersonal relations, too, should hence be governed by hierarchizing discourse. I have tried to demonstrate that people in Saurashtra, meeting in public situations where the parties are unknown to each other do, in fact, construct a temporary hierarchy.

In such open settings, there is a need to define the situation, as well as to determine the relevant identities of the parties. Categories, we have seen, are strategically chosen, as actors tend to identify with the highest ranked category that their counterparts are likely to accept. There is competition for position in defining the situation. When identities cannot be ranked on a common scale, the theme of interaction may provide a frame. But people often present themselves before the theme is known, so that their self-definition may itself be strategically intended to define the frame. There is a large range of possibilities, a game in which a card thrust forward may or may not carry the day.

Still, people range themselves in a hierarchical order ruling the resultant discourse. This discourse often resembles a teaching situation, where the superior gives of his wisdom to others willingly taking in his words. It is hierarchizing in that the emerging superior must take others into account, not as opponents but as relatively, and variably, valuable receivers of information. The contrast to the consciously equalizing concessions often made by Westerners to open a discourse, was striking.

I have tried to analyse this 'game' by using Marriott's concept of hierarchizing transactions (1976). In these transactions, equalization can only be achieved if we assume that differences in rank balance unequal prestations; an inferior prestation gains value in coming from a superior, and vice versa. There is thus a lack of distinction between transacted value and the value, or rank, of the transactors; unlike market exchange, such transactions are indissolubly bound to their (hierarchically structured) social location. I argued that this is the fundamental cultural assumption behind the definition of the situation in the context of unknown altera, which may be analysed as a series of hierarchizing transactions. Such transactions become the elements constitutng relativity in Mead's terms, while the cultural competence to initiate them must be part of emergence.

This does not mean that hierarchizing transactions are the only mode of interaction possible. Thus, to revert briefly to a question posed earlier, we do not need to postulate a hierarchical 'mind'. I have described a situation defined as 'dividing the spoils' in which each sequence takes on a hierarchical form, in that one of us talk and the others listen. No clear hierarchy emerges from the situation as a whole; instead there is rather a respectful acknowledgement of difference. Conversations between friends, too, are often conspicuously equal in spite of differences in rank. I remember discussions where we started from different hierarchical positions, only to find ourselves talking more and more as friends as we came to trust and respect each others' positions. Tandon (1961) cites, as an example of interactional equality, the conversations his mother, the highly respectable wife of a public servant, used to have with the matron of a well-known house of prostitution in Lahore. Kipling (1938) gives us further examples in which interactional equality runs counter to differences in rank. If rank difference, with its concomitant hierarchizing discourse, is a common expectation in India, the individual is conversant with other modes of discourse. Hierarchy would seem to be imperative on the interactional and cultural, not the psychological, level.

We have dealt with interaction rather than discourse. There is no need for every statement in such interactional sequences to be itself an example of the hierarchizing mode. But taken together, the structure created by such interactional sequences, marked as it is by hierarchizing transactions, creates temporary instances of hierarchical order.

CASTE AND COMPLEXITY: INSIDERS AND OUTSIDERS

The overwhelming impression that I am trying to convey, is one of a great deal of continuity between behaviour in the village and in the city, as well as between 'traditional' and 'modern' elements. Family and caste are as important in the city as in the village, while the non-determinace of rank in urban interaction precludes the ordered hierarchy of the 'village community' so often romantically imagined, even by Gujarati writers. But this is equally true of large villages such as Praj. As we turn to the hamlet, village and caste community become practically contiguous, for such hamlets are mostly inhabited by a single caste. But then we shift from the 'cold', 'outside' world of intra-caste relations, to what is effectively the 'inside', the solidary community where, in this particular case, local caste group and village practically become one. In the city, certainly, caste groups are ordered not by ritual hierarchy but rather by relations of power and competition for scarce resources. And, I suggest, it is this uncharitable 'outside' that gives to caste as a social form much of its internal strength.

It is common to misrepresent Tönnies as thinking in terms of a unilateral evolution from community (*gemeinschaft*) to association (*gesellschaft*).[3] Yet Tönnies was equally fascinated by the efforts to create community, especially in his later work (1932).[4] In other words, Tönnies realizes the need of the individual, in complex society, to come out of the cold, creating a communitarian environment around himself.[5] In India, caste readily provides one partial solution to this problem. In town as in village, 'community' is prescribed by caste rather than by geographical boundaries; moreover, even in town they often coincide at the local level. Caste is 'inside' to its members, as opposed to the world outside. This is not the only way Indians have to create 'community', as we have seen. There are forms of organization such as the club which transcend caste barriers. Yet it would be a mistake to think that these various forms of cross-caste organization necessarily weaken caste.

INTRAGROUP RELATIONS

We have noted how an important implication of Dumont's work was to displace our focus from caste units to the hierarchical order itself. Pocock's concepts of inclusion and exclusion (1957a) imply, precisely, such hierarchizing discourse.

I have referred to Pocock's work (1972) on the Kanbi/Patidar caste of central Gujarat. Among Kanbis, political change from without created an elite of tax-collectors, the Patidars. With the disappearance of that political structure, Patidar became a general term of prestige within the caste. Prospering during the last century and a half, more and more Kanbis were able to assume the Patidar title. Others, though claiming to be Patidars, were relegated to the category of Kanbi by their superiors. The distinction between Kanbi and Patidar remains fluid, while the Patidar identification has spread progressively downwards. This, in our terms, is a competitive game of relativity, quite comparable to those we have observed in interaction. But there is also an element of hierarchizing discourse, for the term Patidar carries important implications with regard to all-India standards. Most notable here is dowry marriage, seen as a necessary concomitant of high rank, since the scriptures hierarchize the different forms of marriage, which serve here as the point of reference. Thus rich Patidars pay some of the highest dowries in India, while poor Kanbis still pay bride-price, and a gradually disappearing middle level of the caste marry by exchange (Patel 1961).

Daughters of rich Patidar families may, at considerable cost, marry Anavil Brahmins, the highest caste in central Gujarat. Poor Kanbis, lacking the resources to marry within the caste, are often suspected of 'buying' Koli girls from Saurashtra. It seems that similar hypergamous dynamics obtain between the groups known as Kolis, extending to a large part of the Gujarat caste system an order ruled by hypergamy rather than caste divisions (Shah 1988), and similar fluidity characterizes the lower levels of the Rajput caste (Singhji 1994). This calls for constant discourse on ranking, rather than an order established once and for all: but the point of reference, the cultural ranking of marriage practices, remains fixed.

Pocock extends his argument, stating that large castes with a wide geographical spread cannot have the organization needed to maintain fixed boundaries. They are categories, not groups: if caste boundaries are clear at the village level, they become blurred as we follow kinship networks into adjacent regions, where the same name may denote people whose hierarchical position is different, and where even the name may change. Pocock exempts smaller, densely organized, castes from these observations. Yet they, if they want to marry outside established kinship ties, may have to accept caste mergers and cross-caste ties. Again, constant discourse on hierarchical position is called for. Emigrants from India, who may have difficulty in finding marriage partners within their own community, are faced with the same problem.

In London, I observed problems in hierarchy of a similar kind. My Patidar hostess' sister was married to an Anavil Brahmin, who should have outranked my host, since wife-givers rank below wife-receivers, as well as by caste. Yet the Brahmin had arrived in London with little money, and lived very simply; my host was on his way to economic success. The latter's lack of deference to the former was a challenge to traditional concepts of hierarchy. Yet the result was not a negation of hierarchy but the introduction, by my host, of alternative hierarchical criteria. Their conflict, solved mainly by avoidance, embodied hierarchizing discourse.

The new criteria, in London, came from the identification of the true Patidar with the entrepreneur, who often became patron to other Patidars. While power and economy thus prevailed over traditional values, the new criteria in themselves constituted a hierarchical order. The qualities that made a 'real Patidar' in London were very similar to those that define 'standing' within the caste in Gujarat (Pocock 1972). When ethnic identity is centred on a prototype such as the Patidar entrepreneur, members of the group become hierarchically ranked according to their resemblance to the type. We may have to look for such prototypes in other Indian castes, recognizing the 'typical Rajput', the 'typical Bania' etc., as criteria for standing within their own community.

INTERCASTE RELATIONS

Since the appearance of Mayer's monograph (1960), anthropologists have been aware of an important schism in the caste order. This is the opposition between vegetarian and non-vegetarian castes, disturbing the ranking based on the purity-impurity dimension. The most precise mapping of such inconsistency is probably Marriott's study of food transactions (1968). Later, Beck (1972) showed the schism as fundamental to the division of the right and left-hand castes in Tamil Nadu. Here, as in Saurashtra, the division is more than an anomaly in the ranking. It seems more apt to see it as two competing rank orders,[6] referring to fundamentally opposed ideas in classical Hinduism.

While non-vegetarians refer to sacrifice, vegetarians, in particular the merchants, refer to renunciation. Within each tradition we find hierarchizing discourse: what is the best form of sacrifice? What constitutes real renunciation? But the two traditions also try to outrank each other within a single hierarchical mold. Thus for Heesterman, renunciation is the logical conclusion to the theory of sacrifice (1985: 38-9). The renouncer leaves this world, maintained by sacrifice, by burning his sacrificial utensils (Biardeau 1976: 64; Olivelle 1977). The Jain canon argues that renunciation is the ultimate sacrifice (Heesterman 1985). It is less clear how sacrifice can be the ultimate renunciation. But I have argued that the sacrifice of one's own life, by the hero in war, the woman as *sati*, and by the Charan bard in *traga*, may be interpreted in this way (1995). The discourse on renunciation versus sacrifice is, however, better documented in the classical literature than in today's India. The integration, today, between the two alternative strains of hierarchy, seems to take place on the social, not on the discursive, level. We noted Pocock's view, that recent division and conflict should be opposed to an earlier, more symbiotic relationship (1973). Considering the historical opposition between merchants and rulers, I am sceptical to this. Rather, the two strands of hierarchy have always been in conflict—which, of course, does not exclude an ongoing discourse between them.

A relatively late example is found in the *Sati-gita* of Muktananda (Mallison 1973). This prominent member of the Swaminarayana sect argues against the institution of Sati. He opens by praising the real Sati, the absolutely pure woman, and the benefits that accrue both to herself and her relations by her meritorious act. Then, true to Vaishnava tradition, he exalts renunciation over sacrifice, even the ultimate sacrifice of oneself. Only fools are satisfied with the latter. But finally, he stresses, in the whole world, no woman of such absolute purity is found. Thus the argument moves gradually from hierarchization towards absolute negation.

This negation should be seen in the light of one of Dumont's observations. The sect, in promoting the ideal of the renouncer, is the exception to the rule of hierarchy. Thus, when sects negate hierarchy, the negation results only in the encompassment of the sect within the hierarchical order. When informants maintain that the Swaminarayanas are 'becoming like a caste', they parallel Dumont's view; the dominance of hierarchizing discourse places the anti-hierarchical viewpoints firmly within the hierarchical order.

THE POSITION OF THE KING

The image of traditional society, in Saurashtra, centres on the king and his position is crucial to my argument. My position differs, here, from that of Dumont, who underlines the disjunction between rank and power (1966a, 268-9 and *passim*). To Dumont, this is what Hocart in his essay on sacred kingship (1927) failed to see: the priest has taken over the sacred function of the king, making India fundamentally different from societies where kingship is sacred.

But Saurashtra fits neither the idea of sacred kingship in Hocart's sense, nor the pre-eminent position of the Brahmin implied by Dumont's analysis; rather, one is led towards the view of Heesterman (1985). To him, the Brahmin's sacred position does not benefit the king, whose sacredness derives rather, in quite a Durkheimian sense, from his role as the node of social relationships and symbol of the social whole. Galey (1989) takes a somewhat similar position, in underlining the sacredness of the royal function as different from that of the priest's, while Mayer (1991) stresses the differences between Indian royal traditions: Rajput rulers, according to him, put less emphasis on their sacredness than did, for example, the Maratha rulers of Baroda. In comparing the rulers of Saurashtra with the kings of Puri (Eschmann, Kulke and Tripathi 1978), certainly one of the examples closest to sacred kingship in India, I conclude that the sacredness of the king is, in the Indian context, itself a matter of discourse. There is a world of difference between the concept of royalty found in the *Vishnudharmottara Purana* (Inden 1978) and the heroic robber barons that figure in the foundation myths of the Rajput kingdoms.

Thus the position of the king is part of the hierarchizing discourse. In Saurashtra, this discourse on royalty partakes of the conflict between merchants and rulers. Even if we see the king as the symbolic head of the thirteen castes that dominate rural society, his relationship to the merchants is different. He may be in conflict or alliance with them, but he is not their king: the eulogies of the ideal king in Jain literature did not fit the average ruler in Saurashtra: he, indeed, was the type against which such eulogies were directed. Jain arguments on kingship are structured precisely in terms of hierarchizing discourse; the ideals of Hindu kingship are good, but Jain kings are better (Arai 1978; see also Tambs-Lyche 1997: 256-74).

Indeed, through the Goddess the king worships power, the very quality that Dumont would have relegated to a secondary position, while those who propitiate purer, more transcendental values, be they Brahmins or merchants, represent nobody but themselves. Their ideal order remains an abstract point of reference, while religion as a social practice reflects rather precisely the relations that obtain, on a secular level, between groups. It does not transcend their competition and conflicts: rather, reproducing the same oppositions at a religious level, it serves as ideological arguments in their rivalry.

HIERARCHIZING GODS AND GODDESSES

Not only humans, but also gods and goddesses tend to be hierarchized through discourse. In one story about Khodiyar, there is an interlude on Shiva:

> . . . to please (Shiva), Vishnu had determined to offer him a thousand lotuses. He offered nine hundred and ninety-nine (of them), but due to the enchantment (*lila*) of Lord Shiva, one lotus was found short. Then, Vishnu Bhagwan offered one of his eyes instead of the lotus, saying 'O lord Maheshwari, please accept this as the one thousandth lotus'. Lord Shiva then himself appeared and embraced lord Vishnu. (Mehta 1973)

We see how two great gods of the trinity become ranked; Vishnu is sacrificing to Shiva as his superior, and Shiva blesses him. The point is not to negate Vishnu's divine status, but to exalt Shiva beyond the other god. By placing Vishnu with Ravana the demon among the worshippers of

Shiva, the hierarchical point is underlined. Sacrifice is an idiom apt to express such hierarchization, as the sacrifice at once symbolizes and establishes the hierarchical relation. One might equally make Shiva pay homage to Vishnu. The partisans of each god have here a readymade cliché to hierarchize the gods in favour of their own.

But this is only one way to constitute a hierarchical relation. As the divine nature of the goddess Khodiyar manifests itself, we are told that she and her sisters are 'incarnations of the sixty-four joginis, which form part and parcel of the Goddess Parvati's power' (Mehta 1973). Later Khodiyar, leaving her parents to establish her own abode, appeals to the goddess Jagdamba, stressing the identity of Jagdamba and Parvati. Jagdamba, whose temple is on Girnar, is one of the oldest goddesses of Saurashtra. She appears before Khodiyar, blesses her 'child', and gives her part of her own powers (*shakti*). Here, a hierarchical relationship is established between the two goddesses, yet today, as we have seen, Khodiyar is the most important goddess in Saurashtra.

Similarly, another regional goddess, Shakti Mata, is presented as an incarnation of 'Ambabhawani'—a combination of two goddesses, Amba and Bhawani, who in their turn are seen as forms of Durga. Finally, when the king of Junagadh, Khengar I, is marching towards Sindh to protect the honour of his adopted sister Jasal, he is aided in his enterprise by a minor goddess, Varudi. She performs some of her miracles with the direct aid of Khodiyar, who is the particular guardian goddess of the king.

Again, the hierarchy of the goddesses is made explicit; but this in no way affects the individual personality of each of them. Khodiyar is not seen, by her partisans, as simply an incarnation of Jagdamba or Parvati, and it is Shakti Mata, not her hierarchical superior Ambabhawani, who is honoured for having established the first kingdom of the Jhala clan of Rajputs. We recognize the typical feature of hierarchizing discourse; the inferior element is not negated, just put into place further down the order.

We should note, too, that the place given to the high gods differs from one goddess story to another. The Puranic goddess is sometimes said to be created from the sweat of the gods' bodies. In other cases, she represents their combined shakti or powers and the hierarchical ordering depends on the place given to shakti by the story or its interpreters. In a Shaktist story, the prime position of the goddess is thereby vindicated; in a more Vedantic vein, the goddess becomes, like Maya, an ultimately illusory being created to combat demons in an equally illusory world.

The goddess' hierarchical relation to the gods, then, indicates the cosmological leanings of the author or the interpreter of myth. While hierarchization is a general feature of such representations, the resulting hierarchy differs from one myth to another. In fact the hierarchy of divine beings seems more variable than that of humans.

HIERARCHIZING ARGUMENTS ABOUT COSMOLOGY

The hierarchizing mode of argumentation may be illustrated, finally, by central shifts in the development of Indian philosophy. Classical Sankhya was a dualist explanation of existence, in which a female element *prakriti*, usually identified with power or shakti, has to be tamed, or perhaps better contained, by a male element often translated as form, but sometimes as spirit. This is *purusha*, a word which stands for man both in the general and the gendered sense; its combination with the female element is sometimes couched in terms of marriage or intercourse.[7] Both elements are necessary to the existence of the world. But authors may give preference to any one of them, making it the 'essence' of reality, introducing a hierarchical relation between spirit and matter, male and female, form and power.[8]

The Vedantic revolution identified with Shankara pushes this hierarchical relation to the extreme, making the observable, material world—Maya—but a veil between the human soul and ultimate reality. This reality, however, can no longer be purusha, tainted as he is by consorting with prakriti to form Maya: it has to be something beyond purusha, an abstraction from it, which, ultimately, must be formless. Thus Shankara identifies ultimate reality with Brahman, and spirituality is underlined by the unity of the individual soul, atman, with Brahman. On the individual as well as the cosmic level, then, matter and spirit are opposed as well as hierarchically ordered. But Maya is not a complete illusion; it represents an inferior conception of the world, an imperfect understanding. Instead of negating the Sankhya doctrine, Shankara relegates the dualistic worldview to what we might call a folk model; truth and existence become hierarchically ordered into several levels, more or less true or real.[9]

The most significant opposition to Shankara came from Ramanuja, who stressed the personal nature of ultimate reality. To perceive god as formless was a fundamental misconception. While god might merge with the individual soul, the quest of the latter was not for the formless but for the ultimate form. This form, superior to Brahman, was Purushottama, the ultimate purusha or spirit. Purushottama is Brahman in so far as he is distinct from the Purusha that joins with Prakriti to form Maya, but is beyond Brahman in being the force that inspires, in the imperfectly knowledgeable, the idea of the formless Brahman.[10] Thus the Vedantin who follows Shankara is superior to the simple Sankhya, but inferior to the follower of Ramanuja who has learned to distinguish the real nature of the Godhead. This qualified monism—*vishishtadvaita*—is the philosophical foundation of Bhakti, the religious stream centring on love for god. For Bhaktists, Shankara's views are unacceptable; the object of love cannot be formless; as the object of bhakti is to realize unity between the individual soul and the ultimate reality, they cannot be identical. It takes bhakti to merge them, so unity most be potential, not the preexistent as Shankara implies.

The Swaminarayanas take Ramanuja's argument even further. For them, Purushottama is himself the incarnation of a more abstract principle, Akshara, 'letter' or 'syllable'. We may tentatively translate it by 'logos'. Akshara is not formless like the Brahman nor personalized like the Purushottama, it is depersonalized form. As Akshara incarnates in the head of the sect, the personalization of Purushottama is complete, he being a living person at any time. Akshara is the principle that ensures the truth of the sect's doctrines. To identify the ultimate with Purushottama—as do other Bhaktists—is to confuse the personalized godhead with the principles of ultimate reality. For Swaminarayanas, the element of love in *bhakti* has to be surmounted by knowledge of the ultimate truth. This implies the primacy of moral principles over the experience of love. Needless to say, other Bhaktists are, in the eyes of the sect, closer to the truth than the Vedantist followers of Shankara; who are again immensely superior to the cults that still incarnate the ideas of Sankhya.

The Swaminarayanas do, however, come closer to negating other creeds that their predecessors in Indian philosophy, as their role in Gujarat's religious politics make clear. Pocock (1973) and Williams (1984) have both seen here a significant shift within Hinduism. Yet their mode of hierarchizing discourse is very much in tune with what has gone before. This mode does not negate the point of view of opponents, but surmounts it, relegating it to a lower level of truth.

RELIGIOUS DISCOURSE IN CASTE SOCIETY

Successive Vaishnavite sects have lent themselves rather easily to analysis in terms of hierarchizing discourse since they may be seen as developing, one after another, a single strain of religious philosophy. Turning to the conflict between these Bhaktist views and their Shaktist opponents, we reach a different level of discourse where opposition is, on the face of it, a better term than competition. Yet on another level, we return to the disjunction between power and purity, for Bhaktists tend towards the latter while Shaktists quite literally adore power.

For the Shaktist, power derives from the goddess. Yet in spite of its single source, power may be delegated to a variety of human actors: its religious nature is not fundamentally hierarchical, though the resulting distribution of power may assume a hierarchical form. To the follower of bhakti, however, such power differentials, as indeed the goddess herself, are ultimately Maya and his religion, fundamentally egalitarian, transcends the power hierarchy. It is no wonder that Bhakti cults appeal to those who have no stake in power, while power-holders, traditionally, are followers of the goddess. But this two-fold division, while important for the understanding of religious thought in Saurashtra, is obviously an oversimplification.

Religious variation by far exceeds these two stereotyped forms. Not only must we add others—like the Nagar Brahmins, whose orthodox *advaita* Shaivism sets them apart from either camp, or the Jains, whose social practice assimilates them to the Vaishnavites even though their religion is quite different. Or even the Muslims, some of whom can be construed in Hindu terms as radical Bhaktists while others, representing Islamic orthodoxy, are very different indeed. Above all, this diversity is dynamic. Religious discourse has been perhaps the most important stream in intellectual and political debate in Saurashtra, for a very long time.

This discourse takes a number of forms. Khodiyar's myth of origin, dating probably from the ninth or tenth century (Tambs-Lyche 1997), establishes the fundamental nature of shakti and its importance for life in what other religious traditions, condescendingly, term this world. Discourse about the nature of the world turns on the ontological aspect of the goddess—power or illusion—and becomes intimately tied to the discourse on power in the socio-political sense. Yet the derogatory tone of the goddess' opponents had to be muted in traditional times, for she was after all the deity of kings, and opponents must bow to the strength of traditional political institutions. I have noted (1997: 299-300) how the great sacrifice at Bhuj in the 1830s became a focal point in Swaminarayana's criticism of blood sacrifice, but it must have been an impressive spectacle. On such occasions the presence of learned Brahmins invited from afar lent both prestige and legitimacy to the occasion.

The goddess cults were the most widespread form of religion in Saurashtra and, through their link to kings, the one with the highest political, if not necessarily religious, prestige. Their wide spread was possible only by segmentation, offering to each powerful group a goddess of its own.[11] Such segmentation was certainly made easier by the hierarchization of the goddess cults, from the nameless deities whose stone or tree graces a corner of the field, to the regionally recognized goddesses propitiated by kings.[12]

In their relation to the goddess cults, the Nagar Brahmins are unanimous. It is not that worship of goddesses is abominable or even wrong; it simply reflects an inferior kind of religion compared to the *jnana-marga*—the road of knowledge—on which they base their own worship. Their hierarchizing argument, based on *advaita*, is quite simple. The common people—which in this context includes the king—can realize religion only as devotion to a personal deity, while those who know better recognize the transcendent, impersonal nature of the eternal Brahman through the worship of Shiva. Unlike the sacrificial cults of the goddess, who as prakriti is part of maya, the all-pervading principle (sometimes known as purusha) is attained only through knowledge. Such knowledge is appropriate—and in the opinion of some accessible only—to Brahmins; it opens the way to see beyond the imagery of Shiva to grasp his inner essence.

Thus the *advaita* philosophy of the Nagar transcends the worship of the goddess; it creates a hierarchical relationship between the two. In the myth of Khodiyar, this hierarchy is not so much reversed as denied: the worship of the Charan, the goddess' own people, is shown to be more powerful than that of the Brahmin. In the story, the king, trusting his Brahmin purohit, expulses his Charan bard from the court: Khodiyar, the bard's daughter, emerges as an incarnation of shakti, chastising the king. There is an interminable debate, wherever Shiva and the goddess are present in discourse, as to their relative importance. For the Shaktist, the goddess is the power behind Shiva, and so his discourse takes on a hierarchizing character. Similarly, Heesterman, commenting on Jain criticism of sacrifice notes, '. . . the monk does not condemn the institution of sacrifice as such; on the contrary, he exhorts the brahmins to perform the true sacrifice—that is, the renunciatory life of the monk—and he declares that the true brahmin is the monk' (1985: 42).

POWER AND DEVOTION

What stands out, as to religious debate in Saurashtra, is how competition and hierarchy are integrated through the hierarchizing discourse. Competition is evident, while equally striking is the lack of denial as a form of argument; the tenets of an opposing school are shown, instead, to lead to an inferior form of understanding.

Religious competition takes place, here, between a multiplicity of groups, and there is no religious monopoly (such as a church) or even clear and lasting pre-eminence of any party. The king could not enforce monopoly, as goddess cults legitimized power rather than authority, and his political position, compelling him to play upon factions and alliances, left him unable to clamp down on unorthodoxy without dire results. Thus even the powerful Rao of Kacch restrained his minister when Swaminarayana, though far from popular with the rulers, had been insulted (Tambs-Lyche 1997: 300). As for the Brahmin, he does not hold the position of authority that would enable him to restrain unorthodoxy. Indeed, orthodoxy itself becomes a problematic concept in Saurashtra, as there is no single agent able to, or even said to, represent it.

Thus, religious competition cannot be construed as a controversy between the orthodox and unorthodox. Hierarchizing discourse, then, is not related to an established hierarchy, but to an image of absolute truth, marking all other propositions as relative. This referential position of absolute truth is beyond the actors, as none may monopolize it. Thus in religion, too, the openness of games constitutes a scramble similar to that of power. It is this relatively open contest, for power as well as for prestige, that characterizes political and social life in Saurashtra, and, paradoxically, invests them with their hierarchical character.

THE QUESTION OF INTEGRATION

Looking at the way social situations are defined, we have seen that a concern with ranking is indeed typical of life in Saurashtra. When we gather at Rambhai's guest-house, for example, we are confronted with his Brahmin-centred, hierarchical, view of Indian society and culture. Rambhai, indeed, talks as if he had read Dumont.

But the presence of hierarchical ideas does not produce the integrating hierarchical structure Dumont would have us believe in—not as giving form to the social order. On that level, we have found instead alternative ideologies and interest groups in conflict, such as oppose, in Saurashtra, the king and the remnants of feudal society to merchant interest and ideology. But we cannot rest satisfied with an opposition: we must turn to whatever integrates the two sides to form a whole.

I have tried to provide an answer, on two different levels. One is what Marriott (1976) calls ranking transactions, which we have seen working in everyday situations—even when people are not acting from fixed positions in a known status order. This leads us to interpret social life as a never-ending process of competition for rank: it explains inequality, but not hierarchy. We have to go beyond interaction to look for a truly hierarchical structure, to the implicit levels of discourse. The second level then, which may be seen as the discursive reflection of the first, is what I call hierarchizing discourse.

One evening in Rambhai's guest-house, Rambhai, some neighbours and guests, including myself got to discuss the cult of the goddess. I think it was I who raised some question regarding the different goddesses of the peninsula, who are many and various, preside in several sites and cater to different castes and Rajput clans. Rambhai, who is well read in the Shastras assumed the role of umpire in the discussion: 'As a Brahmin I am able to understand these things. The common people talk in terms of many and different goddesses, giving her different names. But this is not the correct view. They are all one and the same, just different views of the same Goddess.'

In this gathering, where he was not only a Brahmin but also our host, nobody except the naive anthropologist opposed his view. But next morning I met one of the neighbours, a Koli who worked as the clerk of a trucking company renting an office in the back building of the guest-house. 'Of course you were right last night', he told me. 'There are many goddesses and they are all different. The host is a Brahmin, he knows nothing of these matters. If you want to know about the goddess, you should speak to the pastoralists, they know her best. Even I can tell you some things, about my own goddess, who is Bahucharaji.' Unhappily we never got down to a discussion of this interesting goddess, but the point is clear. The hierarchical view is held by Rambhai the Brahmin, and in a multi-caste gathering his prestige carries the day: the many goddesses are 'one and the same'. Once Rambhai is out of view, the perspective changes: now each caste and each clan of Rajputs has its goddess, which they themselves of course know better than others, and who does not intrinsically form part of a ranked order, though their relative merits, like those of their devotees, may be discussed. Thus, whether the object of the discourse is political or religious, the opposition repeats itself. The hierarchizing discourse of Brahmins or dominant castes has its counterpart in a different idiom where this hierarchy is deconstructed. It may even be denied, but that is not the case in my examples here. Rather, instead of taking an overall order as the point of departure (a hierarchical perspective) the same order is produced from its parts (a conflict perspective)—certainly a perspective that is interactional and transactional, seeing the rank order as a result of the relations between parts of the system—and not vice versa.

My point here is that the two perspectives coexist and are contiguous. Only partly is it true that the hierarchical perspective represents the view of those who dominate the system, and this is more true of religious than of political or economic discourse. No doubt the latter two engender a kind of realism, even on the part of the dominant, that is less incumbent on the participant in a religious discourse. Indeed, it is as if the hierarchical view becomes easier to defend if we limit ourselves to the religious field, where physical sanctions are replaced by manifestations of superiority in discourse.

THE HIERARCHICAL VIEW

Let me turn, again, to Dumont's conception of hierarchy, which, some of my colleagues feel, is outdated.[13] We should be wary, however, of throwing out the baby with the bath-water. Dumont changed our perspective on caste, according central importance to the emic conception of the system, as well as to society viewed as a whole. Analytically, it may be well to distinguish the two, which tend to be conflated in Dumont's own writing. According to the second, castes were not to be seen as ethnic groups having their own, distinguishable cultures; each caste must be viewed in terms of its place in the larger system. But whose perspective? Behind the system there is a mind, Dumont seemed to imply, a specifically Indian mind, structuring its conception of society by reference to the hierarchical principle. This is implicit in his view that hierarchy is emically grounded, and leads me to question some of the implicits of Dumont's approach.

The first problem which confront us, is the location of this particular kind of mind. For Dumont, hierarchy is part of what Durkheim (1911) called collective conscience. To me, collective conscience is at best something to be explained; it has no explanatory value. To explain the hierarchical mind I look for some process involving interaction between individual agents. There would then seem to be three possible levels at which the hierarchical principle might be located:

–We may conceive of a hierarchical imperative, present in the mind of each individual, to structure or interpret interactional or discursive sequences. Such an imperative may be culturally conscious, or it may be part of emergence (Mead 1934)—so deeply embedded in the mind that no emic explanation is needed or even possible.

–We may see hierarchical structuring as the form that discourse takes, in analogy to the rules of games theory.[14] Here, we are getting closer to collective conscience, but the level identified is intra-individual rather than transindividual, and must be analysed as a set of semantic rules imposed by actors on their altera.[15]

–Finally, discourse, as well as games, produce consequences that go beyond intentions and rules. It is logically conceivable that a hierarchical structure may result from processes where neither imperatives nor rules are in themselves hierarchical. This third alternative, however, is no longer consistent with Dumont's view: we move from the collective conscience to the collectively unconscious, and our approach is no longer emic. Since I have tried to show that, on the etic level, social form is produced by power relations rather than hierarchical principles, this last alternative loses much of its interest.

I reject the first alternative because my informants seem as capable of opposing this hierarchical principle as of following it. We recall the Koli at Rambhai's guest-house rejecting Rambhai's claim to superior knowledge of the goddess. But the rejection, made separately to me, did not enter the common discourse at the guest-house. This invites us to look at the second alternative: there are rules of discourse which have a hierarchizing effect. This alternative subsumes the third: if the rules of discourse produce hierarchical structures, they are indeed hierarchizing, even if they do not appear hierarchical. The difference between the second and the third alternative boils down to the degree of consciousness actors have, and we cannot a priori exclude such consciousness.

HIERARCHIZING DISCOURSE

These remarks imply that we must deduce the rules of hierarchizing discourse from their effects—we cannot expect to find them stated as explicit norms. We must, therefore, turn to contrastive ideal models[16] of discourse, with evident danger of overstating the contrast.

Opposed to hierarchizing discourse is the supposition that statements tend to be true or false. This excludes hierarchization: the true and the false are each lumped together, and we may discard the lump of false arguments and retain the true. Normally, we assume the opposite of a true statement to be false. In hierarchizing discourse, however, truth is seen as relative: absolute truth is surely difficult to reach, so statements are judged according to their distance from the ideal. The rules of hierarchizing discourse, then, imply that the opposition's arguments are not denied as untrue but subsumed by our own as representing a lesser aspect of truth: the discourse is hierarchizing, for it creates a ranking of arguments. The attempts at reaching truth proceed by englobing—or encompassing—each other, so that an argument in favour of a new proposition consists of showing how alternative formulations are already included or provided for by the new one. The relationship between the theory of relativity and the law of gravity is a hierarchizing relation, since Einstein's theory included and went beyond Newton's thinking—yet most scientists would agree that the latter is still sufficient in many cases, such as calculating the strength of a bridge. Thus hierarchizing discourse is not particularly Indian: my argument is simply that Indians tend to use it in a number of contexts where Westerners do not.

In other words, what hierarchizing discourse does is strikingly parallel to the competition for rank we have seen in interaction, where partners try to assume a position that subsumes the others. And, as in interaction, where a rank order emerges for each situation, so in hierarchizing discourse, each complete sequence of argument constructs a particular, hierarchical order. Evidently, these arguments cannot produce a single order, since ideologies differ: but the different orders remain similar in the one, important respect of being constructed according to hierarchizing rules.

The importance of ranking, in the Indian context, was no news when Dumont wrote. Hierarchy for Dumont is not simply ranking, but 'the ordering of the elements with reference to the whole' (1966a: 92). It follows from the image of the whole, and cannot be generated from relations between parts. And the whole to which arguments refer, in the hierarchizing discourse of Saurashtra, is a particular idea of truth (*satya*).

I see hierarchizing discourse, then, as the baby that should be saved from the contemporary onslaught on Dumont's ideas. If such discourse could be neatly separated from social relations, we might conclude that Dumont is right in insisting on a disjunction between an overt, hierarchical ideology, structuring the image of society, and a web of power relations remaining ideologically unconscious, though having its effect on social form. But the opposition is not so simple. The parallel between rules of discourse, on the one hand, and relativity in social relations on the other, indicates that power dynamics and hierarchical discourse go together. Power is not just important in practice, but actively imagined, and through its focus on the king this image is as present as the Brahmin-centred, hierarchical image is. Conversely, hierarchizing discourse may enter the power game, as when alcohol or animal sacrifice is prohibited by law. Power is not implicit, but highly present on the ideological level, and the hierarchical ideology is powerful in quite a concrete sense.

THE VALVUES OF THE HIERARCHY

Hierarchizing transactions imply value dimensions that apply equally to persons and things. Only by understanding these dimensions can we refer rank differentials back to a conception of the whole. This excludes a ranking constituted by scores in a competitive game. Hierarchy in Dumont's sense cannot be produced by competition. Yet the link between the whole and the parts, between hierarchizing transactions and hierarchy, must be located in the dimensions to which transactions refer for evaluation. Looking for such dimensions in classical texts as well as in ethnographic reports, Marriott came to experiment with three-dimensional models of such value scales (1989). He tried to locate various phenomena in Indian culture with regard to these dimensions, visualized as cubes.

One set of dimensions are the three *gunas* of classical Indian literature. We may tentatively translate *guna* as quality, bearing in mind that one primary use of the term is grammatical. The three *gunas* are *sattva*, *rajas* and *tamas*. We may identify *sattva* with goodness, purity or truth; *rajas* with passion, power or action; *tamas* with darkness, negation and impurity. Note that the three dimensions are not intrinsically related to each other. They identify phenomena by placing them in three-dimensional space.

Marriott's cubes, as I call them, may be approached from several angles. The Brahmin is sattvic and non-tamasic, but tainted with *rajas* since this is a quality necessary for procreation; here he is bettered by the renouncer. The king is rajasic and non-tamasic, but cannot be sattvic since this implies abstaining from the quality, *rajas*, that gives him power. When he is beaten, however, and goes into outlawry, he becomes tamasic, threatening to destroy the order protected by the king. The tantric, rejecting rajasic order as well as sattvic purity, represents the tamasic pole. Near the centre of the cube is found the ordinary farmer.

Turning the cubes, as it were, we may adopt the perspective of the sattvic, vegetarian renouncer, the rajasic king, or the tamasic tantric in turn. The cube always includes the totality as ordered by the three *gunas*, but the priorities change. Thus we are not bound to a single rank order, but to a complex set of relations, which nevertheless follow the same three-dimensional logic.

Marriott's scheme solves several problems arising from Dumont's attempt to align hierarchy around a binary scale of purity and impurity, affording a more precise consideration of the horizontal, as well as the vertical, differences in the hierarchical order, such as the opposition between meat-eating and vegetarian castes. It also helps us to specify the value dimension involved in any hierarchizing transaction. But this is not the main object of Marriott's exercise, which is to identify the dimensions along which Indians themselves think. For Marriott the social is but one of many orders: similar dimensions are found to rule the space in which Ayurvedic medicine, Indian astrology, and other traditional sciences operate.

To demonstrate these parallels Marriott needs metaconcepts beyond the emic dimension. Ultimately, he identifies the dimensions with concepts from Western science: glossed as 'unmarking', *sattva* become an example of non-symmetry; *rajas* as 'mixing' correspond to non-reflexivity; and *tamas* as 'unmatching' to non-transitivity. The dimensions in which Indians think, according to Marriott, thus have their counterparts in certain branches of Western science such as symbolic logic or mathematics.

THE USE OF VALUES IN DISCOURSE

In Saurashtra, it is easy to identify the discourse between meat-eaters and vegetarians, or rulers and merchants, with *rajas* and *sattva* respectively. (It seems far less easy to identify *tamas* with any existing group.[17])

However, when reading the hagiographies of the self-consciously sattvic Swaminarayana sect, we find that their opponents, the goddess-worshippers, are not recognized as rajasic, as they surely are in their own eyes. Instead, the worship of the goddess, with its tradition of animal sacrifice, is qualified as tamasic. In fact, the sect, who opposed the princely states throughout its growth, is 'turning' Marriott's three-dimensional cube at an angle where the rajasic dimension recedes into insignificance. Similarly, the implication of the princely point of view, as represented by Sharpe's criticism of Gandhi's father in his role as Dewan of Porbandar state (1931: 16-18) makes little of the sattvic qualities represented by the merchant castes to which Gandhi belonged. Old Gandhi is represented as somebody who does not understand power. Sharpe, in effect, turns the cube to make the sattvic dimension insignificant.

Hierarchizing discourse, therefore, implies choice. Preference has to be given to one of the three dimensions. In the interactional sequence I have described as 'dividing the spoils', we may suggest that when the Rajput speaks to the teacher and the foreigner, the rajasic dimension is foremost, but replaced by the sattvic dimension when the teacher speaks. I hope we may not conclude that the foreigner's role is tamasic. Yet in some contexts it clearly is, as when, on innumerable occasions, the Westerner is interrogated about the sexual practices of his decadent civilization.

Marriott, in fact, accords considerable importance to this 'turning of the cube' (1989) which he assimilates to Malamoud's conception of revolving hierarchy (1982). These shifts in emphasis help us understand how Indians may live with those 'inner conflicts of tradition' that Heesterman analyses (1985). But if values are variable, the value scales maintain their discontinuous and non-dichotomous character. This is why, in hierarchizing discourse, there is always room for the separate, though inequal, identity of the other. It is here we find the base of that peculiarly Indian 'tolerance' often recognized by Westerners.

THE HIERARCHY OF IDENTITIES AND THE ROLE OF THE INDIVIDUAL

Establishing identity, in the meeting between persons, must therefore consist in allocating qualitative difference—which hierarchizing transactions make possible, and which in turn accounts for their necessity. Discourse must be hierarchizing in order to establish identities that are different as well as ranked; the logic of negation would lead to non-communication, and the logic of gradual ranking along a common dimension would not accord the necessary difference.[18]

But discourse establishes not just hierarchical relationships between units; the categories of language establish these very units themselves, so they assume a reified dimension on the level of meaning. They may, indeed, yet be ethnic groups, without disturbing the notion of hierarchy, as also without prejudice to their form of social organization. Dumont, in fact, may have seen this, stressing 'division' along with 'hierarchy' as a fundamental dimension of the caste system.

In analysing the structure of traditional society I concentrated on interest groups viewed as estates (1997), implying not just a conflict of interest but opposing values. It is not only in the structure of the state, but also that of civil society in Saurashtra, that the integrative role of the Brahmins is conspicuous by its absence. This lack of integration is not only evident at the structural level, but, as I have shown in my examples, on the level of day-to-day interaction, where hierarchical structures are continuously re-created with regard to position rather than person. This leaves an option, not visible from the Dumontian view, for the individual as defined not by roles or statuses extended in time, but as a reflection of the physical agent moving through a succession of chosen positions.

In relation to religion, we have found, this view of the individual can be retained, for religion does not appear as a holistic entity encompassing the individual. Rather, and far more than in Christianity, there is a division between personal religiosity, chosen by the agent, and his inclusion in the religous activities of larger social units. A deviant view of religion does not entail a conflict with his caste. Coming home from the worship of Rama the Rajput individual is free to be a Shakta, a Krishnaite, or an atheist.

The distinction between sect and cult is important here. Basically, the cult is transactional: rendering unto god whatever is his due, the individual may hope to be rewarded for his devotion. This paradigm is paramount in the goddess cults. The rewards of sect membership are not of this transactional nature. Rather, bhakti tradition establishes a bond between deity and devotee which tends towards unity. The reward of the devotee lies, above all, in this feeling of being one with God.

In traditional Kathiawar, the sect remained subsidiary. Until the establishment of the Swaminarayana sect, these groups remained apart from the agrarian core of rural and political society. In other words, though sectarian merchants had power and influence, their religion did not form an integral part of the state structure and their sects had no intrinsic relation to the religious institutions of the state.

THE PRESENT AND THE FUTURE

The elections of 1952 brought the merchant estate to power, and though its dominance has since been contested, Saurashtra as well as Gujarat cannot now be analysed politically without taking the middle classes—ideological successors to the merchant estate—into account. And the transformation from merchant estate to a wider, middle-class constituency cannot be understood without considering the transformation of the Kanbi caste into Patidars and the concomitant growth of the Swaminarayana sect. This is particularly so in mainland Gujarat. In the peninsula, though Kathiawar has become Saurashtra and similar factors are at work, the development has not gone as far. Maybe it never will, since the Rajputs and other Darbar castes are not equally influenced by the sect, and these castes are still a factor to be reckoned with.

It is not just the Swaminarayana sect which has created the new religious discourse which goes with middle-class ascendancy. Its roots are diverse: the Bengal renaissance, the Congress Party, Mahatma Gandhi's work, all stressing a new Hindu identity which goes beyond caste and the older, transactional cults. It is not that I believe in the imminent disappearance of caste, nor of cults such as those of the goddess. Rather, it is the function, of cult as well as of caste, that is likely to change.

The history of India since Independence has shown caste solidarity adapting to democratic conditions, and we may see it as the grassroots foundation of politically potent interest groups which ensures a viable democracy in India. But if the goddess' or other cults have a function in this context, it is quite different from when the goddess represented the king's power. It is doubtful whether the goddess will ever decide the vote. But goddess-worship could well become a symbol of agrarian interests, of the backward castes, in opposition to *bhakti* sects and Congress values. If so, the myth of Khodiyar may gain new significance, and whoever rules in Ahmedabad may be likened to Shiladitya, that last ruler of Vallabhi whose fall Khodiyar provoked. When I was in Saurashtra in 1991, something like this seemed to be happening. The goddess reappeared as a potent symbol of those social forces which merchantization and Congress reforms had pushed aside: the Darbars, the rural interests, and the revitalization of Hinduism under BJP which, at least in Rajkot, seemed to represent these values and interests.

If these trends are significant, they indicate, as Galey (1989) puts it, that the values incarnate in kingship have survived the institution. The goddess may become the symbolic vehicle of these values. If so, we may see the wheel of history turning a full circle: again, regional interests may contest the centralized power that made the *shakti* of the goddess politically superfluous, with her devotee kings and princes: and while the sectarian form of religion, tuned to the challenges of an urban-dominated environment, had expanded to something like the dominant position of Buddhism and Jainism in Vallabhi, they are now again confronted by the goddess.

What I wish to stress, however, is not some inherent circularity of history, but rather that the social function of religion should be seen as a determinant of its form, so that *shakti* and *bhakti* relate not only to a history of ideas but also to social formations which emphasize transaction versus community, power versus devotion, in the role religion plays for society and individual. These two levels imply an understanding of hierarchization as an ongoing discourse, in parallel to the ranking produced by transaction and power. We should not be surprised, therefore, if the idea of the whole, fundamental to hierarchizing discourse, persists in raising its head wherever we discuss ideology.

Even on the level of politics, the assumption of an ordered whole may well underlie conflict, as when a friend described his native village. 'At the time of my father', he said, 'the whole village was like one great community. If the untouchables made some mischief, my father (a leading member of the landowning caste) would get his caste-fellows together and they would beat up the trouble-makers like anything. Nobody dared to make any trouble.'

This village is in north Gujarat, but the contradictions in the statement are as typical as they are important. The ideal of a hierarchically ordered, harmonious community coexists with a realistic assumption that force is needed to keep everybody in their place. In this simple statement, Durkheimian and Weberian conceptions of society meet: society exists both as an idealized whole and as an equation of power relationships. The hierarchical premise applies to the former, while the society about which it is made is seen as a product of conflict and competition, of sanctions and power constellations.

We may see such statements as naïvely inconsistent, or as admitting the futility of containing complex society in simple logical schemes. I prefer to see them as part of empirical reality and the alternative interpretations as equally real: in India as elsewhere, there are people who fail to see the contradiction as well as those who, tongue-in-cheek as it were, present them consciously to show the confusing nature of social reality.

It was Edmund Leach (1954) who first taught us that myth is argument. He departed, of course, from Malinowski's dictum: 'Myth is charter' (1954). Discourse, in short, is at once establishing the units under consideration and ordering them into our conception of what society is. If discourse takes on a constantly hierarchizing form, arguing difference and rank, but persistently pointing to an ideal order that would have integrated these differences were it allowed to function, the charter of hierarchy results.

NOTES

1. Virbhadra Singhji (who is of course a Rajput) makes the same observation (1994: 14).
2. This statement, of course, parallels the conclusions of Raheja (1988).
3. In the English-speaking world, much of this misrepresentation is due to Talcott Parsons (1936).
4. Typically, Tönnies sees labour unions as an effort to recreate community within associational capitalism (1932: 57-8).
5. Brögger (1993) has explored this perspective.
6. Chauhan, writing of Sadri, also stresses this element of competition (1967).
7. For a further discussion of this female element, see my introduction in Tambs-Lyche (ed.) 1999.
8. I rely here mainly on Larson, 1979.

9. This presentation of Shankara's views rely mainly on Tuck 1986.
10. See Esnoul 1964; Dave 1967.
11. As well as to some others, notably the rather independent-minded pastoral communities.
12. We should not forget to add the existence, though less prominent in Saurashtra than in some other regions of India, of functionally specialized goddesses.
13. For one recent view, see Appadurai 1988. In my view, Appadurai underestimates the influence of classical Indian litterature on Dumont's view.
14. The hierarchization of discourse would result, then, from a strategic constraint on the kind of argument acceptable (Barth 1966, Brox 1972, Tambs-Lyche 1980).
15. As such, it may be culturally unconscious to an extent, though we must expect learning the rules of discourse to form part of an—at least partly conscious—process of socialization.
16. Ideal models, then, in Weber's sense of the term.
17. Lunheim tells me he has the same problem in applying Marriott's categories to his Rajasthan material.
18. This, in my view, is the problem of Bourdieu's analysis of 'distinction' (1979) which, reducing prestige in Western society to a single scale, fails to recognize alternative cultural values. Thus our view of Western culture may well be too simplistic: we may be more like Indians than we think.

Bibliography

Amarji, R., 1882, *Tarikh-i-Sorath*, Bombay: Education Society's Press.

Anand, Mulk Raj, 1967, *Lament on the Death of a Master of Arts*, Delhi: Hind Pocket Books.

Anderson, B., 1983, *Imagined Communities*, London: Verso.

Appadurai, A., 1981, 'The past as a scarce resource', *Man*, 16: 201-19.

Appadurai, A., (ed.), 1986, *The Social Life of Things*, Cambridge: Cambridge University Press.

———, 1988, 'Putting Hierarchy in its Place', *Cultural Anthropology* 3: 36-49.

———, 1991, 'Global Ethnoscapes, Notes and Queries for a Transnational Anthropology', in R.G. Fox (ed.), *Recapturing Anthropology: Working in the Present*, Santa Fe: School of American Research Press.

Arai, T., 1978, 'Jaina Kingship as viewed in the Prabandhacintamani', in J.F. Richards (ed.), *Kingship and Authority in South Asia*, Madison: University of Wisconsin.

Ardener, E., 1972, 'Belief and the Problem of Women', in J. La Fontaine (ed.), *The Interpretation of Ritual*, London: Tavistock.

Asad, T., 1972, 'Market Model, Class Structure and Consent: A Reconsideration of Swat Political Organization', *Man*, n.s. 7: 74-94.

Babb, L.A., 1975, *The Divine Hierarchy. Popular Hinduism in Central India*, New York: Columbia University Press.

Bailey, F.G., 1959, *Caste and the Economic Frontier*, Manchester: Manchester University Press.

———, 1960, *Tribe, Caste and Nation*, Manchester: Manchester University Press.

Bailey, F.G. (ed.), 1971, *Gifts and Poison*, Oxford: Blackwell.

Baily, C.A., 1983, *Rulers, Townsmen and Bazaars*, Oxford: Oxford University Press.

Banerjea, J.N., 1956, *Development of Hindu Iconography*, Calcutta: University of Calcutta.

Banks, M., 1992, *Organizing Jainism in India and England*, Oxford: Clarendon.

Barth, F., 1953, *Principles of Social Organization in Southern Kurdistan*, Oslo: Universitetets Etnografiske Museum.

———, 1956, 'Ecological Relationships of Ethnic Groups in Swat, North Pakistan', *American Anthropologist* 58: 1079-89.

———, 1959a, *Political Leadership among Swat Pathans*, London: Athlone.

———, 1959b, 'Segmentary opposition and the Theory of Games', *Journal of the Royal Anthropological Institute*, 89, part 1.

———, 1960, 'The System of Social Stratification in Swat', in E. Leach (ed.), *Aspects of Caste in South India, Ceylon and North-West Pakistan*, Cambridge, Cambridge University Press.

———, 1964a, *Nomads of South Persia*, Oslo: Universitetsforlaget.

———, 1964b, 'Competition and Symbiosis in North East Baluchistan', *Folk*, 6, 1: 15-22.

———, 1996, *Models of Social Organization*, Occasional Paper no. 23, London: Royal Anthropological Institute.

———, 1969, Introduction, in F. Barth (ed.), 9-38.

———, 1971, 'Role dilemmas and father-son dominance in Middle Eastern kinship systems', in F.L.K. Hsu (ed.), *Kinship and Culture*, Chicago: Aldine.

———, 1972, 'Analytical Dimensions in the Comparison of Social Organizations', *American Anthropologist*, 74, 1-2.

———, 1975, *Ritual and Knowledge among the Baktaman of New Guinea*, New Haven: Yale University Press.

———, 1983, *Sohar*, Baltimore: Johns Hopkins University Press.

———, 1987, *Cosmologies in the Making*, Cambridge: Cambridge University Press.

———, 1993, *Balinese Worlds*, Chicago: University of Chicago Press.

———, 1994, *manifestasjon og prosess*, Oslo: Universitetsforlaget.

Barth, F. (ed.), 1969, *Ethnic Groups and Boundaries*, Oslo: Universitetsforlaget.

Basham, A.L., 1967, *The Wonder that was India*, Calcutta: Fontana.

Basu, H., 1995, *Habshi-Sklaven, Sidi-Fakire*, Berlin: Das Arabische Buch.

Bateson, G., 1958, *Naven*, 2nd edn., Stanford: Stanford University Press.

———, 1972, *Steps to an Ecology of Mind*, New York: Ballantine.

Bateson, G. and M. Mead, 1935, *Balinese Character: A photographic analysis*, New York: New York Academy of Sciences.

Beane, W.C., 1977, *Myth, Cult and Symbols in Sakta Hinduism*, Leiden: Brill.

Beck, B.E., 1972, *Peasant Society in Konku*, Vancouver: University of British Columbia Press.

Beidelman, T.O., 1961, *A Comparative Study of the Jajmani System*, Locust Valley: Association for Asian Studies.

Benedict, B., 1968, 'Family firms and economic development', *Southwestern Journal of Anthropology*, 24: 1-19.

Bernier, F., 1916, *Travels in the Mogul Empire*, London: Oxford University Press.

Berreman, G.D., 1961, 'Caste in India and in the United States', *American Journal of Sociology*, 66: 120-7.

———, 1962, *Behind Many Masks*, Ithaca: Society for Applied Anthropology.

———, 1972, 'Social Categories and Social Interaction in Urban India', *American Anthropologist*, 74, 3.

———, 1973, 'Self, Situation and Escape from Stigmatized Ethnic Identity', in J. Brögger (ed.), *Management of Minority Status*, Yearbook of the Ethnographic Museum of Oslo, Oslo: Universitetsforlaget.

Berwick, S., 1976, 'The Gir Forest; an endangered ecosystem', *American Scientist*, 64: 28-40.

Béteille, A., 1965, *Caste, Class and Power*, Berkeley: University of California Press.

———, 1986, 'Individualism and Equality', *Current Anthropology*, 27, 2: 121-8.

Bhardwaj, S.H., 1973, *Hindu Places of Pilgrimage in India*, Berkeley: University of California Press.

Bhattacharyya, N.N., 1977, *The Indian Mother Goddess*, Delhi: Manohar.

Biardeau, M., 1976, 'Le Sacrifice dans l'Hindouisme', in M. Biardeau and C. Malamoud, *Le Sacrifice dans l'Inde Ancienne*, Paris: PUF.

Bloch, Marc, 1975, *Feudal Society*, London: Routledge & Kegan Paul.

Bloch, Maurice, 1977, 'The Past as the Present in the Present', *Man*, n.s. 12: 278-92.

Boelhower, W., 1989, 'Ethnic Trilogies: A Genealogical and Generational Poetics', in W. Sollors (ed.) *The Invention of Ethnicity*, New York: Oxford University Press, 158-75.

Bouez, S., 1985, 'Le sperme et le venin, sur la nature ambiguë de la déesse bengalie Manasa', *Cahiers de Littérature Orale*, 18: 18-39.

———, 1992, *La déesse apaisée*, Paris: Cahiers de l'Homme.

Bourdieu, P., 1972, *Esquisse d'une théorie de la pratique*, Genève: Droz.

———, 1979, *La distinction. Critique sociale du jugement*, Paris: Editions du Minuit.

———, 1980, *Le Sens Pratique*, Paris: Editions de Minuit.

Boyer, P., 1990, *Tradition as Truth and Communication*, Cambridge: Cambridge University Press.

Brent, P., 1972, *Godmen of India*, Harmondsworth: Penguin.

Brox, O., 1972, 'Komparativ analys av marginella lokalsamhällen', in *Struktur-fascismen och andra essäer*, Uppsala: Prisma.

Brögger, J. (ed.), 1973, *Management of Minority Status*, Oslo: Universitetsforlaget.

Brögger, J., 1989, *Prebureaucratic Europeans: A Study of a Portuguese Fishing Community*, Trondheim: Norwegian Universities Press.

———, 1993, *Social Anthropology and the Lonely Crowd*, Delhi: Reliance.

Burgess, J., 1869, *The Temples of Satrunjaya*, Bombay: Sykes and Dwyer.

———, 1882, 'Introduction', in R. Amarji, *Tarikh-i-Sorath*, Bombay: Education Society's Press.

———, 1971, *Report on the Antiquities of Kathiawad and Kacch* (first published 1876), Varanasi: Indological Book House.

Cappetti, C., 1989, 'Deviant Girls and Dissatisfied Women: A Sociologist's Tale', in W. Sollors (ed.), *The Invention of Ethnicity*, New York: Oxford University Press, 124-57.

Carrin, M. and H. Tambs-Lyche, 1993, 'La vengeance des femmes dans ce monde et l'autre', *Cahiers de Littérature Orale*, no. 34: 47-75.

———, 1998, 'You don't joke with these Fellows', Paper for the EASAS Conference, Frankfurt.

Carrin-Bouez, M., 1991, 'Un roi venu d'ailleurs . . . ou la conception santal du roi dans les contes', *Cahiers de Littérature Orale*, no. 29: 89-124.

Carstairs, 1967, *The Twice Born*, Bloomington: University of Indiana Press.

Chaube, 1975, *History of Gujarat Kingdom, 1458-1537*, Delhi: Munshiram Manoharlal.

Chaudhuri, K.N., 1990, *Asia Before Europe*, Cambridge: Cambridge University Press.

Chaudhuri, N.C., n.d., *A Passage to England*, Delhi: Hind Pocket Books.

Chauhan, B.R., 1967, *A Rajasthan Village*, Delhi: Vir Publishing House.

Clémentin-Ojha, C., 1990a, *La divinité conquise*, Nanterre: Société d'Ethnologie.

———, 1990b, 'Image animée, image vivante. L'image du culte hindoue', in A. Padoux (ed.), *L'image divine: culte et méditation dans l'hindouisme*, Paris: Editions du CNRS.

Clifford, J., 1992, 'Travelling cultures', in L. Grossberg, C. Nelson and P. Treichler (eds.), *Cultural Studies*, New York: Routledge.

Cohen, A., 1974, *Two-dimensional Man*, London: Tavistock.

Coomaraswamy, A.K., 1965, *History of Indian and Indonesian Art*, New York: Dover.

CVM (Village Monographs), 1961 Census of Gujarat (*Census of India*, vol. V, part VI.)

- no. 1: *Pacchatardi*
- no. 8: *Chichod*
- no. 9: *Sutrapada Fishing Hamlet*
- no. 10: *Jambur*
- no. 13: *Velavadar*
- no. 16: *Kajarda*

Ahmedabad: Director of Census Operations.

Daniel, V., 1984, *Fluid Signs: Being a Person in the Tamil Way*, Berkeley: University of California Press.

Dave, H.L., 1889, *A Short History of Gondal*, Bombay: Education Society's Press.

Dave, H.T., 1967, *Life and Philosophy of Shree Swaminarayana*, Bochasan: Akshar Purushottam Sansthan.

Davis, R.H., 1998, *Lives of Indian Images*, Princeton: Princeton University Press.

Desai, I.P., 1964, *Some Aspects of Family in Mahuva*, London: Asia.

Desai, S.H., 1973, *Prabhas and Somnath*, Junagadh: The Sorath Research Society.

Dharaiya, R.K., 1970, *Gujarat in 1857*, Ahmedabad: Gujarat University.

District Gazetteers, Gazetteer of India 1961. Gujarat Census:

- Amreli District (abbreviation ADG)
- Bhavnagar District (abbreviation BDG)
- Jamnagar District (abbreviation JMG)
- Junagadh District (abbreviation JDG)

Ahmedabad: Director of Census Operations.

Doshi, H., 1974, *Traditional Neighbourhood in a Modern City*, New Delhi: Abhinav.

Dumont, L., 1957, 'For a Sociology of India', *Contribution to Indian Sociology*, I: 7-22.

———, 1962, 'The Concept of Kingship in Ancient India', *Contributions to Indian Sociology*, VI: 48-77.

———, 1965a, 'The Modern Conception of the Individual', *Contributions to Indian Sociology*, VII: 13-61.

———, 1965b, 'The functional equivalent of the individual in caste society', *Contributions to Indian Sociology*, VII: 13-61.

———, 1966a, *Homo Hierarchicus*, Paris: Gallimard.

———, 1967, 'Caste: A Phenomenon of Social Structure or an Aspect of Indian Culture? in de Reuck and Knight (eds), *Caste and Race: Comparative Approaches*, London: Churchill.

———, 1971, 'Religion, Politics and Society in the Individualistic Universe', *Proceedings of the Royal Anthropological Society for 1970*, London.

———, 1983, *Essais sur l'individualisme: une perspective anthropologique sur l'idéologie moderne*, Paris: Esprit/Seuil.

———, 1986, *L'Ideologie allemande*, Paris: Gallimard.

Dupont, V., 1995, *Decentralized Industrialization and Urban Dynamics: The Case of Jetpur in Western India*, Delhi: Sage.

———, 1997, 'The Role of trade and Traders in Small-Scale Industrial Development: the Example of a Textile-Printing Centre in Gujarat', in P. Cadène and D. Vidal, *Webs of Trade*, Delhi: Manohar, 108-35.

Durkheim, E., 1896, *Le Suicide* (the edition used: 1995), Paris: Quadrige/ PUF.

———, 1911, *Les formes élémentaires de la vie religieuse* (the edition used: 1968), Paris: PUF.

Eck, D.L., 1991, 'Following Rama, worshipping Shiva', in D.L. Eck and F. Mallison (eds.), *Devotion Divine*, Paris: Ecole Francaise d'Extrème-Orient.

Ehrenfels, U.R. von, 1941, *Mother-Right in India*, Hyderabad: Oxford University Press.

Emerson, R.W., 1907, 'Self-Reliance', in *Essays and Other Writings*, London etc.: The People's Library, Cassell & Co., 43-66.

Enthoven, R.E., 1920/1921/1922, *Tribes and Castes of Bombay*, vols. I-III (rpt. 1975, Delhi: Cosmo; vol. II has never been reprinted).

Eschmann, A-M, H. Kulke and Tripathi, 1978, *The Cult of Jagannath and the Regional Traditions of Orissa*, Delhi: Manohar.

Esnoul, A-M., 1964, *Ramanuja et la mystique vishnouite*, Paris: Seuil.

Esser, H., 1996, 'Die Definition der Situation', *Kölner Zeitschriftfür Soziologie und Sozialpsychologie*, 48, 1: 1-34.

Evans-Pritchard, E.E., 1940, *The Nuer*, Oxford: Oxford University Press.

———, 1949, *The Sanusi of Cyrenaica*, Oxford: Oxford University Press.

———, 1962, *Essays in Social Anthropology*, London: Faber.

Firth, R., 1950, *Elements of Social Organization*, London: Athlone.

Fischer, E. and H. Shah, 1971, *Rural Craftsmen and their Work*, Ahmedabad: National Institute of Design.

Forbes, A.K., 1878, *Ras Mala: Hindu Annals of Western India* (rpt. 1973, Delhi: Heritage).

Fox, R.G., 1967, 'Family, Caste and Commerce in a North Indian Market Town', *Economic Development and Cultural Change*, XV, 297-314.

———, 1971, *Kin, Clan, Raja, Rule: State-Hinterland Relations in Pre-industrial India*, Berkeley: University of California Press.

Fruzzetti, L., 1990, *The Gift of a Virgin*, Delhi: Oxford University Press.

Fuchs, S., 1965, *Rebellious Prophets*, Bombay: Asia.

Fuller, R., 1990, 'Misconceiving the Grain Heap', in J. Parry and M. Bloch (eds.); *Money and the Morality of Exchange*, Cambridge: Cambridge University Press.

———, 1992, *The Camphor Flame: Popular Hinduism and Society in India*, Princeton: Princeton University Press.

Furnivall, J.S., 1949, *Colonial Policy and Practice*, Cambridge: Cambridge University Press.

Galey, J.-C., 1973, 'L'état et le lignage', *L'Homme*, XIII: 71-82.

———, 1989, 'Reconsidering Kingship in India: An Ethnological Perspective', in J.-C. Galey (ed.), *Kingship and the Kings*, History and Anthropology, no. 4, London: Harwood Academic Publishers.

Geertz, C., 1973, 'Person, time and conduct in Bali', in *The Interpretation of Cultures*, New York: Basic Books, 360-411.

Ghaddavi, S., n.d., *Causes and Consequences of Conflict in a Saurashtra Village*, Bhavnagar: Cyclostyled.

Ghosh, S.C., 1977, *The Peninsula of Gujarat in the Early Nineteenth Century*, Delhi: Sterling.

Ghurye, G.S., 1962, *Gods and Men*, Bombay: Popular Prakashan.

Giddens, A., 1986, *The constitution of society*, Cambridge: Polity Press.

Goffman, E., 1959, *The Presentation of Self in Everyday Life*, New York: Doubleday.

———, 1974, 'La tenue et la déférence', in *Les rites d'interaction*, Paris: Editions de Minuit: 43-85.

———, 1986, *Frame Analysis*, Boston: Northeastern University Press.

Gold, A.G., 1989, *Fruitful Journeys: the Way of Rajasthani Pilgrims*, Berkeley: University of California Press.

Gould, P. and R. White, 1974, *Mental Maps*, Harmondsworth: Penguin.

Goodenough, W.H., 1957, 'Cultural Anthropology and Linguistics', in P. Garvin (ed.), *Report on the Seventh Annual Round Table Meeting on Linguistics and Language Study*, Monograph Series on Language and Linguistics, no. 9, Washington, D.C.: Georgetown University.

———, 1961, 'Comment on Cultural Evolution', *Daedalus* 90: 521-8.

Grönhaug, R., 1974, *Micro-Macro Relations: Social Organization in Antalya, Southern Turkey*, Bergen: Bergen Studies in Social Anthropology.

———, 1978, 'Scale as a Variable in the Analysis', in F. Barth (ed.), *Scale and Social Organization*, Oslo: Universitetsforlaget.

Hannerz, U., 1992, *Cultural Complexity: Studies in the Social Organization of Meaning*, New York: Columbia University Press.

———, 1996, *Transnational Connections*, New York: Routledge.

Hardiman, D., 1988, 'Class base of the Swaminarayana Sect', *Economic and Political Weekly*, 10 September.

Harlan, L., 1991, *Religion and Rajput Women: The Ethic of protection in Contemporary Narratives*, Berkeley: University of California Press.

Harman, W.P., 1989, *The Sacred Marriage of a Hindu Goddess*, Delhi: Motilal Banarsidass.

Heesterman, J.C., 1985, *The Inner Conflict of Tradition*, Chicago: Chicago University Press.

Hobsbawm, E. and T. Ranger, 1983, *The Invention of Tradition*, Cambridge: Cambridge University Press.

Hocart, A.M., 1927, *Kingship*, Oxford: Oxford University Press.

Homans, G.H., 1958, 'Social Behavior as Exchange', *American Journal of Sociology*: 63: 597-606.

———, 1961, *Social Behavior: Its Elementary Forms*, New York: Harcourt Brace and World.

Hopkins, E.W., 1915, *Epic Mythology*, Strassburg: Trübner.

Hsu, F.L.K. (ed.), 1971, *Kinship and Culture*, Chicago: University of Chicago Press.

Inden, R.B., 1976, *Marriage and Rank in Bengali Culture*, Delhi: Vikas.

———, 1990, *Imagining India*, Oxford: Blackwell.

Ingold, T., 1986, 'Comments to A. Béteille' "Individualism and Equality"', *Current Anthropology*, 27, 1: 129-30.

Ingold, T. (ed.), 1996, *Key Debates in Anthropology*, London: Routledge.

Jackson (ed.), 1972, *Role*, Cambridge: Cambridge University Press.

Jacob, W. Le Grand, 1842, 'Report on village foundation', in *Selections from the Records of the Bombay Government*, no. XXXVII, Bombay: Government Press 1856.

———, 1872, *Western India*, London: Henry S. King.

———, 1894, 'Historical, Geographical and Statistical Memoirs on the Province of Kathiawar', in *Selections from the Records of the Bombay Government*, n.s., no. XXXIX, Bombay: Central Government Press.

Jacobson, D., 1977, 'Flexibility in Central Indian Kinship and Residence', in K. David (ed.), *The New Wind*, The Hague: Mouton.

Jain, J., 1973, *Bavaji und Devi. Besessenheitskult und Verbrechen in Indien*, Wien: Europaverlag.

Janaki, V.A., 1966, *Functional Classification of Towns in Gujarat*, Baroda: M.S. University.

Jeffrey, R. (ed.), 1978, *People, Princes and Paramount Power: Society and Politics in the Indian States*, Delhi: Oxford University Press.

Kakar, S., 1982a, *The Inner World*, Delhi: Oxford University Press.

———, 1982b, *Shamans, Mystics and Doctors*, Delhi: Oxford University Press.

Kapadia, K., 1996, *Siva and her Sisters: Gender, Caste and Class in Rural South India*, Delhi: Oxford University Press.

Kautilya, 1998, *Arthasastra* (présentation de G. Challand), Paris: Editions du Felin.

Keesing, R.M., 1976, *Cultural Anthropology: A Contemporary Perspective*, New York: Holt, Rinehart & Winston.

Kennedy, M., 1908, *Criminal Classes in the Bombay Presidency*, Bombay: Government Central Press.

Khare, R.S., 1984, *The Untouchable as Himself*, Cambridge: Cambridge Universiy Press.

Kincaid, C.A., 1905, *The Outlaws of Kathiawar and Other Studies*, Bombay: Times of India Press.

Kipling, R., 1938, *Lidt om mig selv* (Danish translation of 'Something of Myself'), Copenhagen: Gyldendal.

Kolenda, P., 1990, 'Untouchable Chuhras through their humour: "Equalizing" Marital Kin through Teasing', in O. Lynch (ed.): *Divine Passions*, Berkeley: University of California Press.

Kolff, D., 1990, *Naukar, Rajput, and Sepoy*, Cambridge: Cambridge University Press.

Kosambi, D.D., 1975, *An Introduction to the Study of Indian History*, Bombay: Popular Prakashan.

Lapidus, I.M., 1967, *Muslim Cities in the Later Middle Ages*, Cambridge, Mass.: Harvard University Press.

Larson, G.J., 1979, *Classical Sankhya*, Delhi: Motilal Banarsidass.

Leach, E.R., 1954, *Political Systems of Highland Burma*, London: Athlone.

———, 1961, *Pul Eliya: A Village in Ceylon*, Cambridge: Cambridge University Press.

Levinson, S.C., 1982, 'Caste Rank and Verbal Interaction in Western Tamilnadu', in McGilvray (ed.) *Caste Ideology and Interaction*, Cambridge: Cambridge University Press, 98-203.

Lévi-Strauss, C., 1958, *Anthropologie structurale*, Paris: Plon.

———, 1962, *La pensée sauvage*, Paris: Plon.

Lewis, O., 1954, *Village Life in Northern India* (the edition used: 1965), New York: Vintage.

Linton, R., 1936, *The Study of Man*, New York: Appleton.

Lobo, L., 1989, 'Koli Kshatriyas of North Gujarat', *Eastern Anthropologist*, 42: 171-92.

Lynch, O.M., 1969, *The Politics of Untouchability*, New York: Columbia University Press.

MacMurdo, J., 1894, 'Report and Memoir of the Province of Kathiawar', in *Selections from the Records of the Bombay Government*, n.s., XXXIX, Bombay: Central Government Press.

Majumdar, A.K., 1956, *Chalukyas of Gujarat*, Bombay: Bharatiya Vidya Bhavan.

Malamoud, C., 1976, 'Village et forêt dans l'idéologie de l'Inde brâhmanique', *Archives européennes de sociologie*, XVII: 3-20.

———, 1989, *Cuire le monde*, editions la découverte.

Malinowski, B., 1954, *Magic, Science and Religion*, New York: Doubleday Anchor.

Mallison, F., 1973, *L'épouse idéale. Le Sati-Gita de Muktananda*, Paris: Institut de Civilisation Indienne.

———, 1983, 'Development of Early Krishnaism in Gujarat; Vishnu, Ranchod, Krsna', in M. Thiel-Horstmann (ed.), *Bhakti in Current Research*, Berlin: Dietrich Reimer Verlag.

———, 1991, 'Lorsque Ranachodaraya quitte Dwarka pour Dakor, ou comment Dvarakanatha prit la succession de Dankanatha', in D.L. Eck and F. Mallison (eds.), *Devotion Divine*, Paris: Ecole Francaise d'Extrême-Orient.

Manor, J., 1978, 'The demise of the Princely Order: a Reassessment', in R. Jeffrey (ed.), *People, Princes and Paramount Power: Society and Politics in the Indian States*, Delhi: Oxford University Press.

Marriott, McKim, 1955, 'Little Communities in an Indigenous Civilization', in Marriott (ed.), *Village India*, Chicago: University of Chicago Press.

———, 1968, 'Caste Ranking and Food Transactions: A Matrix Analysis', in M. Singer and B. Cohn (eds.), *Structure and Change in Indian Society*, Chicago: Aldine.

———, 1976, 'Hindu Transactions: Diversity without Dualism', in B. Kapferer (ed.), *Transaction and Meaning*, Philadelphia: ISHI.

———, 1989, 'Constructing an Indian Ethnosociology', *Contributions to Indian Sociology*, n.s., 23: 1-39.

Marriott, McKim and R.B. Inden, 1974, 'Caste Systems', *Encyclopaedia Britannica, Macropaedia*, 3: 982-91.

———, 1977, 'Towards an Ethnosociology of South Asian Caste Systems', in K. David (ed.), *The New Wind*, The Hague: Mouton.

Mauss, M., 1995, *Sociologie et anthropologie* (6e édition), Paris: Quadrige/PUF.

Mayer, A.C., 1958, 'The Dominant Caste in a Region of Central India', *Southwestern Journal of Anthropology*, 14: 407-27.

———, 1960, *Caste and Kinship in Central India*, London: Routledge & Kegan Paul.

Mayne, H., 1921, *History of the Dhrangadhra State*, Calcutta: Thacker, Spink & Co.

McGilvray, D.B., 1982, 'Introduction', in McGilvray (ed.), *Caste Ideology and Interaction*, Cambridge: Cambridge University Press, 1-7.

McGilvray, D.B. (ed.), 1982, *Caste Ideology and Interaction*, Cambridge: Cambridge University Press.

McHugh, P., 1968, *Defining the Situation*, New York: Bobbs-Merrill.

Mead, G.H., 1934, *Mind, Self and Society*, Chicago: University of Chicago Press.

Meghani, Jh., 1927-9, *Sorathi Baharvatiya*, 1-3, Ahmedabad: Gurjar Grantharatna Karyalaya.

Mehta, M.N. and M.N. Mehta, 1896, *The Hind Rajasthan, or the Annals of the*

Native States of India, I-III, Bhadarwa, Rewakantha: Amritlal G. Shah.

Mehta, R.R., 1978, *Shri Khodiyarmata Akhyan* (in Gujarati), Surat: Shri Harihara Pushtakalaya.

Misra, S.C., 1964, *Muslim Communities in Gujarat*, Bombay: Asia.

———, 1981, 'Some aspects of the Self-Administering Institutions in Medieval Indian Towns', in J.S. Grewal and Indu Banga (eds.), *Studies in Urban History*, Amritsar: Guru Nanak Dev University.

———, 1984, 'The Medieval Trader and his Social World', in D. Tripathi (ed.), *Busniess Communities of India*, Delhi: Manohar.

Nadel, S.F., 1957, *The Theory of Social Structure*, London: Cohen & West.

Nevaskar, B., 1971, *Capitalists without Capitalism: The Jains of India and the Quakers of the West*, Westport: Greenwood.

Obeyesekere, G., 1981, *Medusa's Hair*, Chicago: University of Chicago Press.

———, 1984, *The Cult of the Goddess Pattini*, Chicago: University of Chicago Press.

O'Flaherty, W.D., 1973, *Asceticism and Eroticism in the Mythology of Siva*, Oxford: Oxford University Press.

———, 1980, *Women, Androgynes and Other Mythical Beasts*, Chicago: University of Chicago Press.

Olivelle, P., 1978, 'Ritual suicide and the rite of renunciation', *Wiener Zeitschrift für die Kunde Südasiens*, XXI: 19-44.

Oza, K.C., 1946, *Reconstruction of Life and Polity in Kathiawar*, Rajkot: author.

Pandit, K.M., 1965, *Earning one's livelihood in Mahuva*, London: Asia.

Parekh, M.C., 1936, *Sri Swami Narayana*, Rajkot: Sri Bhagwat Dharma Publishing House.

Pareto, V., 1966, *Sociological Writings*, London: Pall Mall Press.

Parmar, V.S., 1989, *Haveli: Wooden Houses and Mansions of Gujarat*, Ahmedabad: Mapin.

Parsons, T., 1936, *The Structure of Social Action*, Glencoe, Ill: Free Press.

Patel, H.G., 1961, 'Status and Prestige by Marriage among the Lewa Patidars of Five Villages in Mehsana District', M.A. thesis, M.S. University of Baroda.

———, 1966a, 'Anawari—the system of social status among the Lewa Patidars', *Journal of the Gujarat Research Society*, XXVII, nos. 1-4.

———, 1966b, 'The Change in Structural Unit and Attitudes towards Marriage by Exchange', *Sociological Bulletin*, no. 2.

———, 1973, *The Change and Resistance in the Few Determinants of Caste-Status among the Lewa Patidar of Western India*, Bhavnagar: Cyclostyled.

———, 1983, 'The Hijada (Eunuch) Culture-Complex: Urgent Research Needs', *Bulletin no. 25 of the International Committee on Urgent Anthropological and Ethnological Research* (Vienna).

———, 1988, 'Human Castration: A Study of Hijada (Eunuch) Community of Gujarat in India', *Man and Life*, 14, nos. 3-4, 67-76.

Pathak, R. and G.D. Patel, 1970, *Agricultural Taxation in Gujarat*, Bombay: Asia.

Pearson, M.N., 1976, *Merchants and Rulers in Gujarat*, Berkeley: University of California Press.

Pehrsson, R.N., 1966, *The Social Organization of the Marri Baluch*, Chicago: Aldine.

Pocock, D.F., 1955, 'The Hypergamy of the Patidars', in K.M. Kapadia (ed.), *Ghurye Felicitation Volume*, Bombay: Popular Book Depot.

———, 1957a, 'Inclusion and Exclusion: Two Processes in the Caste System of Gujarat', *Southwestern Journal of Anthropology*, 13, 9-31.

———, 1957b, 'The Bases of Faction in Gujarat', *British Journal of Sociology*, 8, 295-306.

———, 1972, *Kanbi and Patidar*, Oxford: Clarendon.

———, 1973, *Mind, Body and Wealth*, Oxford: Blackwell.

———, 1981, 'The vocation and avocations of the Guggali Brahmans of Dwarka', *Contributions to Indian Sociology*, n.s., 15, 321-36.

Pradhan, M.C., 1966, *The Political System of the Jats of Northern India*, London: Oxford University Press.

Pramar, V.S., 1988, *Haveli*, Ahmedabad: National Institute of Design.

Qanungo, K.R., 1969, *Studies in Rajput History*, Delhi: S. Chand.

Radcliffe-Brown, A.R., 1952, *Structure and Function in Primitive Society*, London: Cohen & West.

Raheja , G.G., 1988, *The Poison in the Gift*, Chicago: University of Chicago Press.

———, 1989, 'Centrality, mutuality and hierarchy; Shifting aspects of caste relationships in North India', *Contributions to Indian Sociology* (n.s.), 23, 1, 79-101.

Rajagopalachari, C., 1968, *Ramayana*, Bombay: Bharatiya Vidya Bhavan.

———, 1973, *Mahabharata*, Bombay: Bharatiya Vidya Bhavan.

Rangarajan, H., 1996, *Ramanuja Sampradaya in Gujarat*, Bombay and Delhi: Somaiya.

Ranger, T., 1989/1993, 'The Invention of Tradition Revisited', in P. Kaarsholm and J. Hultin (eds), *Inventions and Boundaries: Historical and Anthropological Approaches to the Study of Ethnicity and Nationalism*, Roskilde: Roskilde University.

Ray, 1978, 'Cambay and its Hinterland Records of the Bombay Government', (1856 selections from) vols. XXXVII and XXXIX (n.s.), Bombay: Government Central Press.

Rex, J., 1970, *Race Relations in Sociological Theory*, London: Weidenfeld & Nicholson.

Rosch, E., 1978, 'Principles of Categorization', in E. Rosch and B.B. Lloyd (eds.), *Cognition and Categorization*, Hillsdale, N.J.: Lawrence Erlbaum.

Roth, G., 1995, *Das Gehirn und seine Wirklichkeit*, Frankfurt am Main: Suhrkamp.

Rushbrook Williams, L.F., 1975, *A Handbook for Travellers to India, Pakistan, Nepal, Bangladesh and Sri Lanka*, London: Murray.

Sahajanand Swami, Shree, 1968, *Shikshapatri*, Bombay: Bharatiya Vidya Bhavan.

Sahlins, M.D., 1972, *Stone Age Economics*, New York: Aldine.

Schütz, A., 1964, *Collected Papers, II. Studies in Social Theory*, The Hague: Martinus Nijhoff.

Shah, A.M. and I.P. Desai, 1988, *Division and Hierarchy: An Overview of Caste in Gujarat*, Delhi: Hindustan.

Shah, A.M. and R. Shroff, 1958, 'The Vahimamça Barots of Gujarat', *Journal of American Folklore*, 71: 246-76.

Shah, P.G., 1967, *Denotified Communities of Western India*, Bombay: Gujarat Research Society.

Sharma, R.S. and V. Jha (eds.), 1974, *Indian Society: Historical Probings*, Delhi: People's Publishing House.

Sharma, S.R., 1971, *Maharaja Raj Singh and his Times*, Delhi: Motilal Banarsidass.

Sharpe, E., 1931, *Thakore Sahib Shri Sir Daulat Singh of Limbdi, Kathiawar*, London: Murray.

Sinha, S., 1967, 'Caste in India; its Essential Pattern of Socio-Cultural Integration', in A. de Reuck and J. Knight, *Caste and Race: Comparative Approaches*, London: Churchill.

Sinha, S. (ed.), 1982, *Tribal Polities and State Systems in Pre-Colonial Eastern and North Eastern India*, Calcutta: K.P. Bagchi.

Singh, M.H., 1990, *The Castes of Marwar* (1st pub. 1894), 2nd edn., Jodhpur: Books Treasure.

Singhji, V. 1994, *The Rajputs of Saurashtra*, London: Sangam.

Sjoberg, G., 1960, *The Preindustrial City*, New York: Free Press.

Solanki, P., n.d., *Jay Khodiyar Akhyan* (in Gujarati), Ahmedabad: Mahavir Book Depot.

Sollors, W. (ed.), 1989, *The Invention of Ethnicity*, New York: Oxford University Press.

Sopher, D.E., 1975, 'Indian Pastoral Castes and Livestock Ecologies: A Geographic Analysis', in Leshnik and Sontheimer (eds.), *Pastoralists and Nomads in South Asia*, Wiesbaden: Harassowitz.

Spodek, H., 1974, 'Rulers, Merchants and Other Groups in the City-States of Saurashtra, India', *Comparative Studies in Society and History*, 448-70.

———, 1976, *Urban-Rural Integration in Regional Development: A Case Study of Saurashtra, India*, Chicago: University of Chicago, Dept. of Geography.

Srinivas, M.N., 1952, *Religion and Society among the Coorgs*, Oxford: Oxford University Press.

———, 1953, 'Prospects of Sociological Research in Gujarat', *Journal of the M.S. University of Baroda*, 2: 21-37.

———, 1962, *Caste in Modern India and Other Essays,* Bombay: Asia.

———, 1967, *Social Change in Modern India*, Berkeley: University of California Press.

———, 1988, 'Foreword', in Shah and Desai, *Division and Hierarchy: An Overview of Caste in Gujarat*, Delhi: Hindustan.

Steed, G.P., 1955, 'Notes on an Approach to a Study of Personality Formation in a Hindu Village of Gujarat', in McKim Marriott (ed.), *Village India*, Chicago: University of Chicago Press.

Stein, B., 1977, 'The Segmentary State in South Indian History', in R.G. Fox (ed.), *Realm and Region in Traditional India*, Delhi: Vikas.

Stern, H., 1973, 'Le pouvoir dans l'Inde traditionelle; territoire, caste et parenté', *L'Homme*, XIII, 50-70.

———, 1986, 'Le temple d'Eklingji et le royaume du Mewar (Rajasthan)', in *L'Espace du temple* II; *Purushartha*, 10: 15-30.

———, 1996, *L'Inde des familles: le Rajasthan*, Paris: l'Harmattan.

Stevenson, M.S., 1920, *The Rites of the Twice-born*, London: Oxford University Press.

Strandberg, S., 1976, *Indisk Vardag*, Stockholm: Forum.

Strathern, M., 1996, 'For the Motion', in T. Ingold (ed.), *Key Debates in Anthropology*, London: Routledge, 60-6.

Tambs-Lyche, H., 1973, 'Encompassed Communities: an Essay on Ethnic Minorities in the Metropolitan Setting', in J. Brögger (ed.), *Management of Minority Status*, Oslo: Universitetsforlaget.

———, 1979, 'Kaste som identitet: aa leve i India', Tidsskrift for Samfunnsforskning.

———, 1980, *London Patidars*, London: Routledge & Kegan Paul.

———, 1982, 'The Merchantization of Saurashtra', *Journal of Social Science* (Dhaka), no. 16.

———, 1991a, 'Le roi et les enfants de la déesse', *Cahiers de Littérature Orale*, 29: 61-85.

———, 1991b, 'Om etniske stereotypiers oppbygning og form', *Norsk Antropologisk Tidsskrift* (Oslo), no. 2: 140-50.

———, 1992a, *Power and Devotion: Religion and Society in Saurashtra* (2 vols.), Bergen: University of Bergen.

———, 1992b, 'Heroes in the Hills, Power in the Plains; Patterns of Traditional Politics in Western South Asia', in R. Grønhaug, G. Haaland and G. Henriksen (eds.), *The Ecology of Choice and Symbol*, Bergen: Alma Mater.

———, 1993, 'Flooding the World with Wealth. The Consecration Ritual of the Rajsagar Lake in Mewar', *Journal of the Oriental Institute* (Baroda), 40: 275-91.

———, 1993, 'Interaction by Category; Some Perspectives on Caste', *Man and Life*, 19, 3-4: 163-73.

———, 1994a, 'The Concept of Maya in the Vacanamrta of Swami Narayana', in A. Entwistle and F. Mallison (eds.), *Studies in South Asian Devotional Literature*, Delhi: Manohar.

———, 1994b, 'The Region as Object of Discourse: an example from India', *Social Science Information*, 33, 4: 731-52.

———, 1995a, 'Un défi mortel: le sacrifice de soi en Inde occidentale', *Revue de l'Histoire des Religions*, CCXII, fasc. 3: 327-50.

———, 1995b, 'The Son's Burden: Growing up to Represent the Indian family', in H. Aspen, C. Dahl-Jörgensen, B. Erring and A.K. Larsen (eds.), *The Family: Anthropological Approaches,* Trondheim: Tapir, 138-61.

———, 1996a, 'Réflexions sur les mythes de fondation des royaumes Rajput', in *Les littératures de voix: les épopées. Les rites de fondation.* Textes reunies par N. Revel et C. Champion, Paris: Centre de Recherche sur l'Oralité / INALCO, 37-54.

———, 1996b, 'Unc tradition orale face au postmodernisme: l'exemple des bardes de Saurashtra', in *Traditions orales dans le monde indien, Purusartha* 18, études réunies par C. Champion: 23-37.

———, 1997a, *Power, Profit and Poetry. Traditional Society in Kathiawar, Western India*, Delhi: Manohar.

———, 1997b, 'Le cycle des rites d'une vie hindoue', in *Rites de vie, rites de mort*; textes réunies par Marion Péruchon, Paris: ESF, 57-88.

———, 1998, 'The Urbanity of Non-Violence', Paper for the Conference of the International Association of Sociologists of Religion, Toulouse.

———, 1999, 'Marriage and Affinity among Virgin Goddesses', in Tambs-Lyche (ed.), *The Feminine Sacred in South Asia*, Delhi: Manohar, 63-87.

———, forthcoming a, 'Les langages de l'identité au Saurashtra (Inde)', *Langage et Société.*

———, forthcoming b, 'Les baharvatiyo (hors-la-loi) du Saurashtra', in V. Bouiller (ed.), *Héros régionaux, héros nationaux. Le figure du héros en Inde* (provisional title), Paris.

Tambs-Lyche, H. (ed.), 1999, *The Feminine Sacred in South Asia*, Delhi: Manohar.

Tandon, n.d., *Punjabi Century*, Delhi: Hind Pocket Books.

Tarlo, E., 1997, 'The Genesis and Growth of a Business Community: A Case Study of Vaghri Street Traders in Ahmedabad', in P. Cadène and D. Vidal (eds.), *Webs of Trade*, Delhi: Manohar.

Thomas, W.I., 1923, *The Unadjusted Girl*, Boston: Little, Brown & Co.

Thoothi, N.A., 1935, *The Vaishnavas of Gujarat*, Calcutta: Longmans, Green & Co.

Thorner, D., 1956, *The Agrarian Prospect in India*, Delhi: University Press.

Tod, J., 1971, *Travels in Western India* (orig. publ. 1836 or 1837), rpt., Delhi: Oriental.

Tönnies, F., 1932, *Innledning til Sociologien*, Oslo: Fabritius.

Touraine, A., 1992, *Critique de la modernité*, Paris: Fayard.

Tripathi, D. (ed.), 1984, *Business Communities of India*, Delhi: Manohar.

Trivedi, A.B., 1939, 'Present Industries of Kathiawar', *Journal of the Gujarat Research Society*, 2: 26-72.

Trivedi, H.B., 1961, *The Mers of Saurashtra*, Baroda: M.S. University.

———, 1985, *The Mers revisited*, Baroda: M.S. University.

Trivedi, R.K., 1961, 'General Report on Census', *Census of India 1961*, vol. V, Part I-A, Ahmedabad: Director of Census Operations.

Tuck, D.R., 1986, *The Concept of Maya in Sankara and Radhakrishnan*, Delhi: Chanakya.

Vaidya, K.V., 1945, *The Sailing Vessel Traffic on the West Coast of India. Notes on its present and its future*, Bombay: Popular Book Depot.

van den Hoek, A.W., 1979, 'The Goddess of the Northern Gate', in *Asie du Sud: traditions et changements*, Paris: CNRS.

van der Veen, K., 1972, *I give Thee my Daughter*, Assen: v. Gorcum.

Vaudeville, C., 1980, 'The Govardhan Myth in Northern India', *Indo-Iranian Journal*, 22: 1-45.

Veblen, T., 1934, *The Theory of the Leisure Class*, New York: Modern Library.

Verdier, Y., 1979, *Façons de dire, façons de faire*, Paris: Gallimard.

Vidal, D., 1995, *Violences et vérités. Un royaume du Rajasthan face au pouvoir colonial*, Paris: Editions de l'EHESS.

Wadley, S.S., 1975, *Shakti: Power in the Conceptual Structure of Karimpur Religion*, Chicago: University of Chicago Press.

Watson, J.W. (ed.), 1884, *Gazetteer of the Bombay Presidency*, vol. VIII: *Kathiawar*, Bombay: Government Central Press.

———, 1910, *Statistical Account of Bhavnagar*, Bombay.

Weber, M., 1930, *The Protestant Ethic and the Spirit of Capitalism*, London: Allen & Unwin.

———, 1948, *From Max Weber. Essays in Sociology and Political Science* (H.H. Gerth and C. Wright Mills, eds.), New York: Oxford University Press.

———, 1958, *The Religion of India*, New York: Free Press.

Weinberger-Thomas, C., 1990, 'Cendres d'immortalité: la crémation des veuves en Inde', *Archives de Sciences Sociales des Religions*, 67: 9-51.

———, 1996, *Cendres d'immortalité: la crémation des veuves en Inde*. Paris: Seuil.

Westphal-Hellbosch, S. and H. Westphal, 1968, *Zum Geschichte und Kultur der Jat*, Berlin: Duncker und Humboldt.

———, 1974, *Hinduistische Viehzüchter im Nordwestlichen Indien, I: Die Rabari*, Berlin: Duncker und Humboldt.

———, 1976, *Hinduistische Viehzüchter im Nordwestlichen Indien, II: Die Bharwad und die Charan*, Berlin: Duncker und Humboldt.

Whyte, W.F., 1943, *Street Corner Society*, Chicago: University of Chicago Press.

Wikan, U., 1990, *Managing Turbulent Hearts. A Balinese Formula for Living*, Chicago: University of Chicago Press.

Wilberforce-Bell, H., 1916, *A History of Kathiawad from the Earliest Times*, London: Heinemann.

Williams, R.B., 1984, *A New Face of Hinduism*: *The Swaminarayan Religion*, Cambridge: Cambridge University Press.

Wiser, W.H., 1936, *The Hindu Jajmani System*, Lucknow: Lucknow Publishing House.

Wiser, W.H. and C.V. Wiser, 1971, *Behind Mud Walls, 1930-1960*, Berkeley: University of California Press.

Wood, J.R., 1978, 'Indian Nationalism in the Princely Context: the Rajkot Satyagraha of 1938-39', in R. Jeffrey (ed.), *People, Princes and Paramount Power: Society and Politics in the Indian States*, Delhi: Oxford University Press.

Yajnik, J.U., 1889, *Gaorishankar Udayashankar C.S.I., ex-Minister of Bhavnagar*, Bombay: Education Society's Press.

Zimmermann, F., 1972, 'Gauche et droite, dehors et dedans. Trois études sur des orientations de l'espace et du mouvement dans la culture de l'Inde du Sud' (doctoral thesis): Paris, EHESS.

———, 1982, *La jungle et le fumet des viandes*, Paris: Seuil.

Index

Abu (Mt.) temples 25-6
Ages, mythic pasts 12, 13-14, 15, 34
Aghoris (sect) 115-16
Ahmedabad 81, 171, 193, 195, 207
Alcohol 72-3, 86
Amreli (district) 16
Animal sacrifice (*see also* buffalo sacrifice) 128, 131, 132-3, 134, 135, 263
Ashramas (places of study and meditation) 96, 102-3, 135
Artisans, craftsmen or specialists 22, 67, 187, 233, 236, 244, 263, 271, 276, 277, 287-8, 297-9

Babriawad (region) 16
Barda Hills 16, 260-1
Baroda (state) 118
Barth, F. 15, 18, 157-60, 164, 174, 216-17, 219, 227-8, 270, 289
Bateson, G. 158, 163-4, 214
Bazaars, markets 41, 48, 51, 54-5, 70, 82-3, 233, 238-41
Bedi (port) 43
Berreman, G.D. 20, 162, 223, 255
Bhagavad Gita 176, 184-5, 199, 203, 225-6
Bhajans (devotional songs) 141, 149, 151
Bhakti (devotional religion) 24, 74-5, 132, 141-2, 147, 151, 315-16, 326-7
Bhal (salt flats) 16, 274-7
Bhavnagar (city) 17, 35, 38, 39, 43, 46-50, 54, 55, 57, 66, 69, 72-5, 81, 83, 86, 89, 90-1, 96, 127, 129, 148-51, 172, 176, 200, 207, 214, 293; district 16, 70, 112; state 16, 17, 46-50, 61, 64, 129, 233, 235, 256, 272, 274, 277, 296
Bhuchar Mori (battle) 12, 52
Bhuvo (sacrificer, also called *bhopa*) 134, 253, 288,
BJP (party) 52-3, 85, 112, 327
Bombay (Mumbai) 77-8, 83, 84, 95
Bourdieu, P. 165, 219
Brahmacharya, stage or way of life 200, 201
Brahmakumari Mission (sect) 96-7, 196
British times, *see* colonial period
Buddhists 114, 135, 327
Buffalo sacrifice 123, 125, 132-3, 134, 135, 140, 263
Buses (as social scenes), bus terminals 179, 206-15

Cambay 47, 69
Capitals (general) 33-4, 56-7
Caste, settlement pattern 63, 80-2, 240, 241, 256, 286
Caste, theoretical discussion of 19-24, 29, 63, 78-9, 83, 89-94, 97-8, 155-7, 159, 166, 175, 177-8, 187, 265
Castes and communities: Afgan *see* Pathan, Ahir (also called Gujar, Goala) 20, 42, 51, 82-3, 187, 271, 273; Anavil Brahmin 24, 309; Anglo-Indians 94; Atit 249-51; Audich Brahmin 85, 87; Babar 275; Babria Rajputs 16; Balai 287; Baluch or Baluchi 42, 275; Barber (Nai) 233, 287-8, 298; Barot 234, 238, 253-4, Bava-Sadhu 261;

Bhangi 92, 275, 287; Bharwad 19, 48, 51, 52, 53, 84, 92, 141-2, 169-70, 262, 274-5, 279, 298; Bhatia 42, 44, 83, 108, 293; Bhil 273, 286-8; Bhowsar 83, 193; Bohra or Vora 42, 83, 244; Brahmin (category of castes) 24, 51, 68, 85, 86, 87, 90-3, 94, 98, 112, 127, 128-9, 132, 155, 189, 235, 238, 242, 245, 247-8, 252-3, 275-6, 287, 304-6, 318-19, 325; Carpenter, caste (*mistri*, also *suthar*) 22, 233, 236, 279, 287-8, 298; Chamar 275, 286-8; Chaora Rajputs 107; Charan (caste) 20, 26, 96, 124-6, 152-4, 155, 170, 196, 263, 297, 310, 317, Christians 94; Chudasama Rajputs 42, 131; Daroga 287; Digambaras 12-13, 25; Dhed 236; Doli or Dholi 287-8; Fakir 264; Gadri 271, 273; Garasia Rajputs 235; Ghedia or Ghedia Koli 265; Ghoghalia or Ghoghalia Kharva 265; Girnar or Girnara Brahmins 42, 111; Goala *see* Ahir, Gohil Rajputs 16, 69, 71, 126, 131, 132, 235, 236; Goldsmiths (*soni*) 233, 243, Gugli Brahmin 105, 107-8; Gujar (caste) *see* Ahir, Hajam (Muslim barber) 265; Harijans, *see* Untouchables; Hirole Rajputs 107; Jadeja Rajputs 12, 37; Jat 286-7; Jains 11-13, 25-6, 38, 113, 194-5, 196, 233, 240, 275, 279, 293, 310, 316; Jhala Rajputs 12, 52, 131; Jogi 72, 74, 248, 313; Kanbi, Kanbi/Patidar 20, 23-4, 51, 68, 83, 86, 89-90, 91, 124, 134, 137, 138, 152, 161-2, 198, 235-6, 237, 238, 240, 242-3, 249-53, 273, 274-7, 279-81, 296, 298, 308-10, 326; Kapol 70; Kathi 19, 66, 71, 102, 169, 301; Khalal 287; Khant 42; Khateek 287-8; Khatri 42, 67-8; Kharol 287; Khawas (slaves) 56; Khoja 72, 198-9, 233, 244, 246; Koli 20, 24, 42, 85, 89, 124, 131, 138, 235-6, 238, 240, 242, 243, 249-50, 265, 273, 274-7, 279-81, 298, 301, 309, 319; Koli Kharva 265; Lodhi 42; Lohana 42, 68, 83, 84, 91-3, 95, 185-6, 236, 244; Lohar (blacksmith) 261, 287-8; Machhiyara 265; Mahia, Mahia Rajputs 12, 278-81, 295-6, 298; Margi (also called *sadhu*) 233; Meghwal 279, 287; Memon 53, 67; Mena Rajput *see* Mahia; Mer 170, 277, Mewar Brahmin 90; Miana 263-4, 295; Moila *see* Vanakiya; Muslims 15, 37-43, 53, 62, 63, 67, 70, 71, 72-3, 86, 93-4, 112, 117, 118-19, 130, 147, 198, 233, 234, 242, 243-6, 252, 254, 262-3, 316; Nagar, Nagar Brahmin 11, 38, 42, 43, 56, 81, 93, 154-5, 294, 300-1, 316-17; Palleva or Palival Brahmins 238; Parmar Rajputs 42, 278; Parsi 83, 147; Pathan 11, 42, 93; Patidar (*see also* Kanbi) 21, 23-4, 51, 83, 85, 152, 155, 161-2, 192, 224, 236, 268, 308-10; Potter (*Kumbhi* or *Kumbhar*) 233, 275, 287-8; Rabari 19, 84, 170, 260-2 278; Rajput 12, 13, 15, 19, 28, 39, 50, 51, 52, 53, 56, 82, 92-3, 123, 126, 135, 138, 155, 169, 177, 187, 188-90, 196, 201, 224, 235-6, 237, 238, 240, 242-3, 244, 249-53, 253-4, 257, 273, 276, 279, 286-8, 289, 292-3, 296, 301, 319, 326; Rathod Rajputs 110, 118; Raval 180, 252; Rawat 287; Regar 287; Sandhu (also called Margi) 275, 279, 287; Sagar 261; Sandhi 278; Sanyasi *see* Jogi; Sarasvati Brahmin 42; Sayyid or Saiyad 42, 264; Shoemaker (*mochi*) 22, 233, 244, 279, 298;

Shrimali Brahmin 89, 90-1, 238; Siddi 262-3; Soratha Brahmin 42; Sarthi 42; Svetambaras 12-13, 25, 194-5; Tailor (*darji*) 42, 233, 234, 279, 287, 298; Teli (oil pressers) 72, 287-8; Turki 93-4; Vadel 107; Vaghela Rajputs 42, 188-90; Vagher 107; Vala Rajputs 42; Valand 279, 298; Vanakiya or Vanakiya Kharva 265; Waghri 22, 48, 92, 236, 245, 275; Washermen (*dhobi*) 233; Yogi *see* Jogi

Categories, as reference for identity 20, 185, 225-30, 306

Chital, village and state 71

Chora, Rajput meeting hall 253-4

Chudasama (rulers of Junagadh) 12, 110, 118, 125-6, 131, 300-1

Clubs 86-9

Colonial period, British period 14, 33, 42-3, 47-8, 50, 51, 66-7, 69-70, 77, 107, 262

Community, as feeling of commonality 151-2, 207-8, 232, 307-8

Competition, as central to the caste order 155-6, 186, 287, 304, 310, 317-18

Competition, as observed behaviour 208-9, 212, 219-20, 220-1, 247

Concepts of space, *see* mental maps

Concepts of time, *see* time

Conflicts or brawls 177, 180, 209-10

Congregation, assembly of believers 147-52

Congress (party) 12, 53, 64, 65, 112, 246, 326-7

Consistency, of individual behaviour 185, 225

Constraints (analytical concept) 165-6

Co-operative societies 298

Cotton, cotton mills 62, 66-8, 70

Craftsmen, *see* artisans

Dakor (town and pilgrimage) 104

Daman 44

Darbars (estates) 19, 21, 28, 53, 222, 235, 250, 268-9, 273, 292-3, 300, 324, 326

Deference 211, 215, 227

Definition of the situation 20, 80, 163-4, 206, 213, 215-19, 224-7, 238-9, 255-6, 306

Dharma (moral order) 27, 133, 140, 153, 171, 172, 226, 312

Dholka (town) 275

Dhows, traditional shipping 44, 47, 68-70

Dhrangadhra (city and state) 35-6, 37, 38, 39, 40, 53-4, 77, 81, 138, 141

Dhrol (town) 46

Discussion and discussion groups 84, 85, 88-9, 102, 179, 254

Diu 44

Dominant caste 267-8, 277, 287, 289, 293, 301, 304-5, 319

Dumont, L. 14, 22, 146, 152, 161, 163-4, 173, 175, 186, 202, 229, 305-6, 308, 311-12, 318, 320-3, 326

Durkheim, E. 13-14, 27, 156, 311, 328

Dwarka (town and pilgrimage centre) 16, 37, 46, 100, 101, 104-8, 118-19

Dwelt-in world *see* lived-in world

Egalitarianism, equality 152, 215, 220, 222, 246, 255, 266, 304, 307

Emergence (analytical concept) 20, 160-1, 163-4, 165, 213, 214, 223, 229

Emerson, R.W. 184-5, 225

Entrepreneurs, entrepreneurship 51, 56, 67-8, 74, 82-3, 309-10

Estate (analytical concept) 19-22

Esser, H. 213, 216-19, 223, 225, 228

Exorcism 136-7

Family, as reference for the individual 185-97

Family firms 68, 187, 188, 199

Farming 74, 177, 235, 237

Fathers, fatherhood 188-9, 191-5, 197, 200-1
Field (analytical concept) 83, 292-9
Fields, as social space 176-9
Fisherman 23-4, 72, 94, 264-5, 289

Gadhada (temple and pilgrimage) 101, 102-3, 152, 153, 200
Gandhi, M.K. 27, 49, 75, 195, 197, 198, 326
Gir (forest) 16, 261-2, 296
Girnar, Mt. 11, 17, 40, 100, 101, 113, 114-17, 123, 313
Globalization 60, 76-8, 94
Goddess, goddesses (*Mata*) (general) 13, 25-8, 37-9, 52, 87, 105, 115, 170, 122-43, 191, 196, 198, 201, 237, 248-53, 312-14, 316-17, 326
Goddesses (individual): Ambabhawani 313; Ambaji (temple and goddess) 24-6, 123, 135, 237, 249; Ambika, also called Amba Mata or Jagdamba (temple and goddess) 115, 117, 123, 125, 171, 313; Andheri Mata 135-7; Avad 123; Ashapuri 124; Bahucharaji 124, 137, 138, 319; Bhadrakali 171; Chamunda 123, 171; Durga 123, 124, 127; Hinglaj 37, 123; Jagdamba, *see* Ambika; Jambu Mata 131, 141; Kali 124; Kalka Mata (goddess and temple) 115-16; Khodiyar (goddess) 13, 28-9, 37, 101, 123, 124-33, 141, 171, 249, 312-13, 316-17, 326; Lakshmi, Mahalakshmi 105, 123; Momai Mata 170; Nani Khodiyar (goddess and temple) 127; Parvati 313; Shakti Mata 105, 141, 313; Sita 90-1; Vagheshvari 189, 201; Varudi 313
Gogha (port and town) 47, 68-70, 86-7, 257, 293
Gohilwad (region) 16
Gondal (town and state) 91, 272, 278-81, 295-6
Gopnath (temple) 87
Greetings 238-9, 242, 255
Grönhaug, R. 83, 292
Guest houses and hotels 84-6, 95, 102
Guilds 56, 187
Gujarat unrest of 1974, 195, 198, 237
Gunas (qualities) 92-3, 323
Guru, devotion to a 156, 193, 200-2

Halar (region) 16
Hamlet, as a settlement type 17, 260-72
Hannerz, U. 19, 76-7, 159
Hanuman (god and temples) 127
Hierarchy, hirerarchical order, ranking 13, 78-9, 85, 97, 155-6, 161, 180, 213, 221, 227-30, 238-9, 243, 247-8, 252-3, 253-4, 255-6, 287, 304-7; of settlement types 17, 76, 80
Hierarchizing discourse 13, 85, 221, 227-8, 304-28
Hindu-Muslim conflict 53, 67, 237
Historicity 14-15, 20, 267, 274, 281-2
Hypergamy 188, 224

Imagined community or communities 24, 28-9
Inden, R.B. 186, 190, 192, 213-14, 224, 232, 312
Individual, individualism 142-3, 146-66, 172-6, 184-204, 325-6
Industry, industrialization 49-50, 51, 54, 56, 62, 66-8, 70-1, 106, 147
Ingold, T. 18

Jafrabad (town and enclave) 262
Jagirdars, jagirdari 268-71
Jain temples 25-6, 38, 61, 96, 112-14, 114-15, 233, 240
Jainism 11-13, 25, 38, 97, 196, 312, 317, 327

Jajman as host or patron, ritual and general 253, 273
Jajmani system 268, 281, 288, 297-9
Jamnagar or Navanagar (city) 17, 36, 39, 43-6, 48, 55, 57, 80, 81, 83, 108, 123, 150, 176; state 17, 43-6, 261, 278, 293
Jangal (wilderness) 16-17, 168-73, 237, 261-2
Janjira (state) 262
Jethwa, dynasty of Porbandar 260, 277
Jetpur (town and state) 54, 66-8
Jhalawad (region) 16
Junagadh (city) 11, 15, 17, 36-7, 40-3, 44, 46, 48, 55, 57, 80, 81, 83, 87-8, 93-4, 95, 101, 115-17, 176; district 16, 260; state 12, 17, 20, 41, 43, 66, 110, 112, 117, 125-6, 131, 132, 262, 278-80, 295, 300-1, 313

Kabirpanthi (sect) 151
Kakar, S., theories of 190-2, 194
Kathi states 66, 71, 102
Kathiawad (as region of the peninsula) 16
Khambhalia (town) 44, 46, 107
Kheduts (estates) 19, 294-6
King, ideas of royalty 25-6, 27, 311-12
Kinship 187, 188, 261, 277, 292-3
Krishna (god), Krishnaism 25, 38, 74, 104-5, 149, 170, 176
Kuldevi, clan goddess 123, 189

Landscapes 14, 168-73
Lathi (town and state) 16, 71-2, 80, 235
Leach, E.R. 161-2, 328
Left-hand group *see* right and left-hand groups.
Limbdi (town and state) 35, 131, 141
Lived-in world, dwelt-in world 14, 15, 18, 80, 156-9
Loj (village and pilgrimage) 103

Mahabharata 170
Mahajan (council of guilds) 56, 63, 65, 187
Mahuva (town) 54, 60-6, 80, 81, 85, 207, 257
Maldharis (estates) 19-20, 51, 239, 261
Malia (town and state) 82, 263-4, 273-4, 295
Mangrol (town) 44, 71-2
Marriage 185-9, 191, 196, 200, 224, 261, 287, 308-10
Marriott, McKim 17-18, 164, 175, 213-14, 221, 229, 306-7, 310, 318-19, 323-5
Marital tradition, marital values 14, 24, 250
Maya (philosophical concept) 313-15, 317
Mayer, A.C. 310
Mead, G.H. 20, 160-4, 174, 184-5, 213, 223, 299-300, 307
Mental maps, cultural construction of space 15-17, 241
Merchantization, merchant model 53, 63-6, 68, 77-8, 113-14, 326
Merchants (*see also* Vanias) 12-15, 21, 24-6, 56, 63-6, 68, 71, 113-14, 188, 233, 293-4, 300, 324
Mewar (state and royal house) 25, 287-8
Migration 11, 21, 46, 75-8, 87-8, 90, 91, 93-4, 233, 261-2, 270-2, 279-80, 293-5
Mithapur (town) 54
Models and modelization 160
Modernity 52, 87-9
Moguls 12, 61, 262
Mohalla, *see Para*
Moksha, ultimate release 101, 201
Morality, moral ideas 26-7
Morvi (town and state) 55, 264
Mothers, motherhood 190-1, 193
Multiple pasts, *see* Ages
Music, dance and song 52, 74, 84, 133-4, 141, 149, 150, 151, 249-51

Muslim League (party) 67
Myth (as argument, as charter) 13, 164, 166

Nath (sect) 115
Nathaji (Shri), form of Krishna 25, 103
Nathdwara (temple) 25
Nature, perceptions of 171-2
Naughan (king of Junagadh) 42, 110, 125-6, 132
Navnagar *see* Jamnagar
Networks, social 187, 293-4
Non-vegetarian food, meat-eating castes 72-3, 91-3, 155-6, 310, 324

Okhamandal (region) 16, 106-8
Opposition between merchants and warriors, non-violence and marital tradition 12-13, 15, 24-6, 27-8, 154, 287, 310
Outlaws 16, 263-4, 295-6

Painters and painting 42, 168
Palaces and castles 34-7, 48, 53-4, 61, 82, 235
Palios, memorial stones 237
Palitana (pilgrimage) 100, 101, 112-14, 118; town and state 16, 113, 118
Para or *Mohalla* (quarter of a town or city) 81-2
Past (the past in the present) 14, 133, 163, 173
Pastoralists (*see also Maldharis*) 21, 169-70, 176, 180, 239, 260-2, 271, 296-7, 300
Patriline, patrilineality 188-90, 192
Peasants (*see also* Kheduts) 21-2, 294-6
Pilgrimage 100-8, 111, 113-14, 116-17, 117-19, 129
Pilgrimage tax 113-14, 118-19
Pir, Muslim saint or his grave 198, 254, 262-3
Piracy, pirates 46, 68-9, 106-9
Poets and poetry 49, 124, 168, 250
Pocock, D.F. 23-5, 130, 146, 152, 161-2, 243, 252-3, 308-10
Pol (quarter in a town or city) 81-2, 187
Porbandar (district) 16; town 55; state 16, 261, 277, 300
Portuguese 43-4, 69
Possession 75, 134-7, 198, 249-53
Power, power relations 27-9, 56-7, 70-2, 78, 107-8, 113, 117-19, 229, 256, 286-302, 304-5, 322
Prabhas or Prabhas Patan (town) 80, 110-11
Praja Socialist Party (PSP) 61, 63-6
Prakriti (cosmic female principle) 131, 314-15, 317
Priests, *see Pujari*
Prototype (analytical) concept) 23-4, 162, 309-10
Public and private space (analytical dichotomy) 80-2, 176, 177, 239, 241-5, 256
Pujari (priest) 74-5, 127, 128-9, 135-7, 235, 245, 249, 276, 298, 304-5
Puranas see scriptures
Puritanism 147, 153, 154
Purusha (cosmic male principle) 131, 314-15

Rajkot (city and state) 17, 34, 39, 40, 50-3, 55, 56, 77, 80, 82-3, 85, 95, 152, 207
Rajput-dominated society, social order 13, 123, 292-3, 295, 300
Rajput state, as a state form 25-8, 37-38, 123, 126, 131, 140
Rajula (town) 55, 70-1
Rama (god and temples) 28-9, 37-8, 52, 54, 90-1, 104, 235-6, 240, 275-6, 279
Ramanuja, Ramanujacharya (ancient philosopher) 314-15
Ramayana 90-1
Ranchod (form of Krishna) 104, 107
Ranking transactions 213-14, 221-4, 227-8, 306-7, 318-19
Ravana 90-1, 312-13

Regional caste system 97-8, 305-6
Reinvention or revitalization of tradition 52, 53
Relativity (analytical concept) 20, 160-1, 229
Religious festivals: Annakuta 105; Bhim Ekadashi 105; Dasahra 132, 134, 235; Dolotsav 105; Holi 105; Janmashtami 105; Navratri 132-4, 138; Shivratri, Mahashivratri 101, 106, 115
Renouncer 74, 175, 180, 201-2
Restaurants, cafés and tea-shops 72-3, 89, 233-4, 239, 240, 245-7
Rex, J. 162, 164-5, 204, 225
Right-hand and left-hand group 27-8, 310
Ritual suicide 26-7, 125
Roads, as social space 179-81
Roles, analysis of 184-204, 225-30

Sadhu, *see* renouncer
Saheb, as social type 209-15
Sanyasi (renouncer), *see* renouncer
Sati, form of ritual suicide 125, 189-90, 310-11
Sayla (town) 123, 253
Schütz, A. 157
Science, scientific thinking, popular conceptions of 95-7
Scripture (Hindu or other classical texts, reference to) 85, 90-1, 148, 150, 188, 254, 278, 308-9, 310-13
Sects (general) 146-7, 326
Security, protection or safety, quest for 176, 181, 185-6, 209-10, 215, 295
Service castes, specialists 267-8, 271-2, 275, 297-9
Settlements, classification and discussion of 17, 265-7, 286-302
Shah, A.M. 78, 83, 309
Shaiva or shaivite religion 74, 90, 93, 115, 152, 155, 196, 233, 316-17
Shakti (power, feminine by nature) 140, 142, 313, 316
Shaktism 87, 116, 141-2, 152, 313, 315-17, 327
Shankara, Shankaracharya, ancient philosopher 106, 154-5
Shankaracharya, present religious leader 106
Shetrunji (mountains) *see* Palitana (pilgrimage)
Shipping, traditional, *see dhows*
Shiva (god temples) 74, 96, 106, 109, 122, 124, 127, 155, 194-5, 196, 236, 312-13, 317
Shops 84, 93, 198, 233, 239, 246-7
Sindh 67, 95, 263
Society as construction, as object of discourse 13-14, 21-3
Somnath (temple) 23, 80, 100, 101, 108-12, 118-19
Sons, importance and situation of 188-96
Sorath (region) 12, 15-16
Spodek, H. 7, 33-4, 56-7
Srinivas, M.N. 146-7, 152
Stigmatized castes 23-4, 262
Structure, structuring 162-4
Suffering, as a moral force 26-7, 101
Sultans and sultanate of Gujarat 61, 69
Surat 47, 69, 72, 81
Surendranagar (town) 39, 80
Swaminarayana (sect and temples) 38, 54, 91, 97, 101, 102-3, 142-3, 146-56, 193, 196, 200-1, 202, 311, 315-16, 318, 324, 326

Tantrism 115-16
Temples (general) 38, 240
Ter tansali or thirteen castes (commensal grouping) 22, 28, 51, 53, 249, 251-4, 261, 301
Thoothi, N.A. 23, 91, 229
Time, conception of, how to calculate 15, 267
Town planning 11, 39, 44-5, 48-9, 54, 56-7, 61-2, 80-2
Town walls, and fortifications 39, 40, 45, 48, 68-9, 110, 170, 233
Towns (general), urban society 33-4,

54-7, 60, 72-3, 78-9, 80-2, 97-8
Trade 12, 21, 33-4, 42-3, 44, 46-7, 51, 65-6, 66-8, 68-70, 107-8, 118, 293-4
Tradition (general, analytical concept) 163-7
Traditional society (in Saurashtra) 27, 52, 163, 301-2, 305
Traga, form of ritual suicide 26, 310
Trains, as social scenes 219-23
Travellers 86, 206-23
Tönnies, F. 308

Untouchables, untouchability, *Harijans* 48, 62, 86, 92, 94, 236, 256
Urban-rural relations 17, 57, 60, 62-3, 71-6, 80, 97, 233, 257, 307-8
Urban society, *see* towns

Vaishnava religion, Vaishnavism 74, 93, 102-3, 104-6, 111, 147, 149, 151, 155, 315-16
Vallabhacharya (sect and temples) 25, 38, 61; *haveli* 103, 108, 147
Vallabhi (city and kingdom) 12, 69, 104, 112-13, 123, 124-5, 131, 300
Vanias (estate or category of castes, also called *Banias*) 19, 24-6, 38, 51, 56, 63, 67, 82, 83, 88, 91, 138, 147, 154-5, 187-8, 193, 233, 252-3, 275, 279, 287, 293-4, 300
Varna 91-2, 305-6
Vegetarianism 24, 91-3, 152-3, 155-6, 310, 324
Veraval (town and port) 55, 94, 111
Villages and hemlets mentioned by name: Chichod 278-81, 291, 295-6, 298; Jambur 262-3; Kajarda 263-4, 290-1, 295; Pacchatardi 260-1, 290, 294-5, 296-7; Praj (name invented) 72-3, 76, 80, 89, 130, 134, 176, 195, 198, 199-201, 207, 232-57, 291, 296 Ranawaton-ki-Sadri 267-72; Ratadi 277, 291; Sutrapada 23-4, 264-5, 291; Velavadar 274-7, 291, 296-8
Villages, classification and discussion of 17, 74-5, 267-9, 272-4, 281-2, 286-302
Vishnu (god) 104, 149, 155, 312-13

Wadhwan (town) 39, 66
Wankaner (town) 278
Weber, M. (theories of) 19, 153, 154, 155, 156, 158, 227, 299-300, 328
Western Indian goddesses 123-4
Women, role of 150, 178, 208, 209-10, 239, 242-5

Yogi, renouncer practicing austerities 135

Zamindars and zamindari 20, 260, 269, 277, 295